*Economy and society in
pre-industrial South Africa*

LONGMAN GROUP LIMITED LONDON

Associated companies, branches and representatives throughout the world

© Longman Group Ltd 1980

First published 1980

BRITISH LIBRARY CATALOGUING IN PUBLICATION DATA

Economy and society in pre-industrial South Africa.
1. South Africa—Social conditions
I. Marks, Shula   II. Atmore, Anthony
309.1'68'04   HN801.A8

ISBN 0-582-64655-3
ISBN 0-582-64656-1 Pbk

Printed in Hong Kong by
Sing Cheong Printing Co. Ltd

Economy and society in pre-industrial South Africa

EDITED BY
Shula Marks and Anthony Atmore

Longman

Abbreviations

AC	Archive of the Advisory Council of the Cape of Good Hope
APS	Aborigines' Protection Society
AYB	*Archives Year Book for South African History*
BBNA	*Blue Book on Native Affairs (Cape Colony)*
BMA	Berlin Missionary Archives
BMB	*Berlin Missions Berichte*
BMS	Berlin Missionary Society
BP	Bourke Papers (in Rhodes House Library, Oxford)
BPP	British Parliamentary Papers
CA	Cape Archives
CO	Colonial Office
CO (Cape)	Colonial Office of the Cape Colony
CPP	Cape Parliamentary Papers
CSP	*Collected seminar papers on the societies of Southern Africa*
FCS	Free Church of Scotland
FMC	Free Missions Committee
JAH	*Journal of African History*
JSAS	*Journal of Southern African Studies*
MMS	Methodist Missionary Society
NGK, NGKSK	Nederlandse Gereformeerde Kerk, NGK Sendings Kommissie
NHK	Nederlandse Hervormde Kerk
NLS	National Library of Scotland
PA	Pretoria Archives
PRO	Public Records Office (London)
SANAC	*South African Native Affairs Commission, 1903–5*
SAR/ZAR	South African Republic/Zuid Afrikaanse Republiek
TA	Transvaal Archives
WMM	W.M. Macmillan Manuscripts
WMMS	Wesleyan Methodist Missionary Society

Contents

List of Maps and Figures

ERRATUM
The Map above the caption on p. 125 should
appear on p. 132, and the map on that page
should appear on p. 125.

A Note on Orthography

With contributions from so many authors, who have used sources in Portuguese, Dutch, German, Afrikaans and a variety of African languages, the editors have found it almost nightmarish trying to impose some form of editorial consistency in the spelling of names and footnote citation. All we can claim is that the inconsistencies which remain have been carefully considered.

In general, we have followed the rules of the International African Institute in the spelling of African names and words. Thus for Bantu words we have omitted the prefixes and suffixes (except the case of the Basotho kingdom, to distinguish the kingdom in the south from those of the northern Sotho); where we have referred to events, institutions or persons among the Nguni, we have tried to adopt Nguni spelling, and where among the Sotho, Sotho: the wars of the early nineteenth century are *Mfecane* on the coast and *Difaqane* on the highveld. Certain names posed problems. The current Lesotho orthography of Moshoeshoe for the nineteenth-century founder-king and his successors has been eschewed for Mshweshwe, on the grounds that this is closer to English phonetics than the French-based convention.

For settler place-names we have tended to follow contemporary South African usage, including some curiosities, even of English place-names— Grahamstown but King William's Town—and substituting Afrikaans for Dutch in the original documents—e.g., Blouberg, rather than the more visually elegant Blaauwberg. The one exception is that we have retained Zoutpansberg for present-day Soutpansberg on the grounds that the Zoutpansberg region as the home of the *jagtersgemeenskap* or hunting community was an essentially nineteenth-century concept, intrinsically different from the modern district of the Transvaal. Zoutpansberg died in 1867. This has led to an additional inconsistency: rather than drive ourselves and our printers insane, we have stuck to Zoutpansberg also for the mountains which originally gave the region its name.

There are a number of terms, particularly for official positions and institutions, which passed from colonial Dutch into South African English. We have employed the most common form of these—volksraad, landdrost, veldcornet, Uitlander—without italicising them in the text. A glossary of these terms is to be found on the next page. All other foreign words have been italicised on their first appearance in the text only, unless they are part of a quotation.

Many of the names people called one another in the nineteenth century have become in the twentieth century, for a variety of reasons, terms of abuse, e.g. Natives. Where possible, that is, except in quotations, we have avoided these. Two, however, posed particular problems. The use of 'Hottentot' for the population of the Cape who had descended in the main from the Late Stone Age Khoisan is explained by Susan Newton-King in footnote 4 on p. 201; and we have found it impossible to find an ideal terminology for the settler population of Dutch descent north of the Orange River from the 1830s. To call them Afrikaners is somewhat anachronistic at least until the later nineteenth century; before that we have used the terms Trekker and Boer more or less interchangeably, though we have preferred Trekker for the northern Transvaal in the early days when there was not much evidence of settlers actually engaging in farming—and hence following the vocations of *boers*, that is, farmers. Wherever possible we have tried to avoid the ideologically determined terms 'black' and 'white'.

Glossary

Boerenbeschermings Vereeniging Farmers' Protection Society (Cape, Dutch)
Burgerkryg civil war—usually refers to the Transvaal civil war of 1860
Burgerraad Citizens' Council (lit)—local district board in the Cape Colony
  under the Dutch
bywoner tenant-farmer or squatter, usually white
diensdoenste kaffers lit. service 'kaffirs'—Africans performing tribute labour
  for whites
Difaqane Sotho form of the word applied to the wars waged in south-east
  Africa in the early nineteenth century, associated with the rise of the
  Zulu kingdom. Thus, also, forced migrations
erf/pl. *erven* allotment/landholding (Dutch)
gemeenskap community (Dutch/Afrikaans)
Grondwet constitution (Dutch/Afrikaans)
heemraad/*heemraden* part-time, unpaid district official/s drawn from locally
  resident burghers to assist *landdrost* in administration
huurkaffers lit. 'kaffirs' for hire—African wage labour
ibutho/*amabutho* regiment or age-regiment/s (Nguni)
inboekseling 'apprentice' (Dutch/Afrikaans)
incwala First Fruits ceremony among the Nguni
induna headman (Nguni)
jagtersgemeenskap hunters' community (Dutch/Afrikaans)
jagveld hunting grounds (Dutch/Afrikaans)
Khoi or *Khoikhoi* preferred term for people referred to in the older
  literature as 'Hottentots', members of Late Stone Age herding communities
Khoisan composite term from Khoi (above) and San (below) for LSA
  herders and hunter-gatherers at the Cape when the Dutch arrived
Krygsraad military or war council (Dutch/Afrikaans)
landdrost paid district official in the Cape and Afrikaner republics; the

equivalent of a District Commissioner or magistrate

Libandla   king's Council among the Swazi

lobola   bridewealth

maatskappy   company (Dutch/Afrikaans)

makhadzi   biological sister of the Venda king

mandaaten   exchequer bills

Mfecane   Nguni form of *difaqane* (see above)

morgen $2\frac{1}{3}$ acres

nagmaal   lit. evening meal (Dutch/Afrikaans)—Church service on Sunday evenings, for which Afrikaner farmers would travel to the nearest church often for several hundred miles, three or four times a year

Nederlandse Gereformeerde Kerk/Nederlandse Hervormde Kerk   rival sects of the Dutch Reformed Church in South Africa

ngoma   Sotho term for loan cattle

opgaaf   tax, tribute (Dutch/Afrikaans)

Rixdaller   coin in use in the Cape Colony in the Dutch and early British period, worth about 1s 6d in *c.*1820

schepsel   lit. 'creature' (Dutch)—term of abuse for blacks

sisa   Nguni term for loan cattle

skietgoed   firearms/ammunition (Dutch/Afrikaans)

skillings   coin in use in the Dutch and early British period at the Cape, worth about 2d. There were 8 skillings in a *Rixdaller* (above)

smous   itinerant trader

Staats Courant   lit. State newspaper (Dutch)—Government Gazette

Superintendant van Kafferstammen   Superintendent of African tribes

Superintendent van Naturelle   Superintendent of Natives (lit.)

swart skuts   black 'shots'—hunters or marksmen

Uitlander   foreigner, alien (Dutch/Afrikaans)

Uitvoerende Raad   Executive Council (Dutch/Afrikaans)

umnumzane/abanumzane   homestead head (Nguni)

umuzi/imizi   homestead/s

veldcornet   elected local district official in a ward

Veldwagmeester   Burgher officer in charge of a group of men from a ward

Volksraad   lit. people's council—the Republican parliaments

Zuid Afrikaanse Republiek   South African Republic

zuurveld   lit. sour veld (Dutch/Afrikaans)—area in the eastern Cape between the Bushman's and the Sundays River, contested between Xhosa and Boers in the late eighteenth century. So-called because the grazing was 'sour'—unsuitable for cattle in the summer months

CHAPTER ONE

Introduction *

Shula Marks and Anthony Atmore

Since C. W. de Kiewiet's *History of South Africa, Social and Economic*, written in the 1930s, there has been no broadly interpretative essay on South African history, despite the revolution in the historiography since that time.[1] Although the two-volume *Oxford History of South Africa* was, for the first time, planned and written 'in the belief that the central theme of South African history is the interaction between peoples of diverse origins, languages, technologies and social systems meeting on South African soil',[2] its publication revealed the enormous gaps in research and conceptualisation which needed to be filled before such a re-interpretation could take place. As the reviews of the *Oxford History* suggested, the volumes marked the apogee of the liberal tradition of South African historiography, highlighting both its positive features and its limitations.[3] It was in this context and in an attempt to get beyond the liberal 'problematic'[4] that, over the past few years, we have been running an interdisciplinary seminar at the University of London's Institute of Commonwealth Studies on the societies of southern Africa in the nineteenth and twentieth centuries.[5] Both this introduction and the essays that follow are in large measure its product.

Although our approach is very different, looked at from the vantage point of the late 1970s, the key question still seems to us not dissimilar to that posed by a group of Afrikaner historians in their interpretation of

*This introduction is the outcome of years of cooperative effort and discussion. We wish to thank participants in the seminar on the societies of southern Africa in the nineteenth and twentieth centuries (Institute of Commonwealth Studies, London), as well as students over the years for their help in refining our conception of South African history. We are also most grateful to the contributors to this volume and to Richard Rathbone, Andrew Roberts, Brian Willan and Harold Wolpe for the extremely valuable comments they made on the first draft. We of course remain solely responsible for all the confusions and heresies which remain despite their best efforts, as we are also for all the views put forward in the introduction.

South African history published nearly a decade ago, and curiously entitled *Five Hundred Years*:[6] how has it come about that so small a number of whites has been able to impose itself on a far greater number of African peoples to achieve its present position of dominance, exploitation and power? It is, however, a question that çan be answered only, on the one hand, by seeing the nineteenth century as it happened not as it turned out at the end, and, on the other, as de Kiewiet first pointed out, by relating the history of the white man in South Africa to that of the majority of its inhabitants and to the imperial context in which the sub-continent was set.[7] This volume also moves beyond these formulations: the historical experience of all South Africa's peoples needs to be explored not only at their points of 'interaction', but also in terms of the internal dynamic of their various social formations and their articulation with the nineteenth-century world economy. In one way or another, all the essays in this collection are concerned with these latter issues.

This volume was planned some years ago, and many of the pieces were first presented to the seminar more than five years ago. As working documents, and in order to stimulate further research and discussion, a number were reproduced in *The Collected Seminar Papers on the Societies of Southern Africa in the Nineteenth and Twentieth Centuries*, a mimeographed annual publication which gave them a limited but immediate audience beyond the confines of the seminar room. The authors would be the first to admit that, in a number of ways, the field has moved beyond their original conceptualisations, and to welcome this. Nevertheless, particularly in view of the fact that the early volumes of the *Collected Seminar Papers* series are out of print, and that the series has formed the basis for a widely-publicised attack on the so-called 'revisionist' or 'radical' school of history,[8] we have included in this collection some of the earlier nineteenth-century pieces, as well as a number of more recent essays, which illustrate the scope, method and range of the current historiography. All the papers have been revised for publication to a greater or lesser extent; some, however, are still set in the context in which they were originally written, as the authors and the editors consider that in this form they both reflect an important stage in the historiographical debate and contribute in their own right to our understanding of South Africa's nineteenth-century past.

We make no claim to have presented a comprehensive account of South African history, either geographically or thematically, though in this introduction we hope to place the papers in a more general chronological and geographical framework. In this sense, then, the collection reflects the outstanding gaps in current research, as well as its preoccupations. Its object is to explore, through a series of case studies, three crucial areas in

South Africa's nineteenth-century history: the nature of precapitalist social formations;[9] the ways in which these were affected, if not necessarily yet restructured, by colonial penetration and mercantile capital;[10] and the impact on Africans of the colonial experience and methods of social control.

For all their regional and temporal diversity, these essays are, in general, concerned with the socio-economic basis of societies and its relationship to ideology and politics. Although there are a number of very important differences in emphasis, we have not tried to impose any uniform approach on the essays. This would have done a disservice to the richness and diversity of the research they represent. Over the years, the seminar at the London Institute of Commonwealth Studies has reflected a variety of intellectual concerns. As will be evident in the pages that follow, participants were influenced by the *Annales* school and·the ecological debate; by the rethinking of African history and work on development and under-development; by recent writing on the social history of industrialising Britain and on slavery in the United States; and most recently by the literature sparked off by the French Marxist anthropologists on pre-capitalist modes of production.

Despite the overall concern with the material base of society, by no means all our contributers subscribe to a materialist or Marxist approach. Nor would they describe these essays as simply 'economic history'. Indeed, we positively abjure the implied distinction. They are all, in some sense, an attempt to come to grips with what the *Annales* school have felicitously phrased 'total history'. They are written in the belief that the division of history, and indeed the social sciences, into fragmented, specialised branches of knowledge is at best inadequate, at worst grossly misleading. Like Lucien Febvre, we see this kind of definition as 'a kind of bullying'. We echo his passionate outcry against those who would impose definitions on the historian:

> 'Careful, old chap, you are stepping outside history. Reread my definition, it is very clear! If you are a historian, don't set foot in here, this is the field of the sociologist. Or there—that is the psychologist's part. To the right? Don't go there, that's the geographer's area . . . and to the left, the ethnologist's domain.' It is a nightmare, madness, wilful mutilation! Down with all barriers and labels! At the frontiers, astride the frontiers, with one foot on each side, that is where the historian has to work . . . [11]

Initially, we grouped the essays in this collection geographically for the sake of simplicity. On reflection this became increasingly inadequate. At the same time, a purely thematic approach, following the three broad areas of interest outlined above, raised an equal number of problems. The present arrangement reflects these difficulties, and is a compromise between the geographical, chronological and thematic. During the nineteenth century, the political, social and economic structures of South Africa were, in large measure, regionally differentiated, and although all areas were ultimately affected—albeit unevenly—by the penetration of mercantile capital from the coast, processes set in train in one part of the region in the early nineteenth century were only in evidence much later in another. As this collection clearly shows, in the nineteenth-century southern African social formations were distinguished by their diversity, a diversity partly, but by no means entirely, encompassed by regional political boundaries. Thus, to take the Transvaal as an example, within the territory which became the South African Republic, there were developments as distinct as the hunting economy described by Wagner, the still essentially tributary mode of production of the Pedi state portrayed by Delius, and the quasi-feudal domain of the Afrikaners and their African serfs, all coexisting uneasily between the Vaal and the Limpopo rivers at much the same time.[12] The Cape and Natal present, perhaps, a more unified picture: there the forces of colonial penetration were far stronger; nevertheless, even in the coastal colonies there were sharply contrasting modes of production both within and on their borders.

It is the simultaneous existence of all these societies and the uneven penetration of capital which makes the problem of presentation so acute. Thus, the logical sequence would appear to be precapitalist social formations; the penetration of mercantile capital; and finally the full domination of these societies by a capitalist mode of production. Nevertheless, because of the way in which colonialism spread from the coast and had its most intense effect first in the British coastal enclaves, processes which were in evidence there in the late eighteenth and early nineteenth century were only played out in the interior considerably later. Moreover, while it seemed logical to begin with an analysis of the precapitalist social formations, and therefore—after the broadly introductory essay by Legassick— with the theoretical discussion by Bonner, followed by Guy and Beinart, we are fully aware that the situation they are describing cannot be described as fully 'precolonial'.[13] Although, in varying degrees, the forces of the world economy had begun to affect the coastal areas of south east Africa from the late sixteenth century, Bonner and Beinart in fact are reconstructing the material and social bases of societies which were creations of the nineteenth century; these were shaped in part by the forces impinging in different ways on all southern African societies in the nineteenth century.

Behind this logic lies a further consideration: that if we are to understand the impact of colonialism on African societies in southern Africa, we have to have some kind of understanding of these societies in as near to their precapitalist forms as we can reach, however imperfect this understanding may have to be. Godelier has drawn our attention to the fact that

> As Marx and Engels have endlessly repeated, it is impossible to analyse and understand the forms and routes taken by the transition from one mode of production and social life to another without taking fully into consideration the 'premises' from which this transition develops. Far from their disappearing from the scene of history at a stroke, it is these earlier relations of production and the other social relations which transform themselves, and we must start from them in order to understand the *forms* which the effects of the new conditions of material life will take and *places* where they will manifest themselves within the previous social structures.[14]

From a consideration of the papers by Bonner, Guy, Beinart and Slater we move next to looking at the colonial experience in the Cape. Here we have shifted from theoretical considerations to geographical and chronological ones as well. By the time we come to look at the Cape under the British in the early nineteenth century we are faced with the intrusion of a new kind of colonial state on societies which already had been reshaped and in some cases shattered by the rule of the Dutch East India Company over the previous century and a half. While parts of the Transkei remained outside the orbit of this far more radical colonialism until late in the nineteenth century, it was here, in the Cape Colony, that the transition to capitalism from precapitalist and mercantilist social formations was first inaugurated. The essays included in this collection by Newton-King, Kirk, Bundy, Trapido and Hogan constitute a powerful reinterpretation of Cape history;[15] despite their diversity they are unified by their concern with problems of class formation and social control. In some sense, they are all re-examinations of nineteenth-century liberalism at the Cape.

While in many ways experience in the Transvaal in the nineteenth century may have paralleled that of the Cape in the previous century, we nevertheless felt it more satisfactory to deal with the Transvaal material at the end of the sequence: Trekker society was both a 'spin-off' from the early nineteenth-century Cape Colony, however specific a form it developed in facing the new exigencies of the interior, and also continued to be profoundly shaped by the effects of political, economic and social change in the Cape, and to a lesser extent Natal. So much further from its home base, the impact of these changes was, of course, diluted. Moreover, the capacity of mercantile capital actually to restructure relations of production *of its own accord* is, in general, limited. As elsewhere, merchant capital could only operate under the aegis of the locally dominant class.[16] In the

Transvaal, we would argue that the actual shape of the social formation, was as much dictated by the social and property relations as well as the ideology which the Trekkers brought with them, and what they found when they arrived, than by any dramatic impact of mercantile capital. Nevertheless, the continuing ties with the Cape and Natal markets and the colonial presence are of importance in explaining the transitional forms and complexities of the situation in the Transvaal, well into the nineteenth century. It is only after our period, in the 1880s and 1890s, that, as a result of the mineral discoveries, the Transvaal itself became the pivot of social, economic and political transformation in the whole of southern Africa, through the operation there of international capital.

Broadly speaking, in the nineteenth century there were two new foci of actual or potential surplus extraction in southern Africa, organised at the political level into different state systems.[17] One was the expanding colony on the coast and its Voortrekker offshoots, first in Natal and then in the interior, the second the expanding indigenous states—Zulu, Ndebele, Swazi, Pedi, Sotho and others, largely products of the *Mfecane* (*Difaqane*), the explosive wars in the second decade of the century which originated in Zululand-Natal, and which radically altered the course of the history of a large number of African societies, from the eastern Cape to Lakes Malawi and Tanganyika. So cataclysmic an event was the Mfecane, that for many African peoples it quite over-shadowed the almost contemporaneous appearance of missionaries, hunters, traders and settlers from outside, and conditioned their responses to these new arrivals until well into the nineteenth century. Much—though obviously not all—of southern Africa's nineteenth-century history until the discovery of minerals, is the story of how increasingly powerful African and colonial state systems incorporated their weaker neighbours into their social formations and appropriated their surplus, and of how in time the white and black groups came into conflict with one another, to the ultimate victory of the colonial states.

At an ideological level, their struggle came increasingly to be conceived in terms of the socio-biological accident of the colour of their ruling classes—'black' and 'white'. When, in the last couple of decades of the century, international mining capital came to play the major shaping role in the sub-continent, this was a powerful new dimension to the pre-existing struggle to regulate the means of production of the various social formations within the area, and extract from them their surplus labour power. The demands of mining capital ended any form of independent African state in those still considerable areas where the struggle had not yet been decided in favour of the colonists. Contrary to the conventional wisdom which locates the origins of contemporary *apartheid* on the seventeenth-century 'Cape frontier', it was probably not until this time that a fully fledged ideology of race, nurtured in the material conditions of late nineteenth-century imperialism, came to be enunciated in South Africa as 'the [ideological] means for the reproduction of a particular mode of production'.[18]

Precisely because of the myths surrounding the origins of contemporary South African society, it is necessary before looking in detail at the nineteenth century, to examine the nature of the societies of South Africa before the second British occupation of the Cape in 1806 or the wars of the Mfecane in the next decade. Martin Legassick's piece on the 'Frontier Tradition in the Historiography of South Africa' addresses these issues directly. It is thus the first essay in this collection. This is not only because it deals with the seventeenth and eighteenth century, and is therefore chronologically 'the first'; nor is it that it was written first, though that is significant. Its importance lies also in the enormously stimulating effect it had at the time of its presentation, and subsequently, on South African historiography. The 'frontier tradition', it is true, was overdue for reexamination, and Legassick's extended essay on the nature of this 'tradition' was in itself a major contribution. Even more important, however, was the way in which Legassick redirected attention to the ideological component of that thesis, and to suggest an alternative methodology. The essay raised—and raises—some of the most fundamental questions in South African history, on the relationship of race and class and ultimately on the nature of the relationship between ideology and specific modes of production. Legassick's subject matter encompasses the whole of South African history. By attempting to relocate the 'frontier thesis' in the realities of an industrialising South Africa, he in fact *liberated* the historian from 'the burden of the present'. He alerted us to the dangers of using the past as a kind of ragbag from which the historian can simply pick out elements to show continuity of some chosen element into the present. Although the problem of the correspondence—or non-correspondence—between form and content in social relations[19] is a formidable one, Legassick pointed the way to a new problematic, which demanded an exploration of the past— as of the present—as a totality. In this way, as David Harvey has argued in *Social Justice and the City*:

> Society comes to be seen as a set of structures in the process of continuous transformation .... Within a mode of production states of consciousness are produced not in some arbitrary or instantaneous fashion, but by transformations and pressures which take deeply rooted ways of thought and reshape them so that they become broadly supportive of the existing structure of production in society.[20]

More concretely, Legassick traces the complex development of the concept of the South African 'frontier' and demonstrates on the one hand the large element of mythology and mystification involved, and on the other, the role this notion has played both on the actual course of South African history and on the writing of that history. There are, of course, a number of layers or strands which make up the concept of a 'frontier', some firmly rooted in reality, others less so. As Legassick points out, what is significant about the areas labelled 'frontiers' is that they are zones of interaction between people either subject to different political authorities and/or engaged in different modes of production, or indeed recognising no formal authority at all, and therefore perhaps as individuals marking the precise point of articulation and change between different modes. Moreover, contrary to the usual stereotype Legassick is concerned to show that it is on the frontier that some of the *least* colour-conscious interaction between peoples of different societies took place: the lack of state institutions perhaps meant that there was scope for individual acts of violence and brigandage, but this should not be confused with the much more explicit and rigid racist ideology of the later nineteenth century, or in the slave-owning areas of the more settled western Cape. This point is clearly borne out, as we shall see, in Susan Newton-King's account of the Cape labour market and the contrast it presents to the study by Wagner of the hunting 'frontier' in the Zoutpansberg.[21]

The geographical movement of 'frontier'-type relations, and to a certain extent of actual 'frontiers', was almost continuous during most of the nineteenth century, and much of South Africa experienced these processes at some time or another. This movement or expansion was itself a process, and it is the flux and absence of clear-cut definition at a stage before the colonial state takes over that requires emphasis. Despite the abuse of the term by many historians and social scientists, the concept of a frontier zone is still of importance to aspects of South African history.

'Frontier zones' were not new to South Africa with the coming of white settlement in the mid-seventeenth century. For well over a millennium before the arrival of the Dutch at the Cape of Good Hope, Iron Age farming communities had established their own kinds of 'frontiers' with the earlier Late Stone Age inhabitants of the sub-continent. By the time the first Europeans rounded the continent at the end of the fifteenth century, and indeed in many areas considerably before that time, it is clear that many, if not most of the present day Bantu-speaking peoples of southern Africa had settled in most of the areas in the region suitable for mixed agricultural and pastoral pursuits. In these areas, they had effectively conquered, absorbed or assimilated the earlier hunter-gatherers and herders; outside them, divided by an effective ecological 'frontier',[22] lived the purely pastoral and hunter-gatherer peoples whom the Portuguese and later the Dutch encountered in the more arid winter rainfall areas of the south and south west coast.

As the terms employed above—Late Stone Age, Iron Age, hunter-gatherer, agricultural—suggest, the concept of the 'frontier' here also signifies the meeting and interaction of different modes of production, an interaction which led ultimately to the creation of a new social formation. Although none of our contributers examines the mode of production of hunter-gatherer bands or that of the Khoikhoi herders, four papers address themselves, either directly or indirectly, to the nature of the mode of production of Bantu-speaking agricultural communities in the nineteenth century. All of them deal with the Nguni peoples of the south-east coast: unfortunately, so far this particular approach has not been applied systematically to the Sotho-Tswana societies of the interior, many of which were marked by an even greater division of labour, specialisation and embryonic or actual class divisions.[23] In the arrangement of these essays, we have again defied chronology, and placed Phil Bonner's piece on 'Classes, the mode of production and the state in precolonial Swaziland' first, even though the nineteenth-century Swazi state originated in the same historical conjuncture which Jeff Guy discusses in his 'Ecological factors and the rise of Shaka's kingdom', and followed after it. It seems to us that Bonner's explicit and lucid exposition of the main issues provides a valuable introduction for readers uninitiated into the debate, which has been influenced both by the work of French anthropologists like Rey, Dupré, Meillassoux, Godelier and Terray, as well as Hindess and Hirst's theoretically preoccupied *Precapitalist Modes of Production*.[24]

Before entering the intricacies of the debate over how best to characterise the modes of production among Africans in early nineteenth-century South Africa, it is perhaps as well to set out the intermediate questions. Until quite recently, very little attention had been paid to the nature of the economies of African peoples in the pre-colonial period; though every anthropological monograph has its information on aspects of production and technology, there are considerable difficulties in using this material for the precolonial period: pitfalls which historians ignore at their cost. Nor does it always answer the key questions posed by Ronald Frankenberg in 1968: 'How are the units of production constituted? What is the nature and form of work? Is its organisation associated with relations of hierarchy, subordination, cooperation or exploitation? How are the products distributed and consumed?'[25] Claude Meillassoux put it even more simply in *Economy and Society* in 1972: what we need to know at the outset is 'Who is working with whom and for whom? Where does the product of the labour go? Who controls the product? How does the economic system reproduce itself?'[26] Both Guy and Beinart carefully and deliberately tackle some of these major issues, though in both cases they are concerned more with the internal dynamics of change, than with any static model of social relationships. Slater also deals with many of the same questions in looking at the effects of colonialism on the 'homestead' from the mid-nineteenth century onwards.[27]

By the beginning of the nineteenth century, all the Iron Age societies of southern Africa had long passed from any simple agricultural self-sufficiency or kinship-based political organisation to more complex social formations. Though all the societies involved were based upon mixed agriculture and pastoralism and had a relatively simple technology, they were characterised by communal production and the absence of private property in land, by the social division of labour both between the sexes and between chiefs and commoners, and by the identity of the chiefly class and the state. Even before the rise of the Zulu kingdom, discussed in this collection by Guy, we have to conceive of chiefdoms which were territorially and politically defined. Although agricultural production for subsistence needs was undertaken largely within individual homesteads, grouped in lineage-based villages, co-operation in the production of the socially necessary surplus was also crucial. Some forms of agricultural production based on work-parties, cattle-keeping, hunting and defence cut across homestead boundaries, and had important structural ramifications for consumption, exchange and distribution. Critically, for its reproduction, the homestead (and lineage) had to look outside its confines for wives. Through their overall control of village production and through their control of bridewealth and thus of marriage and the circulation of women (both producers in their own right and the reproducers of labour power) chiefs ensured the continuity of village life. Part of the surplus produced in the village was thus extracted in the form of tribute paid by commoners to the chiefs, who were in turn expected to redistribute at least part of this to the old and needy and in the form of ritual feasts to the community at large.

Bonner, Guy and Beinart show the crucial role played by cattle in the Nguni social formations they deal with. Through their power over cattle the chiefs, or lineage heads, controlled not only a valuable economic resource, but also the pivot of society: it was through cattle in the form of bridewealth or *lobola* that women were brought into the lineage from outside. Bonner shows the significance of this in the expansion of Dlamini authority over the whole of Swaziland in the first half of the nineteenth century, while Guy stresses the enormous importance of Shaka's control over cattle, women and marriage in the rise and consolidation of the Zulu kingdom. Through controlling marriage, and thus population and production, through the regiments, Shaka was able to revolutionise social relations in Zululand-Natal, if only for a relatively short period. In addition, as Beinart shows for the Mpondo, the loaning of cattle by the rich to the poorer members of society was used to create and maintain relationships of clientage at the political level, and as the way of extracting labour in the form of herding from the borrower at the same time. Not only did this relationship (known as *ngoma* or *sisa*) set up obligations on the part of the borrower: it also masked the very considerable inequalities in cattle ownership within the social formation. By controlling the redistribution of cattle, chiefs were able to prevent the excessive accumulation of wealth by overmighty subjects, and to ensure their own continued control.

There are very real difficulties in characterising this mode of production, and a discussion of these difficulties, both at the theoretical level and in their practical application, is the subject of Bonner's essay on 'Classes, the mode of production and the state in precolonial Swaziland'. Taking as his starting point the work of Hindess and Hirst in *Precapitalist Modes of Production*, and in particular their analysis and dismissal of the Asiatic mode of production, he concludes that in southern, and indeed in most of the rest of sub-Saharan, Africa, social formations were characterised by the articulation of two separate modes of production, that of the lineage—termed by Guy the 'patrilineal lineage system', and by Slater 'the homestead production complex';[28] and that of the tributary state which controlled essential economic resources and their distribution—in the case of these African societies, the allocation of land (though the precise powers of the chiefs varied both regionally and over time) and cattle. Through its appropriation of these resources, the state—or, more concretely, the chief—had vital control over the production and reproduction of the lineages which made up the social formation. Given the low level of population, soil fertility and technology, it was control over people which was, as has frequently been pointed out, crucial, and the forcible incorporation of captives through raiding was an important feature of these societies and of their tributary relationships.

Although all the papers dealing with the Nguni in this collection stress the importance of the lineage in south-east Africa, it should be recognised that the lineage is not simply an expression of purely biological or genetic relations: as Rey and Godelier have reminded us, it is a specific social grouping of biological relations which have socially determined functions.[29] 'It is, above all', as Meillassoux has suggested, 'the expression of the relations of production and reproduction' in these societies, and provides their legitimising ideology.[30] Thus, the ideology of kinship was used, even when the lineage mode was dominated by a tributary state, as was the case in both Swaziland and Zululand: the king was still 'father of the people', and norms of redistribution still served to legitimate and to modify the role of the king in surplus extraction. The chief's position was regarded as superior because of his geneaological relationship to the other lineages, though in many cases this was no more than a convenient fiction. Thus within the chiefdom, as David Hedges has recently commented,

> the totality of the social relations of production is constituted by the hierarchical grouping of lineages dominated by a ruling lineage which controls relations between all the lineages, primarily through exchanges of women and cattle so as to maintain its dominance. This means that the social role of the elder of the lineage is not defined primarily by his membership of the lineage, but by his membership of the collectivity of all the lineages.[31]

Within the lineage, it was the individual homestead which was the basic unit of production, as the papers in this section show, though it would be misleading to characterise the mode of production as a whole as the 'homestead mode of production', which some authors have done, for the homestead neither constituted the totality of relations in the mode, nor reproduced itself.[32]

The relative self-sufficiency of the homestead, however, in terms of agricultural production, is of considerable significance. Both Guy and Slater show how, notwithstanding the tremendous changes wrought by the Shakan revolution, and then by the substitution of the colonial state for the Zulu kingdom, the homestead continued to function in much the same way. Indeed, Guy goes so far as to say that, despite the changes in Zulu society when it was forced in the late nineteenth century to become part of the South African capitalist system, the patrilineal lineage structure, which 'was given material expression in the homestead' remained more or less intact. In some ways, this is very reminiscent of Marx's characterisation of local communities in the Asiatic mode of production:

> The simplicity of the productive organism in these self-sufficing communities which constantly reproduce themselves in the same form, and when accidentally destroyed spring up again on the same spot with the same name—this simplicity supplies the key to the riddle of the unchangeability of Asiatic societies, which is in such striking contrast with the constant dissolution and refounding of Asiatic States, and their never ceasing changes of dynasty. The structure of the fundamental economic elements of society remains untouched by the storms which blow up in the cloudy regions of politics.[33]

Yet this is too static a view of the societies with which we are dealing, whether at the political or the economic level. Notwithstanding the resilience of the homestead, and the outward retention of older forms, as both Slater and Beinart show, what is remarkable in the nineteenth century is the way in which African societies were able to respond quickly and effectively to changes in their natural and economic environment. Despite the continued importance of the homestead in nineteenth-century Natal, Slater describes 'a single though complex network of economic choices and relationships' operating in the colony. It is the flexibility of the homestead, rather than its stability, which should, in this context, be emphasised. And—apart from the greater abundance of choice open to Africans and evidence for the historians—there is no reason to assume this flexibility was new in the nineteenth century.

The papers by Bonner, Guy, Slater and Beinart make a collective and cumulative contribution to our understanding of the nature of the precapitalist social formations among the Nguni. They also make an individual contribution to our understanding of varied aspects of southern Africa's nineteenth-century experience. Thus, after his theoretical discussion of the nature of the precolonial mode of production in Swaziland, Bonner moves on to raise two other major theoretical issues which are related to this: whether one can talk of classes and thus of a state in precolonial Swaziland. These issues, too, have wide-ranging implications. African historians have long been accustomed to talk of state-formation—without sufficiently defining either what they mean by 'states', or what the necessary conditions are for states to arise. Here, Bonner takes as his starting point Hindess and Hirst's definition and sees 'the political level . . . as the necessary space for the representation of the interests of various classes, and the presence of a state apparatus as a necessary condition of the maintenance and functioning of the mechanism of appropriation of surplus labour by the ruling class'.[34] He sees in Swazi society an embryonic class structure which emerged through participation in the trade to Delagoa Bay in the late eighteenth century and through the move into southern Swaziland, which presented the ruling class with the opportunity to enforce 'unequal access to the unevenly distributed means of production'. 'Conquest', so often used by historians to 'explain' the rise of new states is shown, following Hindess and Hirst again, to explain only 'the conditions under which the state may be formed . . . not . . . the mechanisms of the formation of the state'.[35]

Bonner traces the emergence of the Swazi state in the last years of Sobhuza's reign and especially during that of Mswati, with the extension of Dlamini control over the economic resources of subject groups and the beginning of 'class society'. In a sense, it was a class society brought with them by the conquerors, and re-established and reshaped in the Swazi context: for the Swazi state bore a strong resemblance to the eighteenth-century states of Zululand and southern Mozambique, which were its forbears. Its key institutions, like theirs, were the age-regiments, through which the king controlled both military activity and production, the *Incwala* or first fruits festival which symbolised royal control over agriculture, and the *Libandla*, or National Council which seems to have been taken over from the earlier Sotho-speaking inhabitants of the area in an attempt to legitimise Dlamini political, economic and ideological hegemony.[36] Bonner also indicates the important part played by captives in Swazi society, once the kingdom extended its hold over the agricultural lands and increased its production after the move to Ezulwini. Raiders captured children both within, but more frequently outside, the frontiers of the Swazi state, and sold captives also to the Boers on their western frontier in considerable numbers. For the Boers, it can be argued, captives had a not dissimilar use, for much the same reasons as Bonner sketches for the Swazi. And in both they constituted a group of 'perpetual minors' rather than a clearly defined class, because of the limitations on market production and also perhaps because of the limited coercive apparatus of both Boer and Swazi states.[37]

Whereas in the early years of the Dlamini move into southern Swaziland the invaders were an army of occupation, gradually 'random and indiscriminate plundering' were replaced by the 'development of more institutionalised mechanisms for the appropriation of surplus, whose volume was at the same time kept within limits by the need to retain the loyalty and co-operation of subject groups against external enemies like the Zulu'. This sequence can be followed, also, in the other offshoots of the Zulu state: whether it be the Ndebele kingdom established by the Khumalo north of the Limpopo, the Gaza kingdom in southern Mozambique or the Ngoni states as far north as Zambia and Malawi. The similarities again suggest that it is not the fact of conquest as such which explains the emergence of these states, or their nature, but the precise articulation of the conquering groups and the social relations they brought with them with those of the societies they subordinated.

Jeff Guy is concerned with the first of these conquest states: the Zulu kingdom itself. Although he alludes briefly to the various theories accounting for the Mfecane, he is not in the first instance trying to establish its 'cause', but to explore one dimension of the evidence. This suggests that by the end of the eighteenth century, Zululand, an area particularly well-suited to stock-keeping cultivators, was nevertheless in the throes of a severe ecological crisis, in which physical resources 'were breaking down under existing systems of exploitation', and that this contributed to the 'radical social change' which took place. From this he examines briefly production in the Zulu kingdom and the way in which surplus was extracted in order to show the king's central position in controlling the exploitation of the environment. Guy is careful to avoid an over-simple geographical determinism in this argument, despite the weight he gives to the dynamic of the ecological environment which he sees as constantly changing in response to human activity.

The mere fact of 'population pressure' or a shortage of resources can no more 'explain' the formation of a state or the specific nature of the state that is formed, than can the fact of 'conquest'. Nevertheless, for any pre-industrial society ecology sets many of the constraints within which societies have to operate; Guy's outline of the micro-environment of Zululand-Natal, which takes account of grasses and soil, rainfall and climate, is a necessary precondition for his examination of the changing social relations. While he does not set out to explore all the intricate factors which lay behind the Mfecane, he is concerned to show the implications of the changes in the military system for power and for productive relations. He suggests that in addition to its being a military force, the Zulu army also gave the king 'fundamental powers of control over the manner and the rate at which the physical environment of Zululand was to be exploited', and at this point his arguments tie in both with those of Bonner on the role of the Swazi kings in production, and with Beinart in his stressing of the importance of the role of Mpondo chiefs even in the absence of age-regiments, in supervising the economy. In the Zulu state the power of the king over the age-set regiments was, however, central: 'by means of the age-set system, the king restricted the rate of demographic expansion . . . and the rate and direction in which processes of production could expand'.[38]

Whatever the precise configuration of forces behind the Mfecane, the economic and social effects were dramatic and far-reaching. While Guy is concerned mainly with the internal changes in production and demography, the rise of the Zulu kingdom and of its offshoots on the highveld, south Mozambique and north of the Limpopo, also had profound external repercussions. Although Shaka's regiments also engaged in agricultural production, in fact the bulk of this was still borne by the homestead, now mainly women, older children and older men. Moreover, each regiment was underpinned, economically and socially—as Guy shows—by many times its number of cattle: one of the outstanding methods of attracting men to the regiments and legitimating their existence would appear to have been through the abundance of cattle, both for lobola and for the conspicuous consumption of meat. Externally, the shortfalls in agriculture and the ever-increasing requirements for cattle were made good by systematic raiding. This became institutionalised among the people living close to the military states, in the form of the extraction of tribute (which sometimes took the form of symbolic raids); among peripheral people, intermittent raids became part of an accepted part of life, which had to be budgeted for and coped with politically, even if neighbouring hills offered physical refuge. Further afield, peoples could take a calculated gamble against the odds of a raid in any particular year.

While this pattern has been most fully charted by David Beach in the case of the Ndebele state and its relations with the Shona in the nineteenth century,[39] the same processes are touched on in this collection by Beinart for the Mpondo in the second and third decades of the century, and by Slater for the Natal Nguni, whose Zulu overlords were replaced in the 1840s by Boer overlords. Wagner in his analysis of African-Afrikaner politics in the northern Transvaal also shows that fear of the raiding propensities of the Ndebele was a continuing theme in the alliances formed in the Zoutpansberg area as late as the 1870s.[40]

From these essays, it is possible to see the continuing importance of the Mfecane in determining the responses of African societies in the nineteenth century to colonial penetration, at both the political and the economic level. On the one hand, the more powerful of the Mfecane-created military states, such as the Zulu, the Ndebele or the Swazi, and to a lesser extent the Pedi, were able to prevent this encroachment until well into the nineteenth century; on the other, the experiences other African societies had had of the Mfecane/Difaqane led to an acquiescence and indeed at times an alliance with the newly arrived Trekkers on the Highveld. For yet others, the fact that they had already had considerable experience of having to produce an extractable surplus enabled them to respond with such alacrity to the newly created markets. Thus, as William Beinart shows in his essay on the Mpondo in the nineteenth century, the changes in the so-called 'traditional' economy were not only generated by contact with the colonial economy: the first situation he looks at is of a post-Mfecane state which has to recoup its losses after Zulu raids have deprived it of its cattle.

In this situation, the Mpondo compensated for their loss of stock by 'more assiduous cultivation and increased hunting'; forced into denser settlements in order in the first instance to defend itself against the Zulu, the chiefdom was, in turn, reorganised for raiding its neighbours. All these activities lent themselves 'to increased control from the centre in the particular circumstances faced by the Mpondo in the early nineteenth century'. Although the paramount chief of the Mpondo, Faku, did not create a military organisation like that of the Zulu or Swazi, the Mpondo state was still more centralised than any other in the Transkei. Moreover, while the initial purpose of the change in emphasis in the economy was for the re-accumulation of stock, the Mpondo were to evidence equal flexibility later in the century in response to the demands of traders for ivory, hides, cattle and later sheep and maize, utilising new technology like iron hoes, draught oxen and ploughs, when it appeared to offer them a return. As the surplus product came to be geared increasingly to the demands of an outside market, however, and the chiefs came to export cattle rather than use it for redistribution, and as the homesteads came to have independent access to the tools which increased the productivity of labour and the market, so Beinart suggests chiefly control over production declined. Whereas at the beginning of the century, 'the dominant form of economic activity had been communal, now production became atomised to the level of the homestead'. As each homestead came to determine its own production and reproduction through its access to outside resources, so it became increasingly independent of the chiefs, thus preparing the way for the emergence of the peasant 'household', in place of the former 'homestead'.

Closer to the areas of colonial settlement these processes were both starker and swifter, as the essays by Henry Slater on the political economy of nineteenth-century Natal, and Colin Bundy on the rise and decline of the peasantry in the Herschel district of the Cape Colony reveal.[41] In both, we are dealing with communities whose experience of the Mfecane had been far more dramatic than that of the Mpondo: in the case of the Natal Nguni and the closely related Mfengu, who fled from Natal into the eastern Cape in the 1820s and who constituted the bulk of the Herschel peasantry, the processes of atomisation and peasantisation occurred somewhat more quickly than in Pondoland, where the local ruling class of chiefs was able to retain a measure of real control over the processes of change until the latter part of the century.

In Natal, in the early days of Voortrekker settlement, it is clear that the Trekkers were unable to develop and maintain regular patterns of exploitation and surplus extraction. Their various attempts to exert their control over the African population generally proved abortive: instead they remained huddled together in small groups, and carried out very little actual farming. They subsisted on hunting and by bartering African produce for cattle. As the many accounts of early colonial Natal make clear, the same was true in the early days of British settlement. The speed with which Africans were able to produce for the newly created market not only belies much colonial literature on the static quality of African economies; it also suggests that these societies were already structured to produce an extractable surplus.

In Natal, Shaka's political and economic transformations laid the basis for its substitution by a new colonial power: in place of the articulation between the lineage mode of production and the tributary state, there was now an articulation of the lineage mode with the colonial state, which extracted surplus through rent and taxation, and to some extent labour. Despite the effects of the Mfecane, the settler state was never powerful enough to totally restructure African society to create a fully proletarian farm labour force. Thus, in the early days, various forms of politically coerced labour were necessary to prevent the crisis over labour reaching a head. The particular fractions of capital involved in Natal led, as Slater shows, to a compromise between plantation agriculture dependent on indentured Indian labour, large absentee landowners interested in speculation, who, while awaiting a rise in land values, extracted surplus through rent, and a dissatisfied small-settler segment, constantly up in arms against the 'evils of kaffir-farming'. It also meant that Africans had a considerable choice of how to produce a surplus—and for whom. It was only at the end of the century, when the discovery of minerals created new markets for agricultural products and sent up the price of land, that this hegemony of rentier-merchant capital shifted, and commercial farmers and industrialists succeeded in their combined effort to cut down this choice—with dire results for the African peasantry living on colonist-owned land. 'Homestead producers' required the direct intervention of the state before they entered the labour market and were turned into a proletariat.

Politically, too, the Shakan revolution paved the way for colonial settlement, both south of the Tugela, and, as Wagner suggests, on the highveld. The Voortrekkers were able to establish themselves in the first instance by utilising the tensions created in African society as a result of the Mfecane/Difaqane conquests. In the north they simply replaced the Ndebele as raiders and overlords, while in Natal they made use of the divisions between Dingane, Shaka's brother, assassin and successor, and Mpande, Shaka's only other surviving brother. In alliance with Mpande, they were able to drive out Dingane, and establish themselves as nominal suzerains over the Zulu king. Whether Mpande ever saw himself as a Boer dependent is highly dubious. With the advent of the British in Natal in 1843, Mpande quickly switched his allegiance and regained complete independence north of the Tugela. The Zulu kingdom within its new boundaries remained intact and independent until its destruction by

British arms and the civil wars of 1879–87.

South of the Tugela, in the area ceded to the Voortrekkers by the Zulu king, the situation was not dissimilar to that on the highveld. For Africans shattered by the Mfecane, the first priority was to resettle themselves on the lands from which they had been driven. If they had, in the process, to accommodate a handful of settlers—and they were no more—this seemed a minor consideration after the upheavals of the past decades. Even here, as more and more Africans returned to Natal from their involuntary exile, it is doubtful whether the Voortrekker Republic could have coped. It was already beginning to show signs of strain when the British annexed Natal to the Cape in 1843.

In Natal in many ways the British were also able to take over at a political level where Shaka had left off. This was not simply because after a long period of civil war, Africans were anxious to re-establish any kind of order; it was also that the colonial administrators were able to take over the centralised powers of the Zulu kings, without introducing a major discontinuity into African life. So long as colonial society remained small and weak, it was forced to work within the modes of thought and control already established in the area. There was thus considerable continuity even at the political and ideological level in African life in nineteenth-century Natal, with Theophilus Shepstone, the Secretary for Native Affairs, taking on, certainly in his own mind, perhaps more questionably in African eyes, many of the attributes of the Zulu kings.[42] Again, as Slater points out, the fact that the land companies were content with extracting a rent and did not try to restructure productive relations among the peasantry, contributed to this sense of continuity, and masked the critical changes which were in fact taking place.

It has been argued recently that it was these particular circumstances in Natal, where the forces of colonisation were weak and had to come to terms with existing structures, utilising the pre-colonial forms and ideology for its own purposes of surplus extraction, but not totally restructuring it, which led to the development in Natal of a policy and ideology of segregation which were to provide late nineteenth-century policy-makers with useful precedents.[43] Thus in Natal, the resilience of African society and the weakness of settler forces together with British unwillingness to pay the cost of totally changing African society (for example, by removing it from the land) meant that from the 1860s even the sugar planters had to rely for labour on indentured Indians, and on Tsonga migrant labour from Delagoa Bay. This reinforced the tendency of the authorities to conserve African society in Natal, while finding other methods of labour control. The result was that many of the forms characteristic of twentieth-century segregationist policies were to be found in nineteenth-century Natal: the allocation of reserved lands for Africans, under 'traditional' authorities, the recognition of customary law and the attempt to prevent permanent African urbanisation through the 'togt' system.[44] These provided the material base for an ideology of segregation, which was not to be found until later in the century in the Cape, where the forces of colonialism had been far stronger and had lasted far longer, at least within the confines of the old colony.

It was in the Cape Colony that African peoples were first most deeply drawn into the world economy. By the time the British occupied the Cape for the second time in 1806, both the hunter-gatherer and herder Khoisan peoples of the western and northern Cape, and the Bantu-speaking Iron Age farmers of the eastern Cape had already had long experience of colonial intrusion. By the eighteenth century, a distinctive settlement had already come into being around Cape Town and in the wine and wheat-growing districts in its environs. Because of the specific ways in which European, slave and Khoisan were enmeshed in the economy, a particular form of class relations, which partly correlated with perceived colour differences, had, as Legassick suggests, already evolved in this more settled region.

For the Khoisan, the impact of the Dutch settlement had been almost wholly negative. Their relationship with the whites had been dominated by the ever-expanding cattle trade, which had ultimately spelt the destruction of their social system and independent existence, though the process took longer and their responses were more complex than is generally realised. By the end of the seventeenth century, most of the Khoisan people in the immediate neighbourhood of the Dutch settlement had lost most of their cattle and had become impoverished; and although some of them recouped their losses for a while, they did this through taking service with the colonists. The initial trading relationship, which had degenerated so easily into one of raid and counter-raid, ineluctably gave way to one of 'master' and 'servant'.[45] By the second half of the eighteenth century, the process had involved most of the Khoisan of the eastern Cape, while the Xhosa-speakers beyond the colonial frontiers were increasingly aware of the implications of the colonial presence.

During the closing years of the eighteenth century, in the declining years of the Dutch East India Company, social relations in the colony were mixed: the wine and wheat plantations in the west were based on slavery, 'master–servant' relations on the cattle-farms of the east were quasi-feudal. Both were dominated by the mercantilist company. Much of the Cape's nineteenth-century history can be seen in terms of the transformation of this company outpost into a more fully capitalist society, and the essays we publish here by Newton-King, Kirk, Trapido, Hogan and Bundy enable a major reinterpretation of the process.[46] The monopolist company was replaced by an industrialising power increasingly motivated by an ideology of free trade and revolutionary notions of the rightful relationship between capital and an unfettered labour supply. When the British took over the Cape they were confronted with a society still deeply committed to both slavery and serfdom, in which the 'masters' were white —and the slaves and serfs were not.

It is the British attempt to grapple with this situation at a time of acute labour shortage that Susan Newton-King looks at in her re-interpretation of early nineteenth-century colonial history. She is concerned to show the unity of the Cape labour market, in which slave, Khoisan and white immigrant labourers had distinct but closely related roles, as the colony came increasingly to constitute a single economic system. She examines the effects on an already labour-hungry society of the abolition of the slave trade, and reveals the increasingly active role played by the colonial state in attempting to remedy the shortage. Of particular significance were the schemes for importing indentured British labour between 1817 and 1823, because they reveal very clearly the material basis for the differentiation between 'free' high-wage imported labour and 'unfree' low-wage indigenous labour. Despite attempts to prevent the desertion of indentured servants and to delay their conversion into settlers, these schemes, as Newton-King points out, brought little profit to their sponsors and less joy to colonial employers.

The early attempts of the administration to stabilise the Khoisan labour supply through the highly repressive Hottentot Codes soon proved an equally dismal failure, and the labour situation deteriorated further with the arrival of 5 000 additional British settlers in the eastern Cape in 1820. Newton-King concludes that Ordinances 49 and 50 of 1828, for so long regarded by both Afrikaner and liberal historians as a triumph of humanitarian and philanthropic principles, were in fact concerned in the main with relieving the labour shortage through the introduction of a 'free market' in labour by removing most of the restrictions on its circulation. Even the provisions granting Khoisan labour 'equality before the law' were directed to improving the labour supply, by encouraging the Khoisan to enter service through ensuring 'fairer treatment', and defusing class struggle—a theme more fully elaborated in Trapido's full-scale treatment of liberalism at the Cape. The limitations of this *laissez-faire* measure, and the readiness on the whole of the British to yield to pressures from white employers, at least if they were considered to represent important economic interests, are indicated by the government's sanctioning the four-year apprenticeship which the 39 000 slaves were forced to enter after official emancipation in 1834.

The 'freeing' of labour was one aspect—albeit a crucial one—of the battery of measures introduced by the British to bring the Cape into line with the requirements of early nineteenth-century British capitalism. The constitutional, institutional, commercial and financial measures of reform do not directly concern us here: though we will return later to their ideological consequences. Nor do any of the essays in this collection relate directly to the purely military actions which the British found it necessary to take to protect, stabilise and—inevitably in the circumstances—to extend the colonial frontier *vis-à-vis* the Xhosa in particular: or the resistance the Xhosa were able to sustain for over three-quarters of a century.[47] It is perhaps worth noticing, however, the contrast between the later Dutch colonial period where the decline of the mercantile company was accompanied by the decentralisation of the state at the periphery, and the much stronger colonial state with an efficient military apparatus established by the British.

'Left to their own devices', trekboers in the Cape Colony at the end of the eighteenth century were being contained if not pushed back on most fronts.[48] The first two wars against the Xhosa had been inconclusive. The colonists had been totally unable to dislodge Africans from the disputed area along the frontier called the Zuurveld. The third war of 1799–1802 when the Xhosa were joined by Khoisan servants, was, as Susan Newton-King points out, economically disastrous. In the same way as, contrary to considerable mythology, Ordinance 50 and the emancipation of the 'Hottentots' were designed to resolve the labour crisis, so the appearance of the British army on the frontier was intended to defend the white settler, not prevent the extermination of the Xhosa. In 1811, 1819, 1835 and 1846 colonial wars were fought to protect the settler—often from the consequences of his own actions. And although the Xhosa were by no means finally defeated in any of these wars, they were increasingly driven back as they lost land to colonial intruders.

It can be argued that the object of both the legal reforms and the series of frontier wars was to establish and legitimate a colonial economy, which would generate sufficient surplus to support itself and provide raw materials and a market for British manufacturers. An early aspect of this was the attempted establishment of a peasantry in the eastern Cape: their close settlement was intended to have the additional advantage of providing a defence against the hostile Xhosa. The importation of British settlers to the Albany district in 1820 was one experiment in this direction; another was the settlement of Khoisan and Coloured[49] people along the Kat River in 1829, which is the subject of the essay by Tony Kirk included in this collection.[50] Both schemes failed, though for very different reasons: the first because it was wholly misconceived from the outset, as the unfortunate immigrants quickly found to their cost. The second, the Kat River scheme, was destroyed by the very success of the Khoisan—and the Mfengu who had joined them—in peasant production, at a time when commercial sheep farmers were enviously eyeing their lands and wanting their labour. The deliberate harassment of the Kat River peasants by capitalist farmers was, as Kirk shows, not simply the result of social prejudice and race feeling: the 'increasingly vociferous attacks' on the Kat River settlement 'were principally inspired by economic pressures resulting from expansion in the British and Cape woollen industries'. The Kat River settlement 'with its numerous streams and fertile soil, lay right at the heart of the finest sheep territory in the eastern division' of the colony, and ultimately the hostility of the British settlers to its very existence, despite the loyal assistance the Kat River inhabitants had rendered the colonists in the war against the Xhosa in 1846, drove the peasants into open rebellion less than five years later. In 1850–1, they joined the Xhosa in war against the colony.

Like the Xhosa, the Khoisan were defeated, and in 1854–5 the Kat River lands were given over to colonial settlement, as Xhosa lands had been piecemeal over the previous forty years. The last episode of the age-old resistance of the Khoisan to colonial intrusion was over: as Macmillan remarked—though he saw it as the triumphant vindication of Ordinance 50 and the 'colour-blind' Masters and Servants Law of 1841—'not only the Hottentot problem, but the very name Hottentot, passed out of recognition'.[51]

For the Xhosa the effects of the 1850–1 war on top of decades in which their social structure had been steadily eroded, not simply through military defeat, but also through its penetration by merchants and missionaries, led to the disastrous cattle-killing of 1856–7. Inspired by the prophecies of Nonqause, that if they killed all their cattle and destroyed their corn, the ancestors would return and restore the prosperity and integrity of the Xhosa people, the Xhosa committed what has been termed 'national suicide', in a millenarian movement of tragic dimensions. Despite a further series of battles in 1877–8, Xhosa capacity to resist white encroachment and pressure was seriously undermined.

Yet what was for many Africans a decade of military defeat and economic immiseration (1850–60), ushered in a period of commercial and agricultural opportunity for other groups of Cape Africans, especially the Mfengu, who had arrived in the Cape as refugees from the Mfecane some thirty years earlier. As Colin Bundy shows[52] in his study of Herschel, one of the newly acquired eastern Cape territories, in the mid-nineteenth century African peasants responded quickly and with efficiency to the demands of the recently established towns of East London, Grahamstown and King William's Town for food, and to the demands of Cape merchants for wool and other animal products for the international market. Bundy's work, here and elsewhere,[53] makes clear how successful the creation of a free peasantry was in the Ciskei and Transkei. Both in the eastern Cape, and at different times in different parts of southern Africa, the creation of new markets awakened a remarkably rapid response among Africans, even before the demands of the tax collector and the labour recruiter made cash crop production a more attractive option than work on white mines and farms, though often with unforeseen and unintended repercussions. Bundy traces the rise of the Herschel peasantry, its considerable prosperity in the 1870s and 1880s—and its decline by the century's end, part of the wider rural underdevelopment which has come to characterise the African 're-serves' of twentieth-century South Africa. It is a theme fully explored for the region as a whole in the recent volume of essays edited by Robin Palmer and Neil Parsons, *The Roots of Rural Poverty in Central and Southern Africa*;[54] here, in addition to the detailed study by Bundy, both Slater and Beinart touch on aspects of the process whereby capitalist development first stimulated the growth of a peasantry by providing the demand for food-stuffs and cash crops—and then helped undermine it in its search for vast quantities of cheap labour, though again the process was far from complete even at the turn of the century.

Further examples to illustrate this process are legion: the Sotho farmers who fed the little towns of the Orange Free State in the 1850s and 1860s, and the immensely increased population of the diamond diggings in the 1870s and 1880s; the Sotho-Tswana who supplied food for the Wit-watersrand far more swiftly and effectively in the first instance than Afrikaner landowners.[55] Through the work of Bundy and others, our picture of South Africa's rural development has been revolutionised. In 1964, Professor Hobart Houghton could write, with confidence, in his *The South African Economy*:

> In South Africa ... there is a ... fundamental line of cleavage which ... is of such importance that there may be said to be two different types of rural economies existing side by side in the same country. One is the essentially market-oriented farming, as practised by white farmers, and the other is the largely subsistence-oriented farming of African peasants in the reserves. The

difference between the two is deep-seated and manifests itself in a variety of ways reflecting cultural differences and fundamental attitudes to the exploitation of the natural environment. . . . The white farmers are scientific and experimental in their approach, while the African is traditional, and even the few progressive individuals are hampered by the communal system of land tenure and other social restraints.[56]

As Bundy, Slater and Beinart so clearly show, here and elsewhere,[57] the 'traditionalism' and 'stagnation' of contemporary African agriculture in the 'reserves' is a consequence not a cause of the way in which the peasantry was integrated into the developing capitalist economy of South Africa in the late nineteenth and early twentieth centuries.[58]

The essay by Beinart enriches our understanding of these processes. As we have already seen, the main concerns of his paper are to chart the economic history of an African chiefdom which was one of the last areas to come under colonial rule, and to examine the relationship of economic change and chiefly power. The significance of Beinart's paper in this context is that it shows us how, in an area for long regarded as 'a haven of traditionalism', the changes induced by the Mfecane and the penetration of mercantile capital led to profound changes in production and ultimately in social relationships, even though many of the forms of the earlier mode of production were untouched. While most of the studies of the responses of Africans to colonial markets have looked at mission communities, or groups of Africans who, for one reason or another, like the Mfengu, had moved away from the lineage or homestead, in Pondoland communal tenure and what Hobart Houghton terms 'other social restraints' remained remarkably intact. Nonetheless, through the nineteenth century, the Mpondo not only changed their settlement patterns in response to the exigencies of defence and production: they also changed their production and productive techniques at least to some extent in response to market demand. The 'conservatism' noted by observers in the 1930s was a result not of an age-old 'traditionalism' but of the underdevelopment which set in in the early twentieth century with the expansion of large-scale migrant labour and the collapse in the market for cattle. For the Mpondo tribesman, and for Herschel's Christian Mfengu, the trajectory of peasant decline was not dissimilar.

One of the distinguishing features of the prosperous peasantry within the Cape Colony, is that in the second half of the nineteenth century it gained access to the franchise. Much of the historiography of South Africa has been concerned to 'explain' this colour-blind franchise in terms of a Cape 'liberal tradition' imposed from outside by imperial humanitarianism, acting largely through the agency of the much-maligned missionaries.

Most of the writing on the subject has been normative and value-laden. The essay by Stanley Trapido which we publish here in considerably revised form, was important even in its original, more tentative form[59] in breaking with this tradition and providing a new conceptual and interpretative framework for the more detailed case studies which have been undertaken since. His concern is to examine the structural conditions which facilitated the growth and continuation of liberalism at the Cape: and he finds these essentially in the interest Cape merchants, missionaries and colonial officials had in the creation of a free and stable peasantry. His work thus both deepens our understanding of the processes of peasantisation explored by Bundy and Beinart, and moves beyond them to a consideration of the relationship of liberal ideology and rhetoric to the political economy in which it is embedded. He draws a distinction between the 'great tradition' of liberalism at the Cape, centred mainly on Cape Town, and propagated by financial and commercial leaders, missionaries and the major newspapers, as well as members of the parliamentary opposition of the day; and a 'small tradition' of merchants, lawyers and administrators in the constituencies of the eastern Cape, who drew their living directly from their alliance with the African peasantry. By looking at 'the conditions which made liberalism in the Cape possible, the purpose which different liberals gave to the institutions which were created' and the changing forms liberalism took under different historical circumstances, Trapido returned the subject to history.

In 'The death and posthumous vindication of Zachariah Gqishela', Neville Hogan shows how important this return has been. Hogan documents 'an instance of the workings of that alliance between independent African producers and white merchant-traders' which Stanley Trapido has called the 'small tradition' of Cape liberalism', through an analysis of a *cause célèbre* in the Cape courts in 1885: the murder of an African labourer, Zachariah Gqishela, by a white farmer; the refusal of the Solicitor-General to prosecute; the outraged response of the retired Indian missionary Don, who was in turn sued for libel and vindicated—by which time the dead Gqishela was quite forgotten in the pursuit of abstract principles. His murderer, Pelser, remained unprosecuted. As Hogan puts it,

> The legal system having once been celebrated in its ideological guise as The Law, could with safety reassume its ordinary predatory course . . . . The public argument was only obliquely relevant to African rights, and its legal resolution resulted merely in those who considered themselves to be British and virtuous gaining a temporary victory over the Dutch element who they fervently believed would abolish The Law altogether—thus inviting retribution from the masses.[60]

Hogan's essay is a contribution to the debate over the nature of the colonial society established at the Cape, and how and why the ideology of its dominant class was accepted at least in part both by the prosperous peasantry, and by the African petty bourgeoisie which grew up in its wake: African teachers, preachers, traders and newspapermen based at this time mainly in the eastern Cape market towns who acted as intermediaries both economically and ideologically between the Cape Africans (peasant and non-peasant alike) and the colonial proponents of liberal ideology. By breaking with the paradigm of 'proto-nationalism', Hogan is able to situate individuals like the newspaper editors Elijah Makiwane and Tengo Jabavu as live actors in their own world, with all its ambiguities, one which, as he says, 'a history of the spectacular fails to take into account'.[61]

Ironically, the Cape schoolmen and their compatriots from the mission stations all over South Africa were in many ways to reach the height of their expectations and aspirations in the mining towns of Kimberley and the Witwatersrand at the turn of the century[62] at the very time when the material base of Cape liberalism was being undermined by the demand from industrial capital for a massive, unskilled and cheap black proletariat. Bundy, Trapido and Hogan all suggest that it was the mineral discoveries in the last third of the nineteenth century and the socio-economic revolution which these brought about which totally changed the nature of liberalism at the Cape. Although the argument is not pursued in any detail here—it lies beyond the chronological scope of this volume—the changes in social relationships which had initially produced Cape liberalism led now to a coalescence of liberalism with late nineteenth-century British social engineering, social Darwinism and paternalism to produce an ideology of segregation: a subject touched on by Legassick's 'Frontier Tradition', and which he deals with elsewhere.[63]

If by the second half of the nineteenth century, the Cape colony presents a relatively unified picture of a colonial society with sophisticated modes of social control, increasingly drawing the African societies on its frontiers under its jurisdiction, and restructuring their productive relations, the situation north of the Orange presents no such uniformity. At this point we have to admit the very large geographical gap in our coverage of nineteenth-century South Africa. There are no papers on Lesotho or the Orange Free State—indeed nothing on the Tswana peoples. We can do no more than regret this hiatus, which is in large measure the result of a lack of research in these areas (at least by historians whose interests would lend themselves to inclusion in this collection); we can, however, direct the reader to the work of Neil Parsons on the 'Economy of Khama's kingdom in Bechuanaland', and to note that a number of scholars are now working on some of the missing pieces.[64] Much of the Transvaal, however—though as yet not the crucial south-west—has been well-served by scholars concerned with aspects of the political economy in the nineteenth century.

Within the territory bounded on the south by the Vaal and the north by the Limpopo rivers, and blocked east and west by the very considerable kingdoms of the Swazi and the Tswana, no single social formation dominated its neighbours: a diversity of societies co-existed uneasily, as the essays by Wagner, Trapido and Delius in this collection make clear. As we have seen, by the beginning of the nineteenth century, there were a number of African societies in the Transvaal, many of them of considerable size and complexity. When in 1801 the first literate observers arrived at Dithakong, the capital of the most southerly group of the Tswana, for example, they were impressed by its political organisation, the general air of law and order, and by the technical expertise displayed by its inhabitants.[65] Early reports of the Hurutshe capital at Kaditshwena, a little further north, suggested an even larger population, flourishing agriculture, a well-organised bureaucracy and a high degree of craftsmanship carried out by a group of specialised skilled artisans. In the north-east, the Pedi, Venda and Lobedu were organised in not dissimilar Later Iron Age polities, though there were culturally and ecologically determined variations. As in the case of the Nguni precapitalist societies which we have looked at in some detail, the social divisions between chiefs and commoners, and the control which the former had over cattle (or alternative forms of bride-wealth in areas where cattle-keeping was more difficult) and women, suggest that in this area too we are dealing with tributary states of considerable size and complexity, though the principles of organisation and the precise emphasis given to cattle-keeping, agriculture and mining varied from area to area.[66]

By the nineteenth century, the peoples of the Transvaal were, like the Nguni of the south-east coastlands, involved in long-distance trading networks, which in their case stretched to the Portuguese entrepots on the east and west coasts. As Peter Delius reminds us in the introduction to his essay on 'Migrant Labour and the Pedi', the Rota paramountcy which probably first rose to prominence in the eighteenth century straddled the west-east trade-route to Delagoa Bay while the Venda and the Tsonga were hunting ivory in the lands on both sides of the Limpopo and trading it with the coast from at least the early eighteenth century.[67] When the Trekkers arrived north of the Vaal, they entered an area with long-term connections with the Portuguese, connections which they only partially cut.

By comparison with these African societies, and contrary to much of the conventional historiography, it is the weakness of the settler societies which entered the highveld in the 1830s that is immediately apparent from these essays. In his examination of the *jagtersgemeenskap*, the hunting community established by the Trekkers in the Zoutpansberg area of the north-eastern Transvaal, Roger Wagner[68] not only returns to the theme of the 'frontier' opened up by Legassick in the first essay in this collection, but also reveals both the reasons for the initial success of trekker settlement in the Transvaal—and its weakness. As we have seen in the case of Natal, the prior eruption of the Difaqane was crucial for the establishment of Trekker communities. In the Transvaal, not only were some of the best-organised of the Sotho-Tswana states totally disrupted and their settlements destroyed on the very eve of the Great Trek; many Africans were only too willing to make use of the newcomers against earlier enemies. By comparison with these formidable Ndebele overlords, the colonists may have looked initially relatively innocuous. In the south and central Transvaal, the Boers totally replaced the Ndebele with their own version of the raiding state, which exercised hegemony over the African inhabitants 'through annual tribute levies, and meeting obduracy with destructive forays, funded out of the attendant plunder'; in the north, on the other hand, white raiders vied with black for control. In the northern bushveld which the Trekkers entered in the 1840s, their presence 'in a disturbed but crowded African world' depended, notwithstanding the Boers' initial monopoly of the horse and the gun, 'upon the acquiescence and even collaboration of African neighbours'.[69] Once that acquiescence and collaboration evaporated, in part as result of the recovery of African societies from the effects of the Difaqane and their acquisition of firearms in their own right, in part because the white hunters were beginning to encroach too precipitately on the trans-Limpopo hunting grounds the Venda and Tsonga considered their preserve, the jagtersgemeenskap in the Zoutpansberg collapsed: 'with only limited resources and extended supply lines, the Boer republic could not sustain its foothold in the north against determined African resistance in the mid-1860s'.[70]

During its twenty-year existence, the relationship of the Zoutpansberg community with the African communities of the northern Transvaal and beyond had an internal and an external dimension: by and large, it did not attempt to confront the major African polities beyond its immediate frontiers, whether the Ndebele across the Limpopo, the Gaza Ngoni to the north-east, or the Pedi to their south. Its caution was shared by the more powerful Boer communities further south, who did not, on the whole, care to make a frontal attack on the Kwena, Rolong or Hurutshe chiefdoms to the west, or the Zulu and Swazi kingdoms to the east—at least after the initial battles of the Great Trek, while they still had an effective monopoly of guns and horses. Internally, however, the community through its Commandant-General and *Superintendent van Kafferstammen* at the head of an army of African allies, attempted to collect *opgaaf* (tribute) whether in cattle, produce or labour. Labour was of the essence, as Wagner shows in his treatment of the system of *inboekselings* ('apprentices') in the north. The notoriety of the Zoutpansberg's slave-raiding and slave-trading activities had important implications both for its political and economic well-being at the time—and for the way in which it has been portrayed by historians. And increasingly, the symbol of Trekker power and the means of production of the hunters' trade—the gun—was diffused through African society, especially as the elephant retreated into the tsetse-fly zone and had to be pursued on foot, rather than, as the Boer hunters preferred, on horseback. While the Boers attempted to retain control over firearms by distributing them and reclaiming them through compliant chiefs, in fact, as Wagner remarks, 'white ownership of a gun in the hands of a black marksman twenty-five miles the other side of the Limpopo ultimately signified very little'. [71] And he goes on to show the potency of this 'portable and lethal' means of production in dissolving social relations not only between African and trekker societies, but indeed within African society itself.

The necessity to retain control over the *swart skuts*, and more generally over African collaborators in raising levies to ferret out tribute, led to the close involvement of Zoutpansberg officials in the internal politics of the African polities in their immediate neighbourhood. The merit of Wagner's essay is the way it illuminates not only the manipulative actions of the colonisers, but also the equally manipulative actions of the African communities. If trekker officials could intervene effectively in African succession disputes, in the Zoutpansberg at least Africans were able to intervene even more effectively in disputes between the trekker officials—as Wagner's carefully drawn account of the succession dispute between Mawewe and Mzila and the Munene 'affair' reveal:

> When Schoemansdal was a charred ruin and the Volksraad tried to apportion blame for the tragedy of 1867, the commission appointed to examine the documents began its account with the Munene affairs—'from which great jealousy and ... rancour arose between Superintendent Albasini and a part of the officials and officers of the district Zoutpansberg ...' [72]

But there was a wider importance to the collapse of the Zoutpansberg *gemeenskap*, because, as Wagner suggests, the colonisation of the north was 'an authentic Boer colonisation of the Trek period, deriving from the same pool of white communities in the eastern Cape which after 1836 colonised Natal, the northern Free State and the western Transvaal';[73] its collapse was presaged in the difficulties we have already witnessed in the case of the Republic of Natal in the 1840s, and suggests the fragility of this movement in the absence of fresh inputs of manpower and capital from the metropole. This impression is reinforced by the repercussions of its collapse—the African 'resurgence in the Transvaal, culminating in the "Sekhukhune wars" of the late 1870s, from which the Boer settlements were rescued by the British annexation of 1877'.[74]

It is the Pedi polity under Sekhukhune which is the main subject of Peter Delius's essay on 'Migrant Labour and the Pedi, 1840–80',[75] which links in a number of ways with Wagner's work on the northern Transvaal. Not only does he confirm Wagner's view of an African resurgence in the 1860s; he is also able to broaden the scope of the argument to take in the development of the Pedi polity in the aftermath of the Difaqane, which had become, by the 1870s, an alternative focus of power for Africans both to the South African Republic and the Swazi state to its west and east respectively. Crucial in this resurgence was the diffusion of guns in the north-eastern Transvaal. As Sir Garnet Wolseley recorded in his diary on a visit to the north-eastern Transvaal in 1879:

> Now that the Native possesses a gun as well as Meinbeer [(*sic*. Probably should be *Meinheer*—a Dutchman colloquially (Editors)] he is even beginning to recognise a master in the black man. This is shown in the number of Boers who in recent years have been paying taxes to Native Chiefs in consideration of being protected by them.[76]

As we have seen, becoming a swart skut was one way of acquiring a gun; but it was not the only way. As Delius shows, as early as the 1840s, but increasingly from the 1850s and 1860s, considerable numbers of Africans from the north-eastern Transvaal, loosely termed Pedi, but containing among their ranks Tsonga, Lobedu and Transvaal Ndebele (but significantly enough not Venda) were making the 'arduous fifteen-day journey' to the south, to take employment on the farms and public works of the Cape Colony. Although they returned home with cattle, blankets, items of clothing—even on occasion horses—the main object was to purchase a gun. In 1862 the German missionaries, to whom we are indebted for much of the detailed eye-witness account of the migration from the 1860s, believed that up to one thousand guns with accessories were brought into the area in any one year.[77]

It has long been known that the Pedi were among the first migrants on the Kimberley diamond fields in any number. Delius shows that even before the opening of the diamond fields in the late 1860s, the Pedi were accustomed to seek work many miles from home. He locates the origins of the flow in the years following the Difaqane, when refugees who attached themselves to the Pedi kingdom in search of security, found the only way they had of accumulating resources, particularly for lobola, was through selling their labour-power on the colonial market. Yet, as he shows, this does not account for the wider involvement of the polity in labour migrancy: and suggests that the paramount, Sekwati, was closely concerned in the initiation and control of this flow, especially in the 1850s when the Pedi were facing a serious threat to their security from their Trekker, Zulu and Swazi neighbours. Early traditions talk of Sekwati's despatching whole regiments to Delagoa Bay and the Cape to acquire firearms, and this may have been so in the early days. By the time the Berlin missionaries arrived, the numbers of men involved, the evidence that some regimental organisation was used and the accompaniment of the migrants by men of high rank to keep charge suggest that the paramount played an important part in the process. Both in Mshweshwe's kingdom, where the men stopped to replenish their provisions on the southward journey and regrouped to form a body on the return, and at the workplace, the chief had his representatives. In the 1870s, again at a time of tension between the Pedi and their neighbours, Sekhukhune tried to tighten his control over the migrants and subordinate chiefdoms in the polity through his agreements with the newly arrived recruiting agents. Perhaps, like the Zoutpansbergers, he was beginning to realise the difficulties of maintaining control over men with guns, although in general his possession of stores of ammunition did enable him to retain a certain degree of authority over the use of firepower.

For Delius, a key question is why the Pedi chose to reaccumulate stock and to acquire firearms through selling their labour so far afield. After all, other African peoples—the Mpondo, the Zulu, the southern Sotho—achieved the same ends through increasing their crop production or selling surplus cattle. As he shows, the Pedi did not have this option open to them; in the early years, they suffered like the Trekkers of the northeast from the absence of a market for produce, while by the 1870s when the alluvial diggings opened up, population pressure, the result both of natural increase and of the influx of refugees, and of drought had led to a relative if not an absolute land shortage. Disease also may have contributed to a decline in production. Despite the development of the alluvial diggings in the eastern Transvaal in the 1870s, the diamond fields remained the preferred workplace: wages were higher and the price of guns lower.

In Delius's account we are also back with many of the pre-occupations we have already noted in William Beinart's work on the Mpondo: the responsiveness of African society to economic change, the range of options open to Africans, and the crucial importance of the chief in organising production. Whereas Delius explores the way in which the Pedi became exporters of labour and increasingly dependent on a technology and goods they could not reproduce, Beinart shows how much the same process of rural dependence could result from peasant production partly based on an outside technology. Like Slater, they are concerned therefore with the way in which these societies, so vibrant in their responses in the nineteenth century, were, in the twentieth, to present a uniformly 'slow decline into rural stagnation'.[78]

In the 1870s this by no means seemed a foregone conclusion. Those years saw 'a welter of legislation' in the South African Republic attempting to force Africans into the service of the farmers. The opening up of new markets in the wake of the diamond discoveries and the alluvial diggings and the growth of the Transvaal's settler population at precisely the moment that Africans were best equipped to resist trekker demands, meant that the laws were more often disobeyed than observed. Over the years, republican officials had been able to do no more than harass the returning migrants with their illegal (under republican law) guns; attempts to impose pass laws simply induced the less powerful chiefdoms in the north-east to move under Pedi 'protection'. Attempts by the Republic to confront the Pedi, whether in 1852 or 1876, had a 'chastening' effect. Their conquest had to be left to the superior arms and military organisation of the British army, fresh from its costly conquest of the Zulu kingdom—another African state the Republics had never dared tackle militarily after the early years.

We return therefore to our opening question: how has it come about that so small a number of whites has been able to impose itself on a far greater number of African peoples to achieve its present position of dominance, exploitation and power? After all, looked at in the 1870s, rather than the 1970s, on the highveld it is the parallels between white and black societies, between African and Afrikaner, that are striking —at least superficially. We have already noted this in relation to the importance of raiding and captives to at least some of the tributary states as well as to the Afrikaner Republics. Wagner writes of the central position of the 'patriarchal' Commandant-General in the Zoutpansberg, where his position in the commercial system of the *maatskappy*, in fixing the price of all commodities and acting as general broker in relation to the sale of ivory,[79] as well as his control over arms and ammunition, is strongly reminiscent of that of the Pedi paramount, or of some of the Tswana chiefs. Wider parallels can be drawn. Thus, in the nineteenth century, both African and Afrikaner societies were, by comparison with the colonial states of the coast, small-scale and closely knit. They were based largely on subsistence agriculture and pastoralism, with wealth accumulated in land and cattle, and the hunt supplying a useful source of animal protein and exchangeable commodities of high value in relation to transport costs.

Within both societies, the position of the ruling class was determined by the control it had over access to land and cattle, but its potential for exploitation was restricted by its dependence on its clients for labour and defence, and the limited means of coercion available. The tendency of the ruling class to fragment, often along lines of kin, was counterbalanced in the nineteenth century by external challenges which initially contributed to the increased centralisation of some of the societies concerned, but ultimately contributed to their downfall at least in their non-capitalist form, as they came to be seen as 'anachronisms' in the face of the intensified pressure of capitalism in the later nineteenth century. Both the African and the Afrikaner depended on Cape, Natal and Portuguese merchants for their arms and ammunition and for high technology agricultural implements, as well as for luxuries like tea, sugar and coffee; ivory, however, was the key means of exchange, and as the elephant frontier receded, both societies found themselves in relations of dependence on outside markets which they could not control.

It would be wrong, however, to exaggerate these similarities. Each of the elements has to be located within the totality of relationships in the societies concerned, in their specific mode of production. In the long run, the differences between the societies were to prove even more crucial, differences which Trapido highlights in the final essay in this collection.[80] In a still tentative attempt to grapple with the formidable problems of class formation and the state in the South African Republic, he shows the crucial importance of the concept of private ownership in land based on documentary records and therefore the very different property relations established by the Boers on the highveld; even though in the early days of the Trekker communities, the Boers were unable to make good their claims to sole effective ownership of the vast tracts of land they allocated themselves, the fact that this allocation was made on the basis of legal ownership of private property and written title deeds which gave them absolute rights of exclusion, profoundly differentiated their society from that of the African chiefdoms surrounded them.

The Trekkers brought a 'fragment'[81] of the society they had experienced in the Cape earlier in the century to the interior of South Africa. Wagner writes of the 'cultural portmanteau of Dutch-Afrikaans language, Calvinist religion, Roman Dutch law, and characteristic patterns of social relations and economic preoccupation'.[82] Trapido suggests 'the reproduction of relationships of power and property which had existed in the Cape Colony from which they had migrated'.[83] Breaking sharply with a nationalist historiography preoccupied with idealist abstractions, Trapido shows the significance from the earliest days of a market in land in the Transvaal, which led to 'rapid accumulation among Afrikaner notables and landlessness among their (white) clients'.[84]

In the early days of the republics, the key route to land and thus wealth lay through office. The shortage of capital in the Transvaal, and the constant need for military expenditure, coupled with the state's inability to extract taxes systematically, led to the payment of state officials through the allocation of exchequer bills, *mandaaten*, backed by land. Not infrequently, landdrosts, veldcornets and higher officials would be granted farms outright for their services for the state: land was the one commodity in abundant supply which could be used to pay for services rendered and even attract additional capital. 'To him that hath, shall be given'— and the ambitious local official was enabled through his position to secure yet more land; he was the first to know of potential sales of land and its value; in addition his access to what limited means of coercion existed, empowered him to extract a surplus from the land more successfully than others—largely, as in Natal, by extorting rents and taxes from the African cultivators who were allocated along with the land grants.

So long as there was sufficient land to go round, and while the land was not used for intensive agricultural production, legal ownership was perhaps of no great moment. Very quickly, however, the accumulation of land in the hands of the 'quasi-feudal notables' was coupled with an increasing landlessness among their followers. This did not necessarily mean immediate impoverishment; in the early years, the notables encouraged Trekker 'clients' to take up tenancies on their land. The clients or *bywoners* provided a ready military force and cleared previously unused land at relatively little cost. As Trapido shows, however, this began to change in the last decades of the century as the opening up of new markets encouraged notables to make use of their lands for market-oriented agriculture. Although the refusal of landowners to allow 'squatters' or bywoners back on to their farms was a much remarked feature of the post-South African war years, even before the war class cleavages were beginning to emerge in Afrikaner society north of the Vaal. The proletarianisation of sections of the Afrikaner society as a result of the accumulation of land both by the notables and to a considerable extent from the 1860s by speculative land companies owned by colonial or metropolitan capital, was significant before the beginning of the twentieth century. Indeed Trapido holds that it was partly an attempt to 'alleviate intra-Afrikaner conflict' which lay behind the 'irregular exactions' made by the notables who controlled the state on the international mining industry, established on the Witwatersrand in the last decade of the century. These exactions, together with the inadequacy of Boer agricultural production to keep pace with the demands of the mining industry for cheap food and the failure of its state machinery to provide the quantities of cheap labour it required, are some of the main reasons for the demise of the South African Republic. It too, had become an 'anachronism'.[85]

Nevertheless, after the war, the existence of the notables enabled the swift establishment of a collaborating class of capitalist farmers among the settlers that was not to happen among the Africans, whose role was now conceived of as that of a mass proletariat. As Lord Milner, British High Commissioner in South Africa (1897–1905), wrote at the time: 'The ultimate end is a self-governing white community supported by well-treated and justly governed black labour from Cape Town to the Zambesi'.[86] Although conquest hastened the proletarianisation also of white, landless Afrikaners, in the long term their fate was to be very different from that of Africans suffering many of the same trauma. As Wolpe and others have shown, a key to this difference lay in the continued access Africans, but not Afrikaners, had to land. Afrikaner social formations were restructured and transformed into a fully capitalist society; the African precapitalist modes of production were subjected to very different processes of conservation and dissolution which are the basis of the contemporary migrant labour system.[87] This 'fatal dichotomy', the fundamental difference in the outcome of the process of proletarianisation of blacks on the one hand and whites on the other, is one of the most crucial issues in the history of twentieth-century South Africa. In addition, the particular historical circumstances of late nineteenth- and early twentieth-century South Africa, and the resulting alliance between capital and the white state effectively prevented the unification of the proletariat, whether at the institutional or the ideological level. This conscious intervention was achieved by the racial division of labour and the incorporation of the white working class—but not the black—into the political processes of the state through the operation of a racially exclusive franchise: a strategy which was facilitated by the development of late nineteenth-century racism and the existence of differentially incorporated modes of production within the social formation, and made necessary by the militancy of the white working class.[88] This, however, takes us well beyond the confines of the present volume into the history of twentieth-century South Africa.[89]

The core of this volume deals essentially with the history of the societies of South Africa up to the 1880s, though some of the papers follow their themes into the twentieth century. In the nineteenth century, our focus has been as much on the continuities as on the discontinuities: the continuity of much of the structure of African societies with their internally changing dynamic which were at the same time flexible enough to respond to crisis and disaster, pressure and opportunity, whether brought by the Mfecane or white intrusion, with resilience and vigour in their own terms; and the continuity in many of the features of Afrikaner society and its adaptability to the new circumstances of the highveld; even a certain continuity, despite its fluctuations, in British imperial intention and purpose in South Africa—although it has not been our concern to explore these here. Discontinuity arose very largely when these entities interacted with one another, either peacefully or more usually in conflict. With the mineral discoveries in the last third of the century, the pace of change was dramatically altered. The thrust of imperialism and the pattern of capitalist development were unlike anything that had gone before. They spelt the end of the nineteenth-century world. For both black and white, the whole tenor and quality of life were to be quite different from what had gone before.

Notes

1 Oxford, 1941
2 L. Thompson and M. Wilson (eds.), Oxford, 1969 and 1971. The quotation is from vol. 1, p. v
3 See, e.g. A. Atmore and N. Westlake, 'A Liberal Dilemma: a critique of the Oxford History of South Africa', *Race* xiv, 2, 1972, pp. 107–36; R. Gray in *Race* xi, 1, 1969 and xiv, 1, 1972; S. Marks, 'Afrikaner and African History', *Journal of African History (JAH)* xi, 3, 1970 and 'Liberalism, Social Realities and the Oxford History', *Journal of Commonwealth Political Studies*, x, November 1972; M. Legassick, 'The Dynamics of Modernization in South Africa', *JAH*, xiii, 1, 1972
4 By a 'problematic' we mean the 'overall framework which puts into relation with one another the basic concepts [used], determines the nature of each by its place and function in this system of relationships, and thus confers on each concept its particular significance'. (N. Geras, 'Althusser's Marxism: an account and an assessment', *New Left Review*, 71, January/February, 1972.)
5 The seminar has thus covered a far wider geographical range than the essays in this collection, which are confined to dealing with the area south of the Limpopo

6 C.F. J. Muller (ed.) Pretoria, 1969
7 See the preface to his *History of South Africa, Social and Economic*. This formulation
   disguises the very different interpretation we have both of the substance of South
   African history and of the imperial context
8 Harrison M. Wright, *The Burden of the Present*, Cape Town, 1977. We are tempted
   here to recall Gareth Stedman Jones's remarks on Herbert Butterfield, who was
   'able to build up an awesome reputation on the basis of an insubstantial little
   pamphlet which warned the unwary against interpreting the past in the light of
   the present', (in 'History: the Poverty of Empiricism', in R. Blackburn (ed.),
   Ideology in Social Science: Readings in critical social theory, Glasgow, 1972, pp. 104–5)
9 Although we have tended to use the terms society and social formation interchangeably in this introduction, by a social formation we mean 'the exact nature
   of the particular diversity and unity of economic and social relations which
   characterise a society during a specific epoch'. Any given social formation may
   be understood through the abstract concept of a mode of production and its
   structure and specific form may be the result of the combination of at least two
   modes of production, one of which is dominant (i.e. subjects them in some way
   to the 'needs and logic of its own functioning system and integrates them more
   or less into the mechanism of its own reproduction'). The problem of defining
   a mode of production is a thorny one: as Robin Law has recently pointed out
   in a review article, ('In search of a Marxist perspective on pre-colonial tropical
   Africa', *JAH*, xix, 3, 1978, pp. 441–52) there is no agreement even among
   Marxists as to the precise meaning of the term, partly because of the impres-
   sionistic way Marx used it himself. Harold Wolpe, also, in an introduction to a
   forthcoming collection of essays on modes of production discusses the diverse
   interpretations of the concept to be found in the literature. Despite the difficulties,
   we find the concept in its broadest form central to our analysis of the social
   formation. We see it as the combination of forces and relations of production
   together with the mechanisms which make possible its continued functioning,
   and include within its definition economic, juridico-political and ideological
   structures. (See Wolpe and Law cited above; the quotations are from M.
   Godelier, 'The concept of "social and economic formation": the Inca example'
   in his *Perspectives in Marxist Anthropology*, Cambridge, 1977, p. 63; see also
   E. Terray, *Marxism and 'Primitive' Societies*, New York and London, 1972,
   pp. 177–9; and for a somewhat different definition of a mode of production,
   B. Hindess and P.Q. Hirst, *Precapitalist Modes of Production*, London, 1975,
   pp. 9ff.) One of the advantages of the term 'social formation' over 'society'
   for the historian is its stress on processes of change: it connotes the forming of
   society as much as its having been formed. As we shall see, this is of particular
   significance when we come to look at the articulation of modes of production in
   the so-called 'frontier zones' of South Africa, situations where one has social
   formations before the creation of state systems
10 By 'affected' we mean that the mode of production as defined above continues
   to function, with its forces and relations of production essentially intact, but
   that it is changed in the sense that there may be a quantitative change in the
   amount produced, or in the 'form' of exchange (i.e. the introduction of money);
   by 'restructured' we mean either that while earlier relations and forces of production have continued to function, the mode of production has become dependent
   on the dominant mode of production for its reproduction, or indeed that new

demands have acted to change both its relations and forces of production. In both these cases there will be different political and ideological implications

11 In *A New Kind of History: from the writings of Febvre*, edited by Peter Burke and translated by K. Folca, London, 1973, p. 31

12 See below, chs. 12 and 13

13 Below, chs. 3, 4 and 5

14 M. Godelier, 'The object and method of economic anthropology' in D. Seddon (ed.), *Relations of Production*, London, 1978, p. 107

15 See below, chs. 7-11

16 This is not to say that over time, and taken in conjunction with other factors, merchant capital may not have a profound effect on the forces and relations of production, as Beinart illustrates below. Cf. G. Kay's analysis in *Development and Underdevelopment: A Marxist Analysis*, London, 1975, p. 155: '... merchant capital can function in any mode of production so long as a significant part of the social product takes the form of commodities. ... Nevertheless, the development of commodity production which merchant capital must necessarily foster inevitably corrodes the pre-capitalist formation in which it operates'. See more generally chs. 5 and 6 for a discussion of the differences between, and therefore different impact of, merchant and industrial capital on precapitalist modes of production

17 Although we do not wish to enter here into the complex debate about the nature and origin of the state, for a justification of the use of the term in the post-Mfecane period at least see P. Bonner, below, pp. 86ff. Clearly the *forms* of the colonial and the post-Mfecane state were totally different, reflecting their different modes of production and class structures

18 H. Wolpe, 'Capitalism and Cheap Labour Power: from segregation to apartheid', *Economy and Society*, i, 4, 1972, p. 429

19 Cf. M. Godelier, 'The non-correspondence between form and content in social relations: new thoughts about the Incas' in his *Perspectives in Marxist Anthropology*, pp. 186-96, where he shows the way in which the Incas made use of 'the old kinship relations and the former village and tribal political relations *without a change in either form or structure*' for a totally new function in a different mode of production. (Italics in original, quotation from p. 188). The same author's 'Modes of Production, Kinship and Demographic Structures' in M. Bloch (ed.), *Marxist Analyses and Social Anthropology*, London, 1975, pp. 3-29 would seem to illustrate a similar point in relation to the Aborigines in Australia

20 London, 1973, p. 295

21 See below, chs. 7 and 13. For a similar impression of fluidity and instrumentality in social relations in the eastern Transvaal, see also P. Bonner, 'Factors and Fissions: Transvaal/Swazi Politics in the mid-nineteenth century', *JAH*, xix, 2, 1978, pp. 219-38

22 For the stabilisation of Iron Age communities on the ecological 'frontier' along the 50-60 cm. rainfall isohyet, see T.M.O'C. Maggs, *Early farming communities on the southern highveld: a survey of Iron Age settlement*, Pietermaritzburg, 1976

23 Neil Parsons, 'The Economic History of Khama's country in Botswana, 1884–1930' in N. Parsons and R. Palmer (eds.), *The Roots of Rural Poverty in Central and Southern Africa*, London, 1977, pp. 113-43, is only a partial exception to this generalisation. For an early attempt to apply the concepts developed by the French anthropologists to southern African material, see J. Cobbing, 'The

Ndebele under the Khumalos, 1820–96', Ph.D., University of Lancaster, 1976, ch. 5; for two contrasting attempts to apply a Marxist analysis to the modes of production in South East Africa, see H. Slater, 'Transitions in the Political Economy of south-east Africa before 1840', D.Phil. Sussex, 1976, and D. Hedges, 'Trade and Politics in southern Mozambique and Zululand in the eighteenth and early nineteenth centuries', Ph.D. London, 1978. In all these, however, the authors are treating people of mainly Nguni origin

24 For an introduction to this literature see D. Seddon (ed.), *Relations of Production: Marxist approaches to economic anthropology*, London, 1978. The individual chapters and the book as a whole have a useful bibliography. Bonner's chapter below is also an introduction to the literature, and to Hindess and Hirst's *Precapitalist Modes of Production*, and the controversies which it has aroused. See also R. Law, 'In search of a Marxist perspective on precolonial Africa' and H. Wolpe, 'Modes of production' *op. cit.*

25 R. Frankenberg, 'Economic Anthropology: one anthropologist's view' in R. Firth (ed.), *Themes in Economic Anthropology*, London, 1967, p. 84, cited in D. Seddon, *Relations of Production*, p. 35

26 Vol. i, no. 1, p. 98

27 See below, pp. 154ff.

28 See below, pp. 112, 154

29 P.P. Rey, 'The lineage mode of production', *Critique of Anthropology*, no. 3, 1975, and M. Godelier, 'Modes of production, kinship and demographic structures', *op. cit.*

30 'The Social Organisation of the Peasantry: the economic basis of kinship' in D. Seddon, *op. cit.*, p. 164. (This is reprinted from the *Journal of Peasant Studies*, i, 1.)

31 D. Hedges, 'Trade and Politics', p. 71. See also C. Meillassoux, '"The Economy" in Agricultural Self-sustaining Societies: a preliminary analysis', in D. Seddon, *Relations of Production*, pp. 146–7

32 See for example, H. Slater, 'Transitions in the Political Economy of south-east Africa before 1840'. For a critique of the terminology, see Hedges, 'Trade and Politics', pp. 14–21. There are, however, problems with his use of 'the lineage mode of production', for the Shakan kingdom

33 *Capital*, i, Harmondsworth, 1976, p. 479

34 Hindess and Hirst, *Precapitalist Modes of Production*, p. 29

35 *Ibid.* p. 199

36 The existence of the *libandla* or National Council is frequently cited as evidence of the greater popular participation in government in the Swazi state as compared with that established by Shaka among the Zulu. It can be argued, however, that some form of national assembly was more necessary to legitimate the rule of the Dlamini with their preferential cross-cousin marriage system, which as Bonner shows maintained both wealth and power within the confines of a relatively narrow group, than among the Zulu, where the system of exogamy widened the base of the ruling class

37 For the Boer use of slaves, see S. Trapido, 'Aspects in the transition from Slavery to Serfdom: the South African Republic, 1842–1902', *CSP*, vi, 1976, pp. 24–31, and his 'Landlord and Tenant in a Colonial Economy: the Transvaal, 1880–1910', *JSAS*, v, 1 October 1978. See also R. Wagner, below, pp. 332–3

38 See below, p. 116

39 D.N. Beach, 'Ndebele raiders and Shona power', *JAH*, xv, 4, 1974, pp. 633–52. See also J. Cobbing, 'The Ndebele under the Khumalos' *op. cit.*

40 Below, pp. 321–2

41 Below, chs. 6, 8

42 See S. Marks, *Reluctant Rebellion*, Oxford, 1970, p. 33–5

43 S. Marks, 'Natal, the Zulu Royal family and the ideology and segregation', *JSAS*, iv, 2, April, 1978

44 See e.g. D. Welsh, *The Roots of Segregation: Native Policy in Natal (1845–1910)* Cape Town, 1971

45 For the processes at work in the seventeenth century, see R. Elphick, *Kraal and Castle. Khoikhoi and the founding of white South Africa*, New Haven and London, 1977; for the seventeenth and eighteenth, S. Marks, 'Khoisan resistance to the Dutch in the seventeenth and eighteenth centuries', *JAH*, xiii, 1, 1972, pp. 55–80

46 Below, chs. 7–11

47 This is a much under-researched area in nineteenth century South African history, notwithstanding the classics by W.M. Macmillan, *Bantu, Boer and Briton*, London, 1929, and J.S. Galbraith, *Reluctant Empire*, Berkeley, 1963, which deal in large measure with the wars in the eastern Cape, very little detailed analysis of the African side of these wars has been undertaken, nor have the older works really been subjected to any fresh scrutiny

48 For a critique of this concept (which comes from L. Gann and P. Duignan, *Burden of Empire*, London, 1968, p. 178) see A. Atmore and S. Marks, 'The Imperial Factor in South Africa in the Nineteenth Century: towards a reassessment', *Journal of Imperial and Commonwealth History*, iii, 1 October 1974, p. 110

49 For a discussion of the terminology, see S. Newton-King, below, n. 4

50 Below, ch. 9

51 W.M. Macmillan, 'The Problem of the Coloured People' in E.A. Walker (ed.), *The Cambridge History of the British Empire*, viii, Cambridge, 1963, pp. 299–300

52 Below, ch. 8

53 'The Emergence and Decline of a South African peasantry', *African Affairs*, lxxi, 285, October 1972, 'The Transkei Peasantry, c.1890–1914: "Passing through a period of stress"', in Palmer and Parsons, *The Roots of Rural Poverty*, pp. 208–20; and his unpublished D.Phil. 'African Peasants and Economic Change in South Africa, 1870–1916, with particular reference to the Cape', Oxford, 1976

54 Though there are certain limitations in this work, and a good deal of unevenness between the different chapters, it is a most valuable addition to the literature

55 See, for example, R.C. Germond, *Chronicles of Basutoland*, Morija, 1967, ch. 31, 'Peace and Prosperity', pp. 319–28. For the Transvaal, see D. Denoon, *A Grand Illusion*, London, 1973, p. 109

56 D. Hobart Houghton, *The South African Economy*, Cape Town, 1964, p. 45. Hobart Houghton appears curiously oblivious to the work of the early pioneer in this area, W.M. Macmillan, whose *Complex South Africa*, London, 1930, provides a good deal of Bundy's empirical material on the Herschel district. Nevertheless, his work is not atypical of both contemporary official and some liberal thinking in the 1960s

57 See footnote 53, and W. Beinart, 'Peasant production, underdevelopment and the traditionalist response, c.1880–1930', M.A., University of London, 1973

58　Cf. G. Arrighi, 'Labour Supplies in Historical Perspective: a study of the pro-
letarianization of the African peasantry in Rhodesia', *Journal of Development
Studies* vi, 1970, pp. 197–234. (Also published in G. Arrighi and J. Saul, *Essays
on the Political Economy of Africa*, New York and London, 1973.)

59　In *CSP*, iv (1973), under the title 'Cape liberalism revisited'

60　Below, p. 285

61　Below, p. 277

62　For an excellent portrayal of this in the Kimberley context, see B. Willan, 'An
African in Kimberley: Sol. T. Plaatje, 1894–98', unpublished paper presented
to the workshop on South African social history, Centre of International and
Area Studies, London, 1978. Unfortunately there has been no equivalent study
of this group on the Witwatersrand

63　See the three papers he presented to a post-graduate seminar at the Institute of
Commonwealth Studies, London in 1973 under the general title 'Ideology and
Social Structure in Twentieth Century South Africa'. See also his 'Race, Indus-
trialization and Social Change: the case of R.F. Hoernle' *African Affairs*, lxxv,
299, April, 1976

64　J. Kimble at the University of Lesotho and T. Keegan at the University of
London are currently preparing work on Lesotho and the Orange Free State
respectively. K. Shillington, also at the University of London, is working on
the economic history of the southern Tswana in the nineteenth century

65　See J. Barrow, *A Voyage to Cochinchina ... to which is annexed an account of a
journey made in the years 1801 and 1802 to the residence of the chief of the Booshuana
nation ...*, London, 1806

66　S. Marks and R. Gray, 'Southern Africa and Madagascar' in R. Gray (ed.),
The Cambridge History of Africa, vol. 4, c.1600–1790, Cambridge, 1975, pp. 407–
19; M. Wilson, 'The Sotho, Tsonga and Venda' in M. Wilson and L. Thompson
(eds.), *The Oxford History of South Africa*, vol. 1, to 1870, *passim*, for the empirical
evidence on which these remarks are based

67　Below, pp. 294–5, and A. Smith, 'Delagoa Bay and the trade of south-eastern
Africa' in R. Gray and D. Birmingham (eds.), *Precolonial African Trade*, London,
1970, pp. 265–89, and Marks and Gray, *op. cit.*, pp. 408–11

68　Below, ch. 13

69　Below, p. 321

70　Below, p. 316

71　Below, p. 331

72　Below, p. 327

73　Below, p. 317

74　Roger Wagner, below, p. 317

75　Below, ch. 12

76　A. Preston (ed.), *Sir Garnet Wolseley's South African Journal, 1879–80*, Cape
Town, 1973, p. 139. One should note, however, Wolseley's vehement anti-
Boer sentiment, and also that these 'taxes' were frequently paid not only to
secure protection but also in exchange for labour which was provided by the
chiefs

77　Below, p. 296

78　Below, p. 293

79　Below, pp. 320–321

80　Below, ch. 14

81 Cf. L. Hartz, *The Founding of New Societies*, New York, 1964, where colonies of settlement are seen as 'fragments' of the metropole

82 Below, p. 317

83 Below, p. 351

84 Below, p. 350

85 The phrase is Sir Bartle Frere's about Zululand in 1879

86 C. Headlam (ed.), *The Milner Papers, vol. 2, South Africa, 1899–1905*, London, 1933, p. 35. Sir Alfred Milner to Sir Percy Fitzpatrick, 28 November 1899

87 See for example H. Wolpe, 'From Segregation to Apartheid', and R. Davies, 'Mining Capital, the State and Unskilled White Workers in South Africa, 1901– 13', *JSAS*, iii, 1 October 1976, pp. 41–69, esp. p. 44. We have not tried to delineate the complexities of these processes which belong to a subsequent volume here, but note the paradox that it was in part the success of the African struggle against proletarianisation and expulsion from the land, and their greater productive capacity compared to Afrikaner '*bywoners*' on the commercial farms which has led to the difference in outcome. This in turn led to the 'different structural conditions' under which unskilled African and Afrikaner labour was produced and reproduced—and in turn the very different nature of the class struggle for each in the industrial work-place.

88 R. Davies, *op. cit.*

89 For a more complete examination some of these themes, see the forthcoming volume of essays on late nineteenth–early twentieth century South Africa, edited by S. Marks and A. Atmore

CHAPTER TWO

The frontier tradition in South African historiography *

Martin Legassick

'Latter-day civilization', argued Eric Walker in 1930, 'has only been proceeding for sixty years; it has not, it could not hope to have, obliterated the deep marks which frontier conditions had impressed on European South Africa throughout two long centuries.'[1]

In some form or other, this sort of hypothesis is a persistent one in South African thought. 'Mr Vorster probably spoke for many', the *Rand Daily Mail* stated in an editorial in 1970, 'when he said some time ago that South Africa would never become a welfare state because it undermined a man's character if things were done for him. This is the philosophy of the frontiersman.'[2]

'Twenty-five years after the landing of van Riebeeck', so the thesis goes, 'a cattle and hunting frontier had already come into existence. The sons of the first generation of free burghers [the settlers established by the Dutch East India Company in 1658 to cultivate crops more expeditiously

---

*We are publishing here for the first time the original of a paper presented to the seminar on the Societies of Southern Africa (Institute of Commonwealth Studies, London) in 1970–1 and reproduced in *CSP*, ii. Although in a number of places the argument and references could have been updated, and the author himself would reformulate many of the propositions contained in it, the paper marked a critical stage in the historiographical debate and sparked off a number of other researchers. (See, for example, R. Wagner, 'Zoutpansberg: the dynamics of a hunting frontier' below, and P. Bonner, 'Factions and Fissions: Transvaal/Swazi Politics in the Mid-nineteenth Century', *JAH.*, xix, 3, 1978.) Its publication in its original form—apart from minor stylistic changes—seemed to us all the more necessary in that it has recently formed the subject of a swingeing attack by Harrison M. Wright in *The Burden of the Present*, Cape Town, 1977, pp. 61–7. Wright seems more concerned with scholastic pedantry than with the substantive issues. In notes to the text we have taken up the points raised by Wright—it is for the reader to judge who is guilty of misreading and distortion. In one section a tentatively phrased paragraph has been altered in the light of Wright's critique.

than the Company could itself do] became, some of them, genuine frontiers-men.'[3] Isolated from Cape Town, isolated from Europe, isolated from government, isolated from markets, isolated from the influences of 'civilisation', isolated from each other, they evolved a new way of life. The 'far-wandering vee-boer', the 'trekking Boer', thus brought into existence, has, it is argued, been 'the most active maker of South African history': he 'was to determine the form of the South African society to be'.[4] Threatened in the nineteenth century by the 'social revolution'[5] instituted in the Cape Colony by the British regime, the frontiersmen fled further into the South African interior. This movement, the Great Trek, was 'the central event in South African history'; 'all that had gone before led up to that; most of what has happened since has been a commentary on it'.[6] In the Transvaal at least, and, it is sometimes argued, in the Orange Free State and Natal as well, the frontier tradition was perpetuated.[7] The Conventions signed by the British with the Trekker Republics in 1852 and 1854 'made it possible for Transvaal attitudes and policies to dominate a far larger area of Southern Africa and thereby radically influenced future history'.[8] And, with the growing integration and economic develop-ment of South Africa, the frontier tradition returned to spread its spell and its hegemony over all South Africa: 'the habits of mind of the Trekkers ... in the course of time, flowed back into the Colony whence they had come, setting the stamp of their thought upon the whole of South Africa.'[9] Or,

> the Union Constitution, in native policy at all events, represented the triumph of the frontier, and into the hands of the frontier was delivered the future of the native peoples. It was the conviction of the frontier that the foundations of society were race and the privileges of race.[10]

It is, indeed, the influence of the frontier on racial attitudes which has been its most persistently argued effect: the frontiersman regarded the non-white only as a servant or an enemy. It was the frontier tradition which was responsible for the job colour-bar in industry, for opposition to African urbanisation, for opposition to the common non-racial but qualified Cape franchise, for hostility to African 'squatters'. But this question was intimately connected with others. The frontier tradition was individual and anarchic, suspicious of and hostile to the authority of government: it explained the anti-war rebellion of 1914, the Rand Revolt of 1922, and the performance of Afrikaner nationalists in opposition or in power.[11] It was associated with an acute and restless land-hunger, a wasteful attitude to land, 'inherited from the days of unlimited space';[12] it inhibited Afrikaners from the practice of intensive agriculture which, with their disdain for 'Kaffir-work', made more difficult their transition to the new South Africa of industry and land-shortage. Moreover, the very land-hunger of these frontiersmen and their indifference to African land-rights and land needs, had deprived non-whites of the possibility of subsistence on the land and made inevitable that economic integration which the frontiersmen were now resisting. Frontier conservatism itself aggravated all these questions and made more difficult the ending of frontier influence.

Thus baldly summarised—and perhaps even caricatured—the argument might not be supported by any who have written of the frontier tradition. Qualifications are usually made, other factors introduced as explanations, while the limits of the frontier tradition expand and contract with the argument and the author. Sometimes—particularly with respect to land-hunger—it extended to all colonists.

> It is a tradition that plays its part wherever advanced and backward races come into contact with each other ... For the British settlers in the Eastern Province of the Cape Colony and in Natal, to go no farther afield, soon learnt the rules of the game that all men of Western civilisation have played ... in touch with tribal natives whose land and labour are desirable.[13]

As such, the frontier process was 'the gradual subjugation of uncivilised native peoples and the absorption of their lands ... by the remorseless advance of white agricultural colonisation'.[14] Only missionaries and officials—and other men who had 'learnt to value reason as a check on the emotions'[15]—opposed themselves to this process. Eric Walker, W.M. Macmillan and C.W. de Kiewiet set out to rescue missionaries and officials from the onslaughts of G. McCall Theal and George Cory, historians with the 'frontier point of view'. The story of the nineteenth century, said de Kiewiet, was not of 'the struggle of settlers for self-expression against a misunderstanding and interfering Home Government', but of the contact between white and black in which the British government, though penurious, overly pragmatic and indecisive, had nevertheless sought to protect African rights and African land.[16] In two influential books Macmillan strove to rescue the reputation of John Philip; far from being an idealistic and meddling political missionary, he argued, Philip was a statesman whose policies of 'protective segregation' had been practised comparatively successfully towards the Cape Coloured and could have alleviated the problem of South Africa's twentieth-century 'Colour Problem'.[17]

Sometimes, however, the frontier tradition was more confined in its influence. It was restricted to Transvaalers—or to the inhabitants of the Republics—or to Afrikaners alone. 'The development of a separate South African racial policy', wrote W.K. Hancock,

can be regarded from three points of view. It can be looked upon as the progressive 'elimination of the imperial factor', or as a victory of the northern
provinces over the liberal Cape, or as the outcome of an inner struggle which
was, and is, being fought out everywhere in South Africa—not merely *between*
north and south, or *between* Britons and Boers, but *inside* the two European
communities.[18]

Hence the alternative tradition could be found not merely in missionaries
and officials but in colonists as well. Here a number of strands of thought
can be traced. At first there was the notion of those who had 'learnt to
value reason as a check on their emotions', the 'less highly-strung', those
who did not follow 'their instincts rather than their intelligence'.[19] British
rule at the Cape, it implied, had fostered among at least some Cape citizens
a sensible and moderate approach to racial questions and politics in
general. Eric Walker's two subjects for biography are significant: Lord
de Villiers who, with his 'central and detached position', was able to see
all sides of a question: 'I would ask any reader, especially any South
African reader ... to read that statement into every page.'[20] And W.P.
Schreiner, who underwent 'a process of conversion' [the word is his own]
on matters of race: 'that is a pilgrim's progress less rare in South Africa
than many would have us believe nowadays.'[21] As Lewis Gann has pointed
out, this argument is based on a philosophy which postulates that

> there is a necessary, underlying harmony, a sort of 'invisible hand' making for
> good. All conflicts are ultimately due to misconception of interest. Provided
> certain economic, social and political institutions, founded in reason itself, can
> be enforced, and provided men can be made to realise their 'true' interests,
> universal happiness must result.[22]

More recently the philosophy of Cape liberalism has been attributed to
the Western Cape (or Cape Town) of the eighteenth century: the atmos-
phere of town and port created greater fluidity, greater tolerance and
benevolence, and this 'Cape paternalism' became, 'with an injection of
British nineteenth-century humanitarianism,' Cape liberalism.[23]

Hence the 'frontier tradition' thesis imposed a dichotomy—sometimes
the dichotomy of missionaries and officials versus colonists, sometimes of
Afrikaner nationalists against their (largely British) opponents, sometimes
of Cape liberalism against Republican frontierism. More recently, the
'frontier tradition' argument has become caught up with the hypothesis
of the 'political factor': that South African economic development has
been plagued by the pursuit of ideological goals which have interfered
with the 'logic of the market'. Here it is the industrialist, the capitalist, the
entrepreneur, who finds himself opposing the forces of the frontier. But
the 'logic of the market' is as much a specious abstraction as the necessary

underlying harmony of interest which Gann argued has been the assumption of South African liberal historians. The very existence of these several dichotomies suggests that the situation is rather more complex. It suggests, indeed, that much closer attention should be paid to 'the frontier' itself: to such questions as what is the frontier, what are its specific influences, and how does it produce and perpetuate them—if indeed it does at all?

Race and class

The origins, nature and significance of white racism have received a great deal of attention in recent years. The profusion of terminology—racism, racial prejudice, racial discrimination, race relations, institutional racism— and the debates engendered—racism and slavery, racism and abolition, racism and industrialisation—suggest a great deal of conceptual confusion. There is, however, increasing convergence in the belief that 'race is only a special case of more general social facts . . . there can be no general theory of race and . . . race relations must be placed within the total institutional and cultural context of the society studied'.[24] Nor can it be doubted that the essential matrix of ideas from which institutionalised racism grew already existed in Europe—perhaps more prevalently in Protestant Anglo-Saxon Europe—at the early stages of overseas expansion. 'Group differences in physical traits . . . considered [as] a determinant of social behaviour and moral or intellectual qualities', which is van den Berghe's definition of racism, characterised the European perception of the Negro in Elizabethan England, for example, as the monumental study by Winthrop D. Jordan, amongst others, has shown.[25] In the societies generated by overseas expansion such attitudes hardened rapidly: 'previous ideological conditioning made possible a racially based slavery, and the growth of that kind of slavery transformed the conditioning from a loose body of prejudices into a virulent moral disorder.'[26] Racist attitudes became a racist ideology which justified the subordination and oppression of blacks.

However the different slave systems created by European imperialism and the expansion of the capitalist world market produced patterns of race relations which were not identical over either space or time. Much of the comparative work to date has concerned itself with the extent to which these patterns were the product of the differences in the European inheritance or of the immediate social and economic conditions of the colonies— what Genovese has called the 'idealistic' and 'materialistic' tendencies.[27] It is possible to subsume these opposites, as Genovese himself has tried to do:

I should prefer to assume both [ideology and economics] within a synthetic analysis of social classes that avoids compartmentalising their constituent human beings. Social classes have historically formed traditions, values, and sentiments, as well as particular and general economic interests . . . If historical materialism is not a theory of class determinism it must accept two limitations. Certain social classes can only rise to political power and social hegemony under specific technological conditions. The relationship of these classes, from this point of view, determines the contours of the historical epoch. It follows, then, that changes in the political relationship of classes constitute the essence of social transformation; but this notion comes close to tautology, for social transformations are defined precisely by changes in class relationships. What rescues the notion from tautology is the expectation that these changes in class relationship determine—at least in outline—the major psychological, ideological and political patterns, as well as economic and technological possibilities.[28]

The essence of this synthesis is, in fact, a relocation of focus. Genovese is insisting here that one must study not race relations as such but class relations:

modern slavery and the white-black confrontation form part of a single historical process, but it does not follow that slavery can best be understood as a race question. No major problem in the socio-economic transformation of Western Society, apart from the pattern of race relations itself, could possibly be resolved on such grounds.[29] *

The approach can be illustrated by the question of the treatment of slaves, provided it is understood that what has been debated under that category

*Wright (p. 65) accuses Legassick here of distorting Genovese's argument in that he fails to acknowledge that Genovese is tackling 'not race relations generally but slavery in the Americas, a distinctly narrower topic' and that Genovese goes on later to say that 'slavery in the Americas had a racial basis and must be understood not simply as a class question but as a class question with a profound racial dimension . . . a class analysis in short is not enough and can only serve as the basis for a much more complex analysis' (*The World the Slaveholders Made*, London, 1969, p. 113). As the context in which Legassick quotes Genovese makes clear, Legassick is also concerned here with slavery—and its connections with the wider issue of a racist ideology. Nor is he unaware of the 'profound racial dimension'—as he later quotes Genovese as saying 'race relations are *at bottom* a class question into which "the race question intrudes and gives . . . a special force and form *but does not* constitute its essence"', and further on, talking of the competition between black and white workers, he suggests that though this seems, at first sight, 'purely "racial"', it should be analysed '*initially*' in class terms (our italics). We agree with Harrison Wright, 'When an historian argues from analogy and from authority, it is not generally considered good practice to misread the analogy and to misstate the authority'. How much more indefensible when the 'authority' is an unpublished seminar paper . . .

includes at least three distinct phenomena, largely independent: day-to-day living conditions, general conditions of life (family security, opportunities for an independent social and religious life, nature of slave culture), and access to freedom and citizenship.[30]

To assess the significance of *race* in this question, as others besides Genovese have pointed out, we need comparisons of the treatment of whites in similar positions: European indentured servants or sailors on ships (slave-trade), European peasants, and, more generally, 'the attitude not only of industrial but of pre-industrial owners of wealth toward the poor, especially in the period 1540–1750 in Europe'.[31] Indeed, treatment, in all three senses, inter-relates with attitude, as does each with the separate matter of degree of exploitation.[32] 'She had', wrote George Eliot of Esther in *Felix Holt, the Radical*, 'a native capability for discerning that the sense of ranks and degrees has its compulsions corresponding to the repulsions dependent on difference of race and colour.' Hence one finds certain stereotypes in all systems of slavery, and probably in all systems in which political coercion rather than the market is used to create an adequate labour force; these are irrespective of race, and can be summarised as the 'slavish personality'.[33] Hence one finds that the notion of the 'proper relations between master and servant', and of the political community as the community of masters, existed in situations other than racial ones;[34] and such a notion, as Philip Mason points out, hardened under challenge. A lady would happily share her bed with her maid in the eighteenth century, but not in the early twentieth.[35] Changing ideas of the nature of 'proper relations' had their effects on social mobility: it is again Mason who points out how social attitudes and marriage patterns in nineteenth-century Britain were formed in terms of what might be called 'class heredity' rather than class status.[36]

The necessary if not sufficient economic basis of modern slave systems was the need to bring into production tracts of fertile land available at little cost in a situation where free labour was dear. The budding entrepreneur could neither derive rent from (scarce) land nor appropriate profit from employing labourers at market prices, since potential labourers had equal access to the means of production unless coerced.[37] During the nineteenth century such systems, at least in their formal sense, were abolished, sometimes violently, sometimes peaceably. As Genovese has cogently argued, the manner in which abolition occurred was not simply a matter of the character of race relations, nor a mechanistic matter of economics. Nor did it depend, in the narrow sense, on the question debated in the United States for over a hundred years, of the profitability of slavery.[38] What was crucial was whether abolition 'became a class question—a question of life and death for a whole class and therefore for a world view and a notion of civilisation'.[39]

A concentration on slavery and its abolition, however, does not, particularly in the South African case, go far enough. If one accepts the argument that race relations are at bottom a class question into which 'the race question intrudes and gives ... a special force and form but does not constitute its essence',[40] then a similar argument must be extended to post-formal-slavery periods. Where slavery was ended 'too soon', it has been argued by W. Kloosterboer—that is, before independent access to the means of production for potential labourers had ceased—it was replaced by various arrangements of forced labour: what Barrington Moore has called labour-repression; and this, in turn, is integrally related to the linkage of the societies concerned to the world capitalist economy.[41] Bearing in mind, with Andre Gunnar Frank, that this is characterised, at the colonial level, by monopoly, we see here a certain congruence with Barrington Moore's argument about the American Civil War:

> Labor-repressive agricultural systems, and plantation slavery in particular, are political obstacles to a *particular kind* of capitalism, at a specific historical stage: competitive democratic capitalism we must call it for lack of a more precise term ... If the geographical separation had been much greater, if the South had been a colony for example, the problem would in all probability have been relatively simple to solve at the time—at the expense of the Negro.[42]

Yet, even in the American South, labour-repression persisted to a certain degree or was revived after the end of Reconstruction; but, significantly, it was revived in a form which united 'poor whites' with plantation owners in a much more explicit defence of white supremacy and white privilege than had ever characterised their relationships before the Civil War.[43]

The slave and post-slavery systems of labour-repression thrown up by the capitalist world market, can be characterised, though by no means fully encompassed, by the relationship of master to servant in differing forms: master to slave, state or enterprise to coerced labourer, etc.[44] Alongside these forms of social relationship can also be found those of landlord-tenant, owner-sharecropper and even commercial company-peasant producer: these differ in that the producers retain some access to the means of production.[45] As many scholars have noted, however, there is a quite distinct 'type' of race relations, characterised by competition— most usually between white workers and black workers.[46] At first appearance, this 'type', which is prevalent in conditions of urban industrialisation, seems purely 'racial'. However, I would suggest that there is no problem in analysing this, too, initially in 'class' terms. Owing perhaps to labour-repression, perhaps to the possibilities of survival outside the industrial economy, perhaps to lower economic expectations, perhaps to compulsions of the sub-subsistence rural economy, black labour under these conditions is willing to accept lower wages than white labour. This is a *structural* fact, determined by previous history, and not a simple ideological issue: the 'class interests', in Genovese's sense, of white and black workers are different, and the structures serve to maintain and perhaps exacerbate that difference.

Race and the frontier

But to return more explicitly to South Africa and the frontier, in the hope that this schematic presentation has indicated the complexity and subtlety with which the problem of racism is now being tackled. This is hardly true in South Africa. By and large, slavery, Calvinism, and the frontier between them suffice to 'explain' present-day race attitudes in South Africa. Little chips have been made in the edifice. As Hancock, among others, pointed out, none of these served to explain the racial attitudes of immigrant white workers at Kimberley and the Witwatersrand.[47] Frederick Johnstone has made explicit the racial discrimination, in terms of the wage colour-bar particularly, practised by mine-owners.[48] Alf Stadler has pointed out other ways in which the master-servant patterns were transformed by industrialisation.[49] Shula Marks has vividly portrayed the exaggerated fears and over-confident wishful thinking of the settlers of Natal, with respect to non-white revolt in particular. She provides a variety of explanations: Natal was 'a frontier society',[50] a 'divided society'; 'there is, it would seem, a natural tendency for the white settler to become authoritarian and despotic in his relationship with conquered colonial people'. She refers to studies on the nation-states' 'image of the enemy', to the stereotype of the African 'enemy' created in the days of Shaka and Dingane and unchanged by any white military defeat of Africans, to 'innate distrust' of the strangers, to the differing institutions of the Cape.[51] The anxieties and tensions, indeed, parallel those of North American slave systems.[52] But there are questions which remain unanswered. Let us, for example, examine the contributions of the frontier to the pattern of race relations.

It was I.D. MacCrone who, in 1937, first formulated in detail the thesis on the frontier in the seventeenth and eighteenth centuries, which he then explicitly suggested underlay race attitudes in the twentieth century and which has since become widely accepted.[53] * In the original Cape refreshment station, he argued, attitudes towards non-whites were shaped by those of Europe, which saw a religious dichotomy between Christian and heathen rather than white and black: baptism was the key to non-white entry to the white community. As white settler numbers grew, however, transforming the refreshment station into a colony, and even more with the growth of a frontier isolated from the parent colony, continues Mac-Crone, the centre of gravity of influence on social behaviour shifted. Each shift, he claims, intensified racial prejudice, so that the gulf came to be between white and non-white rather than Christian and heathen.[54] But, in view of Jordan's claim, this argument is open to an initial qualification: in England—

> the concept embodied in the word Christian embraced so much more meaning than was contained in the specific doctrinal affirmations that it is scarcely possible to assume on the basis of this linguistic contrast that the colonists set the Negroes apart because they were heathen. ... From the first, then ... to be Christian was to be civilised rather than barbarous, English rather than African, white rather than black.[55]

This attitude would seem to apply also to other Protestant and Anglo-Saxon situations. The historical inheritance of South Africa—perhaps, as Genovese argues, because of the bourgeois rather than seigneurial nature of the parent regime[56]—had greater inherent tendencies towards rigid racial definition than in the Catholic Latin American situations. As so many writers have stressed, Calvinism, with its two-class conception of man, was an extreme form of this. And, as Jan Loubser points out, the

---

*Here again Wright takes issue with Legassick (p. 64) on the grounds that 'he is, simply, not describing MacCrone very well' and is being 'inconsistent' in 'ignoring the fact that Eric Walker's *Frontier Interpretation* [sic!] appeared in 1930 and that most of the books by Macmillan, De Kiewiet [sic] and Walker that he himself relies on for evidence of the liberal frontier thesis appeared before MacCrone's'. Since the first sentence of Legassick's essay refers to Eric Walker's piece (actually called 'The Frontier *Tradition* in South African History') as written in 1930, it would be strange if he were at this point in the essay ignoring this fact. Of course, as the context makes clear, Legassick is arguing that MacCrone was the first to formulate *in detail* the thesis on the frontier by using evidence from the seventeenth and eighteenth centuries: we have simply reinforced the original sense by our interpolation of 'in the seventeenth and eighteenth centuries' and 'which he then explicitly suggests underlay race attitudes in the twentieth century'. It is true that MacCrone feels himself able to make this historical leap because the 'continuity' of the frontier tradition had been sketched out by Walker in his essay of 1930. However, Walker does not examine the early frontier in the detail of MacCrone, and it is therefore MacCrone that Legassick takes as his point of departure in reassessing the seventeenth and eighteenth century evidence.

'situations in which Calvinists were confronted with a large population of different cultural background, defined as less civilised', and where two-class categorisation was prevalent, were not confined to those of colour: Prussia provides another example.[57]

The notion of inheritance is further illustrated by the 'children of Ham' justification of black inequality, which South African historians have implied to be a prevalent, curious, and well-nigh unique feature of South African racism. As an explanation of Negro *blackness*, in fact, this argument can be traced to early Jewish texts, with casual references in St Jerome and St Augustine; it re-emerged in Christian writings in the early decades of overseas exploration. According to Jordan, the first specific connection of the 'curse of Ham' with slavery is to be found in 1621, with subsequent seventeenth-century references by Dutch writers.[58] The first reference I have as yet located in South Africa is in 1703, not, significantly, by frontiersmen but by the Church Council of Drakenstein. They wrote to the Convocation of Amsterdam that they wished to convert Khoi 'so that the children of Ham would no longer be the servants of [or?] bondsmen'. The Convocation approved and hoped that 'one day God would lift the curse from the generation of Ham'.[59] In America, notes Jordan:

> The old idea of Ham's curse floated ethereally about the colonies without anyone's seeming to attach great importance to it; one Anglican minister asserted that Negroes were indeed descended from Ham ... but much more often the idea was mentioned by antislavery advocates for purposes of refutation.[60]

At some stage, but probably not predominantly until the late nineteenth century, the 'curse of Ham' became a central part of South African racial ideology. The main earlier references to the question appear to be in the writings of 'anti-slavery advocates' or the equivalent, such as John Campbell, Janssens, De Mist. Even here it seems hardly an entrenched part of belief: 'A brother of Thomas Ferreira who pretends to have some literature, has made the discovery that the Hottentots are the descendants of the accursed race of Ham'.[61]

A similar aspect of ideology which equally needs more study is the notion of the non-white—and, it would seem, exclusively the Khoisan—as a 'schepsel': 'according to the unfortunate notion prevalent here, a heathen is not actually human, but at the same time he cannot really be classed among the animals. He is therefore, a sort of creature not known elsewhere.'[62] Far from being a strange idea of the unlettered frontier, this also has a lengthy intellectual history, deriving from the idea of the Great Chain of Being. Creation, from the inanimate things through forms of life to man and thence to the myriad ranks of heavenly creatures, was conceived as a ranking, but one without gaps, so that the gradations between ranks were merely subtle alterations. Man himself, or rather men themselves, could be ranked on this scale—though there were ambivalence and confusions. But, inevitably, one method came to be racial. Thus we find William Petty, one of the mid-seventeenth-century founders of the Royal Society, writing that, though there were differences between individual men,

> there be others more considerable, that is, between the Guiny Negroes and the Middle Europeans; and of the Negroes between those of Guiny and those who live about the Cape of Good Hope [the Hottentots], which last are the most beastlike of all the Souls [Sorts?] of Men with whom our travellers are well acquainted.[63]

For, of course, the lowest 'men' on the scale were separated from the uppermost 'beasts' by only the most subtle gradation, an argument which leads naturally to the notion of the 'schepsel'.[64]

The ideas, then, were present from the beginning. They hardened into an ideology, I would argue, in response to the nineteenth-century challenge to the system of social relations. There is no reason to suppose they were more prevalent on the frontier. Nor is the ideology as such directly related to behaviour. Clearly, however, the 'European inheritance' was strongly influenced by local circumstances, and if we are to make meaningful initial comparisons, these should be with other areas where the inheritance was similar, i.e. the United States and the Anglo-Dutch Caribbean. What, in particular, were the possibilities for freedom from slavery? (And, since the Cape was a slave society, it seems reasonable to suppose that the 'normal' position of the Khoi was seen as slavery.) And what was the status of such free non-whites?

It is hard to produce figures, particularly for the Khoi. Of slaves themselves, it is estimated that 893 were emancipated between 1715 and 1792, in a slave population which had grown from *c.*2 000 to *c.*15 000.[65] There are no population figures that I know of for free non-whites in the eighteenth or early nineteenth centuries. In contrast, in 1820 in the Southern United States there were 233 634 free Negroes to 1 538 000 slaves and 7 866 797 whites—some sixteen per cent of the black community and two per cent of the total community. In Brazil the free men of colour numbered perhaps thirty per cent of the total coloured community, and about seventeen per cent of the total community.[66] In the Caribbean, free men of colour also were a sizable number, though, in contrast to Brazil, there was a clear separation at the top between 'white' and mixed black persons. In Brazil and the Caribbean, it has been argued, the mulatto/free black was encouraged to serve as a middle class and provide a political and military establishment, a task performed by the white yeomanry in the South.[67] The limited nature of the Cape government, the puny Cape economy, in fact provided little need for such roles, and where they were needed slave labour, given certain incentives, was able to fill them: Malay slaves developed in this period the monopoly of artisan work they preserved in the western Cape for some time, Khoi supplemented military forces, both on the frontier and in the western Cape, and the British, in the nineteenth century, relied heavily in wars against the Xhosa on this supplementing of military force.[68] Furthermore, the frontier—it is far from the usual argument—in fact provided opportunities for non-whites to which they had no access in the capital. The lack of manumission may have been compensated partly, from the slave's point of view, by the opportunities for escape into the interior, of which they availed themselves from earliest times.[69] The free black *burghers* of whom MacCrone speaks may, as he implies, have become subordinated once again, but it is just as likely that they moved on to the fringes of settlement.[70] Groups of 'Bastards' were landholders in the Graaff-Reinet district in the late eighteenth and early nineteenth centuries, in the inaccessible Cedarberg, as well as in the north-eastern Cape beyond the Colony border. From these emerged the so-called 'Griqua' of the nineteenth century—and it is very significant that in the 1820s the Bastards of Graaff-Reinet moved either to the Kat River Settlement or across the Orange to 'Griqualand'. Clearly such people were not regarded by white frontiersmen uniformly as equals, and their claim to land was increasingly challenged; but they did hold it, and on occasion gave help and protection to destitute whites.[71] Thus, in terms of opportunities, as well as ideology, the distinction between the frontier and the western Cape appears to break down, or, if anything, to make the frontier appear in the better light. Indeed, when MacCrone cites examples to demonstrate the denial of opportunity to non-whites, these are, strangely enough, chosen from the western Colony and not the frontier.[72]

Moreover, if in the areas where governmental authority could be enforced legal measures were important in determining non-white status, then the Colony itself played a major part in determining the pattern of race relations. In 1675 it was discovered—as a result, no doubt, of the shortage of white women—that three-quarters of the children born in the colony were 'half-breeds';[73] ten years later Commissioner Van Rheede forbade marriages between whites and full blacks.[74] At about the same time the freeing of heathen slaves was effectively proscribed, and even the 'natural' right of 'mulatto' children to freedom was limited.[75] In 1708 manumission was prevented unless the owners gave a guarantee that the freed men would not be a charge on the public funds for ten years (increased to twenty in 1783): it has usually been assumed that this was because of the poor economic performance of freed slaves, but it is equally likely that masters would manumit only slaves incapable of work.[76] These measures in themselves qualified the relationship of baptism to freedom, though the confusion that persisted in the minds of slave-owners in fact meant that Christianisation of slaves was discouraged by them. In North America the slave-owning colonies had all, by the end of the seventeenth century, passed laws asserting that conversion did not entail freedom—with the co-operation of British officials.[77] Perhaps the more widespread church activities in the North American colonies necessitated such laws; in any case, in the Cape such was not clearly understood by the colonists until the late eighteenth century.[78] Finally, apart from the Graaff-Reinet case, it does not seem that the Company was willing to accord land-rights to individual Khoi save in exceptional circumstances, so that the only way in which non-whites could maintain some title to land was by accepting staffs of office as Khoi chiefs.[79]

Nevertheless, on the frontier, argued MacCrone, the attitudes and practices of the Colony itself were 'stiffened' and accentuated 'almost to a morbid degree'.[80] Why? The key to MacCrone's argument is an assumption about social behaviour: group-consciousness implies greater hostility to those outside the group, greater group-consciousness implies greater hostility, greater hostility fosters greater group-consciousness.[81] The argument is in a sense circular, and rests as much on the claim that the white frontiersmen developed a group-consciousness as on evidence about their racial attitudes *per se*. And the question of group-consciousness involves a further assumption: that the 'frontier' as an environment has distinctive effects on human behaviour. This is a thesis which MacCrone, and the other historians with whom I am concerned, drew explicitly from F.J. Turner, whose essays on *The Frontier in American History* had been published in book form in 1920.[82] But, in fact, both in America and in South Africa assumptions about 'the frontier' had been implicitly present almost from the beginning. It is important to recognise, moreover, a confusion in the notion of 'the frontier'. When Turner spoke of it as 'the outer edge of the wave—the meeting point between savagery and civilisation' —he was concerned primarily with the frontier as isolation from a parent society, as an area where the natural environment had a greater shaping influence on behaviour. The Indians, for him, were 'to be regarded rather as one more savage obstacle than as a constituent element in frontier society'.[83] In spite of the influence of the Indian on American society and character, this attitude is not, in the case of the United States—or for that matter of Canada or Australia—a significant elision in considering frontier influence: for these frontiers were frontiers of exclusion, of near-extermination.[84]

In South Africa, by contrast, the frontier from the start involved inclusion as well as exclusion: in whatever capacity, non-whites became integral parts of the total society. It was indeed one of the merits of such historians as Macmillan and de Kiewiet to emphasise this point:

> it is of the greatest importance to remember that the settlers in South Africa did not, as the North America, sweep the native population away from their path; here alone . . . [the blacks] have persisted as an ever-present factor in the life of what the dominant whites would fain see develop as a 'White Man's Country'.[85]

This is clearly a process to which, in its most general sense, one should be wary of applying the concept of 'frontier': would the Norman conquest of Great Britain be termed a frontier movement? Yet in the South African situation there has been a tendency to move between the idea of frontier as isolation from the parent society and the frontier as meeting-point of black and white cultures, peoples, and societies. The two are not necessarily the same. Moreover, there is an implication that it is to the effects of inclusion rather than exclusion, and the effects of inclusion are not of their nature 'frontier' effects, which we should look as influences on subsequent behaviour. De Kiewiet quite correctly points out that the South African frontier wars have accorded no romantic place to black South Africans comparable to that of American Indians.[86] Yet the period of Indian warfare in the United States produced attitudes of hatred towards the Indians comparable with those attributed to white South Africans; if this is not the attitude which has survived—and for the Indian as opposed to the Negro it is not, as a study by R.H. Pearce has shown—this was precisely because the Indian was exterminated and the black South African was not.[87]

MacCrone is concerned with the frontier as isolation *and as meeting-point with other societies.* * In terms of isolation, he argues that the natural effect of the frontier is the 're-barbarization' of human beings—unless they can

---

*Editors' italics. Here again Harrison Wright (p. 64) does not appear to have grasped Legassick's argument. According to Wright, Legassick ignores 'the fact that he argues later in his paper [see below p. 63] that in the mid-1930's the attitude of the liberals changed significantly, from regarding the frontier as a place of conflict to regarding it as a place of co-operation, a change which would make MacCrone not the first formulator of a new interpretation but an anachronistic, if detailed, perpetuator of an old one'. That Legassick falls into neither of these traps is clear from the two passages we have italicised here and on the following page.

develop a means of preventing this:

> the extent to which any such radical 're-barbarization' took place was negligible in comparison with the successful preservation of its social and racial identity on the part of a group that became progressively more race-conscious and more determined than ever to maintain its integrity as the dispersion increased in scope. ... What [those who believed in necessary re-barbarization] failed to realize ... was the possibility of a new society, with its own group consciousness, being forced into existence by the force of circumstances. For the stock farmer who appeared to be turning his back upon civilised society—as he certainly was in a physical or material sense—was taking with him those of its elements that could be reshaped to form the framework of a new society. It was these psychological elements—these social attitudes, prejudices, and beliefs that were already part of the social heritage—that preserved the social cohesion of the group in spite of isolation and dispersion. The new society retained, as well as discarded, many features of the old [under the selective influence of environment].[88] *

What has happened here is the combining of two traditions in South African historiography. At least since the time of Simon van der Stel, Company officials and travellers bemoaned the consequences for 'civilisation' of the dispersal of pastoral farmers in the interior.[89] Without the constraints of society, of religion, they assumed, man degenerated into the 'war of all against all'. It was an attitude which survived in the attitudes of nineteenth-century British towards the 'Boers' and 'Afrikaners', and may even be detected in some writings of Theal.[90] Similar attitudes may be detected in the writings of eastern Americans about the frontier in the late eighteenth and early nineteenth centuries though, in the differing conditions of America, they were subordinated—at least from, say, 1830 to 1920—by a contradictory tendency, illustrated by Turner's writings, in which the frontier was assumed to have a beneficial and liberating effect on man: Hobbesian thought, crudely speaking, replaced by primitivism.[91] The corresponding contrary tradition in South Africa was that of Afrikaner nationalism, whose historians from the latter part of the nineteenth century celebrated the emergence of the Afrikaner 'volk', and gradually extended its pedigree back in time from the Trek to the eastern frontier rebellions

---

* This quotation, and the other references, would appear to us to refute Wright's allegation that Legassick 'does not, simply, describe MacCrone very well', when he attributes to MacCrone the 'belief that the frontier engendered a sense of group consciousness and of racial enmity towards the African'. We are interested in how Harrison Wright would interpret these passages. Although the passage does not explicitly talk of 'enmity towards the African', the whole object of the book would appear to confirm this interpretation—MacCrone is after all trying to explain 'racial' antagonism in the 1930s.

to the *trekboer*, and finally to Adam Tas and Hendrik Bibault.[92] Though more systematic treatments of these events now exist, the explanation of racism in these terms, loaded with *a priori* reasoning as they are, survives in those who follow MacCrone.[93]

It would seem, in fact, that the last thing that can be said about the eighteenth and early nineteenth-century frontier was that it fostered 'group-consciousness'. The basic social unit of the frontier was, there can be little doubt, the patriarchal family: a master, his wife, his children, and his dependants. Among the emergent Griqua/Bastards there was a tendency for this to shade off into the 'tribe', in which the master became a 'chief'. Among white frontiersmen one might find several families living together or nearby, or an extended family system, or perhaps the local *veldwagmeester* playing a role of authority. Transhumance may have helped or hindered wider social ties. Certainly one cannot ignore the individualism of these basic units, their quarrels over land boundaries—which contributed to their desire for isolation from each other[94]—and the political factionalism of their societies. Moreover, though de Kiewiet argues (and it is central to MacCrone's thesis as well) that 'in the face of the native population their sense of race and fellowship was exceedingly keen', there seems to be evidence that their disputes did involve differences in 'native policy', not towards their dependants on whose continued subjection under their *personal* rule there was no argument, but towards external groups.[95]

Beyond these basic social units, institutions were fragile, or else closely linked with the western Cape—with one exception. The western Cape provided the only market, the legitimation of land tenure and baptism and marriage, the home of one's kin (if one was white, at least), and in numerous cases the home of the owner of the land one occupied. (Absentee ownership, with the land occupied by non-landowning whites, by slaves, or Khoi dependants, needs much investigation.) If the family reunion joined frontiersmen together, if the infrequent *nagmaal* at a church did too, in most cases this also joined western people and frontiersmen. If some frontiersmen sustained and rigidified their religion, and called for the services of teachers and ministers, others were quite indifferent to these matters.

The one possible exception was the commando, and the local officials who grew up with it and later extended their functions. In terms of hard evidence, indeed, MacCrone's case rests largely on the commando as it developed against the San, as the source of intensified group consciousness and racial hostility. 'An unlimited and unconditional loyalty to one's own fighting group was the dominating idea of the frontier', writes Hancock in summarising MacCrone.[96]* The San, argues MacCrone, 'were considered to be so utterly beyond the pale of humanity that they were looked upon as some kind of noxious wild beast, and like wild beasts they were exterminated'.[97] Indeed, merciless warfare was waged between colonists and San, particularly from the 1770s to the 1790s, war the more vicious because of the tactics employed by San against the cattle of the farmers, and the measure of San success in inhibiting territorial expansion. Perhaps, as Shula Marks has suggested, we should speak more accurately of Khoisan resistance, in which Khoi as well as San participated, so that there is a line of continuity from the wars of the seventeenth century up to this period.[98] This was a brutal period; but let us nevertheless look at MacCrone's evidence dispassionately.

First, though the commando developed as an institution of the frontier when the Company could no longer afford frontier defence, the wars with the San were endorsed by the Company. The 'extirpation of the said rapacious tribes' was official policy in 1779, and Woeke and the liberal Maynier, Landdrosts of Graaff-Reinet, both saw the San as enemies to the Colony.[99] Secondly, and in view of this, the attitude of frontiersmen—as

---

*This citation and Legassick's use of the phrase 'the unity of the *white* fighting group' has led to Harrison Wright's allegation: 'at one point what he [Legassick] attacks about MacCrone is apparently his (Legassick's) own substantial misquotation of someone else's somewhat exaggerated summary of what MacCrone had actually said (pp. 64–5). He supports this in a footnote' (p. 120):

> Legassick quotes W.H. Hancock, who refers to MacCrone's idea of the commando as engendering loyalty to 'one's own fighting group'. Legassick apparently quoting this phrase, speaks of the 'unity of the white fighting group'. Hancock's phrase—and MacCrone's intent—allows for the mention of non-white troops in commandos without incongruity; Legassick does not, and he then points out a presumed MacCrone inconsistency.

Again Harrison Wright would appear to be wilfully misleading his readers and equally wilfully misreading both Legassick and MacCrone. In the first place, while Legassick is clearly citing Hancock in the phrase attributed, it is clear that the second phrase is his own synthesis. Secondly, although it is true that both MacCrone and Hancock allow for the presence of blacks on commando, the whole object of MacCrone's analysis of the commando system is because he feels 'Of all the institutions that were most clearly the reflection of frontier life the commando system was most characteristic' (p. 101). And his analysis of frontier society is intended to show that the 'race attitudes' which arose on the frontier 'helped to provide it with those qualities of group unity, cohesion, and self-consciousness ... without which it could not have overcome its difficulties or maintained its integrity' (p. 125). Non-whites were not in any way part of this group—as MacCrone sees it: even the 'Bastards' who went on commando and were closely associated with whites were not actually 'accepted or regarded as part of it'.

expressed in their letters at least—seems comparatively instrumental. In New England it was the prevailing attitude that the white settlers were instruments of God's will in driving the Indian from a land of which he was not making fruitful use.[100] In South Africa the emphasis is more on actual injuries committed,·on the defence of colonial property rights, than manifest destiny: 'an assemblage of robbers ... they were put to flight by the powerful hand of the Ruler of heaven and earth'; 'heathenish evildoers ... united to oppress and injure us ... Oh! that the almighty and our government might be induced by our sighs and prayers to assist us.'[101] That God was on their side seems more a hope than a predestined fact. Thirdly, it is hard to reconcile the 'unity of the white fighting group' with the fact that white burghers were wont to send their Bastard or Khoi servants on commando duty in their place; or with the evidence that the Griqua and Bastard frontiersmen of the Orange River valley dealt with San cattle-thieves just as harshly as white frontiersmen. Nor were the San treated universally as enemies. Further territorial expansion towards the Orange River was based on a change of relationships, guided by concerned local officials but implemented by the frontiersmen themselves. The San were given sheep—and were later to be absorbed as labour to some extent, by both white and Griqua frontiersmen: even MacCrone cannot ignore the evidence of these alternatives to the 'enemy' status.[102] Indeed, Augusta de Mist, travelling with her father and Henry Lichtenstein in 1803–4, writes of an isolated farmer who 'pays a sort of *tribute* in sheep from time to time, in order to "buy off" the rapacity of these savages'.[103] Gifts, tribute, ransom—the right term may be disputed, but the attitude is instrumental rather than transcendental.

Varieties of attitudes and instrumentalism are even more evident in the relations of frontier colonists with the Bantu-speaking peoples in the nineteenth century. South African pro-colonist historians, English or Afrikaner, have presented here a picture of the upright frontiersmen engaged in relentless defensive warfare against implacable Bantu cattle-thieves. The historians under discussion here—Walker, Macmillan, de Kiewiet and their followers—demurred. Writing at a time when segregation, the 'reserves', and African land rights were of acute political concern, they viewed the main struggle as one for land (or, as crucial, water rights):

> in describing frontier affairs it is easy to lay too much stress on cattle. Cattle-stealing and reprisals were a perpetual harassment and at times a *casus belli*; but land and water were the fundamental factors in the problem ... of the frontier.[104]

But whether it was cattle, land or water, conflict was seen as the essence of the relationship; to see conflict as the essential factor seemed to explain the continued existence of that conflict in the urban and industrial situation of the early 1920s: 'that is the story of nearly every native war in South Africa from that day to this, and if for "land" you write "industry" it is the story of the present struggle in South Africa's urban areas.'[105] As South African liberals turned away from ideas of protective segregation, however, to believing that the road to African 'civilisation' lay in participation in urban industrial society, a new element entered the analysis of the frontier. Where before there had been a tendency to see the entry of non-whites into roles of servile labour under whites as an unfortunate consequence of frontier conflict which had to be recognised, this process was now seen in another light:

> The frontier was the stage where, more spectacularly than elsewhere, was taking place the great revolution of South African history . . . these men of opposite race were doing more than quarrelling with each other. Even though they did not know it, they were engaged in the formation of a new society and the establishment of new economic and social bonds.[106]

The change in perception dates, perhaps, from two articles by H.M. Robertson in 1934–5, whose essential assumption is that 'a directly co-operative aspect [of contact] emerges when members of each race jointly take part in the production of commodities. This usually takes the form of the employment of Native workers by Europeans'—and the theme survives in the *Oxford History*.[107] This changed perception has subtly shifted value judgements on key 'liberal' figures in South African history in a manner which suggests a need for reappraisal. John Philip, once viewed as the first protective segregationist, became South Africa's first 'liberal'.[108] The Treaty State policy of 1837–46, once seen as a laudable attempt to check white land-grabbing, now 'maintained a dangerous fiction and staved off the inevitable day when the pretence of a dividing line between black and white would have to yield to the truth that the natives were as much a direct responsibility of government as the colonists themselves'.[109] Sir George Grey, once castigated for transforming the Ciskei into a 'chequer-board of black and white', now became the great civiliser, while Shepstone in Natal fell in historical estimation.[110] By and large, however, it is the British policy-makers who still retain the credit for the 'co-operative' aspects of the frontier, while, moreover, the element of class conflict created by the white employer–African employee relationship has virtually been dismissed.*

Yet the early frontiersman in contact with Bantu-speaking societies did not view the African solely as enemy or as servant. First, although subsistence appears to have played a larger part and for longer in the South African frontier economy than, say, the American, S.D. Neumark's study demonstrated the presence of a strong market element: slaughtered stock, sheep's tail fat, soap, as well as such natural products as ivory, hides and skins, ostrich feathers and eggs, and berry wax were the elements of this trade.[111] It would appear from recent evidence that prior to frontier expansion, Khoi communities acted as middlemen in the circulation of

---

*Wright also devotes more than a page to taking issue with Legassick's remarks in this paragraph, though in an inconsistent way. Those who have read thus far will be aware that this paragraph is hardly central to the substantive argument of the piece, and was intended to initiate debate about changing historiographic approaches to the frontier by liberals. Thus (p. 64) he appears to agree with Legassick that 'in the mid-1930's the attitude of the liberals changed significantly from regarding the frontier as a place of conflict to regarding it as a place of cooperation'. Yet (pp. 66–7) he vigorously attacks the evidence which Legassick marshals to support this argument. Some of this attack is correct in detail. Thus it is true that Walker (1957 ed.) and Macmillan (1963 ed.) retain and add to their criticism of Grey's land policy in British Kaffraria. However Legassick took the crucial phrase 'a chequerboard of black and white' from the 1928 and not the 1957 edition of Walker (see Walker, 1928, p. 297). And the fact that de Kiewiet is cited both as an exponent of the 'conflict' frontier tradition and of the 'co-operation' frontier tradition supports Legassick's argument that the 'conflict' tradition became supplemented rather than abandoned by the introduction of the theme of 'co-operation'. Legassick, however, has made it clear to us that he would be the first to concede that this piece represented an initial and tentative sally into the field of liberal historiography. The following quotation provided by Legassick would suggest in fact that he is incorrect in seeing the conflict frontier tradition as an element of liberal-segregationist historiography; it seems rather that it emerged in reaction against the sort of liberal-segregationism that Smuts was still preaching in Britain in 1929. In other words the 'frontier tradition' and the 'cooperation theory' are aspects of a 1930s historiography which differs in crucial respects from the liberal historiography of the 1920s. The quotation is from a letter from Eric Walker to W.M. Macmillan, 21/1/1930 (WMM Papers):

> I am speaking at Oxford at Coupland's invitation in the middle of February probably on 'The Trekker Point of View and Its Influence on S. A. History/ politics'. This will give me a chance of unobtrusively pointing minds and adorning[?] a tale or two; notably some of the tales that Jannie has been dangling before the British and American publics. Some of our friends over here are very much alarmed at his goings on which have apparently impressed certain highly-placed persons and may have serious effects when the East African Report comes up for debate in the Commons towards the end of February. Of course I shall be strictly historical, but if historical events are found to have a present application. Why. Who can blame me?

goods between the Cape entrepot and the Bantu-speaking communities.[112] Frontier expansion, on this interpretation, was not primarily to acquire land but to displace first the Company and then the Khoi in this trade. But trade shaded into patently unequal barter, unequal barter into theft, and theft into the organised raiding by commandos which characterised the first 'frontier wars'. On the Bantu-speaking side, unfair trading or raiding by whites provoked reprisals, while—and it is here that land and water enter—insofar as the whites insisted on exclusive occupation of any land they claimed, they provoked resistance from peoples used to communal pasturage.

Trade and war, therefore, were but two sides of the same coin: so-called co-operation and conflict both entered simultaneously.[113] Racism may have encouraged more unequal trade and raiding, but it would seem probable that factors of comparative power were at least as significant. Moreover, a similar trading–raiding syndrome also existed on the northern 'Griqua' frontier. The paradox is well illustrated by examining the careers of the so-called 'frontier ruffians'—those lawless characters who are presumed to be integral to any frontier (of isolation or societal contact). Men like Coenraad Buys, the Bezuidenhout family (Coenraad Frederick, Frederick Cornelius, Johannes and Wynand), the Prinsloos, Lucas Meyer, Carl Trichardt, Christoffel Botha and others, occupy a curious position in South African historiography.[114] Afrikaner nationalist historians have viewed the rebellions in which they played leading parts as essential formative phases in the Afrikaner character, even if they have often downplayed the role of these dubious people: Frederick Cornelius Bezuidenhout was the hero of Slagter's Nek rebellion, the man who stood up to the impudent British who dared tell him how to treat his dependants.

Liberal historians have examined the harshness of frontier treatment of non-whites—and the 'frontier ruffians' were among the most notable of the villains—and have seen here the morbidity of frontier racism. Indeed, these men were involved in brutality, murders, forced concubinage of African women. But many of them also lived for periods in Xhosa territory under the authority of African chiefs. And in the rebellions in which they participated against colonial rule they called for assistance from Xhosa rulers such as Ndlambe and later Ngqika. Sheila Patterson finds it strange that the Bezuidenhouts 'were somewhat illogically prepared to make an ally of Gaika an Xhosa chief although he was their erstwhile enemy and a Kaffir in addition'.[115] But it is not at all strange. Ngqika was not an erstwhile enemy, as some of the lesser Xhosa fragments of the frontier area had been. Enemies and friends were not divided into rigid, static categories; non-whites were not regarded implacably as enemies.

On the extreme frontier, indeed, the family-plus-dependants structure of white society shaded off, even among whites, into the 'petty chiefdom'. The activities of the Kok family or the Barends or Afrikaner families among non-whites are paralleled among white 'frontier ruffians'. These men acquired followings of 'clients', 'dependants', 'wives', 'concubines', and operated in this area of ill-defined authority. Coenraad Buys, who did this kind of thing in the Xhosa frontier area in the 1790s, moved later, when British authority was extended effectively to the area, across the Orange to continue the pattern there: other whites, such as Jan Bloem, had indeed preceded him. The Cape-Xhosa frontier ceased to be a 'frontier' in the complete sense of societal isolation, with the establishment of British military authority after 1812. Conflict and co-operation became more sharply differentiated, and the attitudes of 'frontiersmen'—now simply men living on a frontier dividing two societies—were shaped by a new total situation.[116]

Meanwhile, the frontier of isolation had moved across the Orange, where the Griqua, Jan Bloem, Coenraad Buys and others, were followed by a steady trickle of settlers and then by the Great Trek. Even in the Trek itself it may be profitable to examine different groups of participants. Louis Trichardt (son of Carl Trichardt),[117] for example, had lived outside the Colony with Ngqika for several years before the Trek.[118] And while his journey far north into the Transvaal may have been partly to seek a new outlet for trade, and undoubtedly involved some notions of white superiority, yet the fact that he should have gone so far and established himself so deep in African territory hardly suggests that he viewed non-whites as uniformly hostile.[119] Even in Hendrik Potgieter and, more equivocally, in Andries Pretorius, one senses a conflict between their self-conceptions as African 'chiefs' and as white colonists. Part of the perennial tension among the Voortrekkers over the rights of the charismatic leader against the rights of the representative Volksraad may be traced to this conflict.[120]

It is surprising how often Trekkers—particularly Potgieter and Pretorius —were willing to try to obtain the assistance of African societies not only against other Africans but against whites, thus continuing the pattern of the Cape frontier rebels. In the early 1850s, for example, there is some evidence of the intrigues of Orange Free State farmers and Pretorius in the Transvaal with Mshweshwe against British rule in the Free State, and even in 1857 Marthinus Pretorius may have hoped for the assistance of Mshweshwe against the Free State.[121] Hendrik Potgieter is reported to have attempted to enlist Sekwati of the Pedi on his side in his struggles with the Andries Ohrigstad Volksraad in the 1840s: indeed, Potgieter, with his successive moves from Potchefstroom to Ohrigstad to the

Zoutpansberg, with his continual commandos, stands clearly in line with Trichardt and with Coenraad Buys, with whose Bastard son, Doris, he was in close association.[122]

The stereotype of the non-white as enemy, therefore, does not seem to be explicitly a frontier product, whether one examines the San frontier, the Xhosa frontier, the pre-Trek northern frontier, or the frontier that developed predominantly in the Transvaal (the most 'isolated' area) after the Trek. Moreover, we must be careful not to equate the greater violence, brutality and harshness of treatment of dependants in such areas, with greater racism. White frontiersmen expected all their dependants (save their families) to be non-white: they did not expect all non-whites to be their servants. In the same way, Griqua and Bastard frontiersmen expected Kora-and San and, later, Bantu-speakers to be their dependants. As in the case of slavery in the United States, the sociology and economics of the 'master-servant' relationship in South Africa has been clouded in partisan polemics since the early nineteenth century. Up until the Trek, Cape colonists in general expected to employ labour in a slave capacity. Most of the accounts of mistreatment in Khoi refer, in fact, to efforts to retain Khoi in service, often by withholding the expected wage payments in kind, after completion of the 'contract'. In other respects, particularly the question of physical violence and assault, it would be hard to determine whether the frontier areas were in fact more violent than the western Cape rural areas.[123] After the Trek, particularly in the areas where the penetration of the cash and market economy was weak, whites continued to expect the same forms of labour. The supply of Khoi labour had been supplemented (particularly in agriculture) by Bantu-speakers from the fragmented Xhosa groups, from the late eighteenth century—a supply which, on the whole, appears to have been voluntary.[124] In view of British and missionary watchfulness after emancipation, they were unable to practise slavery as such (and indeed their relationship with the Khoi was different from slavery, at least in degree), and turned to 'apprenticeship' for full-time labour and to the labour-tax, negotiated with African chiefs, for sporadic labour. Most of the initial wars in the Transvaal, indeed, appear to have been over questions of cattle or hunting rights, or labour questions (procurement of labour, African resistance to the labour-tax) rather than over land as such.[125] But such violence must again be differentiated both from violence *within* the master-servant relationship and from the intensity of racism *per se*.

It was not, therefore, the frontier, seen as a social system distinct and isolated from a parent society, which produced a new, or even intensified an old, pattern of racial relationships. Indeed, as Owen Lattimore has written,

> frontiers are of social, not geographic, origin. Only after the concept of a frontier exists can it be attached by the community that has conceived it to a geographical configuration. The consciousness of belonging to a group, a group that includes certain people and excludes others, must precede the conscious claim for that group of the right to live or move about within a particular territory .... In large measure, when he [Turner] thought he saw what the frontier did to society, he was really seeing what society did to the frontier.[126]

The pattern of racial relationships established in the eighteenth-century Cape must be seen in the light of the formation of the Cape colonist as a whole, the form of his inheritance from Europe, and the exigencies of the situation he had to face. If there was a trend in class relationships, indeed, it was a trend away from master-slave towards chief-subject or patron-client on the frontier.

Of course, such a formulation opens new problems. Why did some colonists Trek and some not? Why were some able tò accommodate themselves to a new pattern of social relationships and some not? Or did the nineteenth-century Cape indeed establish a new pattern of social relationships? How did the introduction of new patterns or relationships affect the situation, and affect it differently in differing areas: I refer particularly to the rule by the state as opposed to the master over non-white subjects, and also to the landlord-tenant relationship (squatting) that developed over wide areas of South Africa in the second half of the nineteenth century?[127] If the stereotype of the African as enemy cannot be traced to the eighteenth century, when and why did it in fact come into existence?

Notes

1 Eric Walker, *The Frontier Tradition in South Africa: a lecture delivered ... at Rhodes House on 5th March 1930*, Oxford, 1930, p. 3. Also Walker, *The Great Trek*, 5th ed., London, 1965, pp. 1, 13

2 *Rand Daily Mail*, 24 August 1970

3 C.W. de Kiewiet, *History of South Africa: social and economic*, Oxford, 1941, pp. 10–11

4 Sheila Patterson, *The Last Trek*, London, 1957, p. 6; W.K. Hancock, *Survey of British Commonwealth Affairs, 1918–36*, London, 1942, Section II, Part 1, p. 12

5 The phrase is used, for example, in Walker, *Frontier Tradition*, p. 15; de Kiewiet, *History*, pp. 30–1, 46; Walker, *Trek*, p. 90

6 Walker, *Frontier Tradition*, p. 12 and *Trek*, pp. 1, 5, 8, 105

7 Compare P. Mason, *Patterns of Dominance*, Oxford, 1970, p. 202: 'before Durban became a great commercial centre, the Frontier spirit was influential

and Durban grew under the shadow of the Zulu kingdom' and Patterson, *Last Trek*, pp. 23–4, who credits the Free State with 'tolerance', 'harmony', in contrast with the 'unquiet', 'opinionated', 'factious' inhabitants of the Transvaal, its 'anarchy' and 'ineptitude'

8 Patterson, *Last Trek*, pp. 23–4. Also de Kiewiet, *History*, p. 66; Walker, *Trek*, p. 1

9 de Kiewiet, *History*, p. 71; Walker, *Trek*, p. 13, and *Frontier Tradition*, pp. 5, 22; W.M. Macmillan, *Cape Colour Question*, London, 1927, pp. 4, 248, 288; de Kiewiet, *The Imperial Factor in South African History*, Cambridge, 1937, p. 14

10 de Kiewiet, *History*, 150–51

11 See, for example, Walker, *Frontier Tradition*, p. 23. On the frontier tradition and government see also *ibid.*, pp. 9, 11, 14, 18–19; Walker, *Trek*, pp. 52, 63–6, 127, 129, 134, 211–2, 228, 244, 254, 329, 353; Macmillan, *Cape Colour Question*, pp. 19–21; de Kiewiet, *British Colonial Policy and the South African Republics*, London, 1929, pp. 106–109 and *History*, pp. 12, 19, 32, 41–2, 57, 103; Patterson, *Last Trek*. There are important questions here, in the relationship between individualism and cooperation, between anarchy and authoritarianism, between oligarchy (Walker's phrase) or representative government and populism, which I cannot examine here

12 Macmillan, *Cape Colour Question*, pp. 13, 22. See also Walker, *Frontier Tradition*, p. 19; de Kiewiet, *History*, pp. 16–17, 41, 57–9, 69, 191–7; Hancock, *Survey*, II, pp. 2, 22–3, etc.; H.M. Robertson, '150 Years of Economic Contact Between Black and White'. *South African Journal of Economics*, Dec. 1934/March 1935, pp. 40–5. Two problems are connected here: (a) the question of the *original* extensive use of the land, a fact deplored by numerous contemporary commentators from van der Stel to Philip and onwards, as also by Macmillan—though de Kiewiet and others, rather ambivalently, have pointed out that this was in fact an *efficient* use of the land under existing circumstances (*History*, pp. 12–3) and (b) the perpetuation of this 'habit' in changed circumstances of land shortage, implying *conservatism*—a point which emerges in most studies of the 'poor white' problem from at least the *Transvaal Indigency Commission*, Pretoria, 1908, through Macmillan's *The Agrarian Problem in South Africa*, Johannesburg, 1919, to the Carnegie Commission, *Report on the Poor White Problem in South Africa*, 5 vols, Stellenbosch, 1932, and W.M. Macmillan's *Complex South Africa*, London, 1930

13 Walker, *Frontier Tradition*, pp. 24, 21; also, p. 5

14 Macmillan, *Cape Colour Question*, p. 11. Also *ibid.*, pp. 13, 14, 15; de Kiewiet, *British Colonial Policy*, p. 7

15 Walker, *Frontier Tradition*, p. 4

16 de Kiewiet, *British Colonial Policy*, pp. 1–8; and *Imperial Factor*, pp. 1–11. Recent interpretations, e.g. J.S. Galbraith, *Reluctant Empire, 1834–54*, Berkeley, 1963, and C.F. Goodfellow, *Great Britain and South African Confederation, 1870–81*, Oxford, 1966, lay perhaps less stress on the 'native rights' question

17 Macmillan, *Cape Colour Question*, and Macmillan, *Bantu, Boer and Briton*, London, 1928

18 Hancock, *Survey*, pp. 5–10

19 Walker, *Frontier Tradition*, pp. 4, 21, 23. Cf. Macmillan, *Cape Colour Question*, pp. 9, 24 and de Kiewiet in *Foreword* to 1968 Balkema reprint of *Cape Colour Question*, pp. vii–viii

20 E. Walker, *Lord de Villiers and His Times, 1842–1914*, London, 1925

21 E. Walker, *W.P. Schreiner, A South African*, London, 1937

22 L. Gann, 'Liberal Interpretations of South African History', *Rhodes-Livingstone Journal*, 25, 1959, pp. 40–58

23 P. van den Berghe, *South Africa: a study in conflict*, Middletown, 1965, pp. 15–21. Also Patterson, *Last Trek*, pp. 6, 9, 83, 244. The origin of this thesis is in I.D. MacCrone, *Race Attitudes in South Africa*, Johannesburg, 1937, pp. 67–8, 80, 131–2

24 P. van den Berghe, *Race and Racism*, New York, 1967, p. 6

25 *Ibid.*, p. 23. For definitions see also *ibid.*, p. 11: 'racism is any set of beliefs that organic, genetically transmitted differences (whether real of imagined) between human groups are intrinsically associated with the presence or the absence of certain socially relevant abilities or characteristics, hence that such differences are a legitimate basis of invidious distinctions between groups socially defined as races'; John Rex, 'The Concept of Race in Sociological Theory' in S. Zubaida (ed.), *Race and Racialism*, London, 1970, p. 39: 'We shall speak of a race-relations structure or problem in so far as the inequalities and differentiation inherent in a social structure are related to physical and cultural criteria of an ascriptive kind and are rationalized in terms of deterministic belief systems, of which the most usual in recent years has made reference to biological science'. In a sense these definitions are narrow. For early Europe, see W.D. Jordan, *White Over Black,* Harmondsworth, 1969, pp. 3–43; G. Shepperson, 'The African Abroad or the African Diaspora', in T. Ranger (ed.), *Emerging Themes of African History*, London, 1968, pp. 153–6 and his references. Cf. Mason, *Patterns of Dominance*, pp. 30–32

26 E. Genovese, *The World the Slaveholders Made,* New York, 1969, p. 105

27 E. Genovese, 'Materialism and Idealism in the History of Negro Slavery in the Americans' in L. Foner and E. Genovese (eds.), *Slavery in the New World*, New Jersey, 1969, pp. 238–55

28 *Ibid.*, pp. 249–50. Genovese, explicitly influenced by the writings of Antonio Gramsci, the Italian Marxist, has developed his argument in *The Political Economy of Slavery*, New York, 1965, as well as in other writings

29 Genovese, *World the Slaveholders Made*, p. 103. Also *ibid.*, pp. ix, 4, 14

30 E. Genovese, 'The Treatment of Slaves in Different Countries: Problems in the applications of the comparative method' in Foner and Genovese (eds.), *Slavery*, pp. 202–10

31 J. Plumb, 'Slavery, Race, and the Poor', *New York Review of Books*, 13 March 1969. See also Genovese, *World the Slaveholders Made*, pp. 15–16; and 'Treatment', pp. 207–208

32 As the surplus (total product less wage bill—in the case of the slave his cost of maintenance) divided by the wage bill

33 See David Brion Davis, *The Problem of Slavery in Western Culture*, Ithaca, 1966. Also Genovese, *World the Slaveholders Made*, pp. 5–7. Compare Macmillan, *Cape Colour Question*, pp. 28ff

34 Cf. Peter Laslett, *The World We Have Lost*, London, 1965. This notion of proper relationship must also, as J. Plumb points out in reviewing *The World the Slaveholders Made (New York Review Books*, 26 February 1970), lead to a softening of the rigid distinction made by Genovese between bourgeois and seigneurial (feudal) social systems. However, the lines of an analysis of the

British social systems which takes this into account have been sketched, amid much controversy, in Perry Anderson 'Origins of the Present Crisis', *New Left Review*, 23, 1964; Tom Nairn, 'The British Political Elite', *ibid.*; Tom Nairn, 'The English Working-Class', *New Left Review*, 24, 1964; Edward Thompson, 'The Peculiarities of the English', *Socialist Register*, 1965; Perry Anderson, 'Socialism and Pseudo-Empiricism', *New Left Review*, 35, 1966; Nicos Poulantzas, 'Marxist Political Theory in Great Britain', *New Left Review*, 43, 1968; T. Nairn, 'Britain—The Fateful Meridian', *New Left Review*, 60, 1970. The *New Left Review* characterisations, it should be noted, challenge also Barrington Moore's idea of how British liberal democracy emerged: what took place might be better characterised as a 'premature' bourgeois revolution (Barrington Moore, *Social Origins of Dictatorship and Democracy*, Harmondsworth, 1966)

35 Mason, *Patterns of Dominance*, pp. 22–3

36 *Ibid.*, pp. 101–102, 201, referring the reader to such nineteenth-century novelists as George Meredith, Thackeray and Surtees, and citing also G.O. Trevelyan, *Report on India: The Competition Wallah*, on the similarity of social and racial distinctions

37 Cf. Sidney W. Mintz, 'Slavery and Emergent Capitalisms' in Foner and Genovese, *Slavery*, who cites on this point Edgar Thompson, 'The Plantation', Ph.D. thesis (Sociology), Chicago, 1932, and H.J. Nieboer, *Slavery as an Industrial System*, The Hague, 1900. The question of free labour vs. slave labour has been an issue in South Africa since at least 1717 (cf. *The Reports of De Chavonnes and His Council and of Van Imboff on the Cape*, intro. by J.X. Merriman, Capetown, 1918), and has often been discussed, at least implicitly, in relation to free land

38 On the profitability question, see H.D. Woodman, 'The Profitability of Slavery: an historical reappraisal', in F.O. Gatell and A. Weinstein, *American Themes: Essays in Historiography*, London, 1968; Genovese, *Political Economy of Slavery*, pp. 275–87; S.L. Engerman, 'The Effects of Slavery Upon the Southern Economy; review of the recent debate', *Explorations in Entrepreneurial History*, 2nd series, iv, Winter 1967

39 Genovese, *World the Slaveholders Made*, p. 32

40 *Ibid.*, p. 7

41 W. Kloosterboer, *Involuntary Labour since the Abolition of Slavery*, Leiden, 1960, cited by Mintz, 'Slavery and Emergent Capitalisms' in Foner and Genovese, *Slavery*. See Barrington Moore, *Social Origins of Dictatorship and Democracy* especially p. 434 where he defines such a system as 'the use of political mechanisms . . . to ensure an adequate labour force for working the soil and the creation of an agricultural surplus for consumption by other classes'; he does not define 'political' in a narrow sense: 'particularly where the peasant society is preserved, there are all sorts of attempts to use traditional relationships and attitudes as the basis of the landlords' position'. He excludes (a) the American family farm type, (b) a system of hired labour where the workers have considerable freedom to refuse jobs and move about, (c) pre-commercial and pre-industrial agrarian systems where there is a rough balance between the overlords' contribution to justice and security and the cultivators' contribution in the form of crops

42 Moore, *Social Origins of Dictatorship and Democracy*, p. 152

43 I base this assertion on somewhat slender evidence, though I hope to look at

it further: see, for example, Marvin Harris, 'The Origin of the Descent Rule', in Foner and Genovese, *Slavery*, pp. 55–8, and compare it with, for example, the position of poor whites in Hortense Powdermaker, *After Freedom*, New York, 1939; reprint 1968

44 There is a central problem here (rather similar to the problem Moore faces in assessing the balance between protection and surplus appropriation in pre-industrial systems—see note 41 above). Both Genovese and van den Berghe characterise the 'ideal-type' master-slave relation as patriarchal/paternal, though both recognise that various factors will influence its 'harshness' (but see my comments on treatment of slaves). Mason (*Patterns of Dominance*, p. 83) distinguishes 'paternalism' (colonial powers in Africa generally) from 'dominance' (South Africa and Deep South)—Brazil moved from dominant to paternal and Mexico in the other direction: his point is that the relation between father and son is qualitatively different from that between master and slave in that (a) the father hopes the son will be like him, (b) the father expects the son to be independent one day. John Rex ('The Concept of Race' in Zubaida, *Race and Racialism*, pp. 42–3), moreover, rebukes van den Berghe for calling Latin American societies paternalistic—since relations are often brutally exploitative; and substitutes (pp. 39–40) six categories of race relations

45 Genovese would term these variously seigneurial or explicitly capitalist, but I think the problem is more complex

46 For example, van den Berghe, *Race and Racism*, pp. 29–34. A. Stadler, 'Race and Industrialisation in South Africa: a critique of the "Blumer Thesis"', unpublished Seminar Paper, 1971, criticises H. Blumer ("Industrialisation and Race Relations' in G. Hunter (ed.), *Industrialisation and Race Relations*, London, 1965) for failing to recognise that, in South Africa at any rate, the pattern of race relations was transformed and intensified under conditions of industrialisation. The same point might be made for almost any of the societies studied in Hunter's book—and the evidence is in the book itself

47 Hancock, *Survey*, II, part 2, p. 42

48 F. Johnstone, 'Class conflict and colour bars in the South African gold-mining industry, 1910–26', *CSP*, i, 1969–70

49 Stadler, 'Race and Industrialisation'

50 S. Marks, *Reluctant Rebellion*, Oxford, 1970, p. 16. Shula Marks appears to be using frontier in the sense of line of geographical separation between black and white, with implications of lack of communication between sections. She also refers on the same page to stock-farmer isolation from large centres of white population. I take up these questions of definition below

51 *Ibid.*, pp. 10–17, 21, 26, 144–6, 152, 155, and *passim*

52 See, for example, Jordan, *White Over Black*, particularly chs. 3, 4, 10, 11.

53 I.D. MacCrone, *Race Attitudes in South Africa*, London, 1937, pp. 1–135. Among those who accept his basic argument are Hancock, Patterson, van den Berghe, Philip Mason, Andrew Asheron

54 MacCrone, *Race Attitudes*, pp. 6, 40ff., 65, 84–5, 95

55 Jordan, *White Over Black*, pp. 93–6

56 Genovese, *World the Slaveholders Made*, p. 109: 'Wherever we find slaveholding classes with bourgeois rather than seigneurial origins, we generally find a tendency towards more intense racism. It is a happy coincidence for Hoetinck's thesis that Protestantism and capitalism first emerged in the Anglo-Saxon

countries, in which the somatic-norm image has been furthest removed from black. Coincidence or no, we need not deny some validity to the assertion of a biological-aesthetic dimension to racism to insist on the greater force of other factors.' See the same work, pp. 34–7 on Dutch society

57 J.J. Loubser, 'Calvinism, Equality, and Inclusion: the case of Afrikaner Calvinism' in S.N. Eisenstadt, *The Protestant Ethic and Modernization*, London, 1969, pp. 369, 381. He cites C.R. Kayser, 'Calvinism and German Political Life', Ph.D. thesis, Radcliffe, 1961. On Calvinism and South African racialism see also, *inter alia*, MacCrone, *Race Attitudes*, pp. 87–8, 129 *et passim*; Walker, *Frontier Tradition*, p. 7; Hancock, *Survey*, II, part 2, p. 10; Macmillan, *Cape Colour Question*, p. 23; Walker, *Trek*, p. 64; Edward A. Tiryakian, 'Apartheid and Religion', *Theology Today*, 14, 1957; A.G.J. Cryns, *Race Relations and Race Attitudes in South Africa*, Nymegen, 1959, pp. 41–2; van den Berghe, *South Africa*, pp. 14–15; de Kiewiet, *History*, pp. 20, 22–3

58 Jordan, *White Over Black*, pp. 17–20, 35, 40–1, 54–6, 60, 62n, 84–5. As an explanation of blackness it came to be denied more often than affirmed, and by the eighteenth century was replaced by other ideas (see *ibid.*, pp. 243, 245–6, 525). One of the Dutchmen was a poet who had lived at a Dutch fort in Guinea before going to New Amsterdam about 1652

59 Quoted by F.A. van Jaarsveld, *The Afrikaner Interpretation of South African History*, Cape Town, 1964, p. 6 from C. Spoelstra, *Bouwstoffen voor de Gescheidenis der Nederduitsch Gereformeerde Kerk in Zuid-Afrika*, 2 vols., Amsterdam, 1906–7, i, p. 34; ii, p. 15

60 Jordan, *White Over Black*, p. 200

61 Janssens in G.M. Theal, *Belangrike Historiesche Dokumenten*, London, 1911, iii, p. 219. See also J. Campbell, *Travels in South Africa in 1813*, London, 1815, p. 344; A. van Pallandt, *General Remarks on the Cape ...* 1803, Cape Town, 1917, p. 12; de Mist, in Theal, *ibid.*, iii, pp. 256–7; G.D. Scholtz, 'Die Ontstaan en Wese van die S.A. Rasse-patroon', *Tydskrif vir Rasse-aangeleenthede*, July 1958, p. 147 quoting a Cape Colonist of the early nineteenth century. See also de Kiewiet, *History*, p. 20; Macmillan, *Cape Colour Question*, p. 24; Walker, *Trek*, pp. 63–4; de Kiewiet, *British Colonial Policy*, p. 7

62 Landdrost Alberti, Uitenhage, to Janssens, 12 June 1805, (quoted by J.S. Marais, *Maynier and the First Boer Republic*, Cape Town, 1944), p. 73. See also *ibid.*, p. 68 (M. Gouws to Landdrost, rec. 26 June 1790) where the commando leader refuses to take only Khoi on a commando because 'I do not think that I have been appointed to do commandos with Hottentots but with human beings (*menschen*)'. Also Marais, *Cape Coloured People*, Johannesburg, 1939, p. 5, who says the Genadendal missionaries found the term 'schepsel' in fairly general use at the end of the eighteenth century; Van Jaarsveld, *Afrikaner Interpretation*, p. 6, citing *De Zuid Afrikaan*, 22 February 1833; 26 August 1833 for references to Coloureds as 'schepsels'; MacCrone, *Race Attitudes*, pp. 128, 130, who quotes from J. Barrow, *An Account of Travels into the Interior of Southern Africa in the Years 1897 and 1898*, 2 vols., London, 1801–4, 1, p. 398 (farmers referring to Khoi as 'Zwarte Vee') and Landdrost of Stellenbosch to Fiscal, 2 April 1810 ('de Hottentoten die men in 't generaal in die Historien voor de ruwste zoort reekend en dus zo geregeld nimmer denken of kunnen denken als Christenen')

63 Quoted in Jordan, *White Over Black*, pp. 224–5. Also, on European attitudes

to the Khoi, see *ibid*, pp. 226–7, 492–3; MacCrone, *Race Attitudes*, pp. 47–8.

64 On the Great Chain of Being see A. Lovejoy, *The Great Chain of Being*, Cambridge, 1963, and, in this context, Jordan, *White Over Black*, chs. 6, 13. Jordan argues that twentieth-century writers have continually asserted that the Negro was seen *as a beast* but that the matter is more complex: no one denied the Negro had a soul and reason. This needs evaluation in the South African context

65 H.P. Cruse, *Die Opheffing van die Kleurling-Bevolking*, Cape Town, 1947, p. 253. Walker, *History of South Africa*, London, 1957, pp. 71–2, 84–5, claims that manumissions were common, as does MacCrone, *Race Attitudes*, p. 80. Their main source is H.C.V. Leibbrandt, *Requesten en Memorials, 1715–1806*, 2 vols., Cape Town, 1905–6

66 See M. Harris, 'The Origin of the Descent Rule' in Foner and Genovese, *Slavery*, pp. 52–3

67 This is based on Genovese's attempt to synthesise the contradictory positions of Tannenbaum/Freyre on the one hand, and Harris on the other, by drawing on W.D. Jordan's 'American Chiaroscuro: the status and definition of mulattoes in the British colonies', in Foner and Genovese, *Slavery*, 189–201. See Genovese, 'Idealism and Materialism . . .', p. 248; *World the Slaveholders Made*, pp. 106–108. See also Mason, *Patterns of Dominance*, pp. 317–9 who includes South Africa in a discussion of this matter, without much feeling for comparative numbers of population groups at differing periods

68 See, for example, Marais, *Maynier*, p. 53; and *Cape Coloured People*, pp. 131–4

69 This is a topic which requires further investigation but see, for example, Walker, *History*, pp. 40, 71–2, 96

70 MacCrone, *Race Attitudes*, p. 73

71 I deal with these questions in more detail in my Ph.D. dissertation, 'The Griqua, the Sotho-Tswana and the Missionaries, 1780–1840: the politics of a frontier zone', University of California, Los Angeles, 1969

72 MacCrone, *Race Attitudes*, pp. 133–4 dealing with the refusal of three burghers of Stellenbosch/Drakenstein to serve under a 'black and heathen' corporal—though they will serve alongside him—in 1788. In 1787 a Free Corps had been formed to embrace those born not in slavery but out of wedlock, and in the 1790s it was made clear that this Corps was for those 'whose parents had not been born in the state of freedom'. See also note 62, above

73 By Commissioner van Goske

74 The effect of this measure, in relationship to existing attitudes and those which developed, is uncertain. Provided a 'half-breed' population continued to develop through concubinage with whites, marriages would still have been legally possible with these: even if the women were slaves they or their children could be baptised and freed. Concubinage in itself in these conditions is of course a form of sex-race exploitation: see Roger Bastide, 'Dusky Venus, Black Apollo', *Race*, iii, 1, 1961, pp. 10–18. In the early nineteenth century both James Read and van der Kemp married 'full blacks'—a Khoi woman and slave respectively—though another missionary had trouble legitimising his marriage with a Khoi woman. See also A. Sparrman, *A Voyage to the Cape of Good Hope . . . for the year 1772 to 1776*, 2 vols., Dublin, 1786, i, pp. 284–5

75 The first by van Goens the elder; the second by van Rheede. Whereas van Goske (1675) had said that no half-breed children should be kept in servitude,

van Rheede said Christian, Dutch-speaking half-breeds could claim freedom at twenty-five for men and twenty-one for women

76 Cf. G.M. Theal. *The Progress of South Africa*, London, 1901, p. 59: Walker, *History*, p. 72

77 See Jordan, *White over Black*, pp. 92–3, 180–1

78 Cf. MacCrone, *Race Attitudes, passim*; Walker, *History*, p. 84. See also, for example, C.P. Thunberg, *Travels in Europe, Africa and Asia made in the years between 1770 and 1779*, 4 vols., London, 1795, p. 127; O.F. Mentzel, *A Geographical and Topographical description of the Cape of Good Hope* (1787), transl. G.V. Marais and J. Hoge, ed. H.J. Mandelbrote, 3 vols., Cape Town, 1921, 1924, 1944, pp. 130–1

79 This is dealt with in my Ph.D. thesis, 'The Griqua, the Sotho-Tswana and the Missionaries'

80 MacCrone, *Race Attitudes*, p. 101

81 See, generally, *ibid.* pp. 249ff and specifically pp. 98–100, 107

82 See Walker, *Frontier Tradition*, pp. 4, 9 and *Trek*, p. 11: de Kiewiet, *British Colonial Policy*, pp. 113–4

83 G.W. Pierson, 'The Frontier and Frontiersmen of Turner's Essays', *Pennsylvania Magazine of History and Biography*, lxiv, October 1940, 4, pp. 455, 461. On Turner and the Indians see also R. Hofstadter, *The Progressive Historians*, New York, 1968, pp. 104–5

84 On differing types of frontiers, discussed in this light, see O. Lattimore, *Studies in Frontier History*, London, 1962; D. Gerhard, 'The Frontier in Comparative View', *Comparative Studies in Society and History*, i, 1958, pp. 205–29; M. Mikesell, 'Comparative Studies in Frontier History', *Annals of the American Society of Geographers*, 50, 1960, pp. 62–74; W.D. Wyman and C.B. Kroeber, *The Frontier in Perspective*, Madison, 1957

85 de Kiewiet, *History*, p. 24; Macmillan, *Cape Colour Question*, p. 12. See also de Kiewiet, *British Colonial Policy*, pp. 2–3, 116; *Imperial Factor*, pp. 1–2; *History*, pp. 47–9, 78–9, 178–80; Macmillan, *Cape Colour Question*, pp. 24, 65. Sometimes it is the strength of African society, sometimes the lack of momentum of white society (with little immigration) sometimes the efforts of the British Government or the missionaries which is stressed in explaining this. What is not stressed, however, is that the white frontiersmen created an inclusive frontier from the beginning, and non-whites accepted this inclusion more readily than the Indians. The notion of white settler frontiers as inherently exclusive entered European thought, I believe, in the early nineteenth century as the result of American experience of the Indians, and permeated thought on South Africa via the missionaries (especially John Philip) and perhaps British officials

86 de Kiewiet, *Imperial Factor*, p. 2 and *History*, p. 48

87 See R.H. Pearce, *The Savages of America*, Baltimore, 1953. See also Jordan, *White over Black*, pp. 22, 89–91, 162–3, 169, 239–40, 477–81. Jefferson's attitude to Negroes, whom he regarded as almost certainly inherently inferior (and was the first American to be so explicit) and to Indians, in whom there are qualities of savage virtue, is classic

88 MacCrone, *Race Attitudes*, pp. 98–9; also pp. 114, 107–8

89 On van der Stel see for example Walker, *History*, p. 60–61. See also van Imhoff (in *Reports of Chavonnes . . . and van Imhoff, op. cit.* and ms. in the Cape Archives.

Moodie, 'Afschriften'), 1743 : J.W. Cloppenburg ('Annotatien en Remarques', Cape Archives), 1768; H. Swellengrebel ('Journal' in *Suid-Afrika*, September 1932, 9, pp. 131–7), 1739–51; Gov. J. Van Plettenberg (*Bel. Hist. Dok*, I–III), 1778; C. Beyers, *Kaapse Patriotte*, Cape Town, 1929, pp. 12, 230 (citing memorials of 1779, 1784); 'Replies of Van Ryneveld . . . 1797' (*Transvaal Journal of Secondary Education*, September–October 1931); and even Lichtenstein, an explicit 'friend' of the Boers in contrast to Barrow. This is an incomplete list, but these and other sources need to be examined as documents of intellectual history if we are to have a more sophisticated appraisal of frontier life

90 See, for example, van Jaarsveld, *Afrikaner Interpretation*, pp. 117–24

91 On these questions see particularly H.N. Smith, *Virgin Land: the American West as symbol and myth*, Cambridge, Mass., 1950; R. Welter, 'The Frontier West as Image of American Society: conservative attitudes before the Civil War', *Mississippi Valley Historical Review*, 46, 1959–60, pp. 593–614; Hofstadter, *Progressive Historians*, esp. pp. 71–93

92 See van Jaarsveld, *Afrikaner Interpretation, passim* and especially p. 133. An interesting example of how this penetrated English-speaking historiography may be seen by comparing Walker on the frontiersmen at the beginning of the eighteenth century: 'their characteristics became still more marked during the two generations of isolation and dispersion which followed the fall of the van der Stels' (*History*, 1928 ed., p. 69—already influenced by writers such as Fouche and van der Walt); and 'already the colonial born in the outlying parts were calling themselves *Afrikaners* in contrast to the semi-foreign Hollander officials at the Castle' (*History*, 1962 ed.,—based on Franken's article on Hendrick Bibault, in *Die Huisgenoot*, 21 September 1928)

93 For the unromaticised treatment of these events see Marais, *Maynier and the First Boer Republic*; C.F.J. Muller, *Die Britse Owerheid en Die Groot Trek*, Cape Town, 1948; F.A. van Jaarsveld, *The Awakening of Afrikaner Nationalism*, Cape Town, 1961.

94 On this, as opposed to the romantic wish to avoid sight of the smoke of one's neighbour's farm, see P.J. van der Merwe, *Trek*, Cape Town, 1945

95 See above, p. 66, and below, ch. 13

96 Hancock, *Survey*, II, part 1, pp. 10–11; part 2, p. 20. On the commando see also de Kiewiet, *History*, p. 19 who argues it was 'the sum of individual willingness', p. 48; Walker, *Frontier Tradition*, p. 8 and *Trek*, pp. 53–8, who argues that religion as well as the commando held them together

97 MacCrone, *Race Attitudes*, pp. 101, 122–3, 124. His evidence is Sparrman, *Travels*, i, 198; H. Lichtenstein, *Travels in Southern Africa in the years 1803–6*, 2 vols., transl. by A. Plumptre, Cape Town, 1928, ii, pp. 25–6, 281–2 and MacCrone's assertion that San he visited in the Kalahari remembered being called baboons by whites and Bastards

98 Review in *Journal of African History*, xi, 3, 1970, pp. 443–5. As *resistance* the continuity extends to the Khoi revolt of 1799, to the Kat River rebellion of 1851 and even to the revolt in Griqualand West of 1879—but these were 'internal rebellions' in a sense which the earlier ones were not

99 See D. Moodie, *The Record*, Cape Town, 1838–41, Part III, p. 80; A. van Jaarsveld cited by P.J. Venter in *Die Huisgenoot*, 2 March 1934 (MacCrone, *Race Attitudes*, p. 123); Marais, *Maynier*, pp. 28, 36, *et passim*

100 See Pearce, *Savages of America*, ch. 1; Mason, *Patterns of Dominance*, p. 242.

Cf. MacCrone, *Race Attitudes*, p. 101 quoting Turner, *Frontier Tradition*, pp. 44–6

101 Letters in Moodie, *Record*, Part III, pp. 53, 82, in MacCrone, *Race Attitudes*, pp. 105–6, 123

102 See MacCrone, *Race Attitudes*, pp. 124–5 quoting from Jaassens in *Bel. Hist. Dok.*, p. 251; Lichtenstein, *Travels*, 141ff; 76–7; Moodie, *The Record*, Part V, p. 3 (Colonel R. Collins, 1809) and J. Kicherer (an LMS missionary), *An Extract from the Rev. Mr. Kicherer's Narrative of his Mission to South Africa*, Wiscasset, 1805. On this question see also P.J. van der Merwe, *Die Noordwaartse Beweging van die Boers voor die Groot Trek*, The Hague, 1937; J.S. Marais, *Cape Coloured People*, pp. 13–25; also my 'The Griqua, the Sotho-Tswana Missionaries', *op. cit.*

103 A. de Mist, *Diary of a Journey*, Cape Town, n.d., p. 30

104 Walker, *History*, pp. 181 and also p. 115; Macmillan, *Cape Colour Question*, pp. 12, 67; de Kiewiet, *British Colonial Policy*, pp. 10–11, 16–17, 21, 94–5, 113–4, *Imperial Factor*, pp. 100, 104, *History*, pp. 24, 25, 48, 74–8

105 Walker, *Frontier Tradition*, p. 13. Cf. de Kiewiet, *Imperial Factor*, p. 13, and *History*, pp. 89, 91, 166; Macmillan, somewhat ambivalently, tends to emphasise the *contempt* of whites for Africans, nurtured because of a lack of conflict, embittered by war, and then transposed to the urban scene: see *Cape Colour Question*, pp. 19, 24

106 de Kiewiet, *History*, p. 49. See also *ibid.*, pp. 19, 64, 66, 78–9, 84, 87, 179

107 H.M. Robertson, '150 Years of Economic Contact Between Black and White: A Preliminary Survey', Part I, pp. 403–25; Part II, pp. 1–25. See particularly chapters on the eastern Frontier, Natal, and the highveld in M. Wilson and L. Thompson (eds.), *Oxford History of South Africa*, Oxford, 1969, i

108 Compare the attitude of Macmillan, *Cape Colour Question*, p. 174, with Julius Lewin, 'Dr John Philip and Liberalism', *Race Relations Journals*, xxvii, April-June 1960, pp. 82–90

109 de Kiewiet, *History*, pp. 51–2. Compare with, for example, Macmillan, *Cape Coloured Question*, p. 12; *Bantu, Boer and Briton, passim*. But Philip believed that this preservation of African land-rights could equally be achieved under British hegemony: see *Cape Coloured Question*, pp. 291–2; Walker, *History*, pp. 192–3

110 On Grey and the Ciskei compare de Kiewiet, *British Colonial Policy*, pp. 94–5, 134–7; Macmillan, *Bantu, Boer and Briton*, pp. 339–43; Walker, *History*, pp. 287–9, 294–5 with, for example, de Kiewiet, *History*, pp. 64, 84–5; *Oxford History*, pp. 261ff

111 S.D. Neumark, *Economic Influences on the South African Frontier, 1652–1836*, Stanford, 1957. See also W.K. Hancock, 'Trek', *Economic History Review*, 2nd Series, x, 3, 1958, pp. 331–9, who disputes the importance of this market factor, suggesting that the *proportion* of subsistence vs. market production is most important. Even if small, however, it might still be crucial in certain respects

112 See particularly G. Harrinck, 'Interaction between Xhosa and Khoi; emphasis on the period 1620–1750' in L.M. Thompson (ed.), *African Societies in Southern African*, London, 1969, pp. 145–70. Neumark suggests that westward Xhosa expansion in the eighteenth century is related to this trading pattern: Neumark, *Economic Influences*, p. 101

113 There is a partial recognition of this fact in de Kiewiet, *History*, p. 25

114 For these men see particularly Marais, *Maynier and the First Boer Republic*, *passim*; A.E. Schoeman, *Coenraad de Buys*, Pretoria, 1938
115 Patterson, *Last Trek*, p. 16
116 As Shula Marks points out in *Reluctant Rebellion*, the stereotype of enemy is correlated with exaggerated apprehension and exaggerated confidence, and this in turn is correlated with *lack of knowledge* of the intentions of the opposing community. Such a state of mind did exist on the eastern Cape frontier by the 1790 (see Marais, *Maynier*, p. 26, for example). However, (a) this condition is surely mitigated to the extent that *close*—even if hierarchical—relationships exist; (b) Shula Marks fails to recognise that in the case of 'masters and servants' the lack of knowledge is more characteristic of the *masters* than the *servants*; (c) the syndrome, paradoxically, applies to those with whom one *is* associated— the Khoi and Xhosa fragments of the Zuurveld in this instance, so primarily the Africans of Natal in Marks's case—rather than those more distant, such as Ndlambe or Ngqika; (d) the fear of the Zulu in the case of Marks's study may be compared with the 'fear of Communist invasion' characteristic of the Cold War: it was the ideological threat of domestic revolution rather than the (illusory) external threat which was the reason for the development of the ideology. It is interesting that the figure now widely regarded as the founder of British pseudo-scientific racism, Dr Robert Knox, who introduced a new note into racist thought ('Earlier generations had sometimes despised the Africans, sometimes pitied them, but never feared them') served as an army surgeon in South Africa in 1817–20, the years in which the Xhosa launched, under Makana, their first real resistance to land dispossession—their expulsion across the Fish River in 1812 by British troops. (P. Curtin, *Images of Africa* Wisconsin, 1964, pp. 377–80). See also MacCrone, *Race Attitudes*, p. 130
117 Walker, *Trek*, p. 108
118 Walker, *History*, pp. 184–6, 197, 199
119 Cf. G.S. Preller, *Dagboek van Louis Trichardt*, Cape Town, 1938: C. Fuller (ed.), *Louis Trichardt's Trek Across the Drakensberg, 1837–8*, Cape Town 1932. M. Nathan, *Die Epos van Trichardt en Van Rensburg*, Pretoria, 1938; B.H. Dicke, 'The Northern Transvaal Voortrekkers', *Archives Year Book for South African History*, Pretoria, 1941, pp. 67–170; W.H.J. Punt, *Louis Trichardt se Laaste Skof*, Pretoria,.1953, provide a basis for assessing this hypothesis
120 See references in note 11. It is significant that Jacobus Burger, one of the Volksraad party leaders both in Natal and Andries Ohrigstad, as well as Retief and (possibly) Gert Maritz were not really 'frontier' types in the conventional sense—they were comparatively wealthy colonists
121 Cf. de Kiewiet, *British Colonial Policy*, pp. 55–6, 108; Walker, *History*, p. 252
122 C. Potgieter and N.H. Theunissen, *Kommandant-General Hendrik Potgieter* Johannesburg, 1938. This biography 'rescued' Potgieter from the relative obscurity and disapproval manifested towards him in other Trekker histories— but rescued him in terms of Afrikaner values in the 1930s. However it is interesting that in the western Transvaal, Trekker-missionary, and probably Trekker-African relations deteriorated from the time when Pretorius replaced Potgieter as chief authority in that area: see, for example, R. Edwards, 4 Sept. 1849 (London Missionary Society Archives: 24/1/B)
123 On treatment of the Khoi see, *inter alia*, Letters of Janssens in *Bel. Hist. Dok.*, iii; Moodie, *Record*, v (Colonel Collins); Marais, *Maynier*, pp. 70–71; Macmillan,

Cape Colour Question, esp. chs. 3, 12. On this question, there is a great need to escape from the established sources of evidence—early missionaries, travellers in general (Degrandpre and Barrow for example) and even from the 'dramatic' incidents—the Black Circuit for example, and to consider the question in more detail. Perhaps, after 1812, the Court records would be a valuable new source. Marais is the only person to deal with this (though in the 1790s only) through systematic archival work

124 See, for example, Robertson, '150 Years of Economic Contact'
125 See, as an illustration of this, K.W. Smith, 'The Fall of the Bapedi in the North-Eastern Transvaal', *JAH*, x, 2, 1969, pp. 237–52. Material in the LMS archives on the western Transvaal situation in the 1840s and 1850s supports this argument. To see how this affects analysis, Smith's account of even the 1876–8 Pedi campaigns should be compared with de Kiewiet, *History*, p. 104; *Imperial Factor*, pp. 100–104
126 Lattimore, *Studies in Frontier History*, pp. 471, 490
127 T. Davenport, *The Afrikaner Bond*, Cape Town, 1966, pp. 113–8, for example, compares late nineteenth-century Cape Afrikaner and British farmer racial attitudes and finds one element of difference in greater Afrikaner hostility to squatting. But in fact the squatting was taking place in British farming regions, and for economic reasons (see D.M. Goodfellow, *A Modern Economic History of South Africa*, London, 1931, pp. 49–50, 69, 73–4). See also Marks, *Reluctant Rebellion*, p. 21

CHAPTER THREE

Classes, the mode of production and the state in pre-colonial Swaziland

Philip Bonner

The publication of Hindess and Hirst's *Pre-Capitalist Modes of Production* in 1975 has proved an important landmark in our understanding of pre-capitalist societies.[1] By emphasising the primacy of the relations of production as opposed to the forces of production on the one hand,[2] and juridical and political domination on the other,[3] they have prompted a thorough-going reappraisal of much of the work in the area that has already appeared, including their own. This has not always been sympathetic to *Pre-Capitalist Modes of Production*, and indeed Hindess and Hirst have subsequently revised some of their views.[4] Nevertheless, the overall result has been a far more rigorous approach to the subject and the possibility of a more satisfactory framework for study in the field. This paper is largely inspired by that debate. It seeks, in the first instance, to synthesise some of the arguments that have developed about Asiatic, tributary and feudal modes of production, and to find a suitable framework of analysis for African chiefdoms or kingdoms; it then goes on to consider the emergence of the state in African societies, and particularly among the Swazi; and it moves on finally to an examination of class formation among the Swazi and the relationship of internal and external slave raiding to that.

The tributary mode of production

Hindess and Hirst define a mode of production as an articulated combination of relations and forces of production structured by the dominance of the relations of production. The relations of production define a specific mode of appropriation of surplus labour and the specific form of social distribution of the means of production corresponding to that mode of appropriation of surplus labour. On the basis of this formulation they then proceed to reject the concept of an Asiatic mode of production on the grounds that the conditions of appropriation of surplus labour do not transform the labour process or the relation of the labourer to it.[5] This is no small matter, as the mode of production characteristic of most African social formations seems to correspond more closely to the Asiatic mode of production than to any other, and once this is rejected the bulk of African, and indeed other, social formations known to history are relegated to some kind of 'modeless' limbo. An alternative should therefore be found, or else in one guise or other the Asiatic mode has to be revived. What are the possible alternatives? In Hindess and Hirst's classification the two most likely candidates are the feudal mode of production and what they call the second variant of the primitive communist mode.

The second variant of the primitive communist mode of production corresponds to what Rey and others have termed the lineage mode of production.[6] Its identifying characteristics are communal appropriation of the social product and its extended or 'complex' redistribution among the lineage members. Leaving aside for the moment the question of whether the lineage mode of production is characterised by classes or is classless, it is clear that it has been widely distributed across the continent of Africa. Whether or not that means that this has been the dominant mode of production is an entirely different question, for almost wherever one looks one finds the lineage mode combined into other aggregates like the village or the kingdom which themselves require definition in terms of modes of production.

Nor can these larger aggregates be considered as variants of the feudal mode of production because, whereas the feudal mode of production presupposes a ruling class which exists independently of the state machine, direct producers who are politically and legally bound to their exploiters through the right of eminent domain, and the absence of communal production, most if not all of the larger collectivities of which we have been speaking are characterised by communal production, by the absence of an exploiting class independent of the state, and by the absence of private property in land.[7] The differences implied by all this cannot be reduced simply to matters of scale. Samir Amin for example suggests that the feudal mode of production is only a decentralised and regressive variant of the tributary mode of production (which he sees as the dominant mode of production for most of the world's history), in as much as the rights to tribute and to ownership previously vested in the state have reverted during periods of weakness to individual feudal lords.[8]

In fact the difference between the two is more fundamental than this. In the feudal mode of production the mechanism for the appropriation of surplus (feudal rent), and the property relations which go with that, involve extensive and specific control over the labour process on the part of the feudal lord and for this reason this excludes the possibility of communal production.[9] On the other hand, Hindess and Hirst argue that in the Asiatic mode of production no such intensive or continuous structuring of the labour process takes place. Production can be either by the independent peasant or communal, and the exploiter has a purely external relation to the process of production, intervening to exact tribute only once the production process is complete.[10] Consequently the forces of production are not in any meaningful way structured by the relations of production, and the existence of the tributary or Asiatic mode of production remains unproved.

If neither the lineage mode nor feudalism adequately characterise the modes of production encountered in much of Africa, it seems necessary to look more closely at the Asiatic mode of production unless we are to be forced back on some kind of notion of hegemony which is rooted in, but not comprehended by, the lineage mode.[11] Perhaps the most useful starting point here is John Taylor's extended review of *Pre-Capitalist Modes of Production*. As Taylor suggests, the relations of production established in the Asiatic mode of production are in fact only compatible with communal forces of production, and it would seem that this is true of all tributary formations, since other quasi-feudal mechanisms for structuring and reproducing the labour process would be necessary if communal ones were abandoned.[12] What is more, there is no theoretical or logical necessity which precludes the same relations of production organising or governing a multiplicity of labour processes. As Rey's analysis of the lineage mode of production shows, surplus labour in the form of elite goods is extracted by the elders from a combination of labour processes existing in different units of production—the collectively organised process of hunting, production based on a social division of labour in the extended family unit, the individual labours of slaves, etc., and the same can be said of most African tributary formations. Thus as Taylor has pointed out what we need to concern ourselves with is the crucial problem of the inter-relation of labour processes under a particular mode of extraction,[13] rather than the articulation of a unitary labour process with a mode of extraction of surplus labour; or in other words, the subjects of Terray's earlier studies, but in this case shorn of their technicist assumptions.[14]

The problem however does not simply end there, for what still needs to be shown is that in the Asiatic or tributary mode of production the state is an essential condition for the articulation of these labour processes, and therefore a necessary economic condition of production.[15] In South-

East Asian formations Taylor shows that it is, because

> Whether it be by organising armies of labourers to construct dykes and canals for village production to take place along river valleys (the Ankorian dynasties, the Indonesian empires), or by redistributing communal lands to meet the changing demographic requirements of different villages (the Vietnamese kingdoms), or by organising the storing of food for the dry season, the rotation of crops or the production of tools for agriculture, the State fulfils crucial economic functions.[16]

In Africa hydraulic enterprises on this scale have been relatively rare, prompting Godelier to describe the African mode of production as the Asiatic mode without large works.[17]

Other kinds of intervention do nevertheless occur. Among the Pedi, regiments of young men are organised by the chief to build walls and agricultural terracing, while in Guy's view the Zulu state came into being at least partly because of the varied nature of Zulu ecology and the need to rationalise access to diverse pastures and soils.[18] Speaking more generally, Sahlins talks of 'the chiefdom' going beyond the local (i.e. homestead or familial) economy both to organise larger scale activities necessary for its welfare, and to break into the local economy and urge it on. Chiefly pressure, political pressure, intensifies household production beyond household needs, and diverts the excess (surplus) into the collective economy.[19] Specific Swazi and Zulu examples of this process will be given later in this chapter.

Having said all this, however, certain problems remain. To begin with, when we speak of social formations in Asia which secure their reproduction through the intervention of the state in hydraulic agriculture, and social formations in Africa which attain the same objectives in substantially different ways, are we talking of the same thing? Perry Anderson believes we are not. Marxist thinking on the Asiatic mode of production, he argues, has been characterised by two distinct and basically contradictory trends. On the one hand there is Marx's initial notion of a powerful centralised and often hydraulic state, with its concomitant 'generalised slavery' in the form of arbitrary and unskilled labour drafts levied on primitive rural populations by a superior bureaucratic power. On the other hand, there has been the tendency to enlarge it to embrace the first state organisations of tribal or semi-tribal formations, characterised less by large-scale irrigation works and despotic state power than by the survival of rural kin relationships, communal rural property, and cohesively self-sufficient villages. The result, as Anderson argues, is an enormous inflation of the scope of the Asiatic mode of production to include social formations 'unimaginably distant from one another'. An ubiquitous Asiatism replaces the previous universal feudalism and features of a multitude of social formations become blended into a single blurred and analytically worthless archetype.[20]

Anderson is, in my view, correct, and the various social formations of the east should be regarded as being dominated respectively by at least two and probably more distinct modes of production. Africa (and much of what follows applies equally to Polynesia)[21] is different again, with a range of societies spread along an axis of primitive communist, to lineage and tributary modes of production. What is more, these combine in a complex multiplicity of ways. Thus Godelier talks of two separate relations of production in what I have called the tributary mode of production: those of primitive communities still in possession of land and those of the state that controls essential economic resources and appropriates directly a portion of the labour and production from the communities it dominates.[22] At least part of the burden of Assad and Wolpe's critique of Hindess and Hirst is that their conception of mode of production precludes them from considering the articulation of separate modes of production in the same social formation.[23]

Yet for all these criticisms, certain merits in Hindess and Hirst's analysis remain which point the way to a better comprehension of pre-capitalist modes of production, and this is especially true of their chapter on feudalism. As they observe, the conditions of production in all pre-capitalist social formations preclude the effective separation of the labourer from the means of production. Instead the labourer appears as the effective possessor of those means of production and enjoys the capacity to set them in motion: hence the classical Marxist view that exploitation has to be secured by non-economic means (i.e. through the intervention of politics or ideology). This Hindess and Hirst feel is an inadequate formulation since it provides no means of differentiating between pre-capitalist modes of production on the basis of relations of production. What we require instead, they argue, are concepts of separation/possession from the means of production specific to each mode of production. This they attempt to do for the feudal mode of production (though not, it should be added, for the other modes of production they consider).

In the feudal mode of production, they point out, the feudal labourer/ tenant does not control all the elements necessary to the production of the feudal economy, and such restricted capacity as he has only operates within the conditions and period of his tenure. As a result

> although he may *own* the instruments of production, have tenant-right to the land, and be able to organise the production of his subsistence, he does not control the *reproduction* of means and conditions of production. It is primarily

through the control of the reproduction of the means of production that the landlord/exploiter separates the tenant/labourer from the means of production.[24]

This emphasis on different forms of possession/separation, and control over all the elements necessary for the reproduction of production seems to provide a far more satisfactory basis for distinguishing between distinct pre-capitalist modes of production.[25] In South-East Asian formations, for example, this is secured via hydraulic agriculture and demographic redistribution which ensure the reproduction of production in the communal units of production. In lineage formations similar principles apply. As Meillassoux, Dupre, and Rey long ago noted in West Africa, the control that elders exercise over production and over the cadets in their lineages cannot be secured by either coercion or by control of the means of production since these resources are equally available to all, or in the case of physical coercion, more available to cadets. Rather it is exercised through matrimonial exchanges and by control over the goods (elite goods) for which brides are exchanged, which enables the elders as a group to control the demographic reproduction of lineages and thereby the reproduction of production itself.[26]

Lastly African tributary formations share several parallel features, and one sees control over the reproduction of production being exercised in several interrelated ways. To take the Swazi and Zulu cases as examples, the ruling aristocracies can control the size and reproduction of individual homesteads through witchcraft accusations; through the redistribution of homesteads to new areas, and the sub-division and allocation of chiefdoms themselves; through the withdrawal of young men from the familial economy into centralised age regiments, through organising work parties (*umeno*) either for the benefit of the aristocracy or for the wider needs of the community; and through the organisation of 'hunts' which provided for a more substantial proportion of subsistence than is normally acknowledged.

In addition, for the Swazi specifically, access to cattle, with all their importance for subsistence and for access to women, was seriously restricted for the under-classes of society by the system of preferential cross-cousin marriage documented below (pp. 93–4). However, perhaps most significant of all was the impact on physical reproduction of the age regiments system, in as much as it withdrew young men and young women from the reproductive cycle for substantial portions of their lives. This of course was more developed among the Zulu* than the Swazi,

---

*See Jeff Guy, 'Ecological factors in the rise of Shaka and the Zulu kingdom,' ch. 4, below.

but for both these societies and probably for Nguni conquest societies as a whole it represented the *differentia specifica* of this particular tributary mode of production—the mechanism through which the dominant relations of production were reproduced over time.

Social classes, politics and the state

'No classes, no politics, no state' is a passage that recurs in the pages of *Pre-Capitalist Modes of Production*. What are its implications for tributary modes of production in general, and for that of the Swazi in particular? Following Engels, Hindess and Hirst see the existence of the state and of politics as an effect of the social division of labour, i.e. of the existence of social classes. In social formations such as these the political level exists as the necessary space for the representation of the interests of the various classes, and the presence of a state apparatus is a necessary condition of the maintenance and functioning of the mechanism of appropriation of surplus labour by the ruling class.[27] Otherwise, where social classes are absent, the state and politics do not exist and the social formation is only constituted of economic and ideological levels. Given this definition it is obviously important to impart some precision to our notion of class, and to see whether classes can then be identified in a tributary, and particularly in the Swazi, social formation.

In Marxist theory, the separation of society into social classes arises from the social division of labour between a class of labourers who are separated from ownership of the means of production, and use this as the means of appropriating surplus labour. On the basis of this definition Hindess and Hirst reject outright the possibility of social classes in the primitive communist mode of production. Since the mode of appropriation of surplus labour is communal, they insist, there are *ipso facto* no classes, and hence no possibility of politics and the state.[28] Both Rey and Terray take the opposite view, asserting that control by elders over women in the first case and over prestige goods in the second enables the elders to control the surplus product, the partial or total use of which is for the reproduction of relations of dependence between the direct producers and this group, and out of this process they consider class relations to emerge.[29] Without wishing to enter this debate, there does seem to be one point that should be made, which is that if Hindess and Hirst see the process of the formation of the state as identical to the process of transition from primitive communism to some other mode of production, and if they consider transitions from one mode of production to another to be the product of class struggle, some kind of embryonic class formation must be possible in that mode for the transition to ever occur.[30]

It is that kind of embryonic class formation that seems to me to characterise tributary formations in general and that of the Swazi in particular. Its origin may perhaps be traced to the process outlined by Meillassoux:

> Through historical accidents, usually due to contacts with foreign formations, a group takes for all its members the quality of 'senior' in relation to other groups considered collectively as minor. All the economic and social prerogatives of the elder are transferred to the dominant class, usually an aristocratic lineage. Prestations due to the elder become tributes due to the lord who may also gain control over the matrimonial policy of the community, and eventually over the means of production—land.[31]

Meillassoux's conception suffers in some measure from the role it ascribes to historical accidents, which in themselves presumably ought to be explained. However, with the impact of 'foreign formations' (often mercantile capital), it is possible to see these embryonic classes taking firmer shape. To take the Swazi case as an example, participation in the trade to Delagoa Bay and the ruling groups' monopolisation of its profits helped boost the latter's power, which in turn was consolidated still further by their move to the Shiselweni district in the south of modern Swaziland, and the opportunities this presented for enforcing unequal access to unevenly distributed means of production. Part of that process I have dealt with elsewhere,[32] and I now turn to the second phase of Swazi expansion which took place at the beginning of the 1820s.

At this point it is worth noting the comments of Hindess and Hirst on the nature of conquest. Conquest, they point out,

> does not of itself produce state domination. The conquering people are not phantoms, they existed prior to the conquest and they must have a social organisation and a mode of producing the means of subsistence. In the first instance, the conqueror's mode of production will be represented alongside that of the dominated people. The dominant people receive *tribute* which is redistributed according to their social institutions and relations of production. No state is formed by this relation, dominant people/subject people; the means of coercion to obtain tribute are provided by the Gentile constitution of the dominant people, and the subject people regulates its own affairs by its own institutions. The fact of conquest does not produce either class society or the state. The conditions of transition to class society, of the conversion of the conquerors into a non-labouring ruling class, are not *given* in conquest as such. If such a transition does take place then it is on the basis of class society and irreconcilable class antagonism that the state is formed, not on the basis of conquest. Conquest only explains certain conditions under which the state *may* be formed, it does not explain the mechanisms of the formation of the state.[33]

Conditions in the Swazi conquest area almost exactly mirror those outlined above. For several years the Swazi resembled more closely an army of occupation camped out in hostile territory than a settled administration. In those early days, one oral history recalls, there were no chiefs, only princes and leaders of regiments,[34] and the same picture can be derived from the evidence of Swazi messengers to Captain Gardiner when they visited Mgungundlovu in 1835. The capital of Swaziland, they told him, was Elangeni, and a little to the south was another village of Lobamba, which between them housed the entire male population of the Swazi, numbering no more than a few hundred men.[35] The messengers were surely exaggerating, no doubt for Zulu ears, as we know of much more extensive Swazi settlement in this period, especially in the south.[36] Yet in the area of conquest there was an element of truth in what they said. Few of Sobhuza's brothers or sons were assigned chiefdoms in the central areas until the closing years of Sobhuza's life, and the type of 'placing' to which Kuper refers did not occur on any extensive scale until the reign of his successor.[37] The history of Maphalaleni illustrates this trend. Maphalaleni was established for LaNdwandwe, one of Sobhuza's favourite wives, but so late in Sobhuza's reign that by the time she got there Sobhuza was already dead.[38]

The same pattern repeats itself throughout central Swaziland. Neither Maloyi nor Malunge seem to have taken effective occupation of their chiefdoms in the Mbuluzane River area until the reign of Mswati, and on the north side of the Komati River none of the Hhohho district was even allocated until the 1840s and 1850s.[39] In the south things were somewhat different. At least five of Sobhuza's sons were given chiefdoms there, but if Mantintinti is anything to go by, they only took possession comparatively late in Sobhuza's reign.[40] After accompanying Sobhuza to Mdimba, Mantintinti 'never set foot alive' in the chiefdom he had been given, and it was only' during the time of the return of the princes to neighbouring Velezezweni that his successor Mtfonga was instructed to return'.[41] In sum, then, the story told to Gardiner is at least partly confirmed. In the area of conquest the Ngwane were, for most of Sobhuza's reign, a nation under arms. Little of the conquered territory was settled, and the bulk of the population clustered for security in military towns. Only in the final years of Sobhuza's reign did the situation begin to change. Men could now be spared to reinforce the south, and an administrative presence was gradually extended in the conquered zone. Imperceptibly a shift was taking place to a society less overtly parasitic, and less openly reliant on the naked use of force.

The same process of integration accelerated in the reign of Sobhuza's successor, Mswati (1839–65). Very soon after Mswati succeeded his father he was faced with a rebellion by his half-brother Fokoti, and once that had been put down, Mswati's mother Thandile and his paternal uncle Malunge took it as the opportunity to set in motion a series of far-reaching reforms. On the face of it these took mainly political and ritual forms. The ritual supremacy of the king as expressed in annual *incwala* (first fruits) ceremonies was bolstered by ritual importations from the Ndwandwe, and Swaziland's military and administrative structures were systematised by creating nation-wide age regiments as the framework of Swaziland's military organisation, and by establishing a more extensive network of royal villages to serve both as rallying points for regiments and as centres for monitoring and supervising local political activity.[42] However, the rationale behind these changes was not solely political or ritual. The withdrawal of young men from the agricultural cycle of their families' homesteads involved the direct appropriation of surplus labour by the royal house since they were then set to work tilling the king's fields, while changes in the incwala ceremonies and the establishment of royal villages in the provinces were part of a wider process whereby members of the royal family were being dispersed into the regions, as a means of securing control over all aspects of their activities including the process of production.[43] Why this was needed at that time is less easy to judge, but the most likely explanation is Swaziland's declining ability to raid for booty and tribute in the regions to the north and the west in the troubled period following Sobhuza's death. Under Sobhuza such raiding had been widely undertaken. Thonga traditions collected by Nachtigal are full of references to Swazi attacks, and when Trichardt passed by the Pedi in 1836 he was warned that the entire area to the west of the Steenkampsberg was under Swazi control.[44] By the time the Trekkers arrived in the area in the 1840s, however, Swazi raiding had all but ceased, and it may well have been the shortage of surplus from these 'traditional' sources in a period of stress that caused a tightening of the mechanisms of surplus extraction in Swaziland itself.[45]

The programme of reform evoked immediate opposition and before long the regents were forced to back down by a coalition of regional interests.[46] Further action in the matter had to await the mid-1850s as Mswati and his regents were confronted in rapid succession by the rebellions of two of his elder brothers and two massive Zulu attacks.[47] The year 1862, however, marked the end of Zulu invasions, and Zulu energies were henceforth consumed by internal wranglings over the succession.[48] As a result, Mswati was able to bring the country more systematically under his control, as is evidenced by his attacks on the semi-autonomous

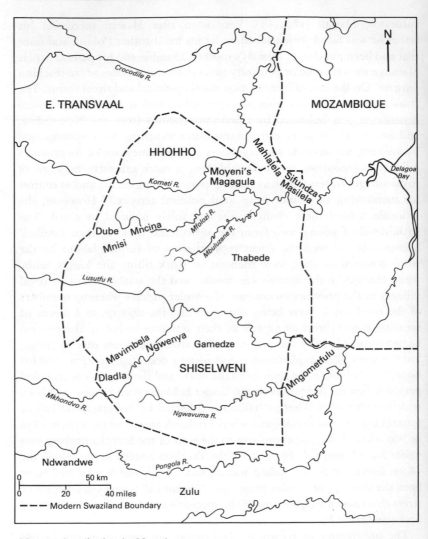

Map 3.1 Swaziland under Mswati

Emakhandzambile chiefs—meaning 'those found ahead', i.e. those chiefdoms which had occupied central and northern Swaziland prior to Sobhuza's arrival from the south. Of the nineteen Emakhandzambile chiefdoms
about which I have definite information, fourteen suffered in some way or
other during this period, and in the cases of the others it required the
intervention of special factors or unusual circumstances to save them from
a similar fate. Thus the Mnisi, the Thabedze, the Gamedze, the Mngomet-

fulo, the Sifundza, the Masilela, and the Mavimbela were all attacked by Mswati's forces, and it is also reported that the chiefdoms of the Mahlalela and Moyeni's Magagula would have experienced similar treatment had it not been for the intercession of chance on the one hand and a trusted royal relative on the other.[49] As for the others, their autonomies were no less completely circumscribed, with the Ngwenya, the Dladla, the Mncina and Moyeni's Magagula being demoted and placed under trusted officers of Mswati.[50]

It would of course be absurd to assume that all this was undertaken in the immediate interests of surplus appropriation. In the case of the Mnisi, for example, their chiefdom was attacked because of the extensive rain-making powers their chief deployed, and ritual factors may have entered into Mswati's attack on others as well.[51] Nevertheless underlying most of these assaults one can see attempts to extend politico-economic control. In many instances it is difficult to separate these two levels. The Mavimbela, for example, were attacked because they refused a royal wife from Mswati, and on the face of it were reacting against the extension of political control. Yet for them there was another dimension to the problem, since marrying a princess involved the payment of inflated sums of bridewealth and so meant a heavy drain of cattle as well.[52] In other cases economic issues are more clearly defined. Thus, when, for example, Mswati tried to extort tribute from the Sifundza and Masilela peoples during a period of drought, his party was intercepted as it returned and stripped of all that it had taken. Mswati did not react immediately but, according to tradition, bided his time until the offenders' fears had been lulled. A more serious consideration was probably fear of the Zulu, since it is likely that these events took place during the drought of 1848. Once the Zulu threat had begun to recede, however, the Masilela were made to pay dearly for their crimes. A hunting party was arranged to which the Masilela were summoned, and they were then surrounded and annihilated by the rest of the assembled host.[53]

The process whereby Mswati extended and rationalised his political and economic control over subject groups I would see as marking the beginning of class society and the emergence of the state. In the place of the random and indiscriminate plundering of Sobhuza's time, more institutionalised mechanisms for the appropriation of surplus developed, whose volume was at the same time kept within reasonable limits by the need to retain the loyalty and co-operation of subject groups against such external enemies as the Zulu. These were closely linked to the emergence of state institutions: the age regiments, which socialised the youth of subject peoples into a sense of national identity (at least partly by providing an avenue of upward mobility for more ambitious elements) and whose labour and booty raiding enriched the dominant class; the expanded *libandla* or national council which represented all interests in the country and whose participation was required for all major political decisions (though here Hindess and Hirst's comments on the means of representation should also be remembered);[54] the annual incwala ceremony in which the king and his people were symbolically renewed each year, and so on. Whether at this embryonic stage they should be considered as existing entirely independently of the ruling groups is obviously open to question. Yet the same question remains open in the case of the feudal state. The extent to which or manner in which this operates as the necessary space for the representation of the various classes in the feudal mode of production is never properly elaborated by Hindess and Hirst, leaving one with the lingering feeling that even here it only partly fulfils that role.

The last question that I wish to consider in this section is the precise configuration of class interests represented in the early Swazi state. Terray, in his article on 'Classes and Class Consciousness in the Abron Kingdom of Gyaman', in the end seems to duck that very question. He begins by defining classes in terms of relations to the means of production, but then goes on to characterise them as a relation of exploitation.[55] This will not do, for as Hindess and Hirst among others have shown, there may be exploitation without classes ever arising, as in the case of banditry and systematised raiding.[56] Can we therefore say we have classes in pre-colonial Swaziland? I believe we can, if only in embryonic form. Firstly, land, the basis of the economic system and the principal means of production, was controlled by the rulers and could be redistributed by them in a variety of ways. Chiefdoms could have part of their territory taken away from them and allocated to other groups; they could be removed *en masse* to other parts of the country or they could have their local rulers replaced by relatives and functionaries of the king.[57] Thus, while each individual subject had access to the means of production, he could have his access restricted to means of greatly inferior worth. Much the same went for cattle and for wives. By a variety of mechanisms such as witchcraft accusations, control over the appropriate combinations of pasturage, variable bridewealth payments, and preferential marriage patterns, the accumulation of cattle could be restricted for the commoners and largely confined to the ruling class.[58] If one adds to this an appropriation of surplus on the basis of these divisions which went to maintain a non-labouring ruling class, one must admit the emergence of class society if only in attenuated form.

The question remains, however, who precisely constituted these classes? In his study of the Abron kingdom of Gyaman, Terray sees a tripartite division between a non-labouring group of aristocrats on the one hand,

and a class of working slaves and tribute-producing peasants on the other, but it seems questionable to me how clear cut this distinction was.[59] Are we to believe, for example, that the Abron aristocracy was an entirely non-labouring class and that neither its women nor its cadets engaged in productive work? Certainly among the Swazi this was not the case, for there a large section of the ruling group took part in such pursuits. Instead we find a more complicated situation, with tribute being extracted from subordinate groups in the various forms that we have mentioned, and then being partly concentrated in the upper echelons of the ruling class and partly filtering down. The important thing to remember here however is the barrier that existed to surplus dribbling down to the groups from which it had been drawn. Essentially this was constituted out of Swazi marriage practices. Unlike their Nguni counterparts the Swazi practised a system of preferential in-kin marriages, which tended to restrict cattle and other wealth to within the ruling class. These restrictions, it is true, were neither permanent nor impermeable. The marriage of matrilateral cross-cousins was much more flexible than its patrilateral parallel variant, which kept alliances within one clan or descent group alone.[60] The Swazi, moreover, married their classificatory cross-cousins and not their actual mother's brother's daughter, and had preferential marriage with a variety of other kin.[61] Finally, a more general political expediency could easily entail an entirely different order of preference and led Mswati to exchange wives with both the leading Magagula chiefs.[62]

From the broader structural point of view, however, the relationships which developed with the conquered were decisively different from those which characterised the first phase of Swazi expansion. Although offering a more flexible range of marriage options than parallel and true cross-cousin marriage, the various Swazi marriage preferences still concentrated them within a restricted group of kin.[63] Marrying a woman from a father's mother's clan, which was perhaps the most popular marriage preference, involved recreating the alliance that one's grandfather had made; while marrying a classificatory mother's brother's daughter, the next most popular Swazi marriage, meant doing the same thing with the alliance of one's father, while avoiding the competition for spouses which direct mother's brother's daughter marriage involved (see Figures 3.1 and 3.2).

Wealth, if anything, tended to follow a still more restrictive route. Even where marriages were contracted outside the ruling group, thereby blurring political divisions between the aristocracy and the rest, property usually followed an entirely different circuit, and was continually funnelling back into the hands of the ruling class. Inflated bridewealths were demanded for female relatives of the king, and this even extended to female captives

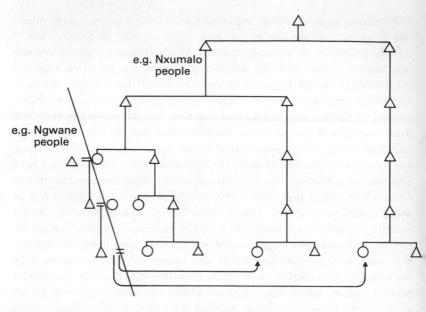

Fig. 3.1 Marriage to a woman of one's father's mother's clan

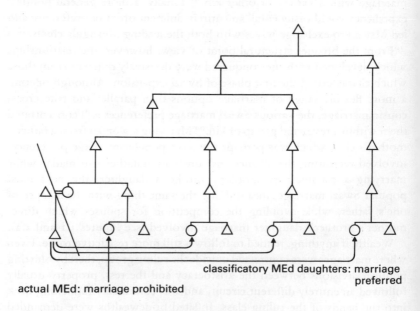

Fig. 3.2 Marriage to a classificatory mother's brother's daughter

attached to the royal house, whereas the king was at liberty to take wives from whoever he wanted without any corresponding bridewealth being levied on him.[64] Nor did the transfer of resources simply end at that point. The heir to a chiefdom, or even household, and hence to most of its property in cattle, would automatically be the son of the chief's royal wife.[65] He in turn would be subject to the typical marriage preferences which would encourage him to recreate ties with his mother's (royal) house, which thus channelled marriage payments in the same direction again.[66]

Small wonder then that nineteenth-century Swaziland is remembered for its gross disparities in wealth. In former days, Kuper remarks, cattle were concentrated largely in the kraals of the national leaders, and the evidence of John Gama and Mnkonkoni leaves a similar impression.[67] According to John Gama, before the time when cattle began to be used for lobola, it was normal practice to use goats as cattle only belonged to the great people, while Giba and Mnkonkoni talk of the small numbers of cattle used in such transactions, particularly during the reign of Sobhuza.[68] The broad effect of these practices, therefore, was that while a degree of social and political mobility was permitted, differences of political and economic status were perpetuated, which persist to this day. In Sobhuza's time these were at their most intense. Marriages were confined politically within the dominant Ngwane, and spatially to their military encampments, while wealth tended to circulate in the same restricted group. Under Mswati there was a blurring at the edges of these categories, but otherwise they remained essentially intact, leaving marriage practices to continue as a crucial determinant of class.

Captives and booty raiding in the tributary mode of production

Jack Goody in his essays on *Tradition, Technology and the State in Africa* sees captives and tributary raiding as an integral part of the tributary mode of production (although he does not use that term). The low fertility of African soils, the relatively low level of technology in most African societies (which make human muscle power virtually the only means of power available), and low population densities make it impossible to extract surplus from peasant communities on a scale similar to much of Asia and Europe, and ensure that it is labour rather than land that is the factor of production which is scarce. Out of this booty-raiding arises as an important means of acquiring surplus, and particularly the raiding of human booty as a source of labour power.[69] Terray in his Gyaman study refines these ideas further. The low level of surplus appropriation from peasant communities, he suggests, is a consequence of the need of ruling aristocracies to enlist the support of peasant communities in the face of threats from outside. At the same time the fear of creating a permanently dispossessed and disaffected slave population, as well as perhaps other factors, ensured the gradual absorption of the captive and his family into Gyaman society, and created the need to secure further supplies of captives as a means of making good that loss.[70] A number of these points apply to Swazi society.

The part played by captives in the Swazi economy was considerably larger than is generally imagined. Whether this was always the case is difficult to say. When the Swazi were centred on Shiselweni in the south of Swaziland between *c.*1770 and 1820, for example, their highly pastoral economy may have meant that their needs for labour power were correspondingly reduced. The situation changed once they moved from Shiselweni to Ezulwini. Here the pasturage was less rich and agricultural production more necessary, and henceforth captives were raided on all sides.[71] According to Ndambi Mkhonta the Ezulwini village once boasted large numbers of captives, and the same is likely to be true of all royal capitals.[72] Other examples which I have come across without direct questioning on the subject are those of the Dube, who were attacked and enslaved in the reign of Mswati, and of the Thabede, who suffered a similar fate at much the same time.[73]

Sources of slaves fell in two broad categories, although the distinction was probably blurred in the early days of the state. The first group comprised non-Swazi who were raided outside their kingdom's boundaries (the *Titfunjwa*).[74] In Sobhuza's early conflicts with the chiefdoms of Magoboyi and Mkise, for example, captives were taken and their presence in Swazi society was used in later years to justify Mswati's right to cede the eastern Transvaal.[75] Later it was the Thonga who bore the brunt of these attacks and who in this case were most usually traded as slaves. The other major source of supply was children seized from households within the Swazi kingdom (the *Tigcili*).[76] As Tikuba told Stuart in 1898

> It often happened that when a person was killed for some crime or other and his cattle and children seized, those children were taken by the Swazi and sold to the Boers in the Transvaal.[77]

The Berlin missionary, Merensky, reported on similar practices after his visit to Swaziland in March 1860. 'Even now', he wrote in his diary,

> if a man of his [Mswati's] people has many daughters or good cattle his soldiers come, surround the Kraal, murder the old, and take the young people and cattle as booty. Children are being sold or given to the 'great of the realm'.[78]

What were the implications of these developments for the emergence of the state and for the development of classes? Terray would have us believe that they signal the emergence of slave classes and of a slave mode of production, but as Hindess and Hirst show a slave mode of production presupposes private property in land and slaves, and a form of commodity exchange corresponding to both.[79] Moreover, given the rights and protection made available to captives in Swazi society, it seems more appropriate to regard them as a group of perpetual minors rather than as a clearly defined class.[80]

The seizure of captives, however, did have other implications for class formation, particularly when considered against the trade in captives to the Transvaal. Without going into any detail this seems to have grown to substantial proportions by the middle of the 1850s, and then to have boomed to new levels for the first half of the next decade.[81] The question that is inevitably raised by these developments is to what extent the seizure of captives for trade became an object in itself in the attacks that were made on offending subject groups, and to what extent (in Rodney's terms) it led to the social degeneration of Swazi society.[82] Or to put it another way, to what extent do we see a robber relation rather than a class relation characterising Swazi society? I would argue that for the most part the seizure of captives did not become the object of these attacks; that they were a by-product of rationalising economic and political control and that once this rationalisation was completed internal captive-taking largely ceased. In its place however, there was a shift of emphasis to Mozambique, the devastation and impoverishment of that area in the pursuit of captives, and perhaps some of the roots of present-day underdevelopment in southern Mozambique.[83]

Notes

1 B. Hindess and P.Q. Hirst, *Pre-Capitalist Modes of Production*, London and Boston, 1975
2 By relations of production, I mean the way in which the means of production (e.g. land, cattle, seed) are distributed, and the form of appropriating surplus labour corresponding to that. By forces of production, I mean the labour process which involves the tools with which it is carried out, the objects to which it is applied, and the human agents with which it combines
3 In pre-capitalist societies the classical Marxist view has been that exploitation is secured by non-economic (i.e. juridical or political) means. Hindess and Hirst attempt an explanation in terms of relations of production (i.e. economic means). See above, p. 84

4 J. Taylor, review article, 'Pre-Capitalist Modes of Production', Part I, *Critique of Anthropology*, 4 and 5, Autumn 1975; and Part II, *Critique of Anthropology*, 6, Spring 1976; B. Hindess and P.Q. Hirst, *Mode of Production and Social Formation—An Auto-Critique of Pre-Capitalist Modes of Production*, London, 1977; T. Assad and H. Wolpe, review article, 'Concepts of Modes of Production,' *Economy and Society*, 5, 1976
5 Hindess and Hirst, *Pre-Capitalist Modes*, pp. 9–10, 183, 196, 225
6 P.P. Rey, 'The Lineage Mode of Production', *Critique of Anthropology*, 3, Spring 1975, pp. 27–9
7 Hindess and Hirst, *Pre-Capitalist Modes*, pp. 184, 189–200, 223–4
8 S. Amin, 'Modes of Production and Social Formations', *Ufuhamu*, Winter 1974, pp. 57–85
9 Hindess and Hirst, *Pre-Capitalist Modes*, pp. 223–5, 229–30, 233–55
10 *Ibid.*, pp. 194, 196–7, 200
11 See for example Rey, 'Lineage Mode'.
12 Taylor, 'Pre-Capitalist Modes', Part I, pp. 136–9
13 *Ibid.*, Part II, pp. 57–8
14 E. Terray, *Marxism and Primitive Societies*, New York and London, 1972, pp. 95–186
15 Cf. Hindess and Hirst, *Mode of Production*, pp. 194–5, 197
16 Taylor, 'Pre-Capitalist Modes', Part I, pp. 136–7
17 See M. Godelier, 'La Notion de Mode de Production Asiatique et les schémas marxistes d'évolution des sociétés', *CERM*, Paris, 1963, cited by C. Coquéry-Vidrovitch, 'Research on an African Mode of Production', *Critique of Anthropology*, 4 and 5, Autumn 1975, p. 41
18 Personal communication from P. Delius; J.J. Guy, 'Ecological factors in the rise of Shaka and the Zulu Kingdom,' pp. 110–11 below
19 M.D. Sahlins, *Tribesmen*, New Jersey, 1968, pp. 25–6
20 P. Anderson, *Lineages of the Absolutist State*, London, 1974, pp. 484–94
21 M. Godelier, *Perspectives in Marxist Anthropology*, Cambridge, 1977, pp. 114–6
22 *Ibid.*, 119
23 Assad and Wolpe, 'Concepts of Modes of Production', pp. 501–5
24 Hindess and Hirst, *Pre-Capitalist Modes*, pp. 226–8, 232–8. The quotation is from p. 238
25 Hindess and Hirst, *Mode of Production*, pp. 43, 63–72
26 C. Meillassoux, 'Essai d'interprétation des phénomènes économiques dans les sociétés traditionelles d'autosubsistence', *Cahiers d'études Africaines*, 4, 1961; C. Meillassoux, 'From reproduction to production', *Economy and Society*, i, 1, 1972, pp. 98–100; G. Dupré and P.P. Rey, 'Reflections on the pertinence of a theory of the history of exchange', *Economy and Society*, ii, 2, 1973, pp. 144–57.
27 Hindess and Hirst, *Pre-Capitalist Modes*, p. 29
28 *Ibid.*, pp. 36–7, 41–3
29 Rey, 'Lineage Mode'; E. Terray, 'Classes and Class Consciousness in the Abron Kingdom of Gyaman' in M. Bloch (ed.), *Marxist Analysis and Social Anthropology*, New York, 1975, p. 107
30 Hindess and Hirst, *Pre-Capitalist Modes*, pp. 278–86, 401
31 C. Meillassoux, 'From reproduction to production', *Economy and Society*, i, 1, 1972
32 P.L. Bonner, 'Early State Formation among the Nguni: the relevance of the Swazi case', paper presented to the Conference on African History, Rand

Afrikaans University, 1975
33 Hindess and Hirst, *Pre-Capitalist Modes*, p. 199
34 Interview with Loncayi Hlophe, 24 May 1970, Lamgabhi, Swaziland
35 A.F. Gardiner, *Narrative of a journey to the Zoolo country in South Africa*, London, 1836, pp. 165, 167
36 P.L. Bonner, 'The Rise, Consolidation and Disintegration of Dlamini Power in Swaziland between 1820 and 1889; a study in the relationship of foreign Affairs to internal political development,' Ph.D. thesis, University of London, 1977
37 H. Kuper, *An African Aristocracy; rank among the Swazi*, London, 1947, pp. 57–8
38 Interview with Sambane Dlamini, 14 May 1970, Maphalaleni, Swaziland
39 Interviews with Mbhuduya, Ganda and Sigungu Magagula, and Mavelebaleni Ginindza, 20 December 1971, Dvokolwako, Swaziland; Bonner, 'Rise', pp. 164–5
40 *Ibid.*, p. 145
41 Interviews with Mpitha Dlamini, Gombolo Nkhosi, John Nhlabatsi, 8 May 1970, Mbelebeleni, Swaziland
42 Swaziland Archives, de S.G.M. Honey, 'A History of Swaziland', MSS, p. 29; Kuper, *Aristocracy*, p. 15; A.J.B. Hughes, *Swazi Land Tenure*, Institute for Social Research, University of Natal, Durban, 1964, p. 43; interview with Makhathi and Mnkonkolote Mkhatshwa and others, 12 April 1970, Elwandle, Swaziland
43 Interview with Mpitha Dlamini; interview with Dlamini informants, 24 June 1970, Mbidlimbidlini, Swaziland; interview with Dlamini informants, June 1970, Kuhlamukeni, Swaziland
44 A. Nachtigal, 'Das Tagebuch des Missionars', 4 vols., typescript, University of South Africa Library, ii, pp. 238–41 (original manuscript pagination); G.S. Preller (ed.), *Dagboek van Louis Trigardt*, Bloemfontein, 1917, p. 215
45 J. Stuart, *De Hollandsche Afrikanen en hunne Republiek in zuid Afrika*, Amsterdam, 1854, p. 189; T.S. Van Rooyen, 'Die Verhouding tussen die Boer, Engelse en Naturelle in die Geskiedenis van die Oos Transvaal tot 1882', *Archives Year Book of South African History*, 1951, i, Cape Town, 1951, p. 3
46 Natal Archives (NA), Pietermaritzburg, Garden Papers, File IV B (Swazis), 58–60, 1158; Cory Library, Grahamstown (CL), Methodist Archives, Minute Book of the Bechuana Methodist Meeting, Report of the Baraputse Mission, 1845
47 Bonner, 'Rise', pp. 86–8, 96–112, 117–9, 134–42
48 *Ibid.*, pp. 113, 116
49 Interview with Mboziswa Mnisi, 16 June 1970, Phumplele, Swaziland; with Mhawu Gamedze, Loshina Gamedze, Moyeni Mamba, 29 June 1970, Mandlenya, Swaziland; interviews with Mandlabovu Fakudze and Mgudwa Masonge, 29 June 1970, Macetsheni, Swaziland; interview with Mjole Sifundza, 28 April 1970, Ka-Shewula, Swaziland; with Hehhane Ngwenya, 9 June 1970, Mgomfelweni, Swaziland; A.T. Bryant, *Olden Times in Zululand and Natal*, London, 1929, pp. 341–4; Kuper, *Aristocracy*, p. 16; Killie Campbell Library, (KCL), Miller Papers, MS 1478, Miller, 'A Short History of Swazieland', from the *Times of Swaziland*, i, 1–3, 6–12, Bremersdorp, 5 June–21 August 1897; interview with Mahloba Gumede, 11 June 1970, eBulandzeni, Swaziland
50 Interview with Hehhane Ngwenya; interviews with Guzana Mncina, LaMnan-

disi, Mncina, Nkunzane and Mchoza Dlamini, 12 June 1970, Silothwane, Swaziland; with Loncayi Hlophe; with Mahloba Gumede; interviews with Mankwempe, Mevane, Mcedzane, Magagula and Mmemo Masilela, 23 June 1970, Madlangampisi, Swaziland

51 Interview with Mboziswa Mnisi. Other probable examples are the Sifundza and the Mngometfulo—interview with Mjole Sifundza, 28 April 1970, ka-Shewula, Swaziland; Kuper, *Aristocracy*, p. 198, Note 1

52 Interview with Hehhane Ngwenya; Kuper, *Aristocracy*, pp. 151–2

53 Arquivo Historico de Moçambique (AHM), *Boletin Geral Colonias*, pp. 87–90; Sw. A., 48/07/2205, Reply to Resident Commissioner Circular No. 9/1907, Assistant Commissioner Ubombo to Government Secretary, 2 January 1908–9

54 Hindess and Hirst, *Pre-Capitalist Modes*, pp. 36, 38–9

55 Terray, 'Classes', pp. 87–8, 90, 92, 100–101

56 Hindess and Hirst, *Pre-Capitalist Modes*, p. 225

57 Bonner, 'Rise', ch. 2, 5

58 *Ibid.*

59 Terray, 'Classes', pp. 107–24, especially p. 119

60 C. Levi-Strauss, *The Elementary Structures of Kinship*, Boston, 1969, pp. 451–2; R. Needham, *Structure and Sentiment: a test case in Social Anthropology*, Chicago, 1962, pp. 14–17; see especially E.R. Leach, *Rethinking Anthropology*, London, 1966, ch. 3, where he argues that asymmetrical (i.e. cross-cousin) marriage alliance is a strategy that can be used to 'seal off' the ruling group from the masses, or to incorporate selectively more groups into the ruling aristocracy. Patrilateral parallel marriage, i.e. to father's brother's daughter, as practised by the Tswana aristocracy, cuts the group off from alliances with any outside group

61 Kuper, *Aristocracy*, pp. 95–6; H. Kuper, 'Kinship among the Swazi' in A.R. Radcliffe-Brown and D. Forde (eds.), *African Systems of Kinship and Marriage*, London, 1950, pp. 104–6

62 Interview with Mbhuduya Magagula; interview with Mankwempe Magagula

63 Needham, *Structure*, pp. 14–17

64 Kuper, *Aristocracy*, pp. 151–2. The same goes for the aristocracy as a whole. As Kuper remarks, cattle come to aristocrats rather than go from them on the marriage market; *ibid.*, p. 152

65 *Ibid.*, pp. 94, 152

66 Kuper also points out that in the early days 'lobola did not end'—a few cattle were paid after marriage, and demands continued throughout the marriage; *ibid.*, p. 98

67 *Ibid.*, p. 151

68 C. de B. Webb and J. Wright (eds.), *The James Stuart Archive of recorded oral evidence relating to the history of the Zulu and neighbouring people*, vol. i, Durban, 1976, p. 138, John Gama, 18 December 1898; pp. 150–1, Giba and Mnkonkoni, 25 November 1898

69 J. Goody, *Technology, Tradition and the State in Africa*, London, 1971, pp. 25–7, 30–31

70 Terray, 'Classes', pp. 125–8

71 Bonner, 'Rise', pp. 36, 61

72 Interviews with Ndambi Mkhonta and four others, 15 May 1970, Ezulwini, Swaziland

73 Interviews with Mlingwa Dube, Machango Kunene, 17 May 1970, Mpholonjeni, Swaziland; with Thabede and Khumalo informants, 21 July 1970, Kwendzeni, Swaziland. For other references see A.B. Nxumalo, 'Oral Tradition concerning Mswati II', Occasional Paper No. I of the School of Education, University of Botswana, Lesotho and Swaziland, Swaziland, April 1976, pp. 30–31, interview with Zwane Gwebu, Helehele, 8 December 1973, 48, interview with Paul Mndvunga Ngubane, Evusweni, 11 March 1974

74 Kuper, *Aristocracy*, pp. 67–8

75 Transvaal Archives, Pretoria, SS 30, pp. 481–2, R.3359/59, interview between C. Potgieter and the Swazi messengers Kappoen and Makwasitiel, 19. December 1859

76 Kuper, *Aristocracy*, pp. 67–8

77 KCL, Stuart Papers, 30091, evidence of Tikuba, 27 November 1898

78 University of the Witwatersrand Archives, A. Merensky, 'Tagebuch unserer Reise zu den Swazi Kaffern', March-May 1860, p. 41

79 Hindess and Hirst, *Pre-Capitalist Modes*, pp. 125–50

80 Kuper, *Aristocracy*, p. 68

81 Bonner, 'Rise', pp. 154–8

82 W. Rodney, *A History of the Upper Guinea Coast, 1545–1800*, Oxford, 1970, pp. 100–118; W. Rodney, 'African Slavery and other forms of social oppression on the Upper Guinea Coast in the context of the Atlantic Slave Trade', *Journal of African History*, vii, 3, 1966, pp. 432–40

83 Bonner, 'Rise', pp. 179–80, 192–211

CHAPTER FOUR

Ecological factors in the rise of Shaka and the Zulu kingdom

Jeff Guy

The rise of Shaka and the founding of the Zulu kingdom in the first quarter of the nineteenth century, with its tremendous implications for the peoples of the sub-continent, has long been a subject of interest to the student of southern African history. In the *Oxford History of South Africa* Leonard Thompson summarised and assessed the various attempts which had been made to explain the Shakan revolution.[1] He dismissed theories of white inspiration, and expressed doubt that the social revolution was due primarily to the effect of trade between the northern Nguni chiefdoms and Delagoa Bay.[2] He was, however, more sympathetic to the suggestion, first put forward by Max Gluckman, and later adopted by J.D. Omer Cooper, that the social disruption which occurred in south-eastern Africa at the turn of the century was the consequence of 'population pressure'.[3] Nevertheless, Thompson felt that

> it has not been conclusively established that population pressure had reached a crucial stage by the time of Dingiswayo. The evidence of demographic trends among the Nguni in the eighteenth century is tenuous and likely to remain so.[4]

Since the publication of the *Oxford History* the demographic evidence has indeed remained tenuous. However, a number of articles have been written which relate to the question of the demography of the region, or the linked problem of the availability of resources, and these have added substantially to the debate. In 1970 I pointed out that an investigation of the grazing potential of Zululand suggested that the major chiefdoms had their origin in areas where a particular configuration of vegetational types existed, and that a closer study of these areas of origin, and the direction of expansion, of the chiefdoms would possibly reveal that one of the factors behind the social revolution of the time was a struggle for diminishing resources.[5] Since then, Daniel and Webb have supplemented documentary evidence with fieldwork and noted the close correlation between the geographical situation of certain pre-Shakan chiefdoms and the physical environment.[6] Phil Bonner and David Hedges have attempted to combine the trade thesis with the environmental arguments and to study in greater detail the differences between the histories of the various chiefdoms in their search for an explanation of the changes which took place.[7] Gluckman has published an article in which he substantiated his previous arguments and Martin Hall has produced dendroclimatological evidence on changing patterns of rainfall which has a bearing on the question.[8]

All these studies have given depth to the debate and I have no intention of taking issue here with points with which I might disagree. However, I believe that there exists further evidence, albeit indirect, which suggests that by the end of the eighteenth century an imbalance had arisen between population density and the resources of the region and that this contributed to the radical social changes which took place. To demonstrate this I intend to summarise the evidence which indicates that the physical environment of the region was particularly well-suited to the needs of stock-keeping cultivators but that, by the end of the eighteenth century, the physical resources were breaking down under existing systems of exploitation. I then want to examine briefly production in the Zulu kingdom and the manner in which the king extracted the surplus upon which the maintenance and continuity of the social formation was based, focusing however not on the manner in which this affected power relations but on how it gave the king control over the rate and degree of environmental exploitation.

Stock-keeping[9] and the physical environment of Zululand

The concept of the 'natural environment', as a stable interplay of geological, climatic, vegetational and faunal forces beyond the disruptive influence of human activity, no longer seems to be accepted by botanists.[10] They also question the empirical validity of studying extant plant communities as stages in a steady succession moving towards a stable vegetational climax, for it is now recognised that for thousands of years the hand and the hoe of man and the feeding patterns of his stock have not only deflected, but in places irreversibly altered, the structure of biotic communities. Certain vegetation types, once thought to be stable plant climaxes, are now considered to depend on continuing human interference. An example of this is the great African savanna, an outlier of which occurs in Zululand where it is called variously thornveld, bushveld or lowveld.

Ecologists now appear to have come to the conclusion that its basic structure of open woodland with a grass understorey is maintained only by the continual action of fire and grazing which holds back the encroachment of the wooded element.[11]

However, although 'natural vegetation' is no longer considered to exist, except perhaps in the remotest corners of the earth, it is still a concept used by botanists and ecologists. Under the name of 'climatic climax community'[12] it provides a theoretical base from which it is possible to reconstruct the direction which vegetational change has taken, and to speculate on the manner in which vegetation will change under certain conditions.

Acocks, in his classic *Veld Types of South Africa*,[13] was well aware of the effect of man on the southern African environment. Although the focus of his attention was the devastation inflicted on the sub-continent by commercial agriculture, he did realise that man had been changing the region's vegetation patterns long before this. Working on evidence provided by known plant successions, vegetational relicts, and also a limited range of documentary sources, he mapped an outline of the possible structure of the climatic climax communities of South Africa, Lesotho and Swaziland. Although the title of this map—'Vegetation in AD 1400?'—reflects his ignorance of the time-depth of farming activity in the area, the map itself is of considerable interest to the historian. On it he indicated that he believed that most of the land between the Drakensberg and the Indian Ocean was covered with 'Forest and Scrubforest', while the low-lying valleys contained tracts of savanna, this latter feature being particularly prominent in Zululand.

Of course a reconstruction of this kind, on a small-scale map, and on a sub-continental level, can only outline the most general vegetational features; it is thus probably most useful to consider the map not so much as a reconstruction of the previously existing, pre-human, vegetation of the region but as an indication of the tendency for the plant communities of the eastern escarpment to move towards wooded vegetation types. However, this tendency has been constantly deflected by the interference of man and a comparison of this map with later known vegetation patterns indicates a high degree of human activity over a considerable period of time.

We can obtain a rough idea of the vegetation of Zululand in pre-colonial times by making use of Acocks's detailed vegetation map[14] and combining it with what we know from historical accounts and our knowledge of the present situation. The forest and scrub forest which dominated Zululand had been reduced drastically leaving forest relics on high wet ridges, and scrub in areas protected from fire, along watercourses and on the coast. In those places where it had been removed, it had been replaced by sour grass. The savanna vegetation types had spread from the depths of the river valleys, and the wooded elements had been reduced by regular burning which favoured the grass understorey. The pronounced deflection of patterns of plant succession was the result of farming activity over a prolonged period of time. We have little detailed information about the manner in which this took place; however, archaeologists have shown that this process had been going on for well over a thousand years before Shaka,[15] and that agriculture probably started in the savanna areas and coastal regions.

This human activity created a complex pattern of interlaced vegetation types which were of particular value to the stock-keeper. Two basic types of 'natural' grazing are recognised by stock farmers in southern Africa and both are found in Zululand. 'Sourveld' is the characteristic grass cover of the higher rainfall areas; its most striking feature is that its nutritive value and palatability decreases as it matures. In the spring and early summer, after the first rains during the growing stage its food value is high and the grass is of great importance to the herdsman. But it can only be fully utilised for about four months in the year before its food value becomes depleted and it loses its palatability. 'Sweetveld' is characteristic of the drier areas. It is usually found in association with scattered trees in savanna vegetation types, where it forms the understorey. It is sparse and easily damaged but it retains its palatability and nutritive value throughout the dry winter. Sweetveld is therefore of particular importance as winter grazing if cattle are to maintain condition. Between these two extremes of sweet and sourveld lie transitional areas of mixed veld which can be profitably grazed from six to eight months in the year.[16]

The occurrence and distribution of these grazing types is determined largely by the amount of rainfall which is in turn affected by topography. Zululand is a country of high relief. Rivers and streams have cut through sandstone layers to the granite beds beneath and, as they retreated westwards, left huge spurs of more resistant material jutting towards the sea. The Thukela, Mhlatuze, Mfolozi, and Phongolo rivers are therefore separated by high-lying ground, at times 2 000–3 000 feet above the river beds, with the sides of the valleys deeply incised by feeder streams, creating much broken country (see Map 4.1 on next page).[17]

This high relief leads to great variation in rainfall over short distances. Rain-bearing winds, coming off the Indian ocean, deposit over fifty inches a year on certain parts of the coastline and there is a general decrease as the distance from the sea increases; but the isohyets are severely distorted

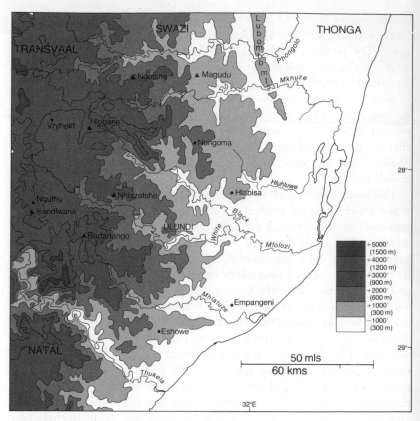

Map 4.1 Zululand: Topography

by the spurs reaching out from the west, and the deep river valleys lie in rain shadow where precipitation can be less than twenty-five inches a year (See Map 4.2). And like most of the sub-continent unreliability of rainfall is a climatic feature.

In Map 4.3 (see p. 108), I have grouped together a number of Acocks's vegetational types to give a rough idea of the distribution of the sweet and sourveld. The coastal belt, with its sour to mixed grazing, is heavily watered, the climate sub-tropical, with hot humid summers and warm

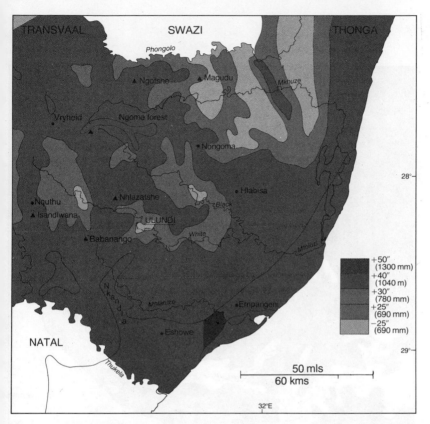

Map 4.2 Zululand: Rainfall

winters. The vegetation in pre-colonial times consisted of large areas of coastal forest, interspersed with coarse, heavy grass which was matted, tick-infested and difficult to burn. In the south, between the Thukela and the Mhlatuze, the 1 500 foot contour lies near the coast, but north of the Mhlatuze it swings further inland, creating a broader coastal plain with reduced rainfall in the western and northern areas. In these drier regions coastal forest and bush give way to thornveld with an understorey of mixed grasses.

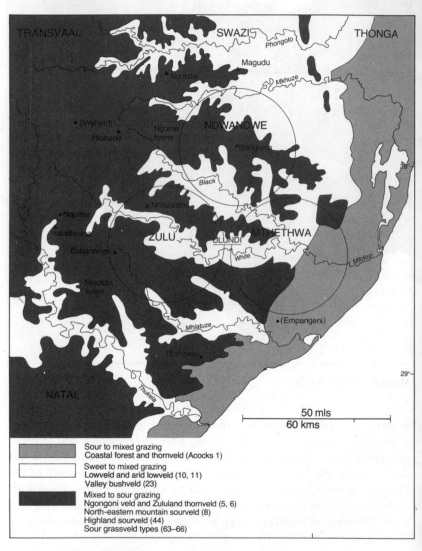

Map 4.3 Zululand: Vegetation

West of the coastal plain, the high ridges of Zululand create rain shadows in the river valleys. It is here that sweetveld occurs as an understorey to scattered thorn trees and bushes. Sweetveld does not occur in areas above 3 000 feet, or in areas where the rainfall is higher than thirty inches per annum. Although the rainfall is low and there is a long dry season, the sweetveld regions are comparatively well-watered by the rivers and streams running down from surrounding hills and ridges where the rainfall is higher. While there are huge tracts of sweetveld in the low rainfall areas of southern Africa, few of them appear to have this somewhat paradoxical feature of being dry but well-watered. Moreover, because of the high relief, it is only a short distance from these hot, low-lying pastures, to the cooler, mixed and sour grazing on the sides and crests of the surrounding valley walls and this creates a variety of grazing types over a comparatively small area. The 3 000 foot contour marks the limit of the sweetveld and above this line pastures become mixed tending towards sour. In Zululand this area included tracts of open sour grassveld on the higher plateaux, while in the wetter regions sour grasses have replaced forest.

It can be seen from Map 4.3 that these grazing types interlace through much of the region. As a result, herdsmen had to be able to move their stock freely if they were to take advantage of the country's grazing potential: to higher areas of sourveld in the spring, to mixed grazing as the summer advanced, and to the low-lying sweetveld in the winter. Because the river valleys penetrated the hinterland, most parts of the country had a sufficient variety of grazing within a radius of some twenty miles of any point. In times of local drought, however, the distance which stock would have had to be moved must have increased.

I have suggested elsewhere that this configuration of different grazing types had a direct bearing on the geographical situation of the pre-Shakan chiefdoms, and the direction of their expansion. Daniel and Webb have established, with considerable precision, the environmental requirements of three pre-Shakan chiefdoms in terms of rainfall and access to different grazing types.[18] Furthermore, during the later history of the Zulu kingdom it is clear that favoured members of the royal house and leading officials were placed in districts which were particularly favourable on account of their proximity to a variety of pastures.[19]

It can be argued that, compared with the rest of the eastern escarpment, Zululand was a particularly suitable environment for stock-keeping cultivators. The region can perhaps be regarded as a transitional area lying between the tropical and temperate zones, with many of the advantageous features associated with both regions. The humid coast and the hot, low-lying valleys can be seen as a southward extension of the more tropical region, with the fecundity associated with it, and yet without the debilitating human and animal diseases of that environment. A botanist has recently suggested that, when studying tropical vegetation, it is useful to move away from considering the 'solar tropics' as the boundary, and he introduces the concept of the 'biological tropics' which lie between 30°N and 30°S latitude.[20] The 30°S latitude cuts the coast just south of Durban. As mentioned above there are vast tracts of sweetveld in southern Africa. However, in the past they could not have been exploited with the intensity that was possible in Zululand. Large areas were infested with tsetse fly, whereas in Zululand this only occurred on the margins of the country or in isolated patches in the deep valleys towards the coast.[21] Furthermore, few other sweetveld regions were as well-watered as those in Zululand.

Apart from the fact that the climate becomes more temperate towards the south, there are some indications that changes in the geological structure have a bearing on sweetveld distribution. The different qualities of the rock strata further south have the effect of creating narrower, more deeply incised river valleys with the result that the rain shadow areas necessary for the production of sweetveld are considerably reduced.[22] Detailed research on the physical environment of pre-colonial farmers in southern Africa would, I suspect, reveal important regional differences which might, in turn, be linked with differences in social development.

Up to this point I have considered the vegetation of Zululand in a somewhat static manner. However, there are indications that the change from climatic climax communities of forest, scrub forest, and savanna, to sub-climaxes of grassland, savanna and forest relicts, was only the initial stage of the series of changes that man wrought on the environment.

It seems possible that once it was no longer easy to convert forest into grassland with the axe, or to increase the grassy elements of the savanna through fire, serious degeneration of the vegetation might well have taken place. The region is subject to severe soil erosion, a process which it is difficult to reverse. This can originate in overgrazing, trampling round water sources and kraals, and too frequent or unseasonal firing of the veld. Sweetveld is particularly vulnerable and once the plant cover has been reduced and the top soil lost, the area is open to invasion by unpalatable bush and thicket. Even under-stocking can lead to pasture deterioration because selective grazing favours unpalatable grasses which eventually invade the pastures. It seems unlikely that the peoples of south-eastern Africa had established a long-term ecological equilibrium with their environment. A society without a scientific knowledge of plant life and nutrition, without the means to control grazing and cattle movements by fencing, or to store and pump water, could not avert pasture degeneration, or bring about pasture regeneration. Concentrated grazing by domestic stock over an extended period of time would have necessarily set in motion a process which steadily reduced the carrying capacity of the pastures.

Shortage of land, decrease in palatable grasses, and population pressure on resources are all aspects of the same problem and they aggravate each other, and can set up a process of continuing environmental degeneration. The increasing rivalry between social groups in Zululand at the beginning of the nineteenth century and the social revolution which took place may have been a response to such a situation. There is evidence that the insecurity and violence of this time was the result of a shortage of resources. In the first decade of the nineteenth century the region experienced a disastrous famine, known as the *Madlathule*, which was long remembered for the suffering it caused and for the fact that, unlike subsequent periods of shortage, it affected the whole country. It seems to have been this famine that James Stuart's informants were referring to when they gave accounts of cannibalism and the grouping of people in large villages for the purpose of defending their grain stores from starving marauders.[23] Martin Hall, using dendroclimatological evidence, has argued that there was a steady decline in rainfall during the 1790s which reached its lowest point at about the time of the Madlathule famine.[24] Certainly the Madlathule occurred at a crucial juncture in Zulu history, at about the time Dingiswayo returned from exile, and Shaka was wandering through Zululand, an outcast looking for protection.

Of course, even it if is assumed that this suggestion is valid, and that by the beginning of the nineteenth century there was a serious shortage of resources in the region, it does not necessarily follow that this should lead to an increase in the size of the social unit. However, as I have mentioned above, there does seem to be a connection between the source and direction of the chiefdoms' expansion and the most desirable grazing areas. And there would be advantages in assuming political control over a larger area of land and an increased number of people; in societies where human energy is the main source of social strength, there is a considerable degree of correlation between demographic magnitude and coercive potential, making the violent appropriation of foodstuffs more effective. Moreover, an extension of territory would give members of the group access to a greater range of grazing and arable land, which is an important factor in a region where local differences in climate create major variations in productive capacity over comparatively small areas. Shaka continued and extended the centralisation process initiated by such leaders as Dingiswayo and Zwide. The most obvious consequence of this was uction of population by warfare. But beyond this, the kingdom he founded was sufficiently large to redistribute cattle over a much greater area than was previously possible. This allowed the Zulu to avoid local concentrations of stock, and to utilise more effectively seasonal variation in the quality of pasturage. Furthermore, by moving herds more freely over a wider area, it was possible to avoid the effects of localised drought and overgrazing. Control of cattle over a large area could not, in the long term, reverse the process of pasture degeneration; but it could retard it, allowing certain areas to rest and regain their grazing potential. This only became possible after the power of the small localised social units had been broken and the peoples of the region brought under centralised control.

Production, reproduction[25] and the Zulu military system

Max Gluckman, in an article written in 1969 and published in 1974, gave additional evidence to support his theory that population pressure was the major factor in the rise of the Zulu kingdom. He argued that an examination of the journals of mariners shipwrecked in the sixteenth and seventeenth centuries 'reveals a description of an increasingly populous land'. The fertility and suitability of the land, he asserted, allowed a rapid population growth but by the mid-eighteenth century there was no more room for expansion. As a result there was a series of rapid changes, initially as individuals built up chiefdoms through conquest, and which culminated in the rise of Shaka who 'solved the land population problem, as tens of thousands of people must have died'.[1]'There may have been', Gluckman continued, 'a process of slowly accumulating quantitative changes in the ratio of population to land, culminating in a rapid change of pattern'. However, Gluckman emphasised that 'the new pattern was still restricted within the limits of the basic technology', for close examination of the changes in social structure brought about by Shaka reveals that they were changes largely of degree. The area in which Shaka did bring about substantial alteration was in Zulu military organisation and this, Gluckman argued, could be traced to the fact that the Zulu king 'was a near psychotic and had a very disturbed psychosexuality'. This demonstrated itself both in his individual actions and, on a wider scale, in 'the extreme development of the military system, with its long-term celibacy'.[26]

I am not convinced that the journals of the shipwrecked sailors reveal as clearly as Gluckman believed that there was a steady increase in population, and find his arguments relating a population crisis to social change mechanistic. Nonetheless, Gluckman's article does tend to confirm the situation suggested by a study of the physical environment, as well as the oral evidence of severe shortage in the region at the beginning of the nineteenth century. However, I disagree that the 'extreme development of the military system' can be explained in terms of Shaka's 'psychosexuality'. Indeed, I would like to suggest in this final section, that a study of the military system in the context of the production processes within the kingdom gives further evidence that the struggle for resources was a major factor in social changes taking place at this time.

Although Nguni social organisation underwent radical alterations at the end of the eighteenth and beginning of the nineteenth centuries, one element remained substantially unchanged up to the time that the Zulu were forced to become part of the South African capitalist system. This was the patrilineal lineage system*, and the basic reason for its longevity and resilience was that it was an expression of productive processes which themselves were not altered substantially over this period. Kinship relations were expressions of production relations and they must be considered together. All Zulu belonged to exogamous lineages, membership being determined by common descent through the male line from a founding ancestor. The lineage structure was given material expression in the homestead (*umuzi/imizi*) of the kingdom. Every man in Zululand on, or soon after, his marriage would set up a homestead of his own. As homestead-head (*umnumzana/abanumzana*) he would rank his wives in segments within the homestead. In time these segments, under the eldest son of each segment, would break from the homestead and establish homesteads of their own. Thus every homestead in Zululand had sprung from a previously existing one and contained within it the seeds of new ones. The process of continual homestead formation gave physical expression to that much abused but most useful concept, the patrilineal segmentary lineage system.[27]

Production in Zululand took place in the homesteads and their immediate environs. There were different types of homesteads, their size reflecting the status and wealth of the homestead-head, but they were all organised on similar principles. If we consider the homestead of the 'common man', that is, the type of homestead in which it was estimated that ninety per cent of the population lived,[28] then it would consist of the homestead-head, two or three wives and their children. Each wife would have her own hut, its position reflecting her status.

*Cf. H. Slater, 'The Changing Pattern of Economic Relationships in rural Natal, 1838–1914', below pp. 148–70 and the discussion in the Introduction, pp. 17–20

Each segment (a wife and her children) formed a production unit within the homestead, the production community. The homestead-head provided each segment with milch cows, plots of agricultural land, and a place for storing the grain it produced. Meals took place within the hut of each wife. Each segment was therefore able to provide its own means of subsistence while a portion of the surplus contributed to the subsistence of the homestead-head.

Labour-power within the homestead was principally expended in the production of cereals and dairy products which formed the basis of the Zulu diet. Supporting activities included hunting, and metal and leather-working. There was a rigid sexual division of labour within the production units of the production community with women involved in agricultural production and men with the other major aspect of production—stock-keeping.

Each homestead was to a large degree materially self-sufficient with one exception—the homestead did not reproduce wives. These had to be obtained by exchanging cattle for women from other lineages, while cattle could be obtained from other lineages for daughters of the homestead. In this manner, through the exchange of surplus from the process of reproduction and production (daughters and cattle), the process of reproduction and production was continued. The ultimate materialisation, or actualisation, of labour-power in cattle is an obvious consequence in an economic formation with few forms of storeable or alienable wealth.

Although it cannot be dealt with here in any detail, this function of cattle as a self-reproducing store of labour-power is a question of great importance. The major relationships in the kingdom were marked by the movement of cattle: between homesteads in exchange for women, from client to overlord, and overlord to client. The accumulation of cattle was directly related not only to political power, but also to material power, as it allowed the cattle-owner to increase his number of wives—that is ultimately the size of the lineage, homesteads, production communities, and number of producers. As we have seen Zululand was particularly well-suited for cattle raising, and centralised control over cattle allowed more effective utilisation of pastures; thus part of the reason for the strength and resilience of the kingdom must have been the physical conditions which allowed a direct transformation of human productivity into cattle and cattle into labour and further productivity.

At the level of the homestead, the correlation between the kinship and lineage systems and the way in which social production was organised is striking. Production groups and lineage and kinship groups were virtually coterminous: the production community consisted of a father, his wives

and their children; production units within the community cons.
ranked segments of wives and their children; wives were introduce
the homestead through exchange of the homestead's surplus cattle;
homestead (production community) had been a lineage segment (production unit) within a previously existing homestead and each homestead
contained incipient production units. The laws regulating the distribution
of property amongst segments within the homestead and inheritance when
these segments became production communities, were defined in terms
of the segmentation of the patrilineal lineage.

The importance of the lineage/productive system in the Zulu kingdom
has to be emphasised because it is often assumed that the lineage system
is somehow of lesser significance in such centralised states as the Zulu
kingdom. Too often analysts approach the subject of their study through
the state, or kinship, and thereby obscure the fundamental fact that the
'driving force' of the social formation was the surplus created by labour
within the homestead, and also that production within the homestead was
given social expression in the patrilineal segmentary lineage system. At
the same time we must remember that the Zulu state consisted of between
100 000 and 200 000 people who considered themselves members of the
kingdom by their allegiance to a king who was the supreme political,
military and religious authority in the land. He ruled in association with
a number of territorial chiefs who, within their chiefdoms, delegated their
authority to local administrators. There were a large number of other
state officials (*induna/izinduna*) who had a variety of specialised roles. The
Zulu kingdom was a stratified state with great diversity in status, wealth
and power. Nevertheless, all married Zulu males, regardless of status,
were members of lineages and the heads of their own production communities.

The basis of the king's power lay in the surplus labour he extracted from
every homestead within the kingdom, by means of the military system.
All Zulu men were members of the state army. From the time they reached
puberty and were recruited into an age-set, or 'regiment' (*ibutho/amabutho*)
until the king gave the age-set permission to marry, perhaps fifteen to
twenty years later, they spent much of their time working for the king.
In the early part of the history of the kingdom they were raiders, going
beyond the kingdom's borders and bringing back cattle. When raiding
ceased during the last thirty-five years of the kingdom's existence, they
concentrated on herding the royal cattle, sowing and reaping the king's
lands, and acted as a coercive force within the country. Thus, through the
'military system' the king was able to draw on the labour of all Zulu men
for perhaps a third of their productive lives. And even when the regiment

to which a man belonged had been given permission to marry, they were liable to a certain amount of service every year. Women were also formed into age-sets but they did not perform service for the king at the royal homesteads. However, they were not allowed to marry until the king gave them permission, which occurred when an associated male regiment had received permission from the king to take wives.

If one understands the fundamental productive processes of the Zulu kingdom and their relationship to the kinship system, then this power of the king to withhold marriage through the military system becomes crucially significant. Let us examine the case of the women first. The rate of population growth is directly dependent on the fertility of women, and obviously if the amount of time between puberty and marriage is increased this reduces marital fertility. Under the heading 'Age of marriage and fertility' a well-known historical demographer has stated:

> One need hardly emphasise the importance of this variable to the fertility levels of any community which does not practise control of fertility within marriage. In such communities the fertility of women is mainly a function of their age. If therefore they spend many of their child-bearing years outside marriage, much reproductive potential is permanently lost. Other things being equal this in itself can result in total fertility levels which differ from each other by a factor of two between a community in which the average age at first marriage is the very early twenties and another where it is about 30.[29]

Krige wrote that 'In Shaka's days there were sometimes women of thirty years of age unmarried',[30] and Sir Theophilus Shepstone reported in 1873 that

> The Zulu Country is but sparsely inhabited when compared with Natal and the increase of its population is checked more by its peculiar Marriage Regulations than by the exodus of refugees ... During our visit we saw large numbers of young women apparently from twenty to thirty-five years of age, all unmarried.[31]

No doubt the age at which women married varied at different points in Zulu history. It is nonetheless clear that Zulu wŏmen married several years after puberty and this necessarily reduced the potential increase in population, and that by means of the female age-set system the king restricted the rate of demographic expansion.

Restriction on the age at which males can take wives and have children does not have this direct effect on population increase. However, 'marriage' in the Zulu kingdom was so much more than taking a wife and conceiving children. It meant that kinship relations were extended, that there was further segmentation of the lineage and that a new productive community was established. The power to control the rate at which this took place lay with the king. Through the 'military system' the Zulu king was able to influence the most fundamental processes of the kingdom—the processes upon which the very existence of the kingdom was based. He could control to an important degree the intensity with which the environment was exploited, the rate of demographic increase, and the rate and direction in which the processes of production could expand. The Zulu military system gave the king the means to control the process of reproduction and production within the Zulu kingdom.

Once this fact is grasped one can understand the inadequacy of the many attempts to see the Zulu military system in crude Freudian terms: that the military system was the consequence of Shaka's disturbed 'psychosexuality', or that it led to an accumulation of sexual energy which was then transmuted into military vigour.[32] While not in any way dismissing the importance of the Zulu army as a military force, we must also appreciate that it gave the king fundamental powers of control over the manner and the rate at which the physical environment of Zululand was to be exploited. And this is surely significant when taken into account with the evidence that suggests that indiscriminate exploitation of grazing had led to a serious deterioration of resources by the beginning of the nineteenth century.

Thus, from a study of the physical environment of Zululand we know that it underwent fundamental changes as a result of the activities of stock-farming cultivators, and that this led to the creation of an environment particularly well-suited to their needs, but one which was also fragile and breaking down under pre-Shakan modes of exploitation. A study of the process of production in the Zulu kingdom reveals that the king had the ability to influence the rate of demographic increase and the creation of new productive communities, thereby solving, by the redistribution of human and animal resources, some of the environmental problems that had arisen.

Although this chapter argues that specific aspects of the physical environment of Zululand and certain developments in the social structure of the Zulu kingdom are related, it is not possible at this stage to identify with any precision the causal connections. We can neither assert that environmental changes 'caused' the Shakan revolution, nor that Shaka necessarily realised that there was a population crisis and solved it by slaughter abroad and contraception at home. To establish the connections between the productive process and ideology in a social formation, or between social being and consciousness in an individual, is the most important and the most formidable of the historian's tasks. At present, however, our ability to identify and conceptualise the most significant elements in pre-capitalistic formations is inadequate, and in the case of pre-Shakan Zululand the paucity of empirical information and our ignorance of the chronology of the development of social change before the nineteenth century makes the task all the more difficult. Nonetheless, the key to understanding the rise of the Zulu kingdom and the events associated with it would seem to lie in the first instance in a study of the productive potentialities of the physical environment and the way in which it was exploited and changed by southern Africa's pre-colonial farmers.

Notes

1 L. Thompson, 'Co-operation and Conflict: the Zulu kingdom and Natal', in M. Wilson and L.M. Thompson, (eds.), *The Oxford History of South Africa*, Oxford, 1969, i, pp. 336–41
2 *Ibid*, pp. 339–40
3 M. Gluckman, 'The Rise of a Zulu Empire', *Scientific American*, 1963, p. 202; J.D. Omer Cooper, *The Zulu Aftermath: a nineteenth-century revolution in Bantu Africa*, London, 1966, pp. 24–7
4 Wilson and Thompson, *Oxford History*, p. 341
5 Zululand in this chapter means the area that became the core of the Zulu kingdom, bounded by the Thukela, Mzinyathi and Ncome rivers in the south and west, to the Phongolo valley in the north, eastwards to the Lubombo range. J.J. Guy, 'Cattle-keeping in Zululand', Research Group on Cattle-Keeping in Africa, School of Oriental and African Studies, University of London, 1970
6 J.B. McI. Daniel, 'A Geographical Study of pre-Shakan Zululand', *South African Geographical Journal*, lv, 1, 1973, and C. de B. Webb, 'Of Orthodoxy, Heresy and the Difaqane', unpublished paper presented to the Conference at the Rand Afrikaans University, 1975
7 P. Bonner, 'Early state formation among the Nguni: the relevance of the Swazi case', unpublished paper, RAU conference, 1975. D.W. Hedges, 'Trade and Politics in Southern Mozambique and Zululand in the eighteenth and early nineteenth centuries', Ph.D. thesis, London, 1978. Unfortunately this chapter was completed before I could consult either Hedges's thesis or that of H. Slater, 'Social transitions in south-east Africa to 1840', Ph.D. Sussex, 1976, which attempts to explain the Shakan period as a transition from a feudal to an absolute state
8 M. Gluckman, 'The Individual in a Social Framework: the rise of King Shaka of Zululand', *Journal of African Studies*, i, 2, 1974; M. Hall, 'Dendroclimatology, Rainfall and Human Adaptation in the Later Iron Age of Natal and Zululand', *Annals of the Natal Museum*, xxii, 3, 1976
9 I have not been able to deal here with the demands of cultivation on the Zululand environment. One problem is that information on such important aspects as yield and growing-period usually refers to modern hybrid types. The introduction of maize to Zululand in the eighteenth century was important not only because of its larger yield but also because it is less labour-intensive than sorghum

or the millets. I suspect that the limiting factor on cultivation in Zululand was not availability of land but availability of labour-power

10 Finally destroyed, it would seem, by the massive tome edited by W.L. Thomas, *Man's Role in Changing the Face of the Earth*, Chicago, 1956. See also A. Thomas, 'Ecology and Human Influence' in W. Davies and C.L. Skidmore, *Tropical Pastures*, London, 1966

11 S.R. Eyre, *Vegetation and Soils: a world picture*, London, 1968, pp. 241–4

12 *Ibid.*, p. 10

13 J.P.H. Acocks, *Veld Types of South Africa*, Pretoria, 1953

14 J.P.H. Acocks, *Veld Types of South Africa*, (Map) Pretoria, 1951, 1:500 000

15 See T. Maggs and M. Michael, 'Ntshekane: an Early Iron Age site in the Tugela Basin, Natal', *Annals of the Natal Museum*, xxii, 3, 1976. Material recovered from an Early Iron Age site in Zululand has apparently been dated to about A.D. 300 (Interview with Martin Hall, Radio South Africa, 4 July 1977)

16 For grazing types see 'Types of Grassland and the Utilization of Pasture', *Handbook for Farmers in South Africa*, iii, Pretoria, 1957, and J.D. Scott, 'Principles of Pasture Management' in G. Meredith (ed.), *The Grasses and Pastures of South Africa*, South Africa, 1955

17 See also the *Natal Regional Survey*, i, London, 1951, and xiii, London, 1957, and *Handbook for Farmers in South Africa*, i, Pretoria, 1957

18 Guy, 'Cattle-keeping' and Daniel, 'Geographical Study'

19 J.J. Guy, 'The Destruction of the Zulu kingdom: the Civil War in Zululand, 1879–84', Ph.D, University of London, 1975, p. 50

20 Davies and Skidmore, 'Problems of Pasture Improvement' in Davies and Skidmore, *Tropical Pastures*, p. 21

21 C. Fuller, *Tsetse in the Transvaal and Surrounding Territories, an historical review*, Pretoria, 1923; D. Leslie, *Among the Zulus and Amatongas*, Edinburgh, 1875, pp. 182–7; Letter by St Vincent Erskine, 22 June 1871, St Vincent Erskine Papers, Killie Campbell Africana Library, Durban

22 M. Cole, *South Africa*, London, 1961, pp. 578, 581

23 C. de B. Webb and J.B. Wright (eds.), *The James Stuart Archive*, Pietermaritzburg and Durban, 1976, i, evidence of Jantshi, p. 201; D. McK Malcolm, 'The Bantu', transcript of broadcast talks, Killie Campbell Africana Library. For other accounts of the Madlathule famine see A.T. Bryant, *Olden Times in Zululand and Natal* ..., London, 1929, pp. 63 and 88, and H. Callaway, *The Religious System of the Amazulu*, Cape Town, 1970, p. 96

24 Hall, 'Dendroclimatology', pp. 701–2

25 The sections on production have been drawn from my paper 'Production and exchange in the Zulu kingdom', *Moblomi (Lesotho)*, iii, 1978

26 Gluckman, 'The Individual in a Social Framework', pp. 137, 139, 140 and 143

27 See also Guy, 'Destruction of the Zulu Kingdom', pp. 21ff

28 A.T. Bryant, *The Zulu People* ..., Pietermaritzburg, 1967, p. 438

29 E.A. Wrigley, *Population and History*, London, 1969, p. 116

30 E.J. Krige, *The Social System of the Zulus*, Pietermaritzburg, 1957, p. 38

31 British Parliamentary Papers, C 1137: 1, enc., T. Shepstone, *Report of the expedition ... to instal Cetywayo, August 1873*, p. 21

32 Furthermore sexual relations between unmarried persons were permitted but were of a kind that did not lead to conception. See J. Stuart and D. Mck. Malcolm, *The Diary of Henry Francis Fynn*, Pietermaritzburg, 1969, p. 295

CHAPTER FIVE

Production and the material basis of chieftainship: Pondoland c.1830–80

William Beinart

During the last few years, a number of researchers have focused attention on the response by African producers to colonial penetration in southern Africa.[1] Their work has shown that in many areas, the availability of market opportunities, or the threat of absorption into the labour market because of rent and taxation, encouraged Africans to innovate and produce an agricultural surplus. The pattern of response varied considerably; both the nature of pre-colonial society and the particular timing and character of penetration were important in determining the variations. A minority of Africans in the eastern Cape, and later in Natal and the Transvaal, became individual farmers on privately owned land, freed from the constraints of pre-colonial society.[2] In areas where whites gained control of substantial tracts of land, many Africans became labour- or rent-paying tenants, farmers-on-the-half or squatters. In the areas that were to become known as the reserves, and later formed the basis for the African 'homelands' or Bantustans, less land was alienated to whites and communal tenure and the redistributive economy remained relatively intact.

None of the studies of 'peasantisation' in South Africa pays sufficient attention to the nature of the economic response to penetration in these latter areas, and to an analysis of continuities in production and social organisation before and after their colonial annexation. The experience of the Mpondo provides a good example for the development of such an analysis. Pondoland, in the north-eastern Transkei, was one of the last annexed areas in South Africa, surviving under independent chiefs until 1894. As late as the 1930s, observers considered the area to be a haven of traditionalism.

> The Pondo is unusually conservative and tenacious of his old culture, and in Pondoland the disintegration of native life is by no means so alarming as in other parts of South Africa.

commented General Smuts in his preface to Monica Hunter's classic anthropological monograph on the Mpondo, *Reaction to Conquest*.[3]

Such characterisations should not disguise the fact that by the turn of the century, the Mpondo were deeply enmeshed in the wider South African economy. Technology, crops, patterns of agriculture and settlement were all changing.[4] White traders provided a channel for the export of pastoral and agricultural produce and the import of an increasing variety of manufactured goods; labour migrancy to the mines on the Reef, although it began later from Pondoland than from other Transkeian areas, was becoming widespread. In trying to understand the nature of economic change in the late nineteenth and early twentieth centuries, a number of problems arose over the nature of the 'traditional' economy. Hunter's work lacked any systematic chronological dimension to the analysis of change. Herding, cultivation, hunting and gathering were, as she shows, always the bases of subsistence. But the relative importance and intensity of these activities varied considerably from the 1820s, when the first literate observers visited the Mpondo chiefdom.[5] Nor—as is often implied in the literature—were changes generated only by contact with the colonial economy.

The first aim of this essay is thus to discover the nature of economic change between 1830 and 1880 and to develop a chronology for the economic history of an African chiefdom; the second is to assess the link between such economic changes and the power of the chieftaincy, because it is clear that the economic relationship between chiefs and people changed very substantially during the nineteenth century. In the earlier part of the century, the chiefs had far greater control over production than they had by 1880; the gradual decline of their control relates to the decline in their political power, and colonial penetration accelerated this process. If it is to be useful in relation to studies of South African chiefdoms, the concept of 'peasantisation' should be expanded to include not only changes in technology and trade relations with the colonial economy, but also such changes in the relations between chiefs and people.

The period of close settlement

During the 1820s, the Mpondo were continually attacked from the north. Zulu impis, and those who fled them, cleared the area between the Thukela and Pondoland of inhabitants. Many sought refuge in Pondoland or clashed with the Mpondo in their flight south.[6] The Zulu themselves twice raided the area, and offshoots from the Zulu state, the Bhaca, Qwabe and Ngwane, collectively and separately known by colonial observers as the 'Fetkanie', presented a continual threat. The Mpondo, under their paramount chief Faku, were victorious in many of the battles they fought. Their success depended on a judicious mixture of strategic retreat into the dense coastal forests and confrontation in battle when the enemy least expected it. But by the time of the second Zulu raid in 1828, Faku had been forced to retreat with most of his people from the eastern side of the Mzimvubu river. The Zulu regiments devastated the Mpondo settlements east and west of the river. Faku, when questioned by the first colonial officer to visit the area ten days after the departure of the Zulu, bewailed the fact that 'his people had lost all their cattle and had nothing to live upon or make clothes of'.[7] Their huts and grain stores had been destroyed.

In order to protect themselves from further raids by the Zulu and the various 'Fetkanie' groups, the Mpondo now concentrated their settlements around Faku's new kraal on the Mngazi river and in neighbouring river valleys. Early missionary visitors, who had travelled up through the Xhosa and Thembu chiefdoms, were struck by the dense nature of Mpondo settlement:

> From one hill near the Great Place . . . [Shepstone in 1830] counted a hundred kraals each of which contained from twenty to forty houses, which after the usual manner of counting in this country, will give more than ten thousand inhabitants; and the view from the hill took in the population of one river, and the parts adjoining.[8]

Some months earlier, Boyce, who was to be the first Methodist missionary in Pondoland, estimated the number of people around Faku's kraal at from 7 000 to 8 000 out of a total of perhaps 20 000 under his control.[9] The homesteads of the Mpondo were closer together and much larger than those of the

> other races of Kaffers nearer the colony, who being from their vicinage to the colonial boundary much more safe from predatory attacks, love[d] to roam at large with their herds, over extensive tracts of country.[10]

The absence of cattle enabled the Mpondo to maintain the close settlement that was so essential for defence, for they had no need of grazing grounds. They remained closely settled in these valleys until at least 1838.

In a period of continual conflict, the army was of great importance for defence. But it was also used to regain cattle through raids. Close settlement, initially a defensive response, facilitated military organisation for offensive purposes. Soon after their defeat by the Zulu, the Mpondo beat the Qwabe and abducted the cattle from the Xesibe great place.[11] However, it was Ncaphayi, chief of the Bhaca and Faku's sole remaining rival in the area after these victories, who captured most of the Qwabe stock. When, within a couple of years, his raiding fortunes turned, some of his people, threatened with starvation, defected to the Mpondo.[12] Faku gave Ncaphayi land on the eastern side of the Mzimvubu in 1832 and together, albeit in an uneasy alliance, they raided to the south-west and west, where cattle stocks among the Bomvana, Thembu and Mpondomise were relatively high. Colonial observers probably over-estimated their joint forces at from 15 000 to 30 000 and some identified the Mpondo, along with the Bhaca, as primarily a raiding chiefdom.[13]

By the first two decades of the nineteenth century, regiments recruited by age group had emerged in Zululand, first among the pre-Zulu confederacies and then, on a larger scale, in the Zulu kingdom itself. Age regiments cross-cut army organisation within the sub-chiefdoms that went to make up these larger polities. Associated with the breakdown of sub-chiefdoms, the disturbance of the agricultural cycle and the constant military demands on the young men that accompanied the rise of the Zulu empire, was the abolition of male circumcision. South-west of the Mzimkulu river, the Mpondo were the only chiefdom to stop male circumcision and it is tempting to suggest that Faku introduced other structural changes similar to those among the Zulu. The evidence, however, does not really support this interpretation. The traditions of the Mpondo and neighbouring chiefdoms are clear that 'the Pondos had no regiments recruited according to age'.[14] The armies were mobilised by sub-chiefs and collected to fight under one of the houses of the paramountcy. Nor is there evidence of military homesteads, a standing army, or female regiments in Pondoland. It is possible too that, contrary to Hunter's belief, the abolition of circumcision in Pondoland took place after the period of close settlement.[15] For some traditions assert that the ceremony was only abandoned when Mqikela, Faku's great son and heir, was due to be initiated in about 1850. Even if the custom was discarded at an earlier date, however, it did not mark major transformations in Pondoland. Military demands were frequent in the 1820s and 1830s and this alone would have made it difficult to set aside the time for ritual and healing necessitated by male circumcision ceremonies.

While Faku may not have transformed the sub-chiefdoms under his control, he did control military expeditions. He alone could authorise the ceremony of doctoring the army, the essential prelude to any military action, and tributary chiefs contested this power at their peril.

> We hear of a war likely to break out between Faku and this rascal Capai [Ncaphayi] the Fitcani chief who this year settled on the Zimvubu; Capai having employed a doctor to wash him with a decoction of roots and 'to make his people strong'. Faku views this as contrary to established usages of pro-

priety on the part of a subordinate chief and as indicating an intention of claiming independence.[16]

Ncaphayi did not challenge Faku, and two years later affirmed to a missionary that he accepted his position: 'I am sitting still and building nor shall I go out to war again unless called by Faku'.[17] Faku not only controlled mobilisation, but also the cattle that were captured in war, which had to be brought to the Great Place immediately they were taken. Captives taken in war were also probably distributed by the paramount. The upheavals of the Mfecane led many groups both large and small, who were seeking a place to settle, to gravitate to Faku, as he emerged as the dominant power on the southern periphery of the Zulu state. Cattle were demanded as tribute or settlement fees, and these accrued directly to the paramountcy; Ncaphayi, for example, paid him about fifty head in 1832.[18]

While some sought refuge under Faku, others fleeing southwards, especially larger parties under their own chiefs, transformed themselves temporarily into hunters and raiders. They had no opportunity to cultivate the land for a number of years and if they did they faced the risk that they would not reap. Nqeto, chief of the Qwabe, for example, always kept his people moving; 'he would not plant crops but depended on marauding expeditions'.[19] The Bhaca also were greatly feared raiders because of their night attacks, and when they came under Faku after a series of migrations that had led them twice over the Drakensberg and back, they still 'never ploughed'.[20] The Ntlangwini, under Dumasi, moved back towards the Mzimkulu after their defeat by Faku and became nomadic hunters for a period, earning for themselves the name *abatwa* as they adopted 'Bushman' hunting techniques. The word came to mean, in the Transkeian area, 'stragling [*sic*] wandering natives of any nation who rove[d] about from Bush to Bush on the outskirts of countries, and who [were] not immediately under any particular chief'.[21] There were a number of these so-called 'Bushmen' groups in the upper Mzimvubu valley, one of whom at least 'subsisted entirely by hunting'.[22]

Conflict with the raiding chiefdoms put great strain on the Mpondo, for the former were not constrained by the agricultural cycle. The Mpondo, however, allowed the cycle to be interrupted for only one year, during which they were forced to live on roots and game. Thereafter, they compensated for the loss of their stock by more assiduous cultivation. Their ability to do so depended not least on the strength of the army which, by its defence of the crops, played yet another important though indirect role in production. The valleys in which the Mpondo were settled were regarded by most contemporary observers as among the most fertile they had seen in South Africa.[23] They often commented on the extraordinary height to

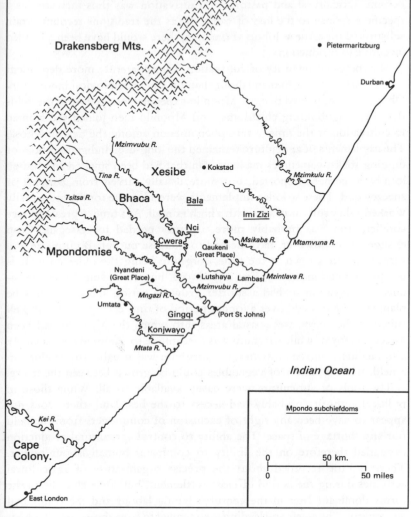

Map 5.1 Location of chiefdoms *c*.1830

which the crops and grass grew. 'In general it may be said of Emampond-weni, "the valleys also are covered with corn; they shout for joy, they also sing",' wrote an excited missionary in the mid-1830s.[24] Henry Francis Fynn, one of the earliest literate visitors to Pondoland, asserted, more prosaically, that, unlike the other Transkeian chiefdoms who were predominantly pastoral, the Mpondo 'having lost much of their stock...

became agricultural and pastoral'.[25] Cultivation was thus increased as a specific response to the loss of cattle. If, as the traditions recount, grain substituted for cattle as lobola at the time, there would have been an added incentive to production.

The increased intensity of cultivation was apparently more dependent on a greater input of human labour than on any technological innovation. Observers commented that the Mpondo expended more effort in the fields than the neighbouring chiefdoms, and Mpondo men joined the women in cultivation at the time, a rare phenomenon among the nearby Xhosa. The implements of agriculture remained the long-used indigenous hoes or digging sticks, sometimes made of iron that had been smelted and beaten locally or perhaps imported, but more usually carved from *msimbiti* or sneezewood. These wooden implements were adequate for the more easily worked valley soils in an area with a high rainfall. At a time of great military conflict, iron was probably more urgently needed for assegais. Crop changes may, however, have helped to increase output. Both maize and sorghum were grown at the time, sorghum being the older crop. It is uncertain when maize was first introduced, but it was suited to more intensive cultivation. It had a shorter growing period and could thus be planted and harvested over a longer period of time each year. It was well suited to the warm, wet coastal areas into which the Mpondo had been forced to retreat, while sorghum was susceptible to damp. Maize probably also facilitated mixed cropping, for sorghum was usually grown alone in a field, while a variety of vegetables could be grown between the maize.

The tools of agriculture were easily available to all. While those in political authority probably had access to the best land, there does not appear to have been any right of exclusion of commoners from the land nor any shortage of space. The ability to control agricultural production depended therefore on the ability to command human labour power. There is little recorded about the precise organisation of agricultural activities during the period of close settlement, but some clues lie in the forms dominant later in the century: family labour and the communal work party. The chiefs and leading men tended to have the greatest number of wives and children and the means to extend their family labour force. If, as is reasonable to suppose, they had first chance to absorb captives taken in war into their homesteads the labour force under their immediate control would have been even larger compared to that available to a commoner. Captives do not seem to have been of great importance in Pondoland at this time, however. The chiefs could also assemble the largest working parties both through the use of their political power and through their ability to provide greater rewards of beer or meat than the commoners. In effect, the wealthier homesteads could extract labour from the poorer, although the relationship was disguised by the idea of communality and by the fact that, potentially, anyone could organise a work party on their fields. The paramount chief, in particular, could command attendance at work parties by the people settled around his Great Place; this right was probably of great importance at the time of close settlement and may even have originated then. Faku does not, however, seem to have been able to use the army for agricultural work as the Zulu chiefs did.

In general, the produce of the land belonged to the possessor of the plot. There may have been some small tribute in grain due to the paramount and, if so, the density of settlement would have made it easier to enforce.[26] Grain from the larger homesteads was distributed largely in the form of beer at parties, but missionary sources suggest that redistribution did not always compensate for the inequalities in production: they talk of starvation among the poorer people during lean seasons, though the influential men remained only partially affected. Their evidence must, however, be treated cautiously for missionaries were not always well disposed to chiefs whom they thought were 'foremost in every species of excess'.[27]

Increased crop production was partly for the purposes of home consumption, and perhaps for internal circulation in the shape of lobola. Consumption was elastic, however, a good harvest being followed by more beer parties. Grain could be stored for a couple of years in pits and store huts, but the threat of attack probably discouraged bulk storage—it was safer to consume the harvest quickly. A reluctance to store may have contributed to the development of trade in crops, particularly with the inland hunting and raiding groups who could cultivate little themselves. The availability of this market may itself have been an incentive to production. As A.G. Bain noted:

> Facko's country may be considered the granary of the eastern parts of Caffre land as they, the Amampondo, annually supply the inhabitants with great quantities of Maize and Caffre corn for which they receive in return hides, beads and cattle.[28]

Tobacco, and probably dagga too, crops grown by all the chiefdoms on the Transkeian coast, were important items of trade throughout the nineteenth century. Mpondo tobacco, more than any other product, became widely known outside the area. It was also used by the Mpondo in the form of snuff after being ground with aloe. In the early nineteenth century, tobacco was traded with grain to the inland chiefdoms and hunting groups. Its production was usually in small garden patches under the supervision of the older members of the homestead and is unlikely to have been subject to chiefly control.

Hunting provided a major source of meat in the 1820s and 1830s as well as important trade goods. Steedman wrote in the early 1830s

> Game is abundant; and since the spoil of their flocks by their conquerors, has mainly supplied them [the Mpondo] with food and enabled them to collect fresh herds from their westerly neighbours by the sale of antelope skins, especially those of the blue buck, the *antilope pygmea*, a favourite and costly ornament, used for the head dress of the Caffer [Xhosa] Belles.[29]

Skins from game were used for clothing, more by the women than the men, who often wore little more than their penis sheaths and decorations in the warm coastal areas. Many other products of the chase—skins, horns, teeth—were important in interchiefdom exchange and in trade with the Europeans who visited the area from the 1820s. Ivory was the primary attraction for European traders and, by all accounts, they found an abundant supply in Pondoland. Fynn spent a considerable time in Mpondo territory in the mid-1820s, where others such as Lochenberg had preceded him, and established a depot for collecting ivory near the Mzimvubu river.[30] Bain collected 2 500 lb. of tusks in three days in 1829 from groups settled near the Mzimvubu river.[31] In the 1830s, regular trading expeditions geared largely to the ivory trade passed through Pondoland on their way between the eastern Cape and Port Natal.

The coastal forests and river valleys of Pondoland did not provide an environment suitable for plains' game—the larger buck, zebra, giraffes—that tended to congregate in large herds. Though some of these animals may have migrated coastwards at times, the nearest concentrations were likely to have been inland and well beyond the Mpondo hunting grounds. Most of the game in Pondoland dwelt in the forests: monkeys, cats, wild pigs and especially small buck which tended to be solitary animals or to collect in small herds. Hippos were restricted to the river valleys though elephants and some of the larger cats—leopards and perhaps lions—were more widely spread in the inland areas. Although traditions collected in later years maintain that the hunting of small game was not controlled by the chiefs, contemporary evidence suggests that the chiefs were able 'to claim the right of hunting in particular forests, allowing no intrusion without their permission being obtained'.[32] They did so not least to protect the buckskin trade, and are reputed to have hired out hunting lands when they did not organise the hunt themselves. It was quite feasible to hunt forest game in small parties, but a good catch depended on the marshalling of a large number of men, some to act as beaters and some with assegais ready to wait for the game as it ran into clearings. Forest hunting on this scale lent itself to central control, though the hunt was far less formal, and did not follow military organisation. Through their control of the forests and their ability to organise hunts, the chiefs probably controlled a substantial amount of the resulting trade.

Traditions collected in the twentieth century report that all tusks were the prerogative of the paramount chief.[33] Fynn's contemporary description of an elephant hunt with the Ntusi sub-chiefdom suggests that at that time the tusks went to the man who threw the first assegai.[34] Bain's experience also suggests that ivory could be traded in Pondoland without Faku's intervention.[35] The Ntusi were a Mpondo sub-chiefdom who always recognised the paramountcy, but they were the only sub-chiefdom to remain on the eastern side of the Mzimvubu during the 1820s and, secreted in the forests of Egosa and Mtambalala, they lived more independently of Faku's control than those settled around him. Faku may only have been able to enforce his right to tusks from them at a later date.

Elephant hunting parties in the period before the introduction of firearms also needed some organisation and chiefs may have had exclusive power to organise hunts in the immediate area of Mpondo settlement. But the evidence suggests that concentrations of elephants were at some distance from the area of dense settlement, inland and towards Natal. These were the hunting lands of the 'Bushmen' and one tradition recorded in the 1920s suggests a particular relationship between the paramountcy and at least some 'Bushmen' groups. When Faku started making overtures to the British, he called for his induna Diko and said:

> Diko my son go and hunt elephants so that I may send government a present of ivory, perchance government will then hear my cry for help and send us aid. Diko assembled the Bushmen who were employed by Faku as hunters in those days. He instructed them to go and kill elephants and bring the tusks. The Bushmen hunted elephants for a month and then returned bringing the tusks. They handed these to Diko saying 'Diko here are your things'. Diko placed the tusks at Faku's feet saying 'My chief here are your things'.[36]

Faku was reputed to have a large stock of ivory, and ivory bangles were conspicuously displayed by chiefs. Apart from trading, Faku made regular presents of tusks to the colonial and missionary authorities. One of the most widespread traditions in Pondoland is that religion was bought with an elephant tusk. In exchange for tusks, it was always cattle that were sought by the Mpondo.

The key feature of the period of close settlement was the increased intensity of raiding, hunting and cultivation, activities which lent themselves to greater control from the centre in the particular circumstances faced by the Mpondo in the early nineteenth century. Faku and his chiefs commanded a good deal of the product of their subjects' labour through their direct control of the organisation of important productive activities, or their control over economic resources. The paramount could thus play a leading role in the inter-chiefdom exchange in the Transkeian area, an activity that has been much neglected by historians and anthropologists. Faku did not create a military state modelled on the Zulu or offshoots of the Zulu kingdom. He could not call on a standing army to work in his fields or herd and hunt for him. But his polity was nevertheless more centralised, geographically and politically, than any other in the Transkeian area. He was able to absorb a great many fleeing groups and he 'governed a people composed of fragments of many different tribes . . . held together and harmonised in a surprising manner by his influence'.[37] Missionary observers and travellers suggest that his individual power was considerably greater than that of the Xhosa chiefs.

The surplus generated in Mpondo society, and the raids on surrounding chiefdoms, were almost without exception geared to the reaccumulation of stock. Cattle were essential for a reversion to a pattern of subsistence and social reproduction more familiar and congenial to the society. They supplied milk, meat and hides, and had probably been the most usual form of lobola. They were the best available store of wealth and they reproduced themselves rapidly with little investment on the part of the owner. Crops on the other hand could not be stored for long and cultivation could not be increased beyond a certain point without investment into technology that was not possible at the time. They also demanded a higher input of labour-time. Other goods were accepted in trade, particularly beads and ivory, but these were generally exchanged again for cattle. Beads were too susceptible to rapid devaluation to be used as a stable currency. Iron, copper and metal goods such as knives and axes were imported, although the Mpondo themselves did smelt. Copper and ivory bangles were status goods which the leading men wore to differentiate themselves from commoners. But it was above all cattle that remained the most prized item of trade in this early period.

Decentralisation and dependence

Between 1838 and 1842 Faku, with most of his people, moved back to the eastern side of the Mzimvubu. His homesteads were built, perhaps a few years later for the move was initially hesitant, between the Mzintlava and Mtsila rivers, about twenty miles from the coast. The threat of another Zulu invasion, a very real fear throughout the 1830s, had been removed by the defeat of Dingane by the Trekkers at Blood River. The Trekkers themselves now raided the Bhaca and planned the removal of African groups in Natal to the area between the Mtamnvuna and Mzimvubu. Faku was keen to stake his claim to eastern Pondoland, and quickly cemented an alliance with the Cape through the Wesleyan missionaries who had settled in his area. On its side, the colonial government was anxious to forestall the complications that could arise from Trekker dominance in Natal, and to secure an ally to the rear of the Xhosa chiefdoms with whom it was in constant conflict. A colonial force, which later participated in the occupation of Natal, was sent to Pondoland and ensured that the trekkers made no attack on Faku. A treaty with the Cape in 1844 defined Faku's boundaries, placing under his paramountcy an area far larger than he could effectively occupy or control. The powers given to him in the treaty made little difference to Mpondo relations with the surrounding chiefdoms, but did secure the area from colonial intervention for a time. With the northern frontier secure, concentrated settlement for defensive purposes was no longer vital, and the sub-chiefdoms began to disperse.

The passing of the period of close settlement heralded a new era of expansion. The area east of the Mzimvubu to which the Mpondo moved was not totally empty. Former tributary groups which would not 'give room for the children of the paramount' were driven out.[38] The Xesibe were pushed further inland towards the mountainous area of present-day Mount Ayliff.[39] The Bhaca first moved politely to make room for Faku himself, but soon confronted the Mpondo and in 1846 were badly beaten in a major battle at Lutshaya where Ncaphayi lost his life. They removed inland and one section established itself in present day Mount Frere district between the Tina and Mzimvubu rivers. Those immigrant groups who were prepared to recognise the Mpondo paramountcy, the Ntshangase, Imizizi, Cwera and others, for the most part settled on the outer edges of Pondoland in the present districts of Bizana and Tabankulu. Some of the Mpondo proper claim to have gone back to the areas which they had occupied before the Zulu raids, but some, under Faku's brothers and sons, were settled at strategic points around the Great Place as if at the end of spokes around the hub of a wheel. The intention was that the Great Place should be thoroughly protected.[40] The immigrant chiefs were allowed to maintain, or refused to give up, a great many of their independent powers although they were subject to mobilisation at the request of the paramount and recognised his court. Some Mpondo sub-chiefdoms also retained their hereditary rulers, although they recognised the seniority of Faku's sons if they were settled nearby.

In the move back to eastern Pondoland, western Pondoland was not neglected. The Konjwayo, Ncamane, sections of Gingqi and the Jali all remained in the Mngazi and adjacent valleys after Faku's departure.[41] In

Map 5.2 Pondoland in the period 1845–80

the mid-1840s Faku sent Ndamase, his eldest son, but not his heir, back over the Mzimvubu river as chief of the Nyanda house. By tradition, the removal of the Nyanda house was arranged by Faku in order to avoid conflict, which had already surfaced, between his heir, Mqikela, and Ndamase.[42] It was not unusual for paramounts to place their sons in new chieftaincies; every son could become a chief, though not all did, and they generally recognised the paramountcy.[43] The eldest son did not necessarily get the largest or most important sub-chieftaincy. Ndamase, however, had distinguished himself in battle as leader of the Mpondo armies since the late 1820s and was by all accounts a popular man. He became chief over all the sub-chiefdoms already settled to the west of the Mzimvubu and took with him a number of followers who became the nuclei of sub-chiefdoms settled around his Great Place near the present town of Libode. Ndamase acknowledged the paramountcy of Faku and of Mqikela, who succeeded in 1867. The Mpondomise and Thembu inhabitants of the area settled by Ndamase were either absorbed under his authority, moved off of their own accord, or were driven out. In less than a decade, the Mpondo succeeded in regaining all the land they had previously claimed, and had occupied or entrusted to tributaries very substantial new areas, particularly away from the coast.

Expansion and dispersion were closely related to the reaccumulation of cattle. The new settlements were nodes from which further movement in search of grazing land took place. By 1861, a missionary complained that 'from the pastoral life which these people lead, the population of the country is a good deal scattered'.[44] Although Faku and his leading men controlled a considerable number of the cattle that were absorbed into Pondoland after the Zulu raids, they did not retain them for their exclusive use. Because they grazed on the open veld, without any fodder except the stubble left after reaping, and because of the configuration of grasses found in the area, stock could not be concentrated in any one place for any length of time. Cattle were kept in small herds at each homestead, kraaled at night and milked daily; they were important to the subsistence of almost every family. The distribution and circulation of cattle within the chiefdom was woven into a wide variety of social relationships.

There is little information on the specific nature of stock ownership and distribution in Pondoland in the mid nineteenth century. Traditions collected and relations observed at a later date must be projected back, to some extent, to supplement the scanty documentation. The paramountcy and minor chiefs distributed cattle through gifts, feasts and loans. Some of the cattle captured in war were given to chiefs and army leaders for distribution among their followers or to men who had distinguished themselves in battle. Outright gifts were also given for special services to the chief; there do not seem to have been any uniform rates of reward, the gift being at the discretion of the chiefs. The men nearest the paramount, chiefs, councillors and induna benefited most, though not exclusively, from his magnanimity. In turn the advisers and councillors of the sub-chiefs would attract their largesse. Slaughtering of animals after a military campaign, or for ceremonies and feasts at the Great Place, was in effect another means of distributing cattle in the shape of meat, but more people benefited.

Loans of stock by the chiefs appear to have been more usual than outrights gifts. A Christian paramount expressed the position years later:

> It must be remembered that in the old days, little was known about work besides the making of pipes, assegais, mats, baskets, pots, and doctoring. Every man looked to the chief for the wherewithal to live. Even important men requested the chief to give them cattle to keep, as did councillors and workers. It was an honour to keep cattle for the Great Place.[45]

The loan beasts would be used by the borrower until they were reclaimed, but ownership would at no stage be transferred. Reclamation would be marked by a ceremony in which the owner would divide up the increase, and perhaps the original stock, giving some to the borrower outright. When the loan was taken from a senior chief—the relationship was not, at least later in the century, confined to chiefs—some service would have to be performed such as helping to construct the chief's cattle kraal. The loan could give rise to a more permanent relationship of service and reward, the borrower becoming an induna (the word could mean anything from a close adviser to a messenger or 'policeman') at the Great Place. The loaning of stock was not the only way in which a man could be appointed induna, but it usually accompanied such a relationship. In addition to the direct service that resulted from the loan, the chief would extract labour in the form of herding from the borrower, which would be materialised in the portion of the increase reclaimed. The extraction of labour was disguised as a loan between two homesteads.

Gifts and loans resulted in the decentralisation of cattle ownership, and, as the Mpondo dispersed, each homestead could have access to the nucleus of a herd which, if looked after, would increase naturally. Inequalities in cattle ownership remained great, however, and there were ways in which the leading men could retain large herds in their immediate possession. Not all the paramount's cattle were distributed. At some time in the nineteenth century, if not before, a pattern of transhumance developed between the coastal and inland areas.[46] In winter, stock was taken down to the coastal plain at Lambasi or to other suitable spots near the sea. The high rainfall—over forty inches a year—coupled with the grass types made for palatable grazing throughout the dry months. The stock was brought back in the spring when the rains in the upland areas produced new grass. Lambasi was reserved for grazing purposes and probably at that time largely, though not exclusively, for the paramount chief. Little or no settlement was allowed on the coastal grazing lands, and herders, either indunas or members of the homestead, were sent down with the animals. This grazing system enabled the paramount, and perhaps others, to maintain in one place relatively large herds which were immediately accessible. It is impossible to estimate how many cattle were kept in the paramount's camp; the number was probably greater than the few hundred that traders kept in this way later in the century. Nor were herds necessarily split up at the death of a chief. A rule of primogeniture governed inheritance, except in the case of succession to the paramount whose Great Wife was not his first. The stock could remain in the Great House for several generations, although the homestead-head often distributed cattle among the minor houses and the law of primogeniture may have been honoured more in the breach than the ideology of succession indicates.

Despite Lambasi, there was limited scope for the accumulation of large herds without some degree of redistribution. The chiefs could not immediately control the bulk of pastoral production. Rather, they attempted to maintain continual redistribution of stock through themselves as representatives of the 'state', and to prevent excessive accumulation on the part of commoners. Cattle came to the chiefs through fines imposed by the courts for a variety of crimes against the state. Most were sanctioned by custom, but new offences, such as the holding of a circumcision lodge, could be created. Death dues, which varied from one to ten head depending on the seniority of the deceased, were regarded by the paramount, and the few other chiefs who had the right to levy them, as of great importance not only because they contributed to revenue but also because through the levy their followers could be identified. Witchcraft beliefs, though of far wider importance than merely disguising the activities of acquisitive chiefs, legitimised the removal or 'eating up' of all the stock in a homestead. The stock of the accused was attached by the chief's induna and taken to the Great Place. Though chiefs in power were generally immune from witchcraft accusations, members of chiefly families were not.

Cattle probably tended to circulate back to the chiefs in their capacity as homestead-heads because they could command higher lobola payments for their daughters. They did, of course, also have more sons, and marrying them off could be an expensive undertaking. Insufficient is known about the marriage strategies at the time to allow an accurate assessment of the effect of lobola payments on stock ownership in the chiefdom. The lobola of the Great Wife of the paramount, usually the daughter of a foreign chief of equal rank, would be paid for by the people. Although the political and social ideas of the society sanctioned the extraction of cattle from the people by the chiefs, this power depended ultimately on the loyalty of his induna and his popularity with the people. Loyalty and popularity were secured not least by generosity in distribution of stock, especially to the induna who enabled him to enforce the decisions of the courts, councillors and doctors.

The reabsorption of cattle into the economy in the 1840s was accompanied by a decrease in the intensity of other productive activities. Male labour appears to have been withdrawn from cultivation at this time. The paramount no longer had direct control over the most important economic activity, and the dispersion of settlement made his rights to labour less easily enforceable. He relied on his ability to extract labour in the form of stock, but this was an area in which the sub-chiefs could compete, for they could also hold courts, loan cattle, arrange witchcraft charges and, in some cases, even claim death dues. Thus, the reincorporation of stock initiated a process of decentralisation in the chiefdom which became more marked as Faku entered old age and Mqikela took over as paramount.

It is particularly important to understand the gradual decentralisation of stock ownership within the chiefdom, for, from the 1860s, when a sufficient surplus had been accumulated and when colonial markets became available, cattle became a major export from Pondoland. Jenkins, the Wesleyan missionary with Faku from 1838 and perhaps the best informed observer of Mpondo affairs, told a visitor in 1866:

> Twenty five years ago not a cow or even a goat could be purchased at any price in all Pondoland. I knew a trader who came with a wagon load of goods for trade, and after spending five or six months, he bought an inferior lot of calves to the value of £7/10/-, which the missionary had previously acquired for his own family use. Now thousands of cattle are bought and sent out of the country annually and there are many successful traders in the country.[47]

In contrast to the period of close settlement, few cattle were absorbed through trading or raiding—the flow had been reversed. For periods in the late 1850s, the 1860s, and the 1870s, the paramounts attempted with some success to prevent the entry of stock from Natal into Pondoland in order to stave off lungsickness and redwater, cattle diseases that broke out in colonial herds.[48] Prohibitions were also placed on the entry of stock from the Cape into western Pondoland at times.

European traders, for the most part British, came to Pondoland from Natal or the eastern Cape, bartered goods for cattle and took herds out to the colonial markets. The development of the trade did not depend on adequate roads, of which there were few in Pondoland, for cattle were highly mobile. They remained an important export until rinderpest killed off most of the herds in 1897. The volume and direction of the trade was affected by the more minor cattle diseases—lungsickness and redwater—

that did eventually find their way into Pondoland, and by fluctuations in price and demand. Oxen varied from £5 to £10, or even more, in Pietermaritzburg, while cows and heifers fetched somewhat less. It is impossible to estimate the number of cattle leaving Pondoland annually, but Jenkins may not have exaggerated. In the decade before rinderpest, one large trading concern in eastern Pondoland usually sent between 500 and 1 000 head to Pietermaritzburg every year.[49] Others may have rivalled them, and there were a number of smaller operators. Exports are not likely to have exceeded a number which could be replaced by natural increase and still have left sufficient for ceremonies and slaughter. The cattle-carrying capacity of land varies through time, and the projection of twentieth-century figures into the nineteenth century is an exercise fraught with difficulty. If, as observers commented, the country was 'swarming with cattle' at the time, the holdings may have exceeded 200 000 or even 300 000.[50]

Pastoral products were also important exports. Hides usually fetched 4d. to 6d. a pound, or around four to five shillings each, in the 1860s and 1870s; horns, a penny to sixpence a pair. With the increase in the number of animals, the number of hides available, given a constant death rate, also increased. Droughts and diseases, while they harmed the cattle trade, helped the hide trade; the two were complementary. The export of hides in any quantity appears to have started in the early 1860s, the time of lungsickness and serious drought.[51] Local demand for hides from which to make shields and clothing was probably declining. Cotton blankets, which were inexpensive, became widespread in the 1860s, while woollen blankets at five to ten times the price were at first luxury goods. (Scarlet was the colour preferred by Faku.)[52] Cotton blankets cost only one or two shillings from Natal dealers and, as competition between the traders in Pondoland controlled the price, the Mpondo could probably have bartered a hide for two or three blankets. By the 1870s blankets were the major import into Pondoland.

Hides had to be collected, salted and dried (or 'poisoned'), and baled before being transported by wagon to East London, Pietermaritzburg or Port St Johns, the only harbour on the Pondoland, and indeed Transkeian, coast at which boats stopped regularly. Bad roads were no great disincentive to the trade, as hides were light in relation to their value. One wagon could carry between 3 000 and 6 000 lb or £60 to £120 worth. As a ready supply of blankets and other goods had to be available for the purposes of barter or exchange for hides and cattle, traders had to establish permanent stations. It was the hide and blanket trades that necessitated a more substantial infrastructure for trade than could be provided by itinerants.

Although there had been a few settled traders in Pondoland since the 1840s, and Port St Johns had been used for trade and small exports of timber, it was only in the 1860s that the number of traders began to increase rapidly.[53] By that time there were at least four in Port St Johns and a decade later perhaps fifty or sixty in the whole of Pondoland.[54]

Interchiefdom exchange did not cease, but white traders became increasingly dominant not only in the barter of manufactured goods for cattle but also in grain and tobacco distribution. As the chiefs could not immediately control the organisation of labour and the product of pastoral activities, the new imports were accessible to most homesteads. The wealthier men could initially afford a wider range of commodities, and some imports such as woollen blankets, horses, guns and liquor became luxuries for the chiefs, but by the 1870s and 1880s even these commodities were widespread. The surplus product of each homestead was increasingly geared to the traders, for the chiefs could not supply the goods desired. At the same time cattle owned by the chiefs was also exported, and the number at their disposal for redistribution was not as great as it had been. Reliance on the chiefs for the means of subsistence was decreasing as were communal productive activities. Each homestead was becoming more self-sufficient in relation to the chiefs. Whereas in the earlier part of the century, the dominant form of economic activities had been communal, now production became atomised to the level of the homestead. The imports of manufactured commodities contributed to and hastened this process.

Firearms, in the hands of European and Coloured hunters, traders and soldiers in search of trade goods and 'sport', finally exterminated large game in Pondoland: elephants by the 1850s and hippopotami a couple of decades later.[55] Hippopotami in the Mzimvubu, their natural home, provided a peculiar attraction for European hunters who delighted in taking pot shots as they surfaced for air. The Mpondo also used firearms in their hunts, but they were not nearly so effective in forest hunting. Nevertheless small game decreased sufficiently in number by the late nineteenth century to render the rights over the forests, if they were maintained, of little importance to the chiefs. Hunting for sport was still regularly organised, but there was little of value for trade in the catch.

When Theophilus Shepstone visited Mqikela in 1871, he came away with the impression that

> The Amampondo are not, and never were, military people, and fighting is, I think, the last occupation they would be likely to adopt. It is scarcely possible to conceive of two tribes living so close to each other as the Zulus and the Amampondos capable of furnishing so complete a contrast.[56]

Not all would have agreed with this view at the time, and Shepstone's familiarity with the Zulu state must have made Mqikela's armies seem to him, as his son Henrique put it, 'a regular ragamuffin lot. Nothing to what a Zulu chief's turnout could be on a similar occasion.'[57] The Mpondo had adopted guns and horses on a large scale, muzzle-loaders in the 1860s and breech-loaders increasingly from the 1870s. The size of the army in eastern Pondoland alone was perhaps over 15 000 if all could be assembled, making it by far the largest in the Transkeian area.[58] Yet Shepstone's assessment was in the long run correct. Guns and horses did not effectively help the Mpondo in raiding and expansion. Mqikela suffered a serious defeat at the hands of the Bhaca in 1867 and soon afterwards, in 1872, the Cape Colony demarcated the Mpondo boundaries at the line of effective occupation. These boundaries were substantially confirmed when the surrounding chiefdoms were annexed in 1878, while the Mtamvuna had been fixed as the boundary with Natal as early as 1866. Mqikela and his councillors were extremely wary of provoking colonial intervention by infringing their boundaries. When relations with the Cape deteriorated sufficiently for the paramountcy to order full mobilisation, such as in 1880, the Cape rearmed the Bhaca and Xesibe and arranged a show of strength on the border. Although occasional sorties were made by Mpondo parties, they were effectively scared off. The paramount could still mobilise an army, but it had ceased to be important in bringing in cattle from raids and Mqikela's right to the spoils of war had become for the most part meaningless.

The Shepstones noticed the lack of regiments and regimental discipline among the Mpondo. The sub-chiefs had always had an important responsibility in mobilising the army and after dispersion were gradually able to consolidate their position. From the mid-1860s some refused to submit to doctoring at the Great Place and independent action in small raids and retaliation across the borders became more common. The paramountcy was not able to control the entry of firearms, and the more ambitious sub-chiefs set about arming themselves and their immediate followers. Ammunition for muzzle-loaders was widely available as traders brought in sulphur and saltpetre for gunpowder and bullets could be made locally from, among other things, broken-down cooking pots. Cartridges for breech-loaders were not as susceptible to local innovation and were perpetually in short supply. There were some centres in Pondoland at which ammunition for these more effective weapons was produced in quantity, partly from colonial scraps. But the paramount did not control these centres exclusively, although he did have the services of the best gunsmiths in Pondoland: the Dorkin family who were settled near the

Great Place.[59] The failure of the paramountcy to control guns or ammunition contributed to the rebelliousness of some of the sub-chiefs during the 1880s, a decade that ended in civil war in both eastern and western Pondoland.

The paramount could still call on members of the homesteads settled near the Great Place to work in his fields, but this right affected fewer people. The sub-chiefs did not have the same power over the labour of the homesteads in their area, although they did have the ability to command greater attendance at a work party. The productive capacity of the chiefs' homesteads was in general much larger, but new technology as much as the ability to command human labour power became increasingly important in production. For, besides the commodities mentioned above, new agricultural implements began to spread through Pondoland, and of all the imports, they had perhaps the greatest long-term significance. In the 1860s the wooden digging spades were widely replaced by imported metal hoes and picks.[60] Although ploughs had been used on mission stations before that time, the Mpondo were slow to adopt them. In the 1870s they were still unusual, but in 1880 the British Resident in Pondoland commented that

> A very noticeable change is taking place in the Pondo system of agriculture. The pick, which some twenty years ago superseded the old wooden spade, is now rapidly being displaced by the plough. Upwards of 500 new ploughs were brought into use by the Pondos for this season's planting.[61]

There were by that time perhaps 1 000 ploughs in Pondoland, and in the next couple of decades their use became widespread. Early ploughs, such as the 'seventy-five', were cumbersome, with fragile cast-iron shares, and were probably not well used. But they did enable the Mpondo to increase the amount of land they cultivated.

The introduction of ploughs was based on an earlier and more radical innovation: the use of oxen as draught animals. In 1856, Faku's sons specifically asked for a team of trained draught oxen to accompany a gift of a wagon made by the Cape government;[62] it was perhaps one of the first wagons owned by the Mpondo themselves, although missionaries, mission people and traders had by that time made them well-known in the area. From the 1860s, the use of oxen as draught animals became general. Wagons, however, did not. The piece of equipment that removed bulk transport from the heads of the women was the sledge, drawn by anything from two oxen upwards, depending on the load. Sledges were manufactured locally from forked trees into which holes were drilled and wooden uprights inserted. They were suitable for transporting small loads around the homesteads and fields and they needed no roads, an important feature in the broken and hilly parts of Pondoland. All the ropes needed for the oxen could be made from hides. Wagons, on the other hand, had to be made by specialist craftsmen, they needed chains, and roads to run on, a full team to pull them, and they were too big for use around the homestead. Only those who made a living by the transport and sale of goods and the wealthier chiefs and agriculturalists found them, at £50 or upwards, a worthwhile investment. The use of sledges and ploughs was intimately linked: the sledge was used to transport the plough to the fields, and the larger harvest that a ploughed land could produce was transported back to the stores by sledge. The use of draught oxen reabsorbed male labour into agriculture for the women were not allowed to handle cattle.

The investment of part of the surplus generated from pastoralism back into cultivation requires some explanation. A preliminary attempt to assess the reasons for the timing of innovations, their significance and effects must suffice. Imported metal hoes and picks did not greatly increase the product of labour put into cultivation, but they did extend the range of land that could be worked. They were more efficient and hardy than wooden implements and more suitable for the open and harder soils to which the Mpondo were moving, especially after protracted droughts such as occurred in the early 1860s. The best hard woods were not so easily obtainable away from the coastal forest. Large-scale importation of hoes coincided not only with drought but with the coming of lungsickness, and the Mpondo may have responded to the loss of stock, as they did in the 1820s, by more intensive cultivation. This phase of innovation was certainly not related to the availability of colonial markets: in 1865 Jenkins noted that 'there is no sale for it [maize] save in our own family and it will not pay traders as land carriage is too far and expensive'.[63] The value of a load of maize—between about £5 and £10 at the time—compared unfavourably with that of a load of hides.

The purchase of ploughs—the usual exchange was a beast for a plough— was clearly a continuation of similar processes. The timing again appears to have been related to drought and cattle disease. In 1877 there was another serious drought in Pondoland—rainfall on the east coast of South Africa rises and declines in a rough seven-year cycle—and redwater began to cause losses in stock soon afterwards.[64] The extension of land cultivated in order to minimise the effect of drought in the late 1870s may have provided the surplus in grain that begins to be mentioned at that time. The traders began to purchase grain and on occasion, export it 'in large quantities' to the small towns and garrisons around Pondoland and to other traders in the Transkeian Territories.[65] They also began to store grain in pits, as the Mpondo did themselves, for resale to certain sections of Mpondo society in times of shortage. The availability of markets for grain no doubt greatly encouraged further investment and production.

Changes in technology and the extent of production should also be considered in the light of the gradually changing patterns of subsistence in Pondoland. The upland pasturages to which sections of the Mpondo moved were not as suited to hunting and gathering as were the coastal areas and game was less plentiful in all parts of the chiefdom. The lower rainfall of the inland areas and the frequent winter frosts made cultivation more difficult and the growing season shorter. Innovation tended to be more rapid in inland areas than on the coast partly because inland transport routes were better but also because the coastal settlements could depend to a greater extent and for far longer on gathering—including the gathering of shellfish—and hunting. Cultivation was becoming more important for subsistence and export even in the coastal areas, and except in the choicest environments demanded substantial investment in technology if it was to be extended.

The pressure on game and resources for gathering related to the increase in both human and cattle populations. Whereas Boyce had estimated 20 000 people under Faku's control in the 1820s, estimates in the 1860s were closer to 100 000 and by the 1880s around 150 000.[66] These estimates may be of no significance at all in calculating the actual increase of population but there was clearly a substantial immigration into Pondoland from the 1820s to the 1880s and there are many reasons for believing that the birth rate exceeded the death rate at least by the second half of the century. Hunting and gathering resources were finite and the investment in agriculture to increase its contribution to subsistence was probably both an effect and cause of population growth. These are indications that pastureland was at a premium. Such assertions are difficult to support and the evidence is not entirely clear. Nevertheless, settlement had moved out to the borders of Pondoland and some groups found their way into areas which were not ideal for cattle. Such areas could, of course, take some settlement and some cattle but were either too broken, or too bushy or had insufficient variation of grasses for large stock. The introduction of woolled sheep—the Mpondo had raised some small stock before— may indicate that an adaptation was being made to less favourable grazing resources. This correlation must, however, be made with great caution for sheep provided a marketable product and were soon to graze with cattle on even the best pasturages. Immigrants from the eastern Cape often brought sheep with them, for Africans in that area had long been involved in wool production. If the country had been heavily stocked for over a decade, as the evidence suggests, grazing may have deteriorated and pressure may have developed for more intensive use of land. Grazing was not entirely finite as bushland was still being cleared. Arable lands were usually made out of bush and forest or in patches of sweetveld grass; ploughs probably did not compete for land with stock at this stage for the plots were relatively small in size and number. The influence of a strain on pastoral resources on investment in cultivation is by no means clear. Whatever the nature of the strain, however, it was not sufficient to stimulate labour migration which was rare except from the mission stations.[67] No doubt the local availability of firearms, one of the great attractions of the diamond fields for Africans elsewhere in southern Africa, contributed to the late development of migration from Pondoland.

Markets, changing resources and patterns of subsistence and the increasing independence of the individual homestead all help to explain the reinvestment in cultivation. The reasons for the decision may have differed in the case of every homestead: the wealthier seeking to market their produce, those in marginal lands seeking to compensate for the lack of grazing resources, the poorer homesteads seeking to produce enough to survive. The acquisition of new implements depended on the availability of a surplus for exchange, and no doubt it was the wealthier homesteads that could first afford ploughs. The chiefs may have found that the new implements compensated to some degree for the declining control they could exercise over labour and tribute. To the people on the other hand, the implements were of great importance for subsistence at the beginning of a less redistributive era. Ploughs allowed for greater independence in the productive process and contributed to the gradual atomisation of production to the level of the homestead. The chiefs were never able to levy tribute in grain as they had in cattle and the more labour absorbed by cultivation, the less they could extract through tribute from each homestead.

The immigration of Xhosa and Mfengu families into all parts of Pondoland served to accelerate individualisation. They had to pay a settlement fee to the paramount and to the local chiefs when they first established their homestead, which may have temporarily bolstered chiefly revenues. But they had less experience of the dominant ideology of chieftainship or else had seen their chiefs defeated. They were often the most progressive and innovative people in Pondoland. Christianity had made little impact outside the mission stations and one or two sub-chiefdoms, but it was to mark and hasten these new developments. Such processes were not nearly as far advanced in Pondoland as in other parts of the Transkeian Territories by the later nineteenth century. The chiefs still had a great deal of authority

—even the paramountcy was to revive briefly under Sigcau—and communal activities did not disappear. In the ensuing decades the chiefs did attempt to defend and adapt their position. But the century had seen the transition from a polity in which the chiefs had a great deal of direct control over production and tribute to one where much of the surplus product of the homesteads was no longer directed to them.

The surplus product of the homesteads, wealthier and poorer, was ever more directed to the traders and through them to the colonial economy. Production of crops necessitated a greater investment in commodities that could not be produced locally. The peasantry relied on the colonial traders for the capital goods which were becoming essential to produce sufficient for subsistence and exchange. Although the Mpondo were highly selective about the imports they would accept, demand for items of consumption such as sugar and salt and articles which undermined local crafts was increasing. The extent of this dependence in Pondoland, one of the last areas to remain free of colonial penetration, was already evident in the mid-1890s, even before the process was accelerated by the disastrous outbreak of rinderpest in 1897.

Notes

1 G. Arrighi, 'Labour Supplies in Historical Perspective: a study of the proletarianisation of the African peasantry in Rhodesia', *Journal of Development Studies*, vi, 3, 1970, pp. 197–234; C. Bundy, 'The Emergence and Decline of a South African Peasantry', *African Affairs*, xxi, 285, 1972, pp. 369–88; I.R. Phimister, 'Peasant Production and Underdevelopment in Southern Rhodesia, 1890–1914', *African Affairs*, xxiii, 291, 1974, pp. 217–28; M. Wilson, 'The Growth of Peasant Communities', *Oxford History of South Africa*, ii, London, 1971, pp. 49–103. See also R. Palmer and G.N. Parsons, *Roots of Rural Poverty in Central and Southern Africa*, London, 1977.

2 C. Bundy, 'Emergence and Decline', and 'The Response of African Peasants in the Cape to Economic Changes, 1870–1910', *CSP*, iii, pp. 24–37

3 M. Hunter, *Reaction to Conquest*, Oxford, 1936, 1964, p. viii; see also H. Rogers, *Native Administration in the Union of South Africa*, Johannesburg, 1933, p. 50.

4 W. Beinart, 'Rural Production and Stratification in South Africa: Pondoland c.1894–1930', paper presented to African History Seminar, School of Oriental and African Studies, October 1975, (unpublished)

5 D.G.L. Cragg, 'The Relations of the Amampondo and the Colonial Authorities (1830–86) with special reference to the role of the Wesleyan Missionaries', D.Phil. Oxford, 1959, is the only detailed work dealing with the Mpondo in the nineteenth century. It is little concerned with changes in Pondoland itself, but I gratefully acknowledge its value in helping to locate mission sources.

6 Victor Poto Ndamase, *Ama-Mpondo. Ibali ne-Ntlalo*, Lovedale, 1927; J. Stuart

Papers, Killie Campbell Library, 61/41, 16ff; Stuart, 62/68, 17. (J. Wright, University of Natal, Pietermaritzburg, has helped with references to material in the Stuart papers).

7 Public Records Office, CO 48/125, Report by W.B. Dundas, 15 August 1828
8 A. Steedman, *Wanderings and Adventures in the Interior of Southern Africa*, ii, London, 1835, p. 268, quoting Boyce's Journal, 29 November 1830
9 Wesleyan Methodist Missionary Society Archives (WMMS), Boyce to Secretaries, 11 May 1830
10 WMMS, SA Box 7, Shaw to Sec., 25 July 1837
11 Cape Archives, Native Affairs (CA NA) 623/1965, 'A history of the Xesibe', Sgd. W.P. Leary, 27 September 1904
12 WMMS, SA Box 5, Boyce to Sec., 2 July 1832
13 WMMS, SA Box 7, Satchell to Secs., 14 October 1834; J. Backhouse, *Narrative of a Visit to the Mauritius and South Africa*, London, 1844, p. 263
14 Stuart, 61/60, 6
15 On circumcision see M. Hunter, *Reaction to Conquest*, p. 165; Cape Parliamentary Papers, *Blue Book on Native Affairs*, G.9–1894; *BBNA*, G.27–1814.
16 WMMS, Boyce, *Diary*, 27 Oct. 1832
17 WMMS, SA Box 7, Palmer to Secs., 10 July 1834
18 WMMS, SA Box 5, Boyce to Secs., 2 July 1832
19 Stuart, 61/41, 18
20 WMMS, SA Box 5, Boyce to Secs., 2 July 1832
21 Cape Archives, Lieutenant Governor, 404, W. Fynn to Hudson, 11 September 1843
22 M. Lister, *Journal of Andrew Geddes Bain*, Cape Town, 1949, p. 118
23 Steedman, *Wanderings*, i, pp. 20, 261, 262, 281; D. Hammond-Tooke, *The Journal of William Shaw*, Cape Town, 1972, p. 167; Lister, *Journal*, p. 111, note 59; W. Shaw, *The Story of My Mission in South Eastern Africa*, London, 1860, p. 402
24 WMMS, Satchell to Secs., 14 Jan. 1835
25 J. Stuart and D. Malcolm, *The Diary of Henry Francis Fynn*, Pietermaritzburg, 1969, p. 24
26 CO 48/125, Dundas report, 15 August 1828
27 WMMS, Boyce to Secs., 21 April 1831
28 Lister, *Journal*, p. 104, note 54
29 Steedman, *Wanderings*, ii, p. 205; see also Shaw, *Story of My Mission*, p. 407.
30 Stuart and Malcolm, *Diary*, pp. 116–7
31 Lister, *Journal*, p. 120
32 Steedman, *Wanderings*, i, p. 258; ii, p. 205
33 Hunter, *Reaction*, p. 95
34 Stuart and Malcolm, *Diary*, p. 104
35 Lister, *Journal*, pp. 115–20
36 Cape Archives, Chief Magistrate of the Transkeian Territories, 3/959, File 6/11/2, F. Brownlee to Chief Magistrate, 4 August 1926; information collected by Brownlee from Maninha, Councillor to Nqwilso, and transcribed by Brownlee
37 WMMS, Cameron to Secs., 24 May 1836
38 Interview Vulizibhaya, Bomvini Administrative Authority, Lusikisiki, 10 February 1977
39 CA NA 623/1965, History of the Xesibe

40 Interview Nelson Sigcau, Ixopo Administrative Authority, Flagstaff, 4 March 1972

41 Interview Ned Xinwa, Gomolo Administrative Authority, Port St Johns, 27 February 1977

42 Poto Ndamase, *Ama-Mpondo*, pp. 17–22

43 Cf. J.B. Peires, 'A History of the Xhosa *c.*1700–1835', M.A., Rhodes University, 1976, chs. 2 and 3

44 WMMS, Mason to Secs., 29 January 1861

45 Poto Ndamase, *Ama-Mpondo*, p. 57

46 CA NA 686/2609, enclosure in Chief Magistrate to Secretary of Native Affairs, 3 March 1903, is one of the few written mentions of the winter grazing grounds

47 W. Taylor, *Christian Adventures in South Africa*, London, 1867, p. 446

48 WMMS, Impey to Secs., 7 June 1858, Mason to Secs., 30 March 1860, Kirkby to Secs., 12 March 1873, Cameron to Boyce, 19 March 1875; WMMS, Jenkins papers, Shepstone to Jenkins, 18 July 1855; Natal Archives, Shepstone papers, H.C. Shepstone, Diary, 5 December 1871, 5 March 1872; and Cape of Good Hope, *Report of the Commission of Enquiry into the Disease Among Cattle, known as Redwater*, G.85–1883, pp. 214, 215, 218

49 Cape Archives, O'Donnell papers, calculated from diaries, 1–8

50 *Kaffrarian Watchman*, 15 April 1876

51 Drought: WMMS, Mason to Secs., 21 June 1861, 30 September 1861, 18 January 1862, 30 March 1863: Lungsickness: WMMS, Natal District Meeting, Jenkins report, 1862, Mason to Secs., 30 March 1863, Allsopp to Secs., 23 August 1865

52 CO 48/380, Maclean to Liddle, 15 June 1856 in Grey to Laboucher, 11 February 1857

53 Shaw, *Story of My Mission*, p. 402; Cato papers, Killie Campbell Library, MS 1557, H.F. Fynn to Cato, 11 July 1849

54 WMMS, Jenkins papers, Jenkins to Shaw, 21 August 1854; WMMS, Mason to Secs., 21 June 1861; CO 48/408, Currie's report, March 1861; *Kaffrarian Watchman*, 15 April 1876

55 B. Holt, *Place names in the Transkeian Territories*, Johannesburg, n.d., p. 1

56 Cape of Good Hope, *Report of Select Committee on Native Affairs*, A.12–1873, p. 74, Shepstone to Harding, 18 January 1871

57 H.C. Shepstone, *Diary*, 16 March 1872

58 CO 48/485, Blyth to Littleton, 10 December 1877, in Frere to Hicks Beach, 22 May 1878

59 H.C. Shepstone, *Diary*, 18 August 1876

60 Taylor, *Christian Adventures*, p. 446

61 Cape of Good Hope, *Blue Book on Native Affairs*, G.13–1880, p. 162; G.21–1875, p. 87

62 CO 48/380, Maclean to Liddle, 16 July 1856, in Grey to Laboucher, 11 February 1857

63 WMMS, Jenkins to Secs., 26 July 1865

64 WMMS, Cameron to Secs., 13 April 1877; M. Benham, *Henry Callaway*, London, 1896, pp. 314–5; *Kaffrarian Watchman*, 10 October 1877; CO 48/485, M. Jenkins, 1 December 1877, in Frere to Hicks Beach, 22 May 1878

65 CPP, *BBNA*, G.13–1880, p. 162

66 F. Flemming, *Kaffraria and its Inhabitants*, London, 1854, p. 121; CO 179/49, Scott to Stanley, 3 June 1858, in Shepstone Acting Col. Sec.; Taylor, *Christian*

Adventures, p. 346; WMMS, Kirkby to Boyce, 21 February 1870, 28 April 1870; United Society for the Propagation of the Gospel, Archives, 1877, Annual Report No. 209; Series D. 1880, Oakes to Secs., 20 January 1880, p. 309

67 Cory Library, MS 15, 391, Jenkins to Boyce, 19 January 1865, mentions Christians going to Natal. R.F. Siebörger, 'The Recruitment and Organisation of African Labour for the Kimberley Diamond Mines, 1871–88', M.A., Rhodes University, 1975, Appendix D, gives origins of workers on the fields. See WMMS, J. Cameron to Secs., 18 May 1876; Cape Archives, NA 162, Oxland to SNA, 13 December 1881

CHAPTER SIX

The changing pattern of economic relationships in rural Natal, 1838–1914

Henry Slater

The 'Dual Economy' model of South African development in the nine-teenth century, which remained unchallenged until fairly recently, is based upon three assumptions. The first is the idea that nineteenth-century South Africa was characterised by two separate economies; an embryonic capitalist economy peopled by whites, and a subsistence economy peopled by blacks. The second assumption is that the subsistence economy made no contribution to the early development of South African capitalism, except insofar as the means of production utilised in the subsistence economy were gradually transferred to the capitalist economy. The third is that this transfer took place only as a result of the latter's greater efficiency and the free interplay of market forces. The transfer is seen to be more or less complete by the beginning of the twentieth century.

The evidence for Natal, however, casts grave doubt on all three assump-tions and thus on the 'Dual Economy' model itself. First, the evidence suggests that there were not two economies in nineteenth-century Natal, peopled respectively by whites and blacks, but that a single though complex network of economic choices and relationships was operating involving all Natalians regardless of ethnic origin. This was the case because Natal already represented one of many peripheral sectors of a single expanding world capitalist economy, albeit a sector made up of an articulation of modes of production based upon different and sometimes contradictory forms of socio-labour organisation along a capitalist–pre-capitalist con-tinuum. Among the pre-capitalist forms, the homestead within the lineage mode of production was particularly important.[1]

Secondly, there is now abundant evidence for Natal which demonstrates the manner in which the early development of South African capitalism, in its merchant and *rentier* forms, rested heavily on the exploitation of the pre-capitalist homestead production complex in a whole range of different ways.

Thirdly, the growing inability of the homestead-based population to support itself during the late nineteenth and early twentieth centuries, and the corresponding entry into labour relationships with an emergent capitalist employer class, cannot simply be explained as the natural result of the economic inefficiency of the homestead as the 'Dual Economy' theorists would wish us to believe. The homestead form of socio-labour organisation was in fact able to meet the needs of the African population of Natal all too well. It was necessary that it first be 'underdeveloped' before homesteads could be made to furnish the means of production, and particularly the labour, essential for the 'development' of a pattern of capitalist social relations. The black near-proletariat created by this process of underdevelopment was as much the product of repressive legislation as of market forces. In South Africa, as elsewhere during the early development of capitalism, the two are inextricably linked. This repressive legislation was firmly rooted in the economic self-interest of white capitalists.

But it is not sufficient to replace the simple dichotomy offered by the 'Dual Economy' model with the new dichotomy of 'development' and 'underdevelopment'. Both are too close to the simplistic dichotomy of race to be entirely satisfactory. Nineteenth-century South African economic and social relationships were more complex and require a more differentiated set of categories. The dynamic of change in the period was furnished by the interaction of a number of social groups and fractions of capital. The attack on the homestead production complex, and its precise character, must be linked to the economic self-interest of particular groups of capitalists. Commercial farmers in Natal, among whom there was probably a high incidence of British settlers relative to those of Afrikaner extraction, were initially the main force operating here.

In the construction of certain parts of this repressive framework, the commercial farmers met as much opposition from certain other white interest groups—notably merchants and *rentiers* and their allies—as from blacks. There was no consensus among the white community at this time as to the form black exploitation should take and the fraction of capital which should benefit principally from it.

Two factors prevented these contradictions within capital from reaching a head in the period covered by this chapter. The first was the importation of 'apprenticed' and later of indentured labour. The second was the fundamental shift in the complexion of the political economy of southern Africa against *rentier* and merchant capital and in favour of employer capital, a shift which can be traced to the Witwatersrand mining developments at the end of the century. It was an uneasy alliance of employer interests which initially came to dominate the new Union Parliament after 1910, and this was reflected in the Natives' Land Act of 1913, though the many loopholes in the Act equally bore testimony to the continuing rearguard action of *rentier* groups with rural interests.

Since the sixteenth century south-east Africa had been loosely linked to the embryonic world economy through trade. By the early nineteenth century the connection had become sufficiently important to attract a permanent coastal settlement of hunter-traders at 'Port Natal', and several overland hunter-trading expeditions from the Cape. The Zulu state, which had emerged as the dominant local power by this time, was initially able to control and benefit from this connection, but as the hunter-trading thrust intensified and sought more freedom of action so the relationship began to sour.[2] In 1838, a further thrust from the Cape, larger and of a somewhat different character, led to a dramatic change in the situation. A branch of the Great Trek, which had left the Cape Colony four years previously, succeeded in winning sufficient local allies, including some of the Zulu forces and the hunter-trading community at 'Port Natal', to defeat the main Zulu armies under Dingane. A new Voortekker Republic of Natalia was established which laid claim to almost all the land between the Buffalo-Thukela and the Mzimkulu rivers. The immigrant population of the Republic should not be over-estimated; by 1842 the community of white settlers still numbered only some 6 000 men, women and children.[3]

Farmers and would-be farmers formed an important section of the new settler community and their needs of plentiful land, security, and a readily available supply of cheap labour feature prominently in the legislative policies of the Republic of Natalia. In theory, the first two conditions could be met relatively easily. The area claimed by the new settlers appeared substantially under-populated, owing to the temporary or permanent migration of the population elsewhere to avoid the regular pattern of Zulu raiding.[4] In the eyes of the settlers, Natal was an empty land ripe for development. All those settlers who arrived in Natal before December 1839 were entitled to claim two farms on the three thousand morgen scale laid down by the original Voortrekker burghership law, and those who arrived subsequently were entitled to one.[5] The commando system would be adequate for the policing of the small indigenous population.

The labour needs of the immigrant community seem to have been met initially by Coloured servants brought on the Trek from the Cape; by the 'apprenticeship' of children supposedly captured during 'legitimate' commando skirmishes with the forces of the Zulu kingdom and other groups which did not accept the new pattern of sovereignty; and perhaps by local people who had been alienated from the means of subsistence during the Mfecane to find entry into a labour relationship with a Voortrekker farmer an attractive possibility.[6] The long-term labour needs of the community were to be met by legislation to ensure that Africans could only gain access to land in return for labour service rendered to the farmers.

The type of society which the Voortrekker farmers desired was never brought about. One factor was the return to the lands now claimed by the Republic of Natalia, and particularly to those on its northern boundary, of large numbers of Africans who had temporarily vacated the area during the time of Zulu oppression. Ironically, the defeat of Dingane by the settler forces had made this return possible. Large numbers of these returnees settled on lands claimed, but often not occupied, by the Voortrekkers. From the settler point of view, these were the first 'squatters'.[7] From 1840 this situation became an increasingly important concern of the Volksraad, partly because of fears for the security of the tiny settler community, and partly because the majority of the returnees resisted the labour and other demands made upon them. It was proposed that wherever such settlements were found they should be broken up and removed, either to south-west Natal beyond the Mzimkulu or back to what were presumed to be their former homes in Zululand. The exceptions were to be parties not exceeding five families to each six thousand acre farm and those others in service with whites.[8] Pretorius, as military commander, was empowered by the Volksraad decision of 2 August 1841 to implement a policy of removing all 'surplus' Africans to an area in the south-west between the Umtavuna and Mzimkulu rivers.[9] In fact the Republic did not control the resources which would have made possible the implementation of such a grandiose design, and more and more Africans returned to the area claimed by the Republic without being controlled by the Republican government.[10]

We can already see evidence in this picture of the close relationship between land and labour questions in Natal, and in turn the degree to which the nature of this relationship in a particular area and at a particular point in time was determined by two other interrelated questions: those of alternative means of subsistence and relative physical force. The Voortrekker farmers' vision of society could not be realised because, for the majority of the African population, other means of subsistence were always available which the Voortrekkers did not control and which they could not therefore barter for labour-service. In turn, there was still land for African settlement because the claims of the Republic could not be backed effectively by force on the scale that would have been necessary.

Another factor which impeded the implementation of the Voortrekker design was the willingness of many of their number to abandon their land claims to speculators. It seems that very few of the farms claimed by settlers were actually ever occupied by them. In the first two years of the Republic some 2½ million acres were provisionally registered in favour of only 254 persons, a mere forty-nine of whom seem actually to have occupied their claims.[11] This was possible under the system by which applications from settlers were entered provisionally in the books of the Volksraad, pending inspection and formal registration. Occupation was not a requirement of provisional registration and youths of eighteen could also hold land in return for the registration fee of twelve Rixdollars. Permanent registration did necessitate occupation, though this again was a technicality easily evaded. Someone, usually an African servant, could be sent to live on the farm until a title had been issued. By the time of the annexation of Natal to the Cape Colony by the British imperial power in 1843, more than a thousand land claims had been registered, many of them ill-defined. Cloete, the Commissioner sent by the British from the Cape to investigate the land situation, was concerned to find that land claims had been staked, not only in every district of Republican Natal, but even in territory claimed by Faku on both sides of the Mzimvubu, as well as north of the Thukela in Zululand.[12]

By 1843 many of the unoccupied claims already seem to have passed into the hands of a class of land speculators. One of the pressures operating may have been the need of poorer claimants to sell some or all of their claims in order to pay or avoid paying the fees necessary for examination and permanent registration. Others may have found more profitable occupations in hunting and in trade with established African communities. The numbers actually working the land in this period seem to have been so few, however, that one is led to wonder just how many of the original claimants had any intention of using it for farming purposes. Research is needed to probe the conventional picture of the Voortrekkers as a socially undifferentiated community of pastoral subsistence farmers. Certainly, at least one of the leading speculators was an official of the Republic, Commandant Gert Rudolph, who was claiming title to forty farms in 1843 amounting to some quarter million acres.[13]

A section of the Republic's white community welcomed the British colonising initiative, whilst others chose to trek once more rather than fall foul of the new power. As yet we do not have a clear picture of the social groupings that were involved here. The effect of the change, however, was to loosen still further the hold of the farmers on the polity. With the arrival of the imperial power they were obliged to compete for their interests with a wider cluster of social groups including merchants, missionaries and *rentiers*, as well as speculators and African homesteaders. Moreover, some of these groups possessed influential metropolitan connections.

In the early years after annexation, Cape and metropolitan capital showed considerably more interest in land speculation and associated activities than in developing new patterns of production.[14] One aspect of this speculation was the continued accumulation of original Voortrekker land claims in the hands of a few speculators. A second involved receiving substantial Crown land grants from the imperial power in return for bringing settlers out from Britain and establishing them on small acreages in Natal. Several schemes were in operation between about 1849 and 1852 involving some 5 000 immigrants. That of J.C. Byrne and his backers was among the most prominent.[15] The operators of these schemes looked for their profit and further working capital in the rapid sale for large sums of money of the large acreages which had been acquired. This depended on settlers actually 'settling' on the land, engaging in successful commercial production, and so pushing up the value of the surrounding lands which were controlled by the speculators. To provide further insurance, the same men who were heavily committed to speculation in land tried to present a picture to potential settlers in England and at the Cape of a rich and fertile land where commercial cash-cropping was already well-established. The founding of a Natal Cotton Company, the encouragement of African commercial production of potential export crops such as cotton, heavy publicity for the arrival in Manchester of a few token bales of Natal cotton, and the spread of favourable propaganda through books and speeches in England, were all part of this programme.[16]

The booming market in land did not materialise. Though some 5 000 settlers did arrive in Natal, they did not settle on the land—either because they were given lots of poor quality and could not farm at a profit, or were urban dwellers who had no intention of becoming farmers. They either sold their lands back to the companies from which they had obtained them, or to other speculators, but in both cases at very low prices.[17] The speculators' 'insurance' scheme was no more successful. Cotton production was a failure and the Natal Cotton Company collapsed.[18] The consequence was that the market in land remained deflated and the operations of the settlement companies ground to a halt. At least some of their holdings seem to have reverted to the Crown. The continued drift of Afrikaner settlers away from Natal during this period further contributed to the collapse in the market for land.

The handful of old and new settlers who genuinely sought a livelihood from the land experimented with the herding of sheep and the cultivation of new crops, including coffee, wheat, arrowroot, indigo, flax, sugar and tea, as well as cotton. Of these new crops, only sugar proved as suited to the coastal environment as maize had·long been proved by African farmers to be suited to the environment further inland. This much had been established by the mid-1850s,[19] but the organisation of production of these crops along capitalist lines depended upon more than the existence of a handful of men with capital. It depended also upon a ready supply of labour being available. Any attempt to recruit this labour locally depended upon the process of primitive accumulation having advanced sufficiently among the African population for some to have become alienated from the means of production to such an extent that they freely entered labour relationships. By the mid-1850s these conditions did not exist in Natal, and any attempt to recruit labour locally would necessarily involve the farmers and the colonial state in a head-on collision with the lineage mode of production which survived from an earlier phase of Natal's development.

[The cornerstone of the lineage mode of production was the organisation of the population into largely self-sufficient units of production based upon the homestead of the extended family. The labour-power of the family, a supply of livestock and seed, and free access to land suitable for cultivation, grazing and hunting were fundamental to the maintenance of the production complex. Equally important was a network of social practices which knitted the production complex together, regulated its relations with other homesteads, and ensured its reproduction. These included polygyny and lobola. The relationship between material resources and these social practices was one of interdependence. Each represented one part of a total production complex. Loss of control over one of the economic resources or the abandonment of a social practice would serve also to undermine the value and the possibility of retaining control over the remainder. Without adequate and suitable land, for example, cattle could not be grazed and crops could not be grown. Loss of cattle would preclude the payment of lobola for wives and so reduce the amount of labour-power available for the tending of crops, and the chance of the homestead reproducing itself. The abandonment of the practices of lobola and polygyny could have equally damaging effects. Loss of control over one of these key resources or social practices would therefore be likely to set off a vicious spiral at the end of which lay the demise of the homestead as the basis of socio-labour organisation.]

I have argued elsewhere that, in certain conditions, the lineage mode of production is a particularly dynamic form capable of generating substantial surplus. This was probably one of the factors responsible for the far-reaching developments which took place in the political economy of the region before the nineteenth century. Under the Zulu state the extraction of surplus was intensified to the point at which it can be argued that the lineage mode was all but destroyed and its resources brought together in a new articulation. Before this process was complete, however, the power of the Zulu state in the Natal countryside was broken.[20]

In the manner already described, the Voortrekkers sought to replace the Zulu state in extracting surplus from the homestead. The attempt was based upon claiming property rights in land, a resource fundamental to the survival of the homestead. Families were only to be allowed access to land in return for rent in labour-power or some other form. Access to land was to bear an 'opportunity cost'.

During the century attempts were made by those who held state power to render land a still more scarce and differentiated resource. By the mid-nineteenth century several different groups lay claim to control it. These included absentee speculators, small farmers largely engaged in mixed farming for subsistence, a few large farmers struggling to establish cash-crop production, missionaries granted land to facilitate their 'civilising' activities among the African population, and the colonial state which controlled lands set aside as locations for sections of the African population and which also controlled the remaining Crown lands which had yet to be alienated. From the African point of view, access to land could be obtained in different ways, though increasingly through the century it came to involve entry into some kind of relationship with the colonisers. The opportunity cost of entry into such relationships differed from one category of land to another, and the balance between these changed during the course of the century. Two themes run through our period on this question. The first is the exercise of African choice with respect to the kinds of relationships which they decided to enter into. The second is the persistent struggle by some white groups to reduce the number of these options for their own ends. Other elements crucial to the independent survival of the lineage also came to be attacked during the course of the century.

During the time of the Republic of Natalia and the early years of British colonial rule, the first of these themes dominates. It was possible to find land bearing a relatively low opportunity cost which not only allowed the maintenance of the homestead population, but also the strengthening of its position through the accumulation of cattle. The net result of the overthrow of Zulu power in the Natal countryside was a remarkable revival in the economic fortunes of the lineage.[21]

There were at least three ways in which cattle and other resources could be built up after 1838 to permit new homesteads to be established or existing ones to be strengthened. One element was African participation in hunting expeditions for ivory. The system might be characterised as 'hunting on the half': that is, guns and ammunition were provided by a white entrepreneur, and the haul of ivory shared between him and the African hunters.[22] The latter could then exchange their share for cattle. This type of relationship was originally established by English trader-hunters before the Voortrekker arrival in Natal, but it continued long after it.[23]

The second element was the barter of an agricultural surplus. Many whites in fact came to depend upon African agricultural produce for their very subsistence. The Voortrekkers, during both their trek northwards from the Cape and their initial sojourn in Natal, supplemented their diet of hunted game together with meat and milk from their herds, with vegetables and grain bartered from African producers. Sheep and goats were amongst the items given in exchange.[24] As the white population of the towns of Durban and Pietermaritzburg increased, so these too came to depend upon maize, vegetables, milk, fruit and wood bartered from Africans living in the vicinity.[25] The large-scale British immigration in the period 1849–52, coupled with the exodus of Boer farmers across the Drakensburg, merely served in the short term to strengthen the position of these African producers. It was usual at Durban for new immigrants to barter their food supplies from Africans until they were well-established, though it would seem that cattle could not be obtained in this way.[26] Fish was supplied by Umnini's people until their removal from land near the sea was enforced. Umnini's trade was said to have been worth between £100 and £200 per year.[27] In this period, Africans from the Zwartkop location were also able to retain their monopoly of the trade in vegetables, maize and wood at Pietermaritzburg.[28] Their trading activities were reported by new settlers to be one of the distinctive features of the colonial social scene in the town. Everywhere there were 'scores of Caffres going in and out with things for sale'.[29]

Such trading operations could probably be undertaken without any major social dislocation. Africans in Natal had always produced a maize surplus for storage against the possibility of failure of the next year's harvest,[30] so that a proportion of this could often be spared for the market. Vegetable cultivation and wood collection could generally also be undertaken without any major reorganisation of the homestead economy. As we have pointed out, capital stocks held in cattle were not alienated through the market. There is in fact evidence to suggest that the accumulation of capital stocks in cattle was one of the main objectives of the trade.[31] The Rev. A. Grout, for example, as late as 1848, noted a reluctance on the part of the inhabitants of the Umvoti area to accept money as a substitute. Cattle would only be exchanged for guns and ammunition, which would have facilitated independent hunting operations and additional security.[32]

Labour in the service of a white employer was the third alternative. It was one which seems to have been adopted reluctantly and with a specific purpose, usually the acquisition of cattle or guns, in mind.[33] It was not regarded as a permanent source of subsistence. White employers complained that no sooner had their African employees learned the skills which made their labour valuable than they returned to their kraals.[34] There was also already an element of competition among white employers for control of this African labour force.[35] There is some evidence that labour in the service of whites was undertaken mainly by those for whom other alternatives were not available, particularly those far from town. It was already being said that most labour, and that which was easiest to manipulate, came from a distance.[36]

The clear import of these developments was not lost on the whites in Natal. The Natal Native Affairs Commission reported in 1853 that 'The Kafirs are now much more insubordinate and impatient of control; they are rapidly becoming rich and independent'.[37] None looked forward to the prospect of Africans in Natal becoming once more totally free from relationships with white society by building up sufficient stocks of cattle to permit a complete return to a pattern of self-sufficiency based on herding, hunting and the cultivation of grain and vegetables. Beyond this, however, whites were divided in their attitude towards these developments.

One school of thought visualised the development of Natal as a self-supporting colony of African peasant cultivators contributing to the imperial economy both a supply of raw materials and a market for British manufactures. This was the vision held out by the report of the Location Commission in 1847, a body whose membership comprised officials and missionaries. Locations were to be set up which would be administered by superintendents and in which industrial schools and missionaries would work to encourage the growing of cash-crops for export while discouraging pastoralism and the social practices associated with it:

> the native locations will become centres of industry and improvement, the whole of the native population in the district and gradually those beyond it, will become consumers of imported articles and producers of articles for export, and after a time with a judicious system of taxation will defray the expenses of their own establishments and furnish an excess to the treasury of the district.[38]

Measures were in fact taken by some missionaries and officials to facilitate the realisation of this vision.[39] There were other interest groups too in Natal who offered tacit if not open approval for these developments. Maize produced by Africans was important to the operations of many Natal traders at this time.[40] Absentee landlords were also beginning to see rent payments from African 'tenant' cultivators as a lucrative business.[41]

At least one section of the Natal white community, however, saw such African activities as a direct threat to their own interests. For the farmers who aspired to commercial production for the market, and others who expected to benefit from such developments, African pastoralism or peasant cultivation, together with the potential for them, were obstacles which had first to be removed. It was the voices of these men that dominated the Natal Native Affairs Commission of 1852–3.

Their complaints were twofold. First, they were concerned that they could not compete with the more efficient African producers, except through a pattern of labour relations based on overt coercion which financial and political constraints prevented. As long as the homestead remained intact there would be an African monopoly in the supply of maize and vegetables to the towns, a monopoly which might yet be extended to other crops.[42]

The second and stronger complaint was that as long as Africans were able to obtain sufficient income from the herding of cattle or the cultivation of the land to meet their own needs, white farmers would be unable to obtain sufficient cheap and long-term labour to make the enterprises to which they aspired feasible.[43] The African homestead had to be broken up and its members forced out into labour for the white man, but how this was to be achieved constituted a problem: 'Kafir labour and management of the Kafirs are what we all want, but how we are to obtain these desiderata is a question easier put than answered'.[44]

It was recognised that the policy adopted with regard to the locations bore an intimate relation to the supply of labour to white farmers.[45] What was required was a reduction in the size of the locations so that they would be insufficient to meet the subsistence needs of the inhabitants.[46] Alternatively the whole of the African population should be removed beyond the Mzimkulu, though under the close supervision of a white official.[47] For those who chose to remain outside these arrangements, entry into a labour relationship with a white farmer would be insisted upon.[48] But measures were also recommended to force people out from areas to be designated as 'African' and into labour relationships with whites. Industrial schools should be set up to instil 'habits of industry', chiefs and magistrates should be obliged to direct labour from these areas to white employers,[49] and the apprenticeship of children to whites should be required.[50] Cash wants had to be created by heavier taxation, by restrictions on the entry into town unless European clothing was worn, by levying additional duties on trade goods for African consumption such as picks, hoes and rough blankets, and perhaps by charging rent for land occupied in the locations.[51]

Polygyny was identified as one of the key factors in maintaining the efficiency of the African homestead so that measures were advocated to control it, either directly, or through a system of differentiated taxation.[52] The retention of property in cattle was also to be discouraged.[53] For the system to be effective, stern measures were needed against 'squatters' on unoccupied Crown or private land, a system of passes to check 'vagrancy' and the undue movement of labour in search of better conditions, and a code of master and servant laws which gave greater freedom to the employer.[54] This blueprint for the creation through coercion of a rightless black labouring proletariat was cloaked in the usual contemporary settler double-think. That is, the recommended measures were asserted to be in the best interests of the African population, one more enlightened step towards their 'civilisation' and 'improvement'.[55] The same language, incidentally, was used by the rival school of thought in advancing its own vision of Natal.

One theme running throughout this period, once the era of cash-crop experimentation was over, was the attempt made by commercial farming interests in Natal to win control of the state apparatus and to use it to implement a version of this blueprint and thus to overcome African resistance to proletarianisation. As we have already hinted, in this attack they were to meet with opposition from some entrenched white interest groups as well as from Africans, while the role of other white groups in the struggle was somewhat ambivalent. Fundamentally the struggle within the ranks of white society revolved around the question of the manner in which an economic surplus was to be extracted from the colonised population. The struggle for the commercial farmers was not easy, and it was not until late in the century that they assumed a supreme position in Natal.

The key targets for the farmers in this struggle were the African landowners and the means which made possible the extension of this class: those who controlled mission lands on which Africans were able to settle and farm independently; the lands set aside by government as locations; the freedom with which mine recruiters were able to operate in Natal; absentee landlords who permitted Africans to 'squat' on their land, and other employers who were prepared or able to offer improved conditions and so were able to attract a labour surplus while their neighbours suffered labour shortage. Quite clearly one stereotype that we must abandon is the picture often presented in the literature of a relatively homogeneous white community more or less united in its 'native policy'. There were several axes of conflict among whites, and several of the more important revolved round the question of African activities.

As we have seen, the problems of the commercial farmers stemmed initially from the fact that Africans had access to sufficient land to meet their needs at a lower 'opportunity cost' than was involved in entry into a labour relationship. Perhaps it is necessary to spell this out a little more clearly and to look at the manner in which it began to change later in the century.

Land in the locations laid out by Theophilus Shepstone, Diplomatic Agent to the Native Tribes and Secretary of Native Affairs in Natal from 1845 to 1875, was probably initially the 'cheapest' available in the sense that neither rent nor labour-service was required from those who chose to live on it and those who did not were likely to be subjected to harassment by the 'legitimate' authorities. The ease with which Shepstone was apparently able to persuade Africans to move on to land in the locations which had been laid out in various parts of Natal is not very surprising. 'Squatting' on unalienated Crown lands or unoccupied purchased lands was a fairly attractive alternative to this in the early period. The entry into some kind of labour relationship with a white farmer was somewhat less attractive, though here a number of other factors had to be considered. Service on a stock farm was not particularly arduous, gave Africans opportunity of running cattle, and, if payment was made in kind, offered them the possibility of accumulating cattle. Labour-service on a commercial farm was probably least attractive of all. The work was arduous, payment was usually in cash or food rather than cattle, and the farmer's concern with marginal costs probably reduced the numbers of African-owned cattle he was prepared to see run on his land. So far as the occupation of mission-lands were concerned, the attraction of access to free land had to be balanced against the social cost of abandoning certain social practices, and this could also involve an economic cost.

The balance between the relative opportunity costs of access to these different categories of land changed during the course of the century. One factor here, for example, was the attempt by those who controlled speculative holdings of land, which they were unable to sell at a profit because of the deflated market, to exact rent from those Africans squatting on their land. This practice came to be known as 'Kafir Farming' and was very prevalent. Rent also came to be charged on Crown lands during the century. Space does not permit a full discussion of the range of changes here, but, as the century wore on, access to all categories of land was becoming, in absolute terms, more expensive. The cost was not, however, the same for all categories. Some were always cheaper than others, though the lands with the lowest opportunity cost were not always the same, and it is probable that there was movement by Africans from one category to another as it became relatively 'expensive'.[56] One category of land, however, was always the least attractive. This was land controlled by commercial farmers, for the reasons outlined. Africans always sought to avoid working for this kind of farmer as labour-tenants, and it is to these commercial farmers probably that the persistent claims of 'labour shortage' during the century should be traced. Neither is it surprising that when sugar production began in the 1860s it was on the basis of a supply of indentured labour from India. In general, commercial farming in Natal came to rely heavily on foreign labour.[57]

During the century the constraints on the African population operating free choice in relation to access to land tended to increase. One factor may have been overcrowding in the locations. More important, however, was the attempt by the commercial farming interest to close off access to those types of land which made possible the avoidance of labour tenancy on their own farms. Earlier measures designed to 'bring forth labour' had not succeeded in the manner in which the commercial farmers had anticipated. Taxation, heavy tariffs on African-purchased imports, the enforcement of European-style dress, fines, and medical fees were among the cash demands made of the African population of Natal as the state sought to exploit the African as a resource and as commercial farmers pressed for means to ease their labour shortage. When these demands are taken together with those of absentee landlords for rent, it is clear that the cash needs which had been forced upon the African population of Natal were quite high. A larger cash surplus had to be produced to meet these demands if conflict was to be avoided. It seems that one section of the African population was able to meet these demands through increased production for the market,[58] while at the same time developing the competitiveness and security of their position by purchasing land. For many of those who were unable to accumulate the necessary surplus through these means, it was still possible to avoid labour-service on a commercial farm by migration in search of temporary employment in the growing urban areas or at the mines. Fresh constraints on African movement and on the range of alternative opportunities open were still needed if the commercial farmers were to gain the labour which they required at the price which they were prepared to pay for it.

This is not to say that the constraints placed on the continuance of

African economic independence were everywhere resisted so successfully. As early as 1852 there is evidence that inroads were already being made into the capital resources of those who could not meet the demands for cash through the sale of a surplus in the market, either because they lived far from town or because they had been located on barren land.[59] Langalibalele's people may have been in such a position.[60] They may well have been among the first people in Natal to be forced out into long-term employment for whites, though not necessarily for white farmers. For those engaged in the independent production of export crops, crops were often pledged in advance to white traders to meet cash demands for tax or items of consumption.[61] Such producers were thereby rendered vulnerable to drought and other factors causing the failure of their crops. Entry into employment for whites offered one way out of these difficulties. Indebtedness was also a means by which white farmers were able to retain their African workforce.[62]

From the evidence so far presented, I would argue that the numbers seeking access to a particular category of land, or seeking a particular type of employment both inside Natal and elsewhere, were related to the relative opportunity costs of these alternatives. Taxation and other legislative enactments did not simply 'bring forth' labour, as white commercial farmers found to their continual consternation. The relationship also involved considerations of the alternative courses available, and these differed from area to area and from time to time. This is clearly indicated both in the fluctuations in the labour force available to the mines and in the lack of 'suitable' long-term African labour for commercial farms, and particularly for plantations, compared with the amount available to other employers whose inducements were a good deal higher.[63] It simply is not possible to talk in terms of a 'Dual Economy'. From the perspective of the African actors involved there was no such thing. There was simply a complex range of possibilities to consider.

Two aspects of the general struggle of the commercial farmers for supremacy in Natal of particular interest are the issues of African 'squatting' and African land-purchase. From the farmers' point of view, 'squatters' were those who avoided labour-tenancy on a white farm by living on Crown or white-owned private land and who paid rent. Well before the turn of the century the farming lobby had succeeded in getting a series of laws on the statute book against 'squatting', but there remained persistent complaints that these laws were not enforced because powerful interests would be threatened. There is even evidence of a similar conflict during the period of the Voortrekker Republic.[64] By 1874 it was estimated that five million acres belonging to private individuals or land companies were occupied by Africans.[65] Foremost amongst the ranks of what were termed the 'Kafir farmers' was the London-based Natal Land and Colonisation Company. In 1871 it owned 675 000 acres in Natal, many of which were rented to African tenants who paid between 5s. and 28s. per year for each hut.[66] But the ranks of the 'Kafir farmers' were not composed solely of land companies controlled by overseas capitalists. The people of Bambatha, leader of the 1906 rebellion in Natal, lived on land in the Umvoti division owned by two Afrikaners, T. J. Nel and P. R. Botha, to whom they paid rent.[67] As the commercial farmers sought legislation to outlaw squatting, they were to meet with determined opposition from those who were exacting profitable rents from African (and Indian) tenants. The same battle was fought on the question of enforcing occupation clauses on white-owned land. Once again the farming lobby's attempts to get these enforced were frustrated and between 1900 and 1908 several attempts to achieve this by levying a special tax on unoccupied land were also blocked.[68]

African land-purchase was a key means by which proletarianisation could be resisted, and as such represented a threat to white employers, and particularly to the commercial farmers. It was a development originally fostered in certain mission locations on the basis of individual tenure in order to encourage the emergence of a black petty bourgeoisie, but later in the century it came to be adopted more generally as a defensive measure against the more overt forms of white exploitation.[69] Not all land was purchased on an individual basis; some was bought through communal subscription.[70] By 1905 in Natal, Africans owned or were in process of acquiring through purchase 238 473 acres.[71] Land-purchase was prominent in the programmes of several social and political movements among Natal Africans at this time.[72] Some of the land purchased in Natal remained in African hands until the sweeping resettlement schemes of the 1960s removed most of the last pockets of African economic resistance.[73]

The tide began to turn in favour of the commercial farmers in the early years of the new century. Land was by that time passing out of the hands of the *rentier* class of absentee speculators and being added to the holdings of the commercial farmers. The Natal Land and Colonisation Company, the largest landholder of this type, was certainly among those who had begun to sell. Capital was only retained in 'Kafir farming' operations through considerable increases in rents.[74] A complex of factors had brought about this change in the political economy of Natal. These included the large-scale immigration of white settlers, the demand of South Africa's new mining and urban centres for agricultural produce, the discovery of a staple crop for the Natal midlands in wattle, and a political climate which was becoming increasingly hostile to the operations of absentee landlords.

The shift of *rentier* capital away from 'Kafir farming' had profound implications for the African population of Natal. Those who had purchased the lands from the absentee speculators were unwilling to perpetuate the existing rent-paying relationship with the people living on these lands. They saw them only as a valuable potential source of labour and tried to force a change in the relationship from one in which payment was in the form of rent to one in which labour-service was required. At the same time they sought seriously to curtail the numbers of cattle that their African tenants were able to hold on the land.[75] Eviction was an alternative, but this was a far more unattractive possibility than it had been earlier in the century. The reserves were now overcrowded, the labour needs of the more easy-going pastoral farmers were already satisfied and the land available for rent-squatting was everywhere diminishing as 'Kafir farmers' sold out to commercial farming interests, mine-owners, and others anxious to use the land more intensively or to use it in order to establish private labour reserves. In addition, the acreage of still unalienated Crown land was now very small, pressure was being placed on the state to break up the mission reserves, and measures were being introduced to block African and Indian land purchase.[76]

For those who were prepared to accept neither of these possibilities willingly, there was one further course of action. By 1905 there was a 'climate of unrest' observed by the authorities in Natal, and soon after there occurred a series of disturbances that have since come to be known as the 'Poll-Tax' or 'Bambatha's' rebellion. The unrest in the Ixopo-Richmond area of the Natal midlands, for example, was probably linked to the fears of eviction prevalent at this time. In this area wattle plantations were expanding rapidly and the Natal Land and Colonisation Company was disposing of lands previously occupied by Africans to white farmers.[77]

One suspects that parallel developments were taking place elsewhere in South Africa at this time, and that the Natives' Land Act of 1913, with its provisions against African land-purchase, rent-tenancy and share-cropping, was the legislative culmination of the shift in the balance of power in favour of farmers and other white employers and should be seen as part of a programme reflecting their real and special interests. It should also be seen, with earlier measures against 'squatting', against absentee landownership, against the continued existence of mission reserves and African locations, against labour mobility, as one in a series of measures designed to reduce African cash-crop competition and to remove those other factors which acted as constraints to the regular flow of cheap and unorganised labour into the enterprises of agricultural and mining capital.

Notes

1 For further discussion of the lineage mode of production and importance of the homestead within it see P. Bonner, 'Classes, the mode of production and the state', ch. 3 above, J. Guy, 'Ecological factors in the rise of the Zulu Kingdom', ch. 4 above, and Introduction, pp. 11–12

2 For an interpretation of early patterns of social and economic relationships in this region see my D.Phil. thesis, 'Transitions in the Political Economy of Southeast Africa Before 1840', University of Sussex, 1977

3 M. Wilson and L.M. Thompson (eds.), *The Oxford History of South Africa*, 2 vols., Oxford, 1969–71, i, p. 364

4 There is considerable dispute over the question of just how 'empty' Natal actually was. Historians sympathetic to the settler cause have argued that Natal was almost totally depopulated at this time, while more recent scholarship suggests that some were able to survive by retreat into defensible concentrations, and stresses the degree to which migration away from the area was temporary

5 Wilson and Thompson, *Oxford History*, i, p. 364. For the text of the law see G.W. Eybers, *Select Constitutional Documents Illustrating South African History, 1795–1910*, London, 1918, pp. 162–4. One morgen is equivalent to $2\frac{1}{3}$ acres.

6 Wilson and Thompson, *Oxford History*, i, p. 367

7 The term is, of course, a loaded one. It implies illegality. That is, use of it indicates an acceptance of the moral right of the settlers to ownership of the land and to dictate who should or should not have access to it

8 Natal Colony, *Proceedings and Report of the Commission Appointed to Inquire into the Past and Present State of the Kafirs in the District of Natal*, Pietermaritzburg, 1852–3, Report p. 8

9 A.F. Hattersley, *The British Settlement of Natal: A Study in Imperial Migration*, Cambridge, 1950, p. 48

10 J.A. Agar-Hamilton, *The Native Policy of the Voortrekkers, 1836–58*, Cape Town, 1928, ch. 3

11 Hattersley, *British Settlement*, pp. 46–7

12 *Ibid.*, pp. 46–7, 76

13 Brit. Parl. Papers 1847–8, xiii (980), p. 125, Moodie to Montagu, 9 March 1847, cited by Hattersley, *British Settlement*, pp. 62, 76

14 I have discussed the theme of land speculation more fully in 'Land, Labour and Capital in Natal: The Natal Land and Colonisation Company, 1860–1948', *JAH*, xvi, 2, 1975, pp. 257–83

15 Hattersley, *British Settlement*, p. 315 and *passim*

16 *Ibid.*, p. 85, draws a firm link between the land speculators and the cotton company; Slater, 'Land, labour and capital', p. 264; on publicity see Hattersley, p. 225; and for books and speeches, Slater, p. 261

17 Hattersley, *British Settlement*, pp. 108, 114, 142, 148, 168, 175, 189, 193

18 *Ibid.*, pp. 135, 229

19 Sugar was first grown experimentally in 1849 and was established as a successful commercial crop by the 1860s. Maize cultivation pre-dates the Voortrekker thrust in the 1830s, but almost certainly not the first contacts with the Portuguese and Dutch in the sixteenth, seventeenth and eighteenth centuries. Wattle, which was to become a staple of the Natal midlands, was not grown experimentally until 1864, and not commercially until the 1880s; N. Hurwitz, *Natal Regional*

Survey, vol. 12, Agriculture in Natal 1860–1950, Cape Town, 1957

20 Slater, 'Transitions', pp. 73–82 and *passim*

21 Its revival, however, may have begun a little before the final overthrow of Zulu power in Natal, as it sought to grapple with the contradictions which beset it; cf. Guy, 'Ecological factors', above, p. 112, who emphasises the continuation of the homestead as the basis of production, despite the destruction of the lineage mode in its articulation with the Zulu tributary state.

22 Cf. also R. Wagner, 'Zoutpansberg: the dynamics of a hunting frontier', pp. 330–1 below

23 For hunting operations from Port Natal before the Voortrekkers' arrival see J. Stuart and D. McK. Malcolm (eds.), *The Diary of Henry Francis Fynn 1803–61*, Pietermaritzburg, 1950, pp. 119, 128, 130, 198 and 213; D.R. Morris, *The Washing of the Spears: The Rise and Fall of the Zulu Nation*, London, 1966, pp. 99, 121, 134 and 136. For the exchange of ivory for cattle see *Natal Native Affairs Commission: Proceedings*, Pietermaritzburg, 1852–3, part 3, p. 27, evidence of Toohey; part 4, p. 13, evidence of Rev. Dohne. For similar operations at a later date see J.E. Methley, *The New Colony of Port Natal*, Leeds, 1850, p. 46. Some may have been hunting independently at this time, *Natal NAC: Proceedings*, part 6, p. 12, evidence of Wilson. Many whites also obtained the bulk of their living from hunting until quite late in the century. Some of these were employed on shares. See, for example, Methley, *New Colony*, p. 72; E.C. Tabler, *Pioneers of Rhodesia*, Cape Town, 1966, pp. 31–2

24 J.C. Chase (ed.), *The Natal Papers, 1498–1843: A Reprint of all Authentic Notices, Descriptions . . . relative to Natal*, Cape Town, 1968, i, p. 111, Retief to Governor of the Cape, 9 September 1837, and pp. 89–91, Roedolf, 'Diary'; J. Bird (ed.), *The Annals of Natal 1495–1845*, 2 vols., Cape Town, 1965, i, pp. 520–1, Pretorius 31 March 1839 and p. 514, Jervis to Napier, 30 March 1839

25 Bird, *Annals*, i, pp. 518–9, Jervis to Napier, 30 March 1839; ii, pp. 212–3, Smith to Napier, 10 July 1843; p. 310, Cloete to Montagu, 10 November 1843; and pp. 360–3, Faure to Montagu, 4 January 1844

26 A.F. Hattersley, *The Natal Settlers, 1848–51*, Pietermaritzburg, 1949, p. 26; A Perthshire Ploughman, *First Impressions of Natal*, Edinburgh, 1850, p. 12; J.C. Byrne, *Emigrants' Guide to Port Natal*, London, 7th ed., 1850, p. 137. Apart from mealies and kafir corn, other types of grain were said to be very expensive because they had to be imported (*ibid.*, p. 108). Meat was supplied by Dick King (Hattersley, *Settlers*, p. 26). Fynn thought in 1852 that more than half the corn consumed in the district was being grown by Africans (*Natal NAC: Proceedings* (1852), part 5, p. 73)

27 *Natal NAC: Proceedings* (1852), part 5, p. 79, evidence of Fynn.

28 (PRO) CO 179/6, Natal Land Commission, minutes of 25 March 1848, evidence of Shepstone

29 Quoted in Hattersley, *Natal Settlers*, p. 32

30 *Natal NAC: Proceedings*, part 5, p. 73, evidence of Fynn

31 *Ibid.*, part 3, p. 32, evidence of B. Blaine, assistant magistrate at the Quathlamba

32 CO 179/6, Natal Land Commission, minutes of 28 June 1848, evidence of Rev. A. Grout

33 *Natal NAC: Proceedings*, part 6, p. 12, evidence of Wilson; part 2, pp. 32 and 36, evidence of Shepstone led by Macfarlane

34 This is what really seems to have lain at the root of the persistent complaints of

'labour shortage' at this time

35 As early as 1842, 'Hottentots', who had been brought up from the Cape with the Voortrekkers, were said to have been leaving the farmers and flocking down to Port Natal. The English residents were apparently quite willing to employ them despite farmers' protests that they were already bound to employers. Bird, *Annals*, ii, p. 125, Smith to Napier, 7 November 1842

36 *Natal NAC: Proceedings*, part 1, p. 47, evidence of Scheepers of Mooi River; part 3, p. 50, Macfarlane

37 *Natal NAC: Report*, p. 27

38 CO 179/5, Report of the Location Commission, 1847

39 The Rev. Allison at Indaleni, for example, applied to government in 1850 for a grant to build a bridge across the Ilovo to facilitate the transport of African produce from his location into town. See S.W.B. Shepstone, *A History of Richmond, Natal, from 1839 to 1937*, Durban, 1937, p. 16. At the suggestion of Sir George Grey, a sugar mill was constructed at the Umvoti in 1860, paid for out of the Native Reserve Fund. It was controlled and operated by Africans for use by African sugar producers in the area. Sir J. Robinson (ed.), *An Old Colonist's Book for New Settlers*, Durban, 1872, pp. 47–8, and pp. 96–7

40 *Natal NAC: Proceedings*, part 5, p. 73, evidence of Fynn. The traders were buying at 4s. per muid in the rural areas to sell in town at 7s. 6d. This is probably the Zwartkop. The Rev. A. Grout had been paying only 2s. at the Umvoti in 1848. Maize was also being exported to Mauritius, probably to form part of the diet of indentured labour on the sugar plantations there

41 This was certainly the case in the area south of Durban and Pietermaritzburg. *Natal NAC: Proceedings*, part 5, p. 76, evidence of Fynn; also part 6, p. 10, Wilson. The latter, a farmer, had earlier been employed by one Smerdon to collect rent from Africans on his land. Part of his salary seems to have comprised the right to take labour from some of Smerdon's 'tenants' in lieu of a rent payment. This appears to refer to the period between about 1846 and 1848. The locality is not clear

42 *Natal NAC: Proceedings*, part 1, pp. 35 and 44, evidence of Cloete; part 2, p. 50, Archbell; part 3, p. 37, Blaine

43 *Ibid.*, part 1, pp. 12, 18–19 and 55, evidence of Struben, Evert Potgieter and D.J. Pretorius; part 2, p. 20, Preller; part 3, pp. 31, 38 and 50, Toohey, Otto and Macfarlane; part 6, p. 32, J. Du Plessis

44 *Ibid.*, part 3, p. 19, evidence of J.M. Howell. Some whites seem to have thought that the Commission existed solely to solve their labour problems, their written evidence actually being addressed to the 'Kafir Labour Commission'. See part 6, pp. 14–15, T. Phipson and George Robinson

45 *Ibid.*, part 6, p. 29, Robinson

46 *Ibid.*, part 1, pp. 31 and 42, evidence of Cloete; part 2, pp. 24, 41–2, 55–6 and 59, Preller, Archbell and Rev. Davis; part 3, pp. 7, 20 and 51, Archbell, Howell and Macfarlane

47 Groups located along the Drakensburg would remain as protection against 'Bushmen' raiding. *Ibid.*, part 1, pp. 20, 22–4, 47, 49, 54–6 and 73, evidence of Potgieter, Scheepers, Spies, Pretorius and Shepstone; part 2, pp. 18 and 36, Preller and J.S. Boshof; part 4, p. 21, Ferreira; part 5, pp. 24–5, J.S. Maritz; part 6, pp. 30–31 and 49, Hatting and Lotter

48 *Ibid.*, part 1, pp. 49, 51, 55–6 and 73, evidence of Scheepers, Pretorius and Shep-

stone; part 2, p. 18, Preller; part 3, pp. 20 and 51, Howell and Macfarlane; part 4, p. 22, Ferreira. There was some dispute as to whether the amount of labour employed by each farmer should be limited. Pretorius, for example, favoured a limit of five families per farm, Cloete, Lotter and Spies were against. See part 1, pp. 27, 54 and 56; part 6, p. 50

49 *Ibid.*, part 1, pp. 12–13 and 18, evidence of Struben and Potgieter; part 2, pp. 48 and 67, Archbell and Rev. Davis; part 3, pp. 21 and 54, Howell and Macfarlane; part 6, pp. 14, 22, 30–32, Phipson, Robinson, Hatting and Du Plessis

50 *Ibid.*, part 1, pp. 47–8, evidence of Scheepers; part 2, p. 67, Rev. Davis; part 3, pp. 10, 22, 35, 42 and 54, Archbell, Howell, Blaine, Otto and Macfarlane; part 4, pp. 21–2, Ferreira; part 5, p. 25, J.S. Maritz; part 6, pp. 20 and 50, Lotter and Robinson

51 *Ibid.*, part 2, pp. 11, 25–6, and 47, evidence of Harding and Archbell; part 3, pp. 10, 25 and 41–2, Archbell, Howell and Otto; part 6, pp. 16, 21 and 48, Robinson and Cleghorn. Tax reductions were proposed for those entering into labour relationships with whites. See part 1, p. 56, Pretorius; part 2, pp. 10–11 and 47–8, Boshof and Archbell; part 3, pp. 21, 10 and 41, Boshof, Howell and Otto; part 4, pp. 21–2, Ferreira; part 6, pp. 15 and 50, Robinson and Lotter. A state of 'civilisation', measured in terms of adherence to the European life-style and cultivation of crops, would still not gain tax exemption, part 2, p. 16, Boshof

52 *Ibid.*, part 1, pp. 15 and 20, evidence of Struben and Potgieter; part 2, pp. 7, 16 and 55, Van Staden (led by Macfarlane), Boshof and Archbell; part 3, pp. 50 and 52, Macfarlane; part 4, p. 17, Rev. Dohne; part 6, pp. 16 and 22, Robinson

53 *Ibid.*, part 1, p. 31, evidence of Cloete; part 2, pp. 26 and 60, Bird and Rev. Davis; part 3, p. 35, Blaine

54 Measures against 'squatters': *ibid.*, part 1, pp. 44 and 73, Cloete and Shepstone; part 3, pp. 20–21, 29 and 52, Howell, Toohey and Macfarlane; part 4, pp. 21–22, Ferriera; part 2, p. 45, Archbell. There is some evidence, however, that hostility to 'squatting' did not always extend to 'rent squatters': part 3, p. 29 and part 6, p. 13, Toohey and Wilson. System of passes: *ibid.*, part 1, pp. 32–4, Cloete; part 2, pp. 10 and 65, Boshof and Rev. Davis; part 3, p. 35, Blaine; part 6, p. 22, Robinson. Code of master and servant laws: *ibid.*, part 1, p. 56 and part 6, pp. 20–21, Pretorius and Robinson

55 *Ibid.*, part 1, pp. 23 and 53, evidence of Potgieter and Maritz; part 2, pp. 42, 49 and 67, Archbell and Rev. Davis; part 3, pp. 10–12, 41 and 50, Archbell, Otto and Macfarlane; part 6, pp. 19–20 and 30–31, Robinson and Hatting

56 This was rendered relatively easy by the dispersal of the different categories of land throughout Natal

57 The importation of cheap labour had been anticipated in some evidence to the Natal Native Affairs Commission of 1852–3. See *Natal NAC: Proceedings*, part 1, p. 54, evidence of Spies; part 2, p. 47, Archbell; part 6, p. 49, Cleghorn. In fact it was already reported that 'numbers of natives from the Zulu country, the Bechuana country, and from the frontier tribes, are in service in this district', part 5, p. 77, Fynn. Labour imported from Portuguese East Africa later became of particular importance for Natal. In 1880 it was said that Delagoa Bay derived its income almost entirely from the proceeds of a £1 tax levied on Africans returning from work on the Natal sugar plantations (W. Macdonald, *The Romance of the Golden Rand*, Johannesburg, 1936, p. 21). By 1939, that is well

after the system of indentured labour from India had been abandoned, at least 40 per cent of the labour employed on the sugar plantations was imported, mainly from Portuguese East Africa. See R.H. Smith, *The Labour Resources of Natal*, Oxford, 1950, p. 42. This pattern persists to this day and acts as a significant wage depressant

58 See, for example, the remarks of the resident magistrate of Upper Umkomanzi district in 1876 on the means by which some members of the African population of his area had dealt with the demand for increased rents: S. van der Horst, *Native Labour in South Africa*, Cape Town, 1942, p. 102. See also Hurwitz, *Natal Regional Survey*, p. 62

59 *Natal NAC: Proceedings*, part 3, pp. 66–7, evidence of Peppercorne, former magistrate at Impafane; part 4, pp. 9–10 and 16, Peppercorne and Rev. Dohne; part 5, p. 76, Fynn; part 6, p. 72, Shepstone. The fact that in 1851, of a total of £1 918 7s. od. paid in taxes by Africans at the Inanda, only £35 was actually paid in cattle (part 6, p. 4) may be partially misleading. It was said that a similar situation prevailed in the Klip River district (part 1, p. 16), but the taxation system was weighted in favour of those paying in cash or crops rather than cattle. There would therefore have been a considerable incentive to sell cattle to a trader in order to get the necessary cash rather than pay directly in cattle. The foundations of at least one South African fortune seem to have been laid in this way: that of the Johannesburg mineowner Harry Struben who accompanied his father on tax-collecting tours of his Klip River magistracy (see Macdonald, *Romance of the Golden Rand*, p. 9)

60 Even Struben, the Klip River magistrate and a man not known for his sympathy to Africans, had thought Langalibalele's location too small. This was more than twenty years before his 'rebellion'. *Natal NAC: Proceedings*, part 1, p. 16. Many were already 'squatting' on Crown or private lands. Colenso found them in poverty in 1856, partly through a fine of one thousand cattle which had been levied by Shepstone; J.W. Colenso, *Ten Weeks in Natal: a journal of a first tour of visitation among the colonists and Zulu Kafirs of Natal*, Cambridge, 1855, pp. 122–4, 130–3 and 147

61 Robinson, *An Old Colonist's Book*, pp. 47–8; Colenso, *Ten Weeks in Natal*, p. 66

62 J.S. Marais, 'African squatting on European farms in South Africa with special reference to the Cape Colony 1892–1913', unpublished seminar paper, London, Institute of Commonwealth Studies, 1967, p. 7

63 It is a persistent theme of southern African history that such employers do not seek to increase the supply of labour available to them by offering improved conditions. The precise reason for this is not clear. Was it simply that they could get away with it? Why then the complaints of 'labour shortage'? Was it traditional prejudice? But Legassick has discussed some of the problems inherent in this kind of explanation. Was it that some other constraint was operating? I suspect that the latter may be part of the answer and wonder whether it was that the market situation was such that large profits could not yet be made from commercial farming, and that many of the farmers were indebted to banks or other sources of credit

64 *Natal NAC: Proceedings*, part 2, p. 8, evidence of Boshof

65 C.W. de Kiewiet, *The Imperial Factor in South Africa: a study in politics and economics*, Cambridge, 1937, p. 192

66 For the operations of this company see Slater, 'Land, labour and capital'
67 S. Marks, *Reluctant Rebellion*, Oxford, 1970, p. 201
68 *Ibid.*, p. 131
69 *Natal NAC: Proceedings*, part 1, p. 73, evidence of Shepstone; Wilson and Thompson, *Oxford History*, i, p. 385; Colenso, *Ten Weeks in Natal*, pp. 50–52; O.H. Spohr (ed.), *The Natal Diaries of W.H.I. Bleek, 1855–6*, Cape Town, 1965, p. 13
70 Marks, *Reluctant Rebellion*, p. 61; Cosmas Desmond, *The Discarded People*, Harmondsworth, 1971, ch. 3, *passim*
71 Marais, 'African Squatting', p. 5, footnote 15
72 Ethiopian churches were thought by whites to have been involved in African land-buying syndicates; B.G.M. Sundkler, *Bantu Prophets in South Africa*, Oxford, 1961, pp. 65–70. For the interest of Congress in the issue see Marks, *Reluctant Rebellion*, pp. 72 and 362; and for other organisations, pp. 359 and 363. For its inclusion among African demands to the 1906 Native Affairs Commission, see *The Times*, 15 November 1906, p. 5. I have argued elsewhere that the issue was a factor in the strength of the ICU in Natal ('A Fresh Look at the Natal ICU', unpublished seminar paper, Sussex, 1971)
73 Desmond, *Discarded People, passim*
74 Slater, 'Land, labour and capital', pp. 277–80
75 *Ibid.*.
76 In 1910, for example, the Natal Land and Colonisation Company was obliged to cancel sales of 897 acres, most of which had been sales involving Africans and Indians (*The Times*, 22 April 1910)
77 Marks, *Reluctant Rebellion*, p. 193

CHAPTER SEVEN

The labour market of the Cape Colony, 1807–28 *

Susan Newton-King

This essay seeks to investigate the labour shortage which prevailed in the colony of the Cape of Good Hope between the years 1807 and 1828. The colony during these years came increasingly to constitute a single economic system, through a process of response to market forces which has been documented elsewhere.[1] From the time of the second British occupation in 1806, the influence of a strong colonial state, both willing and able to intervene in the colonial economy in order to foster its productivity, became a further and powerful unifying factor. Therefore, despite the economic, legal and ethnic divisions which distinguished the various categories of unfree labour from one another and from the handful of free labourers, with respect to the terms on which they could be procured and the manner in which they were employed, the problem of labour supply during this period should be regarded as a single problem and tackled in a single study, seen from the viewpoint of the labour market as a whole.

There is considerable evidence in contemporary documents to show that, at least by the end of the second decade of the nineteenth century, the colony was facing a generalised labour shortage which was more serious in Cape Town and the western districts than elsewhere. The major and irrevocable factor which stood out from the complexity of the elements which contributed to this shortage was the abolition of the slave trade, the effects of which gradually gathered force so that further state intervention in the labour market became a necessity. The government stepped in to tighten the controls over non-slave labour so as to increase its supply and depress its cost, and battle was joined with the missionaries of the London Missionary Society, whose efforts to secure a degree of economic independence for a small proportion of the Khoisan population were

*I wish to thank Peter Richardson for his help in revising this paper (first presented as an MA dissertation at the School of Oriental and African Studies in 1976).

seen as a severe threat. In 1820 the problem acquired new dimensions with the arrival of nearly five thousand British settlers, most of whom were originally settled in the newly created district of Albany, on the eastern frontier. Within a very short time Albany was suffering from a more acute shortage of labour than any other district in the colony, and the troubled Somerset administration was beset with demands that something be done about it. Various schemes were conceived and some had been implemented by 1828, but they did little to alleviate the labour crisis in Albany. In order to understand the failure of these schemes and the depth of the crisis it precipitated, the 1820 settlement should be placed firmly in the historical context of the colonial economy and its labour market, viewed as an integrated whole. From this perspective, it becomes possible to regard the abolition of the slave trade in 1807 and the promulgation of Ordinances 49 and 50 in 1828 as points along a continuum; it is possible to discern an unbroken line of causality which links these major landmarks in the early history of labour at the Cape.

When the British occupied the Cape for the second time, in January 1806, they could not be certain that it was to be a permanent possession. The loss of the American colonies thirty years earlier had increased the significance of India and the Far Eastern trade to the metropolitan economy, and during the Napoleonic Wars Britain came to appreciate the vital strategic importance of the Cape for the maintenance of her dominance in India. At the Congress of Vienna in 1814 British delegates demanded the permanent possession of the Cape of Good Hope, St Helena and Mauritius, not, wrote Castlereagh, 'for their mere commercial value', but because they 'affect essentially the engagement and security of . . . (British) dominion'.[2] Nevertheless, successive colonial governors, both before and after 1814, were required to make the colony pay for the cost of its occupation and administration. The long years of war imposed a severe strain on the British economy, and after the final conclusion of hostilities in 1815 the Liverpool government was in a critical financial position. There was little money to spare for the needs of the Cape government. Thus the prosperity of the colonial economy was of great importance to the metropolitan government, if only because of its contribution towards the colonial budget, the bulk of the internal colonial revenue being raised from tithes, rents, land transfer duties and customs dues. Indeed, the Cape's commercial value was not negligible; by 1820 its total exports had reached a value of nearly £195 000 while its imports, including imports of capital, were worth approximately £367 000.[3]

During this period the most prosperous and most rapidly expanding sector of the economy was pastoral farming. Only small areas of the colony were suitable for arable farming. Transport difficulties, climate, a scarcity of capital and the limited market opportunities for wheat and wine production all combined to produce the dominance of pastoral farming.

Nevertheless, the arable farmers were bigger buyers and bigger spenders than the stock farmers, for their activities were more capital intensive, and hence their importance both to the colonial budget and to the trade of the metropolis should not be underestimated. Moreover, both wheat and wine farming received a boost during the boom which followed the second British occupation. The garrison was increased to nearly five thousand men, as compared with fifteen to sixteen hundred under the Batavians, the removal of restrictions on trade (a reform introduced during the first occupation and upheld by the Batavians) was confirmed, and, under wartime conditions, the number of ships putting into Cape ports was high. From 1815 to 1821 the presence of Napoleon on St Helena increased the demand for all Cape products and helped to offset the adverse effects of the reduction of the garrison in 1817 from 4032 men to 2400 men. In 1806 Baird raised the price of wheat in order to foster production, but despite this, and the generally stimulating climate, wheat farming remained an enterprise of uncertain gain. Wine production, by contrast, was greatly encouraged in 1813 by the reduction of the English customs duty on Cape wines. The effect of the preference led to an expansion in output from 7707 leaguers in 1814 to 19250 leaguers in 1824. In 1825 Britain reduced import duties on continental wines, however, and it is probable that this measure exacerbated the effects of the abolition of the slave trade upon the expanded wine farming sector. The cultivation of vines and wheat was primarily dependent on slave labour while the labourers on sheep and cattle farms were drawn mainly from people of Khoisan and of mixed descent—who came to be known as Hottentots.[4] In the first three decades of the nineteenth century, the colonial government actively demonstrated its appreciation of the economic realities of the colony. Not the least of its activities was intervention in the labour market.

During the period immediately following the second British occupation, it was the labour problems of the important pastoral farming sector which commanded the most urgent attention. From 1799 to 1802 the Khoisan servants of Graaff-Reinet and Uitenhage districts had been in rebellion against their masters. In alliance with the Xhosa of the Zuurveld they had put to flight almost one-third of the estimated 8000 whites who had occupied the area between the Fish and the Gamtoos Rivers during the preceding three decades. Through a combination of coercion, negotiation and conciliation, the Batavian authorities had brought an end to hostilities. They were well aware of the importance of Graaff-Reinet and the Zuurveld to the meat trade; the devastation caused by the war had led to a serious shortage of meat in Cape Town.[5]

The Batavians were unable to expel the Xhosa from the colony but they did succeed in breaking the strength of the Khoi-Xhosa alliance and in compelling many of the Khoisan to return to the service of the farmers, the latter having been coerced and cajoled into returning to their abandoned properties. Although William Freund has argued that without 'the commitment of the Batavian government, affirmed by British successors, to reconstruct the colonial social and economic order . . . the eastern frontier zone would not have been engulfed by colonial South Africa in later times',[6] it is important not to overestimate the extent to which security of property had been restored and control over labour re-asserted by the Batavians. Indeed, it was in response to reports of continuing insecurity in this region, and of continuing difficulties with labour, that the Earl of Caledon dispatched Colonel Collins to tour the frontier in 1808.

In 1809 Collins wrote that those who returned to their lands in the Zuurveld in 1804 'were forced to fly again the following year. The same persons have since made two ineffectual attempts to return to their lands.'[7] And he found much evidence of a continuing labour shortage. Not all the rebel forces had been broken up and successfully distributed among the farmers. Collins writes of 'the late desertion of a Hottentot named Hans Trumpetter, a noted chief of the former insurgents, with several other members, who have since joined the Caffres, and committed several depredations upon the farmers'.[8] But the process was under way. On a farm in the Tarka he found 'two Bosjesman chiefs, named Lynx and Frolic', who had with them

> two hundred of their people at this and a neighbouring farm; Lynx had been one of the most noted depredators, and he and his people now relate with exultation to the farmers their former exploits against them. We . . . prevailed on Lynx to go and reside with a farmer living more inwards.[9]

The proximity of the Xhosa afforded a refuge to many Khoisan who sought to avoid servitude. Thus in Hintsa's territory Collins met Windvogel, who had been with Lynx in a place nearer the colony, and had sought Hintsa's protection after Lynx went to live in the Tarka. At a spot on the coast near Hintsa's Great Place he found a number of Khoisan women living together with an Irishman named McDaniel, a farmer from the colony named Loghenberg and a number of runaway slaves.[10] There were also Khoi living in Nqgika's territory. However, the majority of deserters from service seem to have joined the Gqunukhwebe, who had lived longer in the Zuurveld than the other Xhosa groups and who had long intermarried with the Khoisan. Collins recognised this special relationship between 'Konga's [Cungwa] people' and the 'colonial Hottentots', and recommended that when the government was in a position to expel the Xhosa from the Zuurveld, Cungwa should be removed beyond the Keiskamma River. In general, he advocated the separation of 'Hottentots' from the Xhosa, the dispersion of the former among the colonists[11] and the confining of the latter beyond the Bushman's River, until such time as troops could be spared for the expulsion of the Xhosa beyond the Fish River. Those Xhosa and persons of mixed Khoisan-Xhosa descent who had stronger ties with colonial society than with the independent chiefdoms would be allowed to stay in the colony; that is, they would be treated as 'Hottentots'.

At this time there were many Xhosa in the service of the eastern frontier farmers.[12] The first British authorities, and the Batavians after them, had attempted to prevent the employment of Xhosa, but an exception had been made in the case of

> such Kaffers as had remained quietly with the inhabitants, long before and during the troubles which had of late years prevailed between the Kaffer nation and the inhabitants . . . , orphans, and such as might have been born during their residence with the inhabitants.[13]

These exceptions led to a considerable evasion of the proclamation against the employment of Xhosa herders, and were a cause of concern to the authorities. The reluctance of the authorities to sanction the employment of Xhosa on farms continued throughout the next two decades,[14] or at least until 1826, but under pressure of labour shortage exceptions continued to be made, notably in the case of 'the orphans and abandoned children of the Kaffers' who 'in the visits of veld-cornets to the Kraals . . . might be snatched from destruction and rendered useful to the colony'.[15]

With regard to the London Missionary Society's establishment at Bethelsdorp, Collins's recommendations were consistent with his general awareness of the labour needs of the east. Vanderkemp had persisted in his refusal (made to the Batavian authorities) to turn away deserters from service. Collins noted that among the six hundred strong population of Bethelsdorp, there were 'only forty-three exercising any useful employment' and described the institution as

> the cause of the greatest embarrassment to the inhabitants of the neighbouring districts, whose servants leave them on the slightest pretext to repair to Bethelsdorp, thereby depriving them of the means of preserving their cattle from the [thefts of] Caffres and Bosjesmen.[16]

The institution should be broken up, and its members made to choose between proceeding to one of the Moravian missions, or entering the service of the inhabitants. Missions in general should serve as refuges for the unemployable, training schools for artisans and, on the northern frontier, centres of pacification, with the missionaries acting as intermediaries between the Khoisan and the farmers, until such time as the former had been fully integrated into the colonial order.

This process of integration was, Collins noted, proceeding very successfully in the northern and north-eastern regions of the colony. Many 'Bosjesmen' were already in the service of the colonists and others were entering into partial dependence, performing various services in exchange for gifts of sheep, dagga (Indian hemp) and tobacco. The attitude of the farmers towards the still independent Khoisan on the northern frontier and in the unoccupied areas of the Great Karroo had changed markedly over the past decade:

> several inhabitants of the north eastern districts appear to have exerted themselves with as much zeal to acquire the friendship of the Bosjesmen, as they had before done to blot them from the creation. They have experienced the most happy results from this line of conduct.[17]

The causes of this change in attitude are complex. First, the farmers had been prohibited by the British colonial government from carrying off women and children during commando raids, and this had served to 'damp their ardour' for these expeditions. Secondly 'their great want of servants' had probably led them to the realisation that persuasion rather than force would in the long run secure them a more abundant labour supply. Thirdly, and most importantly, the rapid expansion of the colony towards the north had accelerated the impoverishment of the Khoisan who had retreated thence during the late eighteenth century.

It is possible that expansion in this direction had been a response to the labour shortage in the east, as well as to the continuing insecurity of that region, as many of the new settlers had arrived since the outbreak of the rebellion. This influx would in turn have driven more groups of Khoisan into service as their water sources were appropriated and their game killed off. By 1809 it could be said of those who remained independent on the peripheries of white settlement that they 'often suffer extreme misery, seldom rob but to satisfy their wants, and afford the fairest hope of becoming in time useful to the colony'.[18]

In November 1809, two months after Collins submitted his final report, the British authorities introduced general measures for the mobilisation and control of the Khoisan labour supply. These measures largely confirmed practices which had been the rule for a long time and which had increased under pressure of labour shortage. The colonists took from Governor Caledon's regulations the extra state support which they needed, and they ignored those provisions which contravened their interests. Caledon decreed that every Hottentot was to have a fixed and registered 'place of abode'; if he wished to move from one district to another he had to obtain a certificate from the landdrost; without this certificate he would be 'considered as a vagabond and treated accordingly'. If he wished to move within a district, he had to obtain a pass from his master or from a local official. Any local official or landholder was entitled to demand this pass of any Hottentot. If he had no pass, he was to be delivered up to the landdrost or field-cornet who, 'after due inquiry . . . [would act as] . . . they shall feel incumbent to do'.[19]

These measures had two key implications. First, it was now legal to compel any Khoisan not in government service to serve the colonists, for without a pass he could not legally be anywhere at all, and it was the colonists who controlled the issue of passes. In particular, it was the local officials, the landdrosts and field-cornets, who thus gained the right of total control over the mobility of Khoisan within the colony. They administered the drawing up of compulsory contracts between servants and employers—without a written contract no colonist could claim a Hottentot's service for longer than a month—and they controlled the issue of passes and the allocation of those arrested for being without a pass. The second implication of the Caledon Proclamation was thus that it gave to the local officials extensive opportunities for patronage in the sphere of labour distribution.

The majority of the other provisions were designed to protect the servant against gross ill-treatment, the withholding of wages or detention after the expiry of his contract. The latter clause seems to have been generally ignored and its spirit was in any case nullified by the Proclamation of April 1812, which legalised the ten-year 'apprenticeship' of the servant's children.

It is difficult to say to what extent Caledon's Proclamation was in response to the abolition of the slave trade as well as to the conditions described by Collins. Many writers have drawn a direct connection between the two laws.[20] Thus Macmillan says that 'by the abolition of the slave trade the ordinary labour supply was cut off at the source, and the Hottentots at once acquired a new importance as the obvious means of meeting the sudden deficiency'.[21] Common sense would seem to decree that this should be so. Slaves had been first introduced into the colony in the seventeenth century, because the indigenous Khoikhoi and San could not be induced to work for others on a permanent basis while they still had independent access to land, game and cattle. While the number of slaves had greatly increased over the following 150 years (there were approximately 18 000 by 1795), the Khoisan had gradually lost their independence and had become the servants or the clients of the white settlers. But the latter did not yet have a full monopoly of the natural resources even within the boundaries of the colony. It seems natural enough, then, that when the supply of slaves (whose economic independence had been forcibly destroyed) was brought to an abrupt end, the colonial state should intervene to hasten the destruction of Khoisan independence. A number of practical questions are raised by this formulation, however. We need to know, for example, when the effects of the abolition of the trade first came to be felt and whom they affected, as well as the importance of slave labour to the pastoral farmers at this period.

Detailed statistics showing the annual average number of slaves imported before 1807, or the natural rate of increase of the slave population after 1807, relative to the labour needs of the expanding economy, are difficult to obtain. Nor is it clear to what extent pastoral farmers, as opposed to wine and grain producers, would have been hit by the abolition of the trade. Nevertheless, there is some evidence to refute Isobel Edwards's claim that 'the abolition of the slave trade aroused little comment' and that 'a labour shortage was warded off by an increasing birth-rate amongst the slave population'.[22] This evidence also indicates that, while the effects of abolition built up gradually, they were already being felt before 1809. Thus, Caledon wrote to Castlereagh in July 1807 to request the reduction of the Hottentot Corps, so that the farmers could 'gain the advantage of some useful labourers, a consideration of some importance, especially since the abolition of the slave trade'.[23] Later that year he suggested that the Corps should be entirely disbanded, for 'on account of an increased demand for agricultural products, an additional supply of fresh provision is requisite, and consequently an increase of labour to procure it'.[24] There is no doubt that the demand for meat and related animal products (soap, butter, tallow, candles, hides, etc.) as well as for agricultural products was expanding rapidly during the boom years of 1806–21,[25] and there is some evidence that the pastoral districts were also affected by a shortage of slave labour quite soon after abolition. Thus, in 1812, the Commission of Circuit reported that Hottentots were now better treated since the farmers had an 'essential interest' in their willingness to work, 'as they have not any other persons for herdsmen, neither can they easily obtain people even for other work, in consequence of the present daily increasing dearness of slaves'.[26]

Slaves were used in the pastoral districts for the more labour-intensive work of soap- and butter-making and arable cultivation,[27] but there is no good reason to suppose that they were not also used as herdsmen, despite van Reenen's statement that they deserted to the Xhosa more readily than Hottentots[28] and despite the acknowledged skill of the Khoisan herdsmen and wagon drivers. Collins makes frequent mention of 'slaves and Hottentots' who had deserted from the frontier farms to join the Xhosa. One Stoffel Lombard had lost eleven slaves in this way.[29] And, fifteen years later, Somerset could write with regard to the eastern frontier that slaves were 'the only labouring class obtainable to the colonists'.[30] He had granted lands between the Koonap and the Fish Rivers to a number of Dutch farmers, in recognition of 'their services in defence of the frontier', and he observed that if a clause prohibiting the use of slave labour was inserted into these grants, this would 'exclude all the means at the disposal of the grantee to avail himself of the lands granted him' and would 'tend to excite the most serious discontent'.[31] Between them, the 147 applicants owned 459 slaves.[32]

Somerset may have been exaggerating the extent to which the colonists of the interior were dependent on slave labour, but there is further evidence to this effect in the report made by the Inspector of Lands to the Colonial Secretary in 1826. He wrote that a general prohibition on the use of slave labour on new grants of land would discourage the legalisation of land occupancy in the frontier areas and the conversion of loan rent to quitrent tenure in the more settled districts, and that it might encourage the farmers concerned to move beyond the frontier.[33] Contrary evidence was adduced by the Commissioners of Inquiry, who wrote that they believed that the Boers 'beyond the frontiers' possessed 'few slaves' and that herding work was done by 'the Hottentot Bastaards and Bushmen employed within their service'.[34] Nevertheless, by 1828 there were 3 569 male slaves and 3 029 females slaves in the five eastern districts of George, Uitenhage, Albany, Somerset, and Graaff-Reinet, out of a total slave population of 18 383 males and 13 860 females. In the latter district alone there were 1 265 male slaves and 1 001 females.[35]

Whatever the relative quantitative significance of slave labour in the east, there is little doubt that the general effects of abolition—an increasing pressure on supplies of 'free' labour, and a rise in its price—were felt in the eastern regions as in the west.[36] These pressures may have built up fairly slowly. It seems that it was some time before regulations were introduced to guard against the smuggling of slaves into the colony. After January 1809 all slaves landed at Cape Town were to be forfeited and were to be apprenticed as 'prize negroes' for a period of fourteen years, after which they were to re-engage themselves to their present masters, or would be given passes to seek new employment. By 1825 there were an estimated one thousand such persons under indenture in the colony.[37] Slave ships continued to call at the Cape until the abolition of the Portuguese slave trade in 1823, and while Somerset declared in 1816 that 'no successful attempt had been made to smuggle slaves ashore since the passing of the Abolition Act',[38] the compulsory registration of slaves was not introduced until 1816 and does not seem to have been very effectively carried out.

Nevertheless, the number of slaves added to the labour force by illegal means could not have been large. By the end of the following decade and the beginning of the next, the strain in the labour market was very apparent. The price of slaves had risen rapidly. In 1826 the Advisory Council was informed that

> the average value of slaves in the year succeeding the abolition of the slave trade (1808) was £75—at this time it may be reckoned at £150, being an increase of 100 per cent in eighteen years. The average price before the abolition was £60, which gives an increase of 150 per cent.[39]

Slaves could be hired out at fifteen to twenty Rixdollars per month plus subsistence and lodging;[40] by 1826 it was reported that 'a full grown male [slave] could always earn at least one Rixdollar per diem and even a child of ten years old from eight to ten Rixdollars per mensum'.[41] It was little wonder that Somerset had described slave property as 'the most valuable in the colony'.[42]

With regard to the slave birth-rate, I have only the evidence of T.F. Dreyer, of Tygerberg, who told the Commissioners of Inquiry that in his opinion the slave population had not greatly increased since abolition. 'In my own establishment', he said,

> I have taken every care of my slaves but in the course of twenty five years they have not replaced their numbers. Out of ten women only five have had children and although these have produced twenty there are only six surviving.[43]

He added that many slave-owners had taken the care of slave children upon themselves in order to minimise infant mortality. By 1828 there were 32 243 slaves in the colony, as compared with 29 394 in 1806, but this increase appears to have been quite inadequate in relation to the expanding labour needs of the colonial economy.

The pressures on the Khoisan labour supply built up steadily during the 1810s, as can be seen from the intensification of conflict between the local authorities and the missionaries of the LMS during that decade. These pressures were greater in some regions than in others. Thus, at Bethelsdorp, Vanderkemp and his successors, Read and Ulbricht, were in constant conflict with Cuyler, the Landdrost of Uitenhage, from 1806 onwards, whereas at Hooge Kraal (Pacaltsdorp), in the district of George, relations between the mission and the local authorities were amicable until the death of Pacalt in 1819. While this amity could be partly ascribed to the character of Pacalt, it was also due to the fact that, in 1814, when Pacalt first came to live among the Khoikhoi at Hooge Kraal, this part of the country was

> a new district, thinly peopled, and most of the farmers were then in possession of slaves and Hottentots, and did not find it in their interest to force the Hottentots into their service; but in 1819, when the deputation visited the station, a considerable alteration had taken place. The abolition of the slave trade began to be felt; the population and the trade of the district had increased; the colonists began to feel a scarcity of servants; and as they found the people of Pacaltsdorp made good servants, they began to grudge them the liberty and independence they enjoyed.[44]

The result was an unsuccessful proposal that the mission should be broken up.

By the mid-1820s the shortage of non-slave labour was such that Dreyer could tell the Commissioners, 'free labourers cannot be procured in the country'.[45] And the Inspector of Lands and Woods could ask:

> Where can they get free labour and replace that of their slaves? The equivalent of that labour would not be obtainable in the present state of the colony, and that which they could perhaps partially obtain, would be at a price which they could not afford to pay ... By a reference to the comparative sketch of procurable field labour, made out by me in July 1823, it will be seen that the said procurable field labour, including the Hottentots and slaves, stands at *one* male (comprising boys of twelve years of age) to every 772 acres! ... the free labour ... hitherto consists only of Hottentots, and does not amount to anything like 8 000 males for the whole colony.[46]

The effects of this intense demand for 'free' labour on the wages paid to Hottentots appear to have varied very widely. Thus, on the one hand, the Deputy Fiscal reported that average rates of hire for both Hottentots and slaves (probably in the western Cape) were between fifteen and twenty Rixdollars a month plus subsistence and lodging.[47] And Stoll, Landdrost of the Cape District, told the Commissioners in 1824 that in Cape Town

> a common labourer of any description cannot be hired under one Rixdollar a day, and generally one and a half, and a mechanic from two and a half to three Rixdollars a day, including subsistence, but sometimes these rates are given beside subsistence.[48]

On the other hand, Philip reported that a Hottentot impressed by a local authority, 'to serve *himself* or his friends', might be given from two to three shillings a day, or, on occasion, as little as ten Rixdollars a year.[49]

It thus appears that those who had access to the patronage of the local authorities, or who could draw on a supply of tied Hottentot labour, were able to obtain it at a low cost, while those to whom such patronage was not extended, or who did not control such a supply, were obliged to bid for the labour of the small proportion of Khoisan who escaped the net of the local authorities and the other farmers. I shall return to this subject.

The full extent of the labour shortage during the second decade after the abolition of the slave trade can best be seen in its effect upon the wages of the white labourers and artisans introduced into the colony between 1817 and 1823. During this period, the average wages of white unskilled workers whose labour-power was offered on the free market were between twenty-five and thirty Rixdollars a month, plus subsistence and lodging, or one to one and a half Rixdollars a day, sometimes with food. White artisans selling their labour-power on the free market could command forty to forty-five Rixdollars a month, or two to three Rixdollars a day.[50] The disparity between these wages and those received by the Hottentots was a function of the greater mobility of the white workers or of their greater freedom 'at the level of circulation'. However, as will be seen, not all the white labourers and artisans introduced into the colony during these years were possessed of this freedom, and hence not all could command these wages. Moreover, those who could did not necessarily reap the benefits for themselves.

With the exception of the sixty-nine men who, with their families, made up the 'Independent Parties' assisted by English parishes during the 1820 emigration, and those working-class members of the same emigration who were able to pay their own deposits, all British workers who came to the Cape between 1817 and 1823 came as indentured servants, under contract to the men who had organised their transportation and contributed towards its cost. However, these contracted servants, or 'apprentices', can be broadly divided into two categories, according to the circumstances of their entry into the Cape labour market. In the first category were those whose emigration was organised by persons who did not require their labour for themselves, but who intended to profit from its transfer to others. These workers were literally the stock-in-trade of private speculators. In the second category were workers brought out by those who intended to profit directly from their labour, and who consequently wished that their servants' wages should be kept as low as possible.

The majority of these workers were brought to the Cape during the 1820 emigration, as subordinate members of parties headed by 'Sole

Proprietors'. They were contracted to work for varying periods, normally three years, at average daily wages of 6d. (under one-third of a Rixdollar in 1820) for an unskilled labourer and 1s. (under two-thirds of a Rixdollar in 1820) for a 'mechanic'.[51] However, the boundary between these two categories of 'apprentices' was not absolutely clear, for some of the people brought out by speculators were retained by the latter to work on their estates and were consequently bound to the terms of their original contracts, and it is possible that a number of the 'Sole Proprietors' hired out their indentured servants to others when their own enterprises failed.[52]

The first speculative emigration was organised in 1817 when Benjamin Moodie, elder brother of the more famous Donald Moodie, applied to the British Government to aid him in emigrating to the Cape of Good Hope, with a party made up 'of persons from the Highland estates of the Marquis of Stafford who were ejected to make room for sheep farms and were every day embarking for the United States'.[53] It is probable that he intended the government should meet part of the cost of transporting his apprentices, while he himself would retain control over their labour so as to profit from its proceeds after his arrival in Cape Town.

Moodie's hopes that the government would aid him had been raised by rumours which had been circulating since 1813 to the effect that the British Government was planning some sort of assisted emigration to the Cape. These rumours were not entirely without foundation, for, since the failure of Cradock's attempt to expel the Xhosa from the Zuurveld in 1812, Cape officials had been impressing on their superiors in London the need to implant a densely settled population in the frontier zone, and had suggested that 'some of the unemployed' might be transported from Britain for this purpose. The increasing distress and discontent of the unemployed, the under-employed, and the over-taxed did indeed pose a threat to the ruling classes in Britain at that time. However, despite this, and despite the disfavour with which it regarded voluntary emigration to America, the Liverpool government was not then prepared to meet the expense of aiding individuals to emigrate to the Cape Colony.

Moodie therefore entered into a private partnership with one Hamilton Ross, already at the Cape, through the latter's agent in Scotland. Ross at first agreed to take half shares in the shipment of two hundred young Scotsmen, selected by Moodie 'from above 1500 persons who, in the course of a few weeks offered to accompany him from the south of Scotland'.[54] The plan was that Moodie and Ross would pay the expenses of transportation (initially estimated at £30 per person for the journey from Leith to Cape Town, but later reduced to £20 a head), and that each emigrant would be bound to repay them £60 from the proceeds of his labour, after his arrival in Cape Town. In June 1817 Moodie arrived at the Cape with the first shipment of fifty Scotsmen. It was then, as he later wrote, that his troubles began.[55]

It appears that during the preceding months, Hamilton Ross had publicised the venture in Cape Town circles and, to his chagrin, had encountered much hostility. The majority of Cape Town's inhabitants were slave-owners and many of them derived a considerable income from the hire of their slaves to the surrounding farmers.[56] The richer among the latter likewise derived profit from this source.[57] They thus objected to any scheme which might depress the value of their slaves.

Ross declined to contribute to the costs of any but the first shipment and Moodie, who had little or no capital, was obliged to request a loan from the government-controlled bank in Cape Town. This was granted and the indentures were handed over to the bank as security. He found no difficulty at all in disposing of the first fifty men, nor initially, of the hundred and fifty who followed them. The majority were employed in Cape Town itself, for, as Moodie later observed, 'in Cape Town there is capital to support the labour' and consequently it was there that the highest wages were offered.[58]

It was in Moodie's interest that his apprentices should be paid high wages, or at least high nominal wages, because this would enable him to recoup his expenditure and reap a profit as quickly as possible, through the deduction of substantial monthly sums from their earnings. Thus he would transfer the contract of service to the new employer, on condition that the latter would guarantee the payment of these monthly sums, or would pay them himself in advance. The success of the speculation consequently rested on the preservation of the contract between the apprentice and the person to whom Moodie had transferred his services, and on the willingness of the latter to stand by his guarantee. It was the non-fulfilment of both these conditions which led to the failure of Moodie's venture and was largely responsible for his bitterness towards the Somerset regime.

Moodie's apprentices fiercely resented being forced to submit to high deductions from their monthly wages. They did everything possible to secure their release from Moodie's clutches. Some adopted the strategy of making themselves so obnoxious to their contracted employers that they were returned to Moodie's hands and he was forced to support them without profit. Others simply deserted from the service of those who had made arrangements with Moodie, and hired themselves to other individuals. In neither case was Moodie able to secure effective government support for the enforcement of the original contracts. In his view, the Governor's attitude was consistently unsympathetic and in accordance with this attitude, the 'degraded and dependent Bench' declined to punish the deserters or those who harboured them.[59]

Given the sensitivity which the colonial government had shown in the past to the needs of employers, its attitude in Moodie's case at first sight appears surprising. But in fact it was precisely this sensitivity which lay behind the reluctance to support Moodie; for the claims he made on his apprentices forced up their wage demands, rendered them discontented and made them liable to desert. Cultural factors may also have played a part. Thus Moodie observed that:

> The employers, accustomed to slave labour, were indolent, took little trouble to support their claims . . . even the English were disposed to consider the power which the master claimed over a white servant in a colony where blacks only laboured, an encroachment on liberty.[60]

Moreover, the white servants had behind them a tradition of resistance and their spirited opposition to coercive exploitation may well have taken the authorities unawares.

However, Somerset did take one important step to remedy the situation, which, although it was little use to Moodie, was to give considerable support to the employers of white workers brought to the Cape during the next decade. In June 1818 he issued a Proclamation especially designed to prevent the desertion of white indentured servants and apprentices. They were not to leave their masters' service without written consent, on pain of up to two months' imprisonment and a fine of twenty-five Rixdollars for a first offence, and corporal punishment for a second offence. Juvenile apprentices could be imprisoned for up to three months for a second offence. Persons who harboured such contracted employees without the consent of their masters would be fined two hundred Rixdollars for the first offence, five hundred for the second and could be imprisoned for up to six months for a third offence. Finally, there was a provision which was perhaps designed to delay the conversion of imported workers into independent settlers: no person discharged from his master's service could claim the right of residence in the colony, except with the express permission of the governor.[61]

Moodie commented drily that the new law was simply another weapon with which the colonial government could favour its friends and oppress its enemies. He was reluctant to proceed against his apprentices, fearing that failure would further weaken his position. Had he possessed the means, he might have been able to face his apprentices with the choice between compulsory employment under his own direction, and at low wages, and employment with others on the terms laid down by him. He did, in fact, take some of them to work on a farm which he had bought in the interior, but was unable to prevent them from deserting and returning to Cape Town. He could not force them to work for others. All he could do was prosecute them, or those who harboured them, when they did so without his agreement. Thus, in his case, the net effect of the new law was to discourage 'respectable persons' from employing them, 'as their demands were incompatible with Mr M.'s legal claims on them'.[62] As a result, the apprentices were driven from pillar to post in search of employers who 'chose to incur the risk of paying them their wages'.[63] Eventually Moodie capitulated and allowed them to pay him in their own time. Many of them did so, but in the meanwhile the interest accumulated on the loan he had received from the bank, and he thus derived little profit from the whole undertaking.

The next large-scale importation of white workers into the colony took place in 1820, as part of the 1820 settlement scheme, in terms of which between 4 000 and 5 000 British emigrants were settled in the Zuurveld area, to provide an effective barrier against the attempts of the Xhosa to reoccupy the land from which they had been driven in 1819. From the perspective adopted in this essay, the importance of the 1820 emigration was that it drew together and threw into relief the features which had come to characterise the labour market of the colony over the past thirteen years.

Because the settlement was conceived primarily as a strategic measure, two important restrictions were placed upon the leaders of the parties of settlers. The first was that the parties were to consist of a minimum of ten men and that the leader (or the group, in the case of many of the independent parties) was to be granted one hundred acres per man. The second laid down that the settlers would not be allowed to employ slaves on their land.[64] This prohibition has often been attributed to humanitarian motives; no doubt these played a part, but uppermost in Bathurst's mind was the fear that if slaves were allowed to be held on the lands adjoining the Fish River, slave-raiding expeditions might be sent across the border into Xhosa territory, thereby disturbing the precarious peace which had been concluded in 1819.[65] In consequence of these restrictions and perhaps also because of the government's awareness of the scarcity of labour at the Cape, the 1820 settlement was to be based more or less exclusively on white labour.[66]

From the published sources it is difficult to estimate accurately the number of white articled servants included in the emigration. Edwards gives a list of some seven parties headed by 'Sole Proprietors', comprising 184 men, but the list is not complete.[67] Moreover, many of the parties listed as 'Independent' included articled servants.[68] Pringle wrote that some two-thirds of the emigrants were of working-class origin and not possessed of 'worldly substance'.[69] Some of these, however, had come as independent emigrants, or as members of parties subsidised by their parishes.

The high wages available in Cape Town and the employment opportunities for artisans and tradesmen in the new settlements of Grahamstown and Port Elizabeth, as well as in Graaff-Reinet, which at this time was rapidly expanding, offered ready incentives for the desertion of the emigrant servants. As early as May 1820, Somerset's Proclamation of 1818 was invoked against them by the Landdrost of Albany. They were warned that they would be imprisoned if they absconded and they were not allowed to leave the locations without the written consent of their masters. However, the rapid decline in the fortunes of the latter was to lead, at the end of 1822, to the relaxation of the pass restrictions; when their crops failed for the third time, they were compelled to acquiesce in the desertion of their remaining employees for they could ill afford to continue supporting them. Many artisans and labourers from the independent parties likewise left Albany to seek their fortunes elsewhere.[70] The majority found lucrative employment. John Ingram, who had had the foresight to release his employees relatively early,[71] reported in 1823 that

> they were all in full employment in different services, and getting six times as much wages as Mr. Ingram gave them ... [they] have watches in their pockets, and are perfectly well clothed—men who had not a stitch of clothes on when they left Ireland.[72]

The leaders of the parties could not so easily leave their locations, for they had sunk their capital in them and many were deeply indebted to the government. They stayed on in considerably reduced circumstances, some dependent for their welfare on handouts from the Fund for the Relief of Distressed Settlers, of which the London Missionary Society missionary, John Philip, was the chairman.

By early 1823 the dissatisfaction of these people was well known in England, and two Commissioners were dispatched to the Cape, with instructions to enquire into the general state of the colony and 'particularly ... into the circumstances connected with the settlements lately formed and the probability of their success and advancement'.[73] They were also instructed to enquire into the general condition of slaves and Hottentots. Macmillan has attributed the inclusion of the latter instruction to the influence of Wilberforce, urged on by Philip;[74] he is probably right, but there is one telling sentence which suggests that the home government was also specifically concerned with the problems of labour supply in Albany:

> You will refer to the relations of the colonial government with Hottentots and the means of introducing labour, the nature of free labour, especially in the frontier districts where the climate may be less well suited to Europeans.[75]

In May 1823 the Colonial Office took a step which provides concrete evidence of the existence of such a concern. Wilmot Horton (Under-Secretary for War and the Colonies) concluded an agreement with John Ingram in terms of which Ingram was to convey two hundred men, fifty women and one hundred children from the south of Ireland to the Cape, at government expense. In addition, Ingram was to convey fifty persons at his own expense. The four hundred emigrants were all to be under indenture to Ingram for three years and he undertook that they would not be made chargeable on the colonial revenue during that period. He was to be fully responsible for the organisation of the emigration. In his correspondence with Wilmot Horton, Ingram gave the distinct impression that the emigrants were destined for Albany. He said 'his motive in returning home [to Cork] was to secure European labourers, as he perceived that a pledge had been given that slave labour was not to be applied on the new grants'.[76] He assured Horton that his scheme would be attended with the happiest results by 'providing for some of the poor Irish and ultimately by destroying slavery'.[77] Nevertheless, he added (untruthfully) that he had the means to employ all of the emigrants himself.

If the Colonial Office really was under the impression that Ingram's apprentices were destined for Albany, its ready acceptance of his proposals at this date seems extraordinary. In the first place, although Horton and Bathurst were aware that the servants brought out in 1820 had deserted their masters and that there was consequently a serious shortage of labour in Albany, they also knew of the distress of the abandoned employers, and there were grounds to fear that labourers imported now would go the same way as those who had preceded them. In the second place, Ingram's scheme was conceived by him as a speculative venture similar to Moodie's. It would thus be attended by many of the same disadvantages—chiefly high wage demands and an increased incentive to desert—as had attended Moodie's emigration of 1817. Moreover, it should have been clear to the Colonial Office that a profit-seeking entrepreneur, as Ingram was, would take his commodities to the best market, which at that date was indisputably located in Cape Town and the surrounding districts.

The story of Ingram's apprentices is a long one and can only be briefly told here. Well over four hundred men, women and children were recruited in Cork and the surrounding countryside, and conveyed to Cove to await departure. However, the ship was delayed for a month because, among other reasons, the government inspector found the provisions Ingram had bought to be of inferior quality and a new supply had to be obtained from the navy stores. In the interim, 154 of the original recruits decided against going with Ingram.[78] He attributed this to the influence of the Catholic priests, but it seems that a more important influence was that of an unnamed inhabitant of Cove, who had recently returned from the Cape and who described it as a 'land of monsters and starvation'.[79] The delay had already cost Ingram a considerable amount of money and he was compelled to make up the complement as quickly as possible from among the unemployed populations of Cork and Cove.

On 31 December 1823 Ingram arrived at the Cape with 341 apprenticed servants, 176 men, fifty-nine women and 101 children.[80] Several of the apprentices had signed indentures on board the ship, after its departure from Cove, and some protested that they had been forced to do so, as Ingram had threatened them with the witholding of food and with imprisonment on arrival. Twenty-five had persisted in their refusal to sign. The attitude of the colonial courts to these latter stands out in marked contrast to that evidenced towards Moodie's apprentices six years earlier. Thus the Court of Justice upheld on appeal the decision of the Sitting Commissioner that those who had refused to sign the indentures should nevertheless be presumed to have acquiesced in their terms, 'from the fact of their embarkation at Cork'[81] and from the publicity allegedly given by Ingram to the terms of service. During the course of 1824, Ingram instituted proceedings against twenty of his apprentices, on various charges of breach of contract, and in nearly every case the defendant was sentenced to a short term of imprisonment with hard labour and compelled to return to Ingram's service. A shoemaker, John Rocke, was flogged for his second refusal to pay Ingram the sum he required of him.[82]

A number of reasons can be adduced for this change in attitude. The greater number of prosecutions can be ascribed partly to Ingram himself— to his greater ruthlessness and to his specific situation. For unlike Moodie, he possessed an effective sanction against his apprentices, in that he could compel those who refused to pay him to work on his estate at Sonnebloem, on the outskirts of Cape Town, where he was engaged in building a wine store. But this does not sufficiently explain his willingness to prosecute, nor the consistent support given to his claims by the Sitting Commissioners and the Chief Justice. The more fundamental explanation lies in the growing awareness of the importance of imported labour to the Cape labour market. Thus, although the western Cape was undergoing a mild recession during the early 1820s, all but fifty-two of Ingram's apprentices found employment at high wages within a few weeks of their arrival. Of the fifty-two, it was said that they too could find employment if they were not needed by Ingram. Of the men 117 were artisans and their labour was particularly in demand,[83] but there was also a demand for farm labourers, restricted only by the inability of the farmers to pay the high wages required by the indebted apprentices. Landdrost Stoll was asked by the Commissioners whether he thought there was a demand for labour 'of this description' in the country districts and he replied:

> I think the demand for labour in the country is even greater than in Cape Town, for I know some *wealthy* farmers, who have fewer ploughs upon their land than they formerly had, solely in consequence of their inability to procure labourers, and I also know that considerable tracts of land in this district remain un-cultivated from the want of hands ... Mr Dreyer once mentioned to me that he had in contemplation to write to England for twenty labourers ... I have heard others express how glad they would be to obtain assistance of this sort upon their farms. I have heard Mr Sebastian van Reenen say so.[84]

The only disadvantages said to accompany the use of white labour on the farms were its cost and, according to some witnesses, the unwillingness of the apprentices to submit to the discipline imposed upon the slaves and the rest of the labour force.[85] The Commissioners concluded their report on Ingram's emigration with the recommendation that further emigrations should be encouraged, but that they should not in future be organised by private individuals, because of the adverse effects of the heavy indebtedness of the apprentices which was a function of such speculative ventures.

The recovery of the fortunes of the Albany settlers, which can be dated approximately from the beginning of 1825, gave even greater importance to the question of imported labour. By that date, Somerset's attitude to the settlement had changed, and the shift of the settlers' activities from arable farming to pastoral farming and frontier trading was finally given sanction and encouragement. Credit was extended on condition that the settlers began to pay taxes in 1826. But one major drawback remained to inhibit the prosperity of the settlement: the acute shortage of labour in the district.

In July 1824, Thomas Carlisle had written to the Commissioners, asking them to back his request that the government assist him to convey a party of labourers from England to Albany for, he wrote,

> It is decidedly the opinion of the settlers in general, that no measure whatever can go further in removing the difficulties by which they are surrounded, than a constant and gradual importation of labour ... servants cannot be procured for double the wages they monthly obtained before arriving in this colony.[86]

According to him, current wages of labourers in Albany were between twenty-five and thirty Rixdollars a month, 'with provisions and spirits, which additions almost double the first amounts, bread and corn being as high as from twenty to twenty-two Rixdollars per muid'.[87] However, Carlisle stressed that the ability of the settlers to profit from the proposed emigration would be entirely dependent on the extent to which the government was prepared to contribute to the cost of transport, for the settlers had not the capital to do so themselves. Were government to bear the expense, he said, Albany could probably absorb two hundred to three hundred men annually, 'for a considerable time'.[88] In March 1825, Somerset wrote to Bathurst in essentially the same terms, declaring that the want of labourers in Albany threatened the success of the whole settlement scheme and enclosing a detailed proposal for the supply of six hundred youths aged between eleven and sixteen years and 250 girls aged between ten and fourteen years.[89] They should be brought out at government expense and 'be bound respectively to the Government of the Cape of Good Hope, who should be charged with procuring them good and humane masters amongst the English settlers'.[90]

Speculative immigration had thus been rejected as a solution to the labour problems of Albany, for it was generally recognised that the settlers were not in a position to pay the high wages which were required by the victims of 'speculating individuals', or the indemnities demanded by the latter, as the case of Ingram had shown, and that this, combined with the relative attractions of the Cape Town labour market, would inevitably lead to the desertion of labourers thus procured.

The only way to avoid this system, however, was for the home government to bear the entire expense, and this it was not prepared to do. It might have been possible for the government to demand repayment upon the transfer of the apprentices to their new masters, but this would carry with it disadvantages similar to those of the speculative immigration, though in a less extreme form. Moreover, even if no debt were involved, the normal rate of wages which the settlers proposed to offer to the apprentices was below that in Albany itself and nearer Cape Town, so that—

> the same spirit of discontent and disappointment that was so fatal to the engagements made between the settlers and their former labourers and that occasioned so much embarrassment to the local authorities on the first emigration would not fail to show itself as soon as the labourers acquired a knowledge of the actual demand for their labour in the colony and of the benefit which their engagement would prevent them from reaping.[91]

It is a measure of the seriousness with which both the English settlers and the colonial government regarded the labour shortage in Albany that correspondence on the subject of assisted emigration schemes continued after the departure of the Commissioners of Enquiry, despite the latter's gloomy opinion of the efficacy of such measures. It had become clear by 1828, however, that if the urgent labour needs of the settlers were to be met and the strategic settlement thereby rendered viable, an alternative would have to be found to plans for the introduction of indentured servants from Britain.

Such a strategy had in fact been in the process of elaboration during the preceding two years and on 21 April 1827, following extensive deliberation, it had received the official sanction of the Governor-in-Council. On that day the Advisory Council requested the Lieutenant-Governor

> to cause the draft of an ordinance to be prepared as usual for removing all existing prohibitions to the employment of the natives of the interior as free labourers, and for establishing the necessary regulations for the introduction and management of these people.[92]

This was a major reversal of official policy, for, as we have seen, the colonial and imperial governments had, since the first years of the second occupation, attempted to discourage all intercourse with the indigenous peoples across the borders of the colony.[93]

The first indication of a change in official thinking regarding their employment as herdsmen and domestic servants came in Somerset's dispatch of 31 March 1825, in which he appealed for a supply of apprentices from Britain. He informed Bathurst that over the past twelve months the influx of refugees from the war-torn lands beyond the Orange River had increased:

> Many of these have since wandered into the Graaff-Reinet district and it has become a question how to dispose of them—I have therefore taken upon me to direct that they should be apprenticed to the English settlers in Albany for terms (none exceeding seven years) according to their ages, under very strict conditions as to good treatment etc.[94]

Bathurst minuted 'approve'. Four months later Somerset reported that there were now some three hundred 'Mantatees or Goes' in Graaff-Reinet and Somerset districts, 'in a state of dreadful want and emaciation'.[95] He had, however, deviated from his original intention that they should be apportioned among the settlers in Albany. Instead he had authorised Landdrost Stockenstrom to distribute them provisionally among any farmers or other residents of Graaff-Reinet district who were not slaveholders. Those 'not disposed of' would be sent to Albany.

In his correspondence with Stockenstrom, Somerset stressed that there had been no change in the general policy of denying entry into the colony to people from beyond its borders. An exception had been made in the present case only because of the destitute condition of the refugees. Nevertheless, in July 1826, after he had left the colony, Somerset wrote to R.W. Hay, Permanent Under-Secretary at the Colonial Office, drawing attention once more to 'the great scarcity of labourers' at the Cape and recommending

> that such individuals of these tribes 'Mantatees and Goes' as are not disqualified from age or infirmity should be invited into the colony with the understanding that they are to be apprenticed for a term of years (seven or ten) and children until they attain the age of eighteen the same as the Hottentots.[96]

Bathurst forwarded this letter to the Lieutenant-Governor, Sir Richard Bourke (Somerset's replacement), asking him to take an early opportunity of bringing the proposal before the Advisory Council. It was clear that the Secretary of State had no quarrel with the substance of Somerset's suggestions, though he did object to the idea that the individuals referred to should be indentured 'in the same manner as prize negroes'.[97]

Thus in February 1827, the proposal was laid before the Council. By this time, however, it had become much wider in scope. The obscure designation 'Mantatees and Goes' had been broadened to include all individuals of 'the neighbouring nations'. The Council asked the land-drosts of the four eastern frontier districts to consider whether it was expedient to invite such people into their districts as servants of the colonists and under what conditions they should be admitted. Though the minutes of the Council proceedings do not betray any special concern with the interests of the English settlers, a different impression was created by Bourke. In a private letter to the Landdrost of Albany, he stated that he had

> written to the Secretary of State to suggest the expediency of allowing the farmers in Albany to engage Caffres in their service as labourers under such regulations as might ensure an equitable arrangement between them. His Lordship has approved of the suggestion and given permission to Caffres being engaged by settlers in Albany not owning slaves ... I think you appeared convinced of the utility of this measure.[98]

The other landdrosts appeared to have been similarly convinced, though Andries Stockenstrom withheld his approval until the terms upon which the 'savages' were to be admitted had been clarified. The discussion of these terms occupied the landdrosts and the Council intermittently for nearly three months and the opinions they expressed are of considerable importance, for they reveal a fundamental shift in attitude towards the problems of the exploitation and control of labour in the colony. The landdrosts were asked to consider whether the incoming Africans should be indentured to the colonists for long periods, whether they and their children should simply be made subject to the controls then exerted over the Khoisan, or whether they should be left free to change masters as they wished. At issue, was the whole system of forced labour which had been reinforced in colonial law since the abolition of the slave trade.

Stockenstrom expressed himself more forcefully on this subject than did the other three landdrosts, yet his views were shot through with ambivalence. He had once referred to Caledon's Hottentot Code of 1809 as 'the greatest blessing hitherto conferred on that people',[99] yet he made it clear in his correspondence with the Colonial Secretary that it was the spirit of that code which he praised, not the practice. Opposing the principle of apprenticeship in the present case, he pointed out that 'it will only tend to generate that feeling of rancour and prejudice between the colonists and the apprentices which pretty nearly the same system has established between the farmer and the aborigines of the soil'.[100] He gave a vivid description of the way he thought the conflict would develop:

> For some time the parties will be happy together, the master because he is relieved from his own labour, the savage because he is released from a bloody enemy and gets once more a sufficient meal; but no sooner will the latter be recovered from the panic caused by the battle-axe of the foe or the terror of starvation, no sooner will he have discovered the liberty of some of our laws that the power of his master is not absolute over him, than he will show his aversion to his fetters, become obstinate; the master resists, the apprentice deserts, is retaken and punished, all mutual kind feeling is lost—the magistrate is a couple of hundred miles distant, the apprentice harasses the master by vexatious complaints and dragging the latter for weeks after him to defend himself at the seat of authority—for want of proof neither party can get satisfaction—the offended master in his turn takes his revenge at home where he is despotic, and the upshot is that they try to do each other as much mischief as they can.[101]

He was adamant that Africans should not be 'decoyed' or 'enticed' into the colony—any attempt to use force would lead to the desertion of the apprentice who would 'leave the master, the indenture and the colony after perhaps having learned the use of our arms, being entrusted with these and knowing the weakness of our frontiers'.[102] Only those driven into the colony by starvation could be expected to become useful servants. In this regard, Stockenstrom showed a clear and coldly cynical understanding of the process of proletarianisation taking place on the eastern frontier. In February 1827 he wrote that a large influx of free labourers could not be expected 'as long as the interior is in a state of peace and space aplenty'.[103] The following year, as he was preparing to expel the Xhosa chief Maqomo from his lands on the Kat River, he informed the Colonial Secretary 'that there can be no doubt that in a very short time as many Caffres will avail themselves of said enactment (Ordinance 49) as it will be convenient for the government to admit'.[104] In his opinion, these people should regard the Ordinance as a greater benefit to themselves than it was to the colony, for it would relieve them of the need to plunder for food. Persuasion would thus be as unnecessary as it was impolitic: 'the machine must be left to work itself'.[105] In the meantime, the colony could count on the services of refugees from the north.

Stockenstrom's advocacy of free labour was not unqualified, however. He held that while the new recruits should be left free to dispose of their labour-power as they wished, the decision as to whether they should dispose of it at all was not to be left to them: 'they shall have some fixed abode and honest occupation, on pain of being taken up and severely punished as vagabonds if they go about or collect in gangs'. Like the Hottentots, 'they should be made to work—unless they can prove that they can live without'.[106]

The reader who is familiar with the practical effects of similar provisions in the Caledon Code[107] may conclude that the existence of this contradiction in Stockenstrom's argument renders the whole of it nonsensical. But to do so would be to ignore the evidence, borne out in the testimony of the other landdrosts, that by this time the administration had real reasons for questioning the efficacy of the forced labour system, not only with respect to the employment of Africans, but also with respect to the Hottentots, though the factors involved in the two cases were not identical. Thus the landdrosts of Somerset and Albany, drawing on their experience with the 'Mantatees', concurred with Stockenstrom in his opinion that compulsion would provoke resistance and desertion, if it did not first lead to loss of life.[108] General Dundas of Albany drew the Council's attention to the fact that Africans sought work with the colonists only in order to accumulate cattle, with which they would sooner or later return whence they came. They had no intention of remaining in the colony indefinitely and should not be encouraged to do so against their will.

It is perhaps significant that a dissenting opinion was expressed not by a government official but by a meeting of the white inhabitants of Uitenhage, called to discuss the proposed ordinance, though their landdrost, Colonel Cuyler, had not distinguished himself in the defence of free labour prior to this date. The Uitenhage colonists argued that long indentures (from five to seven years) were necessary in order to suppress 'the vagrant disposition of the Hottentots and other natives'.[109]

Summing up, the Council came down on the side of the three landdrosts, though it noted that 'setting aside, for the moment, the justice of the case, there can be little doubt that the boon would thus be far more valuable to the colonists if the means of compulsion were safe and easy'.[110] However (setting aside the justice of the case) the Councillors found consolation in the discovery that the majority of Africans would prefer to return eventually to their places of origin, rather than to remain in the colony:

> Whilst the colony is thus likely to be relieved from the fear of being overburdened with the old and helpless, it is impossible not to be gratified with the prospect of the blessings of civilisation being at the same time, in this manner, gradually and naturally introduced amongst these ignorant tribes.[111]

The final draft of the ordinance laid down that no engagement, whether verbal or in writing, was to be binding for longer than one month, unless drawn up in writing before a Clerk of the Peace, Justice of the Peace, or any person specially appointed by the Clerk of the Peace with the approbation of the governor.[112] Such written contracts might be binding for up to one year. Yet Stockenstrom's contradiction was well embedded in the framing of the ordinance. Africans seeking work were forbidden to move about without passes, which they were required to show on demand to any official or landholder. Those found without a pass could be press-ganged for up to twelve months. The ordinance thus provided a legal buttress for informal coercion similar to that contained in the Hottentot Code of 1809. It also made limited provision for the institution of child captivity which was so important in frontier society.[113]

There is of course a great danger in attempting to infer the existence of a given pattern of social relations merely from a study of legislation. Insofar as various forms of labour tenancy, rather than full-time service, existed in the frontier districts, legislation designed to restrict or facilitate the mobility of servants had only a partial relevance to actual practice.[114] Also, given the wide dispersal of settlers in the early nineteenth-century Cape, the extreme difficulties of communication and the thin spread of administrators, it is unlikely that legislation which countered settler interests was frequently enforced. Hence until more is known about the actual relations of exploitation which governed life in the frontier districts, no adequate examination of labour legislation is possible.

Nevertheless, there is evidence that the concern of government officials with the use of coercion in labour relations was not without roots in local conditions. If the provisions of Ordinance 49 leave one in doubt as to the depths of such concern, the same cannot be said of Ordinance 50, promulgated on 17 July 1828, just three days after the promulgation of

Ordinance 49. This measure repealed the Caledon Code and the laws which compelled the apprenticeship of Hottentot children and affirmed the right of Hottentots to ownership of land. Oral contracts of service were henceforth to be binding for one month only and registered contracts for a maximum of one year. Domestic punishment of servants was no longer admitted in law, but penal sanctions could be invoked against the servant (but not the master) for breach of contract. Thus, while the state continued to sanction the use of violence in the regulation of labour contracts, the most severe legal restrictions on the mobility of Hottentots were removed. Indeed, after the passage of Ordinance 50, the legal category 'Hottentot', ceased to exist.

Ordinance 50, like Ordinance 49, represented an attempt to increase the labour supply available to the colonists. However, its origins and purpose were rather more complex and obscure. It seems at least arguable that it was primarily a response to the resistance of the Hottentots themselves to the brutal controls which had been imposed on them. It was thus an attempt to diminish and depoliticise this resistance and thereby to increase the stability and productivity of this section of the colonial labour force.

Mention has already been made of the 'rancour and prejudice' which the enforcement of the Caledon Code had produced. This rancour was expressed in many ways through, for example, deliberate loafing, theft and destruction of the master's property, and desertion. The full scope and effect of Hottentot resistance to servitude after the collapse of Cape Khoikhoi and San independence has yet to be investigated by historians.[115] Let it suffice here to observe that the settlers' repeated complaints of the 'inertia', 'moral debasement' and 'vagrant disposition' of their servants should not be taken at face value. The same can be said of the 'increasing frequency of crimes committed by the Hottentots' which the Commissioners of Inquiry had noted in their Report on the Hottentot Population.[116] They wrote that

> the effect of angry words upon the Hottentots will sometimes lead them to commit violence, and not unfrequently cause them abruptly to leave their [masters'] service. Idleness and inebriety are habits to which they are fatally addicted, and the offence of cattle and sheep stealing is that for which they are most frequently brought before the courts of justice.[117]

It is well known that the refuge which their servants found at the missionary institutions was a source of particular annoyance to the colonists and that the missionaries, especially those of the London Missionary Society, played a prominent role in the campaign for Hottentot emancipation. But historians have tended to represent the LMS missionaries only as paternalistic protectors of a passive and helpless people. Insufficient attention has been paid to the process by which the Hottentots made the missionaries aware of their grievances and by which the missions, despite the pervasive paternalism of many of the missionaries, became foci for their collective politicisation.

Perhaps in the majority of cases and for much of the time the response of the indigenous people to their servile status took a turned-inward and self-destructive form, expressing itself in alcoholism and internecine conflict. This too awaits historical investigation. But in the present context it is necessary to point out that even a 'negative' response such as this, despite its advantages in the sphere of social control, would entail considerable costs for a colonial economy which was in the throes of a labour shortage.

In the view of those who promoted it locally,[118] Ordinance 50 could be expected to counteract these varied responses in a number of ways. Two principles were central to the arguments of those who advocated the granting of civil rights to the Hottentots: that they should have 'liberty to bring their labour to the best market'[119] and that they should be secure in their right to whatever property they were able to accumulate.[120] The operation of these two principles would remove the root cause of the apathy and 'lack of industry' so much complained of, and reduce the incidence of desertion and theft. Thus, the Commissioners of Inquiry pointed out that when Hottentots worked on their own account or on that of missionaries or 'builders and merchants', who paid them relatively well, they gave no sign of that 'want of energy' said to be inherent in their character.[121] Dr Philip likewise argued that, given adequate incentive, the Hottentots were as capable of physical and intellectual achievement as any other inhabitant of the colony. As to desertion, Philip averred that many of the aborigines of the colony, particularly those then living on its peripheries, preferred a life of extreme hardship in barren areas and even death, to service with the colonists under a system akin to slavery.[122] In his view, this situation would be reversed if labour coercion was 'outlawed:

> —make the coloured population in your colony free . . . permit the natives to choose their own masters—secure to them, inviolate from the grasp of colonial violence, the right which God and nature have given them to their offspring— allow them to bring their labour to a free market, and the farmers will no longer have occasion to complain of a want of servants.[123]

The architects of emancipation may also have hoped it would give means of depoliticising the class struggle within the colony. If the free (non-slave) coloured population of the colony were no longer singled out by repressive laws as a group apart from the whites, they would be less likely to regard themselves as 'a distinct class of the population',[124] and hence less likely to feel a sense of common grievance. Certainly it was expected that class differentiation among them would increase and that some would become independent peasant farmers, who would willingly make common cause with the frontier colonists in the defence of the colony against the Xhosa. Such was the inspiration of the Kat River settlement scheme.[125]

Further, emancipation would, in theory, remove the need for the missionary institutions to serve as 'houses of refuge'. The missionaries need no longer 'train up the Hottentots as a separate people',[126] for under the new dispensation they would, according to Dr Philip, willingly take service with the colonists, and the missionaries would be permitted to minister to them at the villages nearest their place of work and on the farms themselves. The mission stations could then be gradually run down and funds diverted to the propagation of the gospel throughout the colony. The Commissioners of Inquiry proposed that 'individuals who [had] acquired property at the institutions' and who had resided on mission grounds for a considerable period should be granted freehold tenure and that only the schools and church buildings should remain under the jurisdiction of the missionaries.[127]

The passage of Ordinance 50 may also have been intended to affect the labour market of the colony in ways which were less directly connected with Khoisan resistance. For example, the abolition of the Caledon Code and related legislation would (again in theory) divest local officials of the extensive powers of patronage which they had possessed with respect to the distribution of labour-power: until more is known about the degree of commercialisation and capitalisation attained by Cape agriculture at this period, about the structural divisions within it and about the prevalence of relations of labour tenancy, the possible effects of such an elimination of patronage cannot be projected. It cannot be assumed that increased labour mobility would favour the more efficient and more highly capitalised farmers. Suffice it to say here that the activities of local officials in this regard had met with the disapproval of the Governor some time before the introduction of the ordinance.[128]

It would of course be incorrect to suppose that the motives suggested above were shared equally by all who promoted emancipation in government circles. Dr Philip in particular was genuinely outraged by the suffering of the colonial Khoisan and had devoted a large part of his life to their cause. Certainly his first concern was not with the labour needs of the colony. But his arguments may have influenced others for whom such a concern was dominant. More important, it would be incorrect to assume that the colonists in general were convinced of the need for a measure such as Ordinance 50. Indeed, it is well known that, in general, they were not. But, while it may be that historians have accepted too uncritically the evidence of settler opposition to the ordinance, the existence of such evidence does not invalidate the hypothesis advanced above concerning the origins and purpose of this measure. For Ordinance 50 was not introduced in isolation from other attempts at state intervention in the labour market. It was introduced together with Ordinance 49. The latter measure was designed to increase the labour supply in the frontier districts, particularly in Albany, where the shortage of labour was most acutely felt, and hence to stabilise the economic, political and military situation in this vitally important part of the colony.[129] It thus enabled the colonial government to undertake an initially unpopular review of colonial labour legislation, a review which was necessary in the light of the resistance of the Khoisan, the protests of the missionaries on their behalf and the inconveniences of the previous system of labour control.

Seen in this way, both Ordinances 49 and 50 need to be regarded as instances of state regulation of the Cape labour market. Indeed, they may be regarded as the culmination of attempts at labour market regulation over the two decades since the abolition of the slave trade. Both were responses to the development of the Cape labour market as a whole. Taken apart from that whole, they cannot be satisfactorily understood. In the case of Ordinance 50, explanations which rely exclusively on the role of the missionaries should be discarded in favour of an investigation of the class struggle which took place within the context outlined in this essay.

Notes

1 S.D. Neumark, *Economic Influences on the South African Frontier, 1652–1836*, Stanford, 1957

2 *Memorandum on a Maritime Peace*, 1814, quoted in I.E. Edwards, *The 1820 Settlers in South Africa: a study in British colonial policy*, London, 1934, p. 1

3 C.W.G. Schumann, *Structural Changes and Business Cycles in South Africa, 1806–9*, London, 1938, Table 3, p. 44

4 For the use of slave labour in the east and the increasing demand for non-slave labour in the west, see above, pp. 178–82. The term 'Hottentot' was used in the early nineteenth-century Cape as both an ethnic and a legal category. As an ethnic category it was used loosely to refer to the descendants of the indigenous Khoikhoi pastoralists who were distinguished in colonial parlance from the 'Bosjesmen' living on the peripheries of the Colony and from the Xhosa on the eastern frontier. This usage was necessarily imprecise, for the distinctions between Khoikhoi and San ('Bushmen') had been blurred even in pre-colonial

times and were no less confused in the early nineteenth century. See Richard Elphick, *Kraal and Castle: Khoikhoi and the Founding of White South Africa*, Yale University Press, 1977, and Shula Marks, 'Khoisan Resistance to the Dutch in the 17th and 18th Centuries', *JAH*, xiii, 1, 1972. Furthermore, the process of colonisation was accompanied by racial admixture and by far-reaching cultural change which still awaits research. The racial heterogeneity of the 'Hottentots' was sometimes recognised in colonial discourse. Thus the off-spring of Khoisan and slaves (and of Khoisan and Xhosa) were sometimes known as 'Bastard Hottentots' and the offspring of whites and Khoisan were sometimes known as 'Colonial Bastards'. Yet 'Hottentot' remained a port-manteau term.

As a legal category, it referred to all those who were actual or potential victims of the pass law of 1809 (known as the Hottentot Code) and the pro-clamation of 1812 which regulated the forced apprenticeship of 'Hottentot' children. It thus distinguished this category of unfree workers from slaves, prize negroes and white indentured servants. As the foregoing remarks have shown, these people were not all of pure Khoikhoi or San descent. However, because of the perjorative connotations of the term 'Hottentot' they will be referred to as Khoisan in this essay, except where nineteenth-century colonial usage is quoted or paraphrased. It should be stressed that the adoption of the term 'Khoisan' does not imply any prejudgment of the process of economic and cultural change which the people concerned were undergoing during this period. It does, however, remind us that they had a pre-colonial past.

5 In 1803 Dirk van Reenen observed that 'The wealth of the Colony in cattle and sheep depends, for the greater part, on this area' and that 'in those districts most of the cattle and heaviest animals are produced, the pasture being excep-tionally rich and luxuriant'. D.G. van Reenen, *Die Joernaal van Dirk Gysbert van Reenen, 1803*, Van Riebeeck Society publication, No. 18, pp. 275 and 291–3, quoted in Neumark, *Economic Influences*, pp. 111–2

6 W.M. Freund, 'The Eastern Frontier of the Cape Colony During the Batavian Period (1803–6)', *JAH*, xiii, 4, 1972, p. 645

7 Col. R. Collins, 'Supplement to the relation of a Journey into the country of the Bosjesmen and Caffre People', July 1809, in D. Moodie, *The Record*, Cape Town, 1960, Part V, p. 15

8 Collins, 'Concluding Report', 6 Aug. 1809, in Moodie, Part V, p. 20

9 Collins, 'Journal of a tour to the North-Eastern Boundary, the Orange River and the Storm Mountains, 1809', in Moodie, Part V, p. 6

10 Collins, 'Notes made on a journey to the southern branches of the T'Ky, and through Kaffraria', July 1809, in Moodie, Part V, p. 41

11 'They should be able to reside with the inhabitants, except such of them as are in the service of government, or at the missionary institutions, or as understand trades, which it would be desirable to encourage them to exercise at the several drostdies': Collins, 'Concluding Report', in Moodie, Part V, p. 22

12 Collins, 'Supplement . . .', in Moodie, Part V, pp. 15, 16

13 Stockenstrom (the elder) to Bird, Graaff-Reinet, 19 October 1808, in Moodie, Part V, p. 60

14 Cf. CO 48/69, Bird to Stockenstrom, 27 August 1823; Plaskett to Stockenstrom, 21 July 1825

15 Collins, 'Concluding Report', in Moodie, Part V, p. 21

16 *Ibid.*
17 Collins, 'Supplement . . .', Part V, p. 8
18 Collins, 'Concluding Report', p. 24
19 Proclamation issued by the Earl of Caledon, Nov. 1809, quoted in full in J. Philip, *Researches in South Africa*, London, 1828, Appendix II
20 See for example W.M. Macmillan, *The Cape Colour Question*, London, 1937, p. 160; I.E. Edwards, *Towards Emancipation*, Cardiff, 1942, and Philip, *Researches*, p. xvii
21 Macmillan, *ibid.*
22 Edwards, *Towards Emancipation*, p. 52
23 Quoted in Neumark, *Economic Influences*, p. 116
24 Quoted in *ibid.*
25 See above, p. 173, and *ibid.*, 125–32. Between 1806 and 1824 the number of livestock in the Colony increased by 70 per cent (Neumark, *Economic Influences*, p. 127, and Table 8).
26 Quoted in Neumark, *Economic Influences*, p. 117
27 Cf. *ibid.*, p. 163
28 Quoted in *ibid.*, p. 112
29 Collins, 'Notes made on a Journey . . .', in Moodie, Part V, p. 38
30 CO 48/70, Somerset to Bathurst, 1 October 1825
31 *Ibid.*
32 CO 48/70, Enclosure No. I, Bigge and Colebrook to Somerset, 20 August 1825
33 CO 48/106, D'Escury, Inspector of Lands and Woods to Plaskett, 4 July 1826
34 CO 48/106, Commissioners to Bourke, 20 July 1826
35 Neumark, *Economic Influences*, Table 13, p. 162
36 It is even possible that the number of slaves held in the eastern districts increased as free labour became relatively more expensive and difficult to procure.
37 CO 48/79, Report of the Commissioners of Inquiry on the Emigration of Mr Ingram's Settlers and Apprenticed Servants in the Year 1823, June 1825
38 Edwards, *Towards Emancipation*, p. 50
39 CO 48/84, Proceedings of the Council on the Subject of the Tax on Slaves, proposed by H.M. Commissioners of Inquiry, 15 December 1826, enclosed in letter from Bourke to Bathurst, 17 December 1826
40 CO 48/79, Enclosure No. 8, evidence of van Ryneveld, Deputy Fiscal to the Commissioners of Inquiry, 13 August 1824. It was common practice for the wine farmers to hire their slaves to the corn farmers 'during the short interval when their waggons are sending their wine to market'. CO 48/79, Enclosure No. 11, evidence of Mr Stoll to the Commissioners, 27 August 1824
41 CO 48/84, Proceedings of the Council . . ., 15 December 1826. By a Proclamation of 1806 the Rixdollar was fixed at its nominal (1795) value of 4s. However, it rapidly depreciated until it was officially devalued to 1s. 6d. in 1825. Neumark, (p. xiii) gives the following values:

Year	Rate s.	d.		Year	Rate s.	d.
1875	4	0		1820	1	9.00
1805	3	4.00		1821	1	8.00
1816	2	1.00		1822	1	8.00
1817	1	9.25		1823	1	6.75
1818	1	9.00		1824	1	5.50
1819	1	10.05		1825	1	6.00

42 CO 48/84, Proceedings of the Council . . .
43 CO 48/84, Annexure 13, extract from the evidence of T.F. Dreyer to the Commissioners. Dreyer owned a wine farm and a corn farm
44 Philip, *Researches*, Appendix VI
45 CO 48/84, Annexure 13, extract from the evidence of T.F. Dreyer to the Commissioners of enquiry
46 CO 48/106, D'Escury to Plaskett, 4 July 1826; cf. also CO 48/79, Enclosure No. 8, van Ryneveld to the Commissioners, 13 August 1824. In the same year there were 48 699 whites at the Cape. The estimated size of the Hottentot population in 1823 was 30 549. (T. Pringle, *Narrative of a Residence in South Africa*, Cape Town, 1966. Pringle took the figure from G. Thompson, *Travels and Adventures in South Africa*, London, 1827.)
47 CO 48/79, Encl. 8, van Ryneveld to Commissioners, 13 August 1824
48 CO 48/79, Encl. 11, Stoll to Commissioners, 27 August 1824
49 Philip, *Researches*, p. 314 (emphasis in the text), and p. 354. There were eight skillings to the Rixdollar. This disparity reflected more than a difference in the manner of remuneration between town and country, for Philip noted that in the rural areas of Albany and Somerset, Hottentots could earn ten Rixdollars a month or fifty Rixdollars per annum while Hottentots impressed by the local authorities to work in the villages of the interior might get as little as two or three skillings a month. *Researches*, pp. 312, 354
50 CO 48/79, Encl. 10, evidence of William Reeves to the Commissioners, 28 August 1824; Encl. 11, Stoll, 27 August 1824; Encl. 12, B. Moodie, 28 August 1824; Encl. 21, Rocke, 16 November 1824; Encl. 25, summary of J. Ingram's Statement to Wilmot Horton (May?) 1823; CO 414/11, Mr Benjamin Moodie's Statement of the Circumstances attending the emigration of his apprentices from England; CO 48/82, Royal Engineers' Office to Bourke, 12 May 1826
51 CO 48/79, Ingram to Wilmot Horton, 5 May 1823
52 *Ibid.*; John Ingram wrote of the articled servants he brought with him in 1820: 'on their arrival in the Colony they found such farming mechanics got six shillings per day and labours [sic] three shillings per day. They became clamourous and at length on Lord Charles Somerset taking into consideration the great exertions I had made to fulfil the intentions of Parliament per his letter of the 8 January 1822 . . . I discharged my people to let them work for themselves'. In a summary of the contents of Ingram's statement to Horton, relating to his proposal to transport apprenticed servants from Ireland, it is written: 'He proposed to make similar terms with the fifty men that he had with the former ones'. Thus one may conclude that in 1822 he had profited from the transfer of the services of the people he brought with him in 1820. Others may have done the same.
53 CO 414/11, Mr Benjamin Moodie's Statement of the Circumstances attending the emigration of his apprentices from England
54 *Ibid.*
55 *Ibid.*
56 CO 48/79, Encl. 11, evidence of Stoll to the Commissioners, 27 August 1824
57 See note 45
58 CO 48/79, Encl. 12, evidence of B. Moodie to the Commissioners, 28 August 1824: about one quarter of the apprentices were employed 'in the labours of agriculture'

59 CO 414/11, Mr Benjamin Moodie's Statement

60 *Ibid.*

61 CO 48/79, Encl. 24, Proclamation of His Excellency Lord Charles Somerset, 26 June 1818

62 CO 414/11, Mr Benjamin Moodie's Statement . . .

63 *Ibid.*

64 CO 48/106, Bathurst to Donkin, 20 May 1820

65 Cf. CO 48/106, Bathurst to Somerset, 9 January 1826; CO 48/106, Bathurst to Bourke, 30 October 1826. Given the prevalence among the established frontier farmers of the practice of taking Xhosa captives, this fear was not without foundation. See above, p. 175 and Pringle, *Narrative*, pp. 15 and 170

66 CO 48/106, Somerset to Bathurst, October 1825; Somerset wrote that '. . . the only principle upon which grants were directed to be made to them [the settlers] was founded on the extent of means [human labour being the principal one] they possessed. These emigrants . . . were bound to bring their own labour with them who were also freighted by government . . .'

67 I.E. Edwards, *The 1820 Settlers in South Africa*, London, 1924, Appendix A. For example, Captain Grant's party (400 men), J. Bailie's party (101 men), T. Phillips' party (twenty men), E. Damant's party (twenty-five men) and John Ingram's party (twenty-seven men) are not listed either as 'Independent' or as headed by 'Sole Proprietors'. The men in the parties of Ingram and Phillips were nearly all articled servants

68 That of William Parker, for example (124 men). And Thomas Pringle's small party of twelve men included three servants

69 Pringle, *Narrative*, p. 13

70 'Artisans and labourers' is perhaps not the best phrase with which to describe the varied occupations of these people but it was difficult to find another. They included shepherds, gardeners, hatters, willow cutters, vine-dressers and many others

71 See note 57

72 CO 48/79, summary of Ingram's statement to Horton, May (?) 1823.

73 *British Parliamentary Papers*, 1826, xxvi, pp. 332–54, 'Instructions for Commissioners to the Cape of Good Hope and Elsewhere', quoted in Edwards, *1820 Settlers*, p. 100

74 Macmillan, *Cape Colour Question*, p. 184. He suggests that the whole idea of the appointment of a Commission was inspired by Wilberforce and by LMS criticisms but I think Edwards (*1820 Settlers*, ch. VI, *passim*) has shown this to be incorrect

75 *British Parliamentary Papers*, 1826, in Edwards, *ibid.* p. 101

76 CO 48/79, Encl. 25, summary of Ingram's statement to Horton, May (?) 1823

77 CO 48/79, Encl. 25, Ingram to Horton, 5 May 1823

78 CO 48/79, Encl. 2, Return of the names of persons who executed indentures with Mr Ingram but did not proceed to the Cape

79 CO 48/79, Encl. 15, evidence of Daniel Kennedy to the Commissioners, 18 April 1825

80 The government had enjoined Ingram 'not to take away the heads of families, and to leave their wives and families as a burden on the country' (*ibid.*, Encl. 17. Ingram to the Commissioners, 18 April 1825). Several of the children were under the age of eight

81 CO 48/79, Report of the Commissioners of Inquiry, June 1825
82 CO 48/79, Encl. 1, Case of John Rocke. Since Rocke had not signed an indenture, Ingram was able to raise the sum of 300 Rixdollars to 400 or 500 Rixdollars. Rocke had refused to sign because Ingram had thrown his wife off the ship at Cove and had then brought him to the Cape against his will. He was supported in his defence by William Forbes, the boot and shoemaker who was then employing him. Ingram told the court which judged the case that its support was essential to him, for he was 'convinced if he be not supported it . . . [would] be impossible for him to keep such a number of people in order, who are partly instigated by evil disposed persons, who have their own private views, and partly by an ill-placed spirit of compassion which was . . . evinced for his settlers, contrary to all reason, by persons of high respectability, whereby the seeds of disobedience and insubordination have been widely spread amongst them' (Ingram to the Court of Justice, 18 October 1824)
83 CO 48/79, Report of the Commissioners, June 1825
84 CO 48/79, Encl. 11, Stoll to the Commissioners, 28 August 1824. Benjamin Moodie told the Commissioners: 'The demand is considerable and the farmers are eager to employ persons of any description, but in the present distressed state of the agricultural community, they find a difficulty in paying the wages in currency that they would be willing to give—those who are willing to accept payment in produce can readily obtain service.' (*Ibid.*, Encl. 12.)
85 CO 48/79, Encl. 8, van Ryneveld to the Commissioners, 13 August 1824, and Encl. 12, B. Moodie to the Commissioners, 28 August 1824
86 CO 48/79, Encl. 23, Carlisle to the Commissioners, 29 June 1824
87 *Ibid.*
88 *Ibid.*
89 He averred that 'the lowest price at which a very indifferent labourer can be obtained is two Rixdollars (three shillings sterling) per diem with food and a bottle of wine, for a mechanic five or even six Rixdollars (from 7s. 6d. to nine shillings sterling) per diem, with the same allowance for food—your Lordship will easily perceive that nothing which the earth can be made to produce can repay such an expense in cultivation, exclusive of which it places the labouring class out of its proper sphere and demoralises it' (CO 48/68, Somerset to Bathurst, 31 March 1825); and Memorandum Relative to the Supply of labourers from Great Britain, enclosed
90 *Ibid.*
91 CO 48/100, Commissioners to Wilmot Horton, 24 September 1825
92 AC 1, Minutes of a meeting of the Advisory Council, 21 April 1827
93 See p.
94 CO 48/68, Somerset to Bathurst, 31 March 1825
95 CO 48/69, Somerset to Bathurst, 30 July 1825
96 AC 7, Somerset to R.W. Hay, London, 27 July 1826, Encl. in Bathurst to Bourke, 20 August 1826
97 AC 7, Bathurst to Bourke, 20 August 1826
98 BP Letterbook of Lt-Gov. Bourke, 1827, Bourke to Dundas, 9 February 1827
99 AC 7, extract of a letter from the Landdrost of Graaff-Reinet to the Commissioners of Inquiry, January 1824, Encl. in Stockenstrom to the Col. Sec, May 1827
100 AC 7, Stockenstrom to Col. Sec., 20 February 1827

101 *Ibid.* Stockenstrom's reference to 'the liberty of some of our laws' betrayed his ambivalence on the subject of labour reform. He held firm to his opinion that slavery and other forms of forced labour were unjust and that they degraded both master and servant and produced discontent and apathy in the latter, but he maintained that as long as such a system was in force, the master's right of tyranny over the servant should not be interfered with. ('Slavery without hope of freedom is impossible without the lash'.) On these grounds he had opposed the proclamations of 1823 and 1826 which placed minor restrictions on the violent punishment of slaves. He had also defended the flogging of Hottentot women (C.W. Hutton (ed.), *The Autobiography of the Late Sir Andries Stockenstrom*, C. Struik, Cape Town, 1964, pp. 263–6)

102 AC 7, Stockenstrom to Col. Sec., 20 February 1827

103 *Ibid.*

104 Co (Cape) 336, Stockenstrom to Col. Sec., 24 November 1828

105 *Ibid.*

106 AC 7, Stockenstrom to Col. Sec., 20 February 1827

107 See above, pp. 177–8

108 AC 7, W.M. Mackay, Landdrost of Somerset, to Col. Sec., 20 February 1827, and W.M. Dundas, Landdrost of Albany, to Col. Sec., 10 April 1827. Dundas nevertheless recommended the imposition of indentures not exceeding two years

109 AC 7, Roselt, Secretary of the Landdrost of Uitenhage, to Col. Sec., 19 February 1827

110 AC 2, Minutes of a meeting of the Advisory Council, 21 April 1827

111 *Ibid.*

112 Ordinance No. 49 of 1828, Clause v

113 See S. Trapido, 'The Long Apprenticeship: captivity in the Transvaal, 1843–81', unpublished paper presented to the Conference on Southern African Labour History, University of Witwatersrand, April, 1976, and 'Landlord and Tenant in a Colonial Economy: The Transvaal, 1880–1910', *JSAS*, v, 1, 1978, pp. 26–58

114 See Trapido, 'Landlord and Tenant', for a comprehensive investigation of tenancy on Boer farms in the Transvaal. No such study has yet been undertaken with respect to the eastern and central Cape in the early nineteenth century

115 But see Elphick, *Kraal and Castle* and Marks, 'Khoisan Resistance', which provide a valuable starting point for such research. See also J.S. Marais, *Maynier and the First Boer Republic*, Cape Town, 1944

116 Report of the Commissioners of Inquiry, Hottentot Population, Cape of Good Hope, 28 January 1830, p. 6, in *British Parliamentary Papers*, xx, p. 272

117 *Ibid.*, xxii, p. 120

118 Among these were Captain Andries Stockenstrom, Rev. John Philip, Thomas Pringle, Lieutenant-Governor Bourke, the Commissioners of Inquiry (though they were divided in their opinion at the time of their departure from the Colony) and, on at least one occasion, the notorious Colonel Cuyler, Landdrost of Uitenhage

119 John Philip to T.F. Buxton, 1 July 1828, quoted in Macmillan, *Cape Colour Question*, p. 217. See also Philip, *Researches*, i, pp. xxx and ii, p. 329; AC 7, Stockenstrom to Commissioners of Inquiry, 5 January 1824; T. Pringle, *Narra-*

tive, p. 267; CO 48/100, Commissioners to Bathurst, 30 September 1825

120 Report of the Commissioners of Inquiry, Hottentot Population p. 21; AC 7, Stockenstrom to Col. Sec., 20 February 1827; Philip, *Researches*, p. 324 (and *passim*)

121 Report of the Commissioners of Inquiry, Hottentot Population, pp. 21–2

122 Philip, *Researches*, pp. 320–2

123 *Ibid.*, p. 329

124 Report of the Commissioners of Inquiry, Hottentot Population, p. 22

125 CO (Cape) 336, Stockenstrom to Col. Sec., 13 December 1828

126 Philip, *Researches*, p. xxx

127 Report of the Commissioners of Inquiry, Hottentot Population, pp. 22–3

128 CO 48/108, Bourke to Bathurst, 29 January 1827

129 There is evidence that the labour supply in the frontier districts increased dramatically following the passage of Ordinance 49. Sir Lowry Cole referred in 1830 to an assertion that 'the price of labour [has] fallen to the low rate of 1s. 6d. per month'. The assertion was grounded on the contracts entered into by Africans and frontier farmers under the provisions of Ordinance 49 (CO 48/106, Sir Lowry Cole to Sir George Murray, 18 July 1830)

CHAPTER EIGHT

Peasants in Herschel:

a case study of a South African frontier district *

Colin Bundy

The Ciskei district of Herschel is a triangle of high-lying land in the north-eastern corner of the Cape, bordering on the Orange Free State and Lesotho. For over twenty years before it became the magisterial district of Herschel, it existed as the Wittebergen Native Reserve: as such, it was an early experiment in a 'reserved' area; its creation exemplified missionary pressures in frontier politics, and its social and economic structure underwent substantial changes.

Its intrinsic interest apart, there is a further incentive to study the social and economic history of Wittebergen/Herschel. It was visited in the late 1920s by W.M. Macmillan, who painstakingly assembled a set of valuable data[1]—data which provide a comparative framework against which to assess earlier evidence. Thanks to Macmillan, Wittebergen/Herschel is a fruitful field of enquiry into the emergence in the latter half of the nineteenth century of an African peasantry in the Cape Colony: a phenomenon to which Professor Monica Wilson has usefully drawn attention, that in 'one community after another', African peasants experienced 'a period of early prosperity', followed only later by the falling productivity, over-crowding, and underdevelopment characteristic of those areas today.[2]

The main stream of South African historiography has overlooked or underestimated this 'early prosperity' of African peasants, and failed to realise its significance. I have argued elsewhere[3] that there was a substantially more positive response by African agriculturalists to market opportunities than has usually been suggested; that an adapted form of the traditional subsistence methods provided for scores of thousands of Africans in the

*This study of the Herschel peasantry was originally undertaken as part of a wider study, 'African Peasants and Economic Change in South Africa, 1870–1913, with particular reference to the Cape' (D. Phil. thesis, Oxford, 1976). A slightly fuller version appears as a chapter in my *The Rise and Fall of a South African Peasantry*, London, 1979.

Cape a preferable alternative to farm labour on white colonists' terms; and that a smaller group of African farmers made considerable adaptations, departing from the traditional agricultural economy, and emerging as small-scale commercial farmers.

The subsequent checking, or blunting, of the peasant response cannot be explained in terms of the failure by Africans to adapt their tribal economy, nor simply in terms of population pressure on land. In the first place, the manner in which the peasantry was integrated into the developing capitalist economy of South Africa in the late nineteenth and early twentieth centuries was greatly affected by policies pursued by those (whites) who had access to political and economic power. Such policies reinforced and perpetuated the impact of other factors—droughts, diseases, fluctuating market prices, and the like—that tended to disadvantage the African peasantry, The peasant's capacity to produce an agricultural surplus was diminished, and his control over the disposal of that surplus was weakened; and at the same time that the possibilities for accumulating wealth were being restricted, the penetration of the capitalist economy into the peasant sector was raising the demands for a cash income.

Secondly, the frequently reiterated explanation of 'population pressure' or 'land shortage' is incomplete. That Africans were forced to find subsistence upon a sharply reduced land surface is patent; what has not been examined is the extent to which competition for the land available was heightened by certain linked consequences of the penetration into the peasant sector of a capitalist economy and novel social relations. These consequences included a breakdown of the existing mechanisms for maintaining roughly equal allocation of resources; a division of peasant society into distinct strata or classes; and the pursuit of new interests by methods (such as collaboration, litigation, economic exploitation) that widened the gap between 'haves' and 'have-nots'. While the shortage of land was

> the key to the status of inferiority, exploitation, poverty, lack of culture, in a word the status of underdevelopment . . . of [peasants] who participate all too fully in the social process of capitalist development,[4]

that shortage was greatly exacerbated by the creation in peasant communities of different social classes, a resultant unequal distribution of resources and the pursuit of antagonistic interests, as well as by the increasing control over Africans' lives by the state and the debilitating effects on agriculture of migrant labour.

There is not space here to add to this skeletal outline of the theoretical considerations; it is hoped that the following narrative account of social and economic change in Wittebergen/Herschel will illuminate what has been said. Finally, it should be noted that what took place in Herschel has a more general explanatory value. While minor variations are visible from place to place, the broad pattern of the process in Herschel holds true for most eastern districts of the Cape; the district was, commented Macmillan, typical of, although probably better off than most, other Ciskei areas in the 1920s.[5] Indeed, the process in Herschel is something of an 'ideal type' in that the peasant community there was almost wholly 'non-European': the 1891 Census Report remarked that in the Colony proper Herschel had the lowest percentage of whites, 'and 99.23 blacks in every hundred of the population'.[6]

Herschel appears to have received a settled African population for the first time in the 1830s, when refugees from the *Mfecane* and from the frontier wars peopled this remote and rugged area, although it had been a San stronghold before that. In the late 1840s, the Wesleyan Methodist Missionary Society was permitted by Mshweshwe (and Morosi) to set up stations on either side of the Orange[7] and one of these was established at Wittebergen, in the south-west area of what became known as Herschel district. In July 1850, under promptings by William Shaw of the same missionary society, an area of about 150 square miles was promulgated as the Wittebergen Native Reserve, for occupation by 'aboriginals' only.[8] Further land was added during the 1850s, as the population swelled, and in 1870 the Wittebergen Reserve area became the magisterial district of Herschel, with an area of 684 square miles.

The population was built up by successive infusions of refugees: a group of Thembu, several thousand strong, entered in 1852, and numbers of Sotho (perhaps some four thousand) moved southwards from the Free State-Basutoland hostilities in the later 1850s.[9] There were remnants of other Southern Sotho groups (Phuthi, Tlokwa), a small group of 'bruin-menschen' (variously described as Hottentots, bastards, descendants of slaves) under their own captain, and—the largest single group of the population—Mfengu of Hlubi, Zizi, and Bhele origin.[10] Missionary estimates put the total population during the late 1860s at between 17 000 and 20 000; the magistrate in 1878 adjudged the total to have reached 24 500, of which he designated 12 500 as 'Fingoes'.

An important feature of this heterogeneous and largely refugee population was the absence of any powerful traditional leadership, and hence an absence of opposition by chiefs to agricultural and other innovations. Macmillan noticed that the district had 'no big chiefs and no cohesion',[11] and this had been noted as early as 1850. 'We have got quite a mixed population' wrote the Wesleyan missionary, J. Bertram, and he attributed to the number of clans and their refugee status the fact that the inhabitants were 'thus not so bound under the influence of heathen authority'.[12] Again, a report drawn up for Sir Bartle Frere described the population (which had 'no principal chief') as grouped into 'locations' or villages', each a few hundred strong, under some sixty headmen, some of whom were 'under government pay at from £5 to £10 per annum'.[13]

In the 1850s and 1860s particularly, Wittebergen attracted enterprising peasants. In 1868 a missionary spoke of Africans who had

> accumulated a little flock of sheep or a few cattle. They will not take their hardly earned property into the Independent Native States, from which they first came, for fear of its being 'eaten up' by their greedy relatives or envious chiefs.[14]

The Reserve, in other words, was largely free of the traditional sanctions against the accumulation of wealth by individuals. It is interesting, in this respect, to observe that alternative 'non-traditional' social and political pressures could and did emerge. In 1869 and again in 1870, groups of Africans associated with Brigg's mission station at Wittebergen petitioned the Cape Parliament against the illegal activities (including summary justice, 'eating up', and destruction of property) of headmen, African 'Reserve Constables', and the Frontier Mounted Armed Police. The Governor, Sir Philip Wodehouse, agreed that the administration of the reserve had been carried out 'on a mixed principle' that 'would not bear the test of strict legal enquiry'.[15] The petitioners requested that they be brought under 'British law', and the upshot was the incorporation of the Reserve as a magisterial district of the Cape in 1870.[16]

Given the favourable social climate for enterprise and accumulation, given the fairly fertile and well-watered nature of the terrain, and given the proximity of Southern Sotho grain-trading activities, conditions favoured the appearance in Wittebergen Reserve of an African peasantry, agricultural and trading activities, and the establishment of a cash economy. The evidence for the 1860s bears this out strikingly.

In 1862, the Civil Commissioner for Aliwal North congratulated the Reserve:

> At present, the inhabitants raise large quantities of grain, kafir corn, maize, and wheat; and are fast becoming stock farmers also. From being some ten years ago a source of perpetual annoyance to the farmers of Albert and Aliwal North, owing to their thieving habits, they are now one of the best-regulated native communities on the frontier.[17]

Three years later a Commission on Native Affairs was told that 'very large quantities of all kinds of grain are sold annually' out of the Reserve.[18] The Superintendent of the Reserve wrote that there were 'many' Africans in the Reserve who could qualify for the property franchise; that the majority of the population wore European clothing, and, he added,

> I have observed a very considerable advancement in the social position of the people generally. Many wagons are bought annually, and also many ploughs. The old Kafir picks have fallen much into disuse.[19]

This testimony is echoed in the following year, 1866, by Arthur Brigg, a Methodist missionary who spent fifteen years in Herschel: all classes were 'making marked advances in civilization'; the adoption of the plough was widespread, so that men were doing most of the tilling; square houses were being built; and merchandise was being transported within the territory and exported from it on the wagons of African peasants.[20]

In 1868 the same witness indicated that considerable crop diversification had taken place in Wittebergen. While maize and sorghum were the principal crops and staple foods, 'many cultivate in addition wheat, oats, beans, and potatoes, for which they find a ready sale'. Mfengu, Sotho and 'Hottentot' peasants were active in transport-riding:

> they own wagons and spans of oxen, with which they convey merchandise between the various towns of the colony. . . . By these earnings they gradually rise to a condition of considerable respectability. A good wagon, such as some of them possess, is worth £100 or upwards, and a full span of oxen not less than £70.[21]

After 1866, the amount of wheat exported to the Orange Free State from Lesotho declined, providing an opportunity for the peasants of Wittebergen to extend their markets. The following description of peasant activity and prosperity comes from the pen of H.H. Dugmore, one of the most senior and most experienced missionaries in South Africa at the time, who visited Wittebergen in 1869:

> The extent of cultivation carried on is something surprising. *Ploughs* were at work in all directions, and kafir picks where ploughs could not work. Wagons and even horse carts were to be seen at several of the native establishments. The quantity of wheat, mealies and kafir corn raised is such as to bring buyers from among the farmers on all sides, and even as far as Colesberg. Indeed, the 'Reserve' since the Basuto war has been the granary of both the [Cape's] northern districts and the Free State too.[22]

In addition, Herschel peasants were able to take advantage of the spurt in trade and the rising demand for foodstuffs occasioned by the discovery of diamonds—not only on the Fields themselves, but also along the routes between the ports and the mines.

These 'boom' conditions remain clearly apparent during the first half of the 1870s. The existence of a healthy peasant economy in the district—that is, of a peasant economy offering not only subsistence from agricultural effort but also the opportunity to meet the demands of the state and the attractions of the store-keeper by the disposal of an agricultural surplus—is confirmed by the magistrate's report for 1873. In that year, when 1 400 cattle and (significantly) 14 000 sheep were brought into the district by migrant peasants who had received them as wages, the district produced

> about 1 000 bales of wool, 6 000 bags of wheat, and 30 000 bags of kafir corn and mealies *more than was required for consumption,* and these, with a large number of slaughter and draught oxen, were, owing to the diamond fields demand, sold at unprecedentedly high rates. [23]

A good year, indeed—so much so that in 1875, Africans in the Herschel district offered to spend £2 000 for the building of school premises if the government would assist. [24] John Noble, who was markedly impressed by the level of production in Herschel, said that Africans there raised

> immense quantities of maize, wheat, etc., and like the farmers of the ward of New England, which they adjoin, supply the country for a considerable distance, as far as the diamond fields. About 35 000 sacks of grain is estimated to be the annual amount raised. This is the country to which natives retire after a time of successful service down in the colony, and to which they are continually returning. [25]

In Herschel, however, as elsewhere, rising peasant market production and trade did not confer equal gains on the entire community. Instead, one finds as early as the 1870s that Herschel was exhibiting the symptoms of greater pressure on the land available, of stratification of the population into layers of 'have' and 'have-not', and of migratory responses to economic and social pressures. It has been remarked that Wittebergen/Herschel attracted peasants who had already accumulated a certain amount of capital, and that the absence of powerful traditional political structures facilitated further accumulation. Social stratification proceeded apace in what was an almost purely African district. Apart from those peasant farmers who could afford the considerable outlay of £170 for a wagon and the requisite span of oxen, it was reported that

> Others of the native men are becoming adept as brickmakers, builders, thatchers, blacksmiths, roadmenders, basket makers, and tanners; and many more find employment as farm servants among the Boers; or as wool-washers, warehousemen, constables, grooms and waiters in the town. [26]

Emigration from the Reserve was of two kinds. First, as the letter just quoted suggests, there was a growing need for some of the population to work as labourers. A proportion of these, certainly, may have done so in preference to living by peasant agriculture, or as a means to the accumulation of capital whereby the more effectively to farm—the presence of semi-skilled trades as well as of relatively well-paid seasonal labour (wool-washing) fits this hypothesis. On the other hand, service as road-menders and as farm labourers were usually indications of proletarianisation, of the pursuit of labour through necessity rather than through choice. In 1875, about 2 500 Africans left the district in search of work.

Secondly, there was permanent emigration out of the reserve by peasants who had accumulated considerable herds and/or flocks, but who found access to additional land blocked by the increasing competition within the peasant economy for available land. From *c.*1870 to at least 1900, there appears to have been conflict between Herschel peasants who were primarily agriculturists and those who were primarily pastoralists over the correct use of land. Several reports by civil servants alluded to dissension over the extension of arable land: would-be farmers sought new ploughing 'gardens', and the headmen, whose authority derived from their land allocation powers, were keen to grant these, even at the cost of encroaching upon commonage. This incurred the antagonism of those who were primarily stock-farmers, and of the more successful peasants, who already had sufficient arable land and opposed any diminution of grazing lands.[27] In moves strongly reminiscent of the migrations by similarly circumstanced Mfengu and Thembu in the mid-1860s, sizable groups of peasants left Herschel in search of greater opportunities and fresh land, particularly to 'Nomansland' (East Griqualand). Those migrating included some of the 'most wealthy' stock-owners, who took with them 'large numbers of cattle, sheep and horses'. Their places, predicted the magistrate, 'will soon be filled up by those with less stock, who will depend more upon agriculture'.[28]

The difficulties of a section of the peasantry were heightened by the droughts and depression of the late 1870s. In 1878, it was reported that 'bad seasons have brought much poverty among them'—although, significantly, in the light of what has been said of the growing discrepancies between haves and have-nots—the same informant noted that 'the occupations of the people are agricultural. There is a very extensive cereal trade with the Colony, and they are rich in flocks and herds'.[29] Worse years followed. In 1883, a great number of passes were issued to those seeking wage-employment, and in the following year not only was the drought very severe, but money was scarce: '[The] natives generally barter in cattle and sheep for grain; instead of paying in cash'.[30]

There is continual evidence of the difficulty encountered by an increasing number of peasants in getting enough land to farm at a subsistence level. In a single report, a magistrate mentioned land disputes, over-stocking, over-grazing, and the creation of *dongas* (gullies).[31] The quitrent plots granted in the 1850s and 1860s had fallen into administrative confusion; these areas jostled others held on communal tenure; boundaries, obligations, and ownership were all sources of friction; land matters bred 'continual disputes, jealousy and wrangling'.[32] Many peasants asked for permission to move to Griqualand East or the Transkei, 'complaining they had insufficient land to cultivate', and others simply found subsistence from peasant agriculture impossible—'the labour market was well supplied'.[33] Nevertheless, during this same depressed period, certain Herschel peasants continued to export a surplus, to acquire cash, and to spend it on a range of consumer articles eloquent of their relative affluence. The magistrate told a government enquiry that Africans were selling wool, wheat and other grains, and he said of certain mission-attached peasants

> their children are sent to Heald Town for instruction, and they have fruit gardens, decent houses, tables, chairs, stools, plates, cups, saucers, knives and forks, wagons, ploughs, clocks, and some iron bedsteads.[34]

Some had houses on surveyed plots. A local businessman testified that

> Goods sold are approximating more and more to those sold in European towns ... [Africans] bought articles previously not known amongst them—e.g. blacking, sponges, concertinas, chairs, trunks, lace, ribbons, pomatum, scents, almanacs, date cases, clocks, watches, dictionaries, ready reckoners, etc.[35]

Another telling sign of social stratification—and of a breakdown of the traditional communalism and egalitarianism of Nguni society—was the emergence of employer and employee divisions. In 1883, the magistrate noted that 'The Fingoes are now trying to engage refugee Tambookies from Basutoland as servants as they pass through the district in search of work', and another observer stated that Herschel Africans 'frequently' employed servants who came 'generally from an inferior tribe or from very poor families'.[36]

Although Herschel was geographically remote, its economic health remained intimately bound up with the fluctuations of the South African economy as a whole. The economic recovery attendant on the Witwatersrand discoveries was mirrored in Herschel. The prices of oxen and grain had, by 1889,

> advanced at least one hundred per cent during the past year, in consequence of the demand for transport to the gold fields, and the drought. A considerable number of trek oxen have been purchased at these advanced rates, as also large quantities of grain and this together with the substantial rise in the price of wool has been the means of circulating a large amount of money in the district.[37]

Enough money was available for the peasant community to pay £3 500 owed for taxes in arrears, in addition to the normal taxes for that year.

Similarly, the 1891 census indicates that a considerable amount of wheat, maize, sorghum, oats, oathay, barley, pumpkins and beans, as well as small crops of tobacco, lucerne, potatoes and sweet potatoes, were raised in Herschel. There is no information as to what proportions of the produce was exported and what consumed within the district, but certain pointers suggest that a considerable amount would have been sold as surplus. Apart from the evidence by the magistrate that large quantities of wool, grain and stock were sold, it is noteworthy that more wheat was grown than either maize or sorghum, the staple foods; in the same way, oats, barley, and oathay were predominantly export products, as were, of course, the 451 000 lb of wool and the hides, skins and horns.[38]

Between 1895 and 1899, peasant production in this district was disrupted by droughts, locusts, and rinderpest. Here, as elsewhere, numerous Africans were reduced to the most severe poverty—thousands left the district in search of work, while others stayed, living on edible weeds. Almost certainly, there were peasants in Herschel who experienced for the first time in the late 1890s the failure of peasant activities to provide sustenance. An Anglican missionary wrote in the aftermath of the cattle disease of the many who were compelled to leave the district in search of work, including 'men who other years stayed home'.[39]

Certain factors aided the partial recovery which took place, foremost amongst them the return of good crops and the proximity of troops during the Anglo-Boer war. Africans from Herschel were in great demand for military labour at what were relatively high wages: almost £7 000 was paid to those who served in a single capacity, as Mounted Police during the war.[40] The army also paid inflated prices for remount ponies, grain, and draught oxen.

In the period of recovery after rinderpest, locusts and war, it was easier for those peasants who had already accumulated some reserve capital, or who were naturally more enterprising, to recoup their losses. The corollary to this is that 'marginal' peasants were forced below the subsistence level, either to be fully extruded from the land, or to become migrant labourers. The evidence for Herschel in the early twentieth century confirms this, and also suggests that the stratification noted in the 1870s and 1880s increased substantially in the 1890s and early 1900s.

In this context, the magistrate's report for 1895 is of interest: a total of 24 000 peasants possessed 44 000 cattle, 89 000 sheep, 236 wagons and 1 348 ploughs.[41] The relatively small number of wagons and ploughs suggests a concentration of wealthier (or at least, less poor) peasants at the top of the continuum. Nor can one assume that the stock was evenly distributed: apart from anything else, the 236 wagons would account for something like two and a half thousand cattle, while the possession of ploughs also predicated the ownership of a number of cattle. In 1898, it was reported that 105 500 sheep in Herschel were held in only 1 465 flocks.[42] Contemporary reports were littered with signs that the limits of arable land had been reached; that endemic squabbling and litigation about land rights persisted; and that the magistrate spent much of his time trying to quiet 'the clamour of those who have no garden lands'—that is, peasants without access to the means of production.[43]

The gulf between haves and have-nots that had developed by the 1890s is graphically illustrated by the gaoler of Herschel district. This functionary told a government inquiry that not only white landowners but also wealthy African farmers complained in good seasons of a want of labour, and that twenty to thirty well-to-do African farmers in the district had applied to him for the use of prison labour, batches of eight or ten convicts at a time (for 9d. a day), to do their reaping.[44] The facts of stratification were clearly enunciated by another official in 1904:

> The position now is that many men set up the right to 10, 15 and in some cases as many as 20 lands of varying extent, while, on the other hand, there are a large number of persons in the District paying precisely the same hut-tax, with only one or two lands, and in some instances no lands at all.[45]

Corroboration came from another witness:

> The Headman and his particular friends have large lands and all the good ground, whilst others have either small lands or none at all. . . . I have almost daily complaints of the well-to-do men (who are the headman's friends) having been given or taken land which they have no claim to have.

Some individuals owned and grazed over a thousand head of small stock, he continued, besides cattle and horses—

> These men, owing to their wealth, ride roughshod over their poorer brethren, and I regret to say it appears to have been the tendency to encourage and assist these men to the detriment and starving of the poorer and struggling class.[46]

So there were peasants in the early years of this century who were relatively well off: the 'Headman and his particular friends', those with wagons and large flocks, and those who possessed sufficient capital to be able to counter competition for land by purchasing plots in other districts.[47] A limited number of peasants, in Herschel as in many other Cape districts, found that by entering quasi-feudal relations of mutual assistance with white land proprietors—especially by 'farming on the halves'—they could derive a fair subsistence income.[48] But for probably a majority of the peasant population of the district, for 'the poorer and struggling class', fortunes were in sharp decline by the early 1900s. Their lot was sketched in these words:

> They cannot be compared with those of twenty years ago. This, I take it, is because they have acquired more European habits, which is detrimental to their health. Their present resources are not as good as in former years. . . . So far as I can see, the cost of living is increasing every year.[49]

Following the drought year of 1903, the magistrate managed to draw a consoling moral from the distress he described:

> Natives have been compelled to barter away a lot of stock in exchange for grain. The Natives are very averse to parting with their stock, being their capital, but I think this compulsory alienation of their capital in order to obtain food supplies will do good, in that it will bring home to them . . . the advantage of going out to work.[50]

The reports of the next few years attested further to the facts of decreasing resources and a higher cost of existence. In poor seasons, Africans sold off their grain as soon as they had reaped, and then later had to buy it back at prices of up to fifty per cent more. This was a far cry from the grain-exporting peasantry of thirty and forty years before, and indicative of the demands upon individuals for ready cash. Large quantities of maize and sorghum were imported into Herschel in 1909 from the Orange Free State. Roles had been reversed, and 'granary' had become hungry customer.

The details cited above bring this survey to about 1910, and the act of Union; but the decline of peasant prosperity which has been charted did not end then, and was not a temporary phenomenon. The dwindling wealth and failing social health of the district, the fall in resources, in earning capacity, and in economic resilience, and the mounting pressures of population growth (intensified by unequal distribution) all persisted over the next decade or two, until in the late 1920s, Professor Macmillan conducted his on-the-spot investigation into Herschel's economic well-being.

He discovered that about forty thousand Africans lived in the 684 square miles of the district, an area easily distinguished from its 'white' neighbours because 'it [had] obviously received no tangible or visible benefit from public expenditure on its needs', and lacked attention to the simplest material wants like bridges, roads, and public buildings.[51] Despite being 'relatively well-suited to the production of the two great staples, wheat and wool' (p. 161), Herschel was desperately impoverished. All the available data suggested that 'the district is barely self-supporting even with regard to foodstuffs' (p. 160). '*In a good year* it may have produced grain enough to last perhaps as much as six months' (p. 160, emphasis added). In broad terms, Macmillan indicated that there was an annual shortfall of expenditure over income of £35 000 to £50 000. This deficit was made up (a) by large credit advances and the accretion of indebtedness; and (b) by the sale of labour, mainly as migrant labour. Overall, conditions in the district were worse than they had been ten years earlier (p. 184), and Macmillan came to the measured and sombre conclusion that 'a large proportion of the community here depicted exists almost on the very lowest level of bare subsistence' (p. 185).

His argument is underpinned by a series of statistical findings. Details are drawn from official statistics, adjusted in accordance with local observation and information. He aimed at drawing up an economic balance-sheet for an average or fair year in the 1920s, and collated the figures for about a decade to arrive at a mean. Figures for production consumed locally, pointed out Macmillan, were very difficult to obtain, but he concluded that not even in a good year was enough maize and sorghum grown to meet an (estimated) need of 67 500 bags. The calculation of produce exported from Herschel was 'more measurable and perhaps more significant' (p. 157), and it is to these figures that we now turn.

Macmillan found that about £35 000 worth of wheat, wool, mohair, stock, animal products and miscellaneous items were exported each year—i.e. produce worth 17s. 6d. per capita of the peasant population. The total of £35 000 might be raised to £45 000 with 'a singularly favourable combination of high yield and good prices' (p. 168).

Using data for the years 1873 and 1891 (for which times the available evidence is fairly detailed), I have drawn up a table comparing the peasant production and income for those years with Macmillan's figures for an average year in the 1920s. The basis for the calculations for 1873 and 1891 are, respectively, the magistrate's report for 1873 and the Census Report for 1891, modified and interpreted in the light of other evidence, where available.[52] The prices obtaining in 1873 and 1891 for agricultural and pastoral products have been taken from the *Bluebook for the Cape Colony, 1873*, and the *Statistical Register* of 1891. All values are expressed in current prices. Wherever there was room for doubt or for informed speculation, estimates for 1873 and 1891 have deliberately been kept to the lowest probable figure. In particular, it will be observed that in most instances the prices obtained for produce have been estimated at rather less than the prevailing quotations for the average in Aliwal North and/or the eastern districts: it seems fair to assume that African peasants, suffering from lack of access to markets and with a modest agricultural technology, might have had to sell at reduced rates especially to traders.

Table: Comparison of the amount and value of peasant production in Herschel

Product exported	1873		1891		1921-29 (average)	
Wheat	6 000 bags	£12 000 [a]	45 000 bushels	£13 500 [g]	15 000 bags	£15 000
Maize and sorghum	30 000 bags	£15 000 [b]	nil [h]			£10 000
Wool	1 000 bales	£12 500 [c]	450 000 lb [i]	£8 500	250 000 lb	
Mohair	no information		33 500 lb [i]	£850	60 000 lb	£3 000
Hides and skins	(e)	£1 225	2 000 and 7 800 [k]	£1 750	4 000 and 10 000	£2 000
Stock	'large number' [d]	£13 750	(l)	£2 700	stock,	£5 000
Barley, oats, horns, misc.	no information		(m)	£2 150	barley, oathay, estimated	
TOTAL VALUE		£54 475		£29 400		£35 000
African population		23 000 [f]		25 000		40 000 [n]
Income per capita		£2 7s. 4d.		£1 4s. 0d.		17s. 6d.

Notes:

a) 6 000 bags = 18 000 bushels, at 12s. 8d. per bushel, which is lower than figure for Aliwal North, 17s. 6d.

b) 30 000 bags seems high—although partly corroborated by Noble (p. 6, footnote 4) and other contemporary evidence. It equals 90 000 bushels at 7s. 6d. a bushel, or £30 000—I have arbitrarily halved this.

c) At 435 lb per (unwashed wool) bale = 435 000 lb; at 8d. per bale for unwashed wool (lower than average for eastern districts, 1873) would be £14 10s. per bale; cf. *Eastern Province Herald*, 29 July 1871, 'when the value of a bale of wool averages from £15 to £20'—I have lowered the bale's value to £12 10s.

d) 500 cattle and 1 000 sheep seems a conservative estimate of what the magistrate deemed a 'large number'; one remembers that inflated prices were obtainable for stock on the diamond fields, which induced sale of stock. Both cattle and sheep have been assigned a slightly lower value than the prevailing average prices: cattle £10 each, sheep 10s. each.

e) No figures exist for such sales, but as some stock must die every year, it seems safe to assume such sales. I have halved the 1891 figures for hides and skins, at slightly lower than the prevailing 1873 prices; i.e. 1 000 hides at 17s. 6d. (£875) and 3 750 skins at 2s. (£350).

f) Without any explanation, the 1875 Census simply omits a population figure for Herschel! This estimate derives from missionary estimates (17 000 to 20 000) of late 1860s and the magistrate's figure of 25 000 in 1878.

g) Of the 50 000 bushels raised, I have allowed 10 per cent to be locally consumed or bartered, although contemporary sources stress that wheat was raised for sale.

h) Taking the same dietary needs as Macmillan uses, a population of 25 000 would need 42 175 bags grain. Only 82 000 bushels (or 28 000 bags) were raised, according to the Census. Although contemporary evidence shows that these grains were being sold, and makes no mention—in the early 1890s —of such grains being imported, it is perhaps most satisfactory to conclude that sales of maize and sorghum were made within the district, from 'big' to 'little' peasants, etc., and to suppose that none was exported.

i) At 4½d. per lb.

j) At 6d. per lb.

k) Hides at 10s.; skins at 2s. 9d.

l) Impossible to estimate accurately: we know that in 1889 'large numbers' of stock were sold, so say that (only) 400 cattle at £5 10s. (£2 200) and 1 000 sheep at 10s. (£500) were sold in 1891.

m) 1 605 bushels oats at 5s. = £400; 5 000 bushels barley at 3s. = £750; also horns, rye, oathay, peas, beans, potatoes, tobacco raised—say a total export from these sources of £1 000; total £2 150.

n) Macmillan revised the census figure for 1921 of just over 39 000 to an estimated figure for the late 1920s of 40 000.

How informative is the table? While making due allowance for the uncertain nature of many of the figures, and accepting a generous margin of error, the broad outlines of the story the statistics tell seem clear enough. In Wittebergen/Herschel, the African peasantry over the period 1870–1920 became relatively and absolutely less well off. Overall production fell; per capita income fell; and the number of 'independent' peasants fell correspondingly. The total income for 1873 was in the region of £54 000 (or £2·7s. 4d. per capita) and might (see table; notes (a) to (e)) have been considerably higher—say £70 000 plus (or over £3 per capita). In 1891, the total income was about £30 000, and the per capita figure £1 4s. od. It will be appreciated that, given the lower taxation and rents, as well as lower spending on education and goods, in 1873 and 1891, the diminished purchasing power of the per capita income was even more marked than the sums suggest.

If the 1873 figure seems startlingly high, then, when compared with Macmillan's totals, there are nevertheless substantial grounds for accepting it. The relative wealth that the figure indicates is consistent with the descriptions of the peasant community of Wittebergen/Herschel made at the time.[53] It is consistent, too, with estimates made of other successful African peasant communities at the same time—thus in Fingoland (total population 44 000) we are told in 1874 that 'At the lowest computation, the value of the import and export trade represents £150 000 p.a.'[54] And in neighbouring Basutoland, in 1873, two thousand bales of wool (worth say £25 000) and 'upwards of 100 000 muids of grain' (say £75 000) and also much stock, were exported.[55]

Finally, the figures seem wholly consistent with the nature of social and economic change as presented in this paper. By the 1870s, the peasant community of Herschel had responded to economic opportunity and changes; individuals had adapted and diversified the traditional agricultural economy, accepting innovations in their social organisation as well as in their economic life. And it seems indisputable that that population was in almost every economic respect better off than it was by the 1920s. The Herschel peasantry was, in 1873, more productive, more self-sufficient, and more prosperous; it was less crowded, less indebted, and less dependent on migratory labour. About a hundred years ago, this area was called 'a beautiful settlement of well-watered fertile hill and dale',[56] and its popula- tion described as 'loyal, peaceful and contented'.[57] Fifty years later, the same area had become congested, eroded, over-stocked, suffering from 'thoroughly unsound economic conditions' and 'general depression', while the population was 'seething with discontent', 'poor in production and very low in consumption'.[58] Oliver Goldsmith described the erosion of a very different peasant community, but a few lines from *The Deserted Village* serve as a not wholly inapt coda:

Ill fares the land, to hastening ills a prey,
Where wealth accumulates, and men decay:
Princes and lords may flourish, or may fade;
A breath can make them, as a breath has made:
But a bold peasantry, their country's pride,
When once destroyed, can never be supplied.

Notes

1 W.M. Macmillan, *Complex South Africa*, London, 1930, pp. 144–86
2 M. Wilson and L. Thompson (eds.), *The Oxford History of South Africa*, 2 vols., Oxford, 1971, ii, p. 55
3 C.J. Bundy, 'The Emergence and Decline of a South African Peasantry', *African Affairs*, lxxi, 285, October 1972, pp. 369–88
4 A.G. Frank, *Capitalism and Underdevelopment in Latin America*, New York, 1969, p. 136
5 Macmillan, *Complex South Africa*, p. 184
6 Cape Parliamentary Papers (CPP), G.6-'92, *Report of the Census in the Cape Colony for 1891*, p. xix
7 Wm. Shepstone, the missionary concerned, took occupation 'by consent of the colonial and nearest native authorities'; Methodist Missionary Society (MMS) Archives, SA Box XVII, 'Bechuanaland 1838–57', 1850 file, J. Bertram's letter to WMS, 5 July 1850
8 *British Parliamentary Papers (BPP)*, 1851, xxxvii (1360), Sir H. Smith to Lord Grey, desp. 120, 12 May 1850 and encl., for annexation of Wittebergen
9 CO 879/13, Confidential Print African No 154, p. 192
10 A. Brigg, *'Sunny Fountains' and 'Golden Sands': Missionary Adventures in the South of the Dark Continent*, London, 1888, pp. 106–7, 134–6; also CPP, G.5-'86, *Bluebook for Native Affairs (BBNA)*, p. 23
11 Macmillan, *Complex South Africa*, p. 147
12 MMS, SA Box XVII, 'Bechuanaland 1838–57', File 1850
13 Conf. Print Africa No. 154, p. 192
14 MMS, SA Box XVIII, 'Bechuanaland 1868–76', File 1868, A. Brigg to General Secretaries and Committee of WMS, 13 August 1868
15 CPP, *Votes and Proceedings*, 1870, App. I, ii, message from Governor to House of Assembly, 16 April 1870 (minute xxx, 1870)
16 CPP, C.2-'69, 'A Petition from certain inhabitants of the Wittebergen Native Reserve', and A.9-'70, 'Petition of Inhabitants of Wittebergen Native Reserve'
17 *Bluebook for the Cape Colony*, 1862, p. JJ39
18 CCP, *1865 Commission on Native Affairs*, App. I, p. 105
19 *Ibid.*
20 *Wesleyan Missionary Notices*, 3rd Series, xlv, January 1867, Brigg's letter of 20 July 1866

21 MMS, SA Box XVIII, 'Bechuanaland 1868–76', 1868 file, A. Brigg to Gen. Secretaries and Committee of WMS, 13 August 1868

22 MMS, SA Box, 'Queenstown 1868–76', 1869 file, H.H. Dugmore to the Secretary WMS, 1 November 1869 (emphasis in the original)

23 CPP, G.27–'74, *BBNA* for 1874, p. 10 (emphasis added)

24 PRO, CO 879/13

25 J. Noble, *Descriptive Handbook of the Cape Colony*, Cape Town, 1875, p. 224. (Although in the text a little ambiguous, it seems clear—from a comparison with census figures—that the 35 000 sacks 'raised' refers to the surplus raised.)

26 MMS, SA Box XVIII, 'Bechuanaland 1868–76', 1868 file, A. Brigg, 13 August 1868

27 See, among others, CPP, G.9–'94, *BBNA* for 1894, p. 22; G.42–'98, *BBNA* for 1898, p. 33; G.31–'99, *BBNA* for 1899, p. 28. And see *Queenstown Free Press*, 2 September 1892, for a report of a meeting of over five hundred Herschel Africans with their new Resident Magistrate over this issue. The Headmen, charged the magistrate, were permitting new land—including commonage—to be ploughed without first getting permission as laid down in Circular 1/1890

28 CPP, G.21–'75, *BBNA* for 1875, p. 64

29 CO 879/13. Conf. Print Afr. 154, p. 192

30 CPP, G.2–'85, *BBNA* for 1885, p. 27

31 CPP, G.13–'80, *BBNA* for 1880, p. 188

32 CPP, G.5–'86, *BBNA* for 1886, p. 24

33 CPP, G.2–'85, *BBNA* for 1885, p. 27

34 CPP, G.4–'83, *Commission on Native Laws and Customs*, Appendix D, Part II, p. 317, evidence of Capt. Hook, magistrate

35 *Ibid.*, p. 319, evidence of O. Brigg

36 *Ibid.*, pp. 317, 319

37 CPP, G.4–'90, *BBNA* for 1890, p. 12 (magistrate's report)

38 CPP, G.6–'92, *Census for the Cape Colony for 1891*, pp. 448–9

39 United Society for Propagation of the Gospel Archives, EMSS, 1898, ii, letter by J.H. Bone, 31 December 1898

40 CPP, G.25–1920, *BBNA* for 1902, pp. 21–32; G.12–1904, *BBNA* for 1904, p. 13

41 CPP, G.5–'96, *BBNA* for 1896, p. 32

42 CPP, G.35–'98, *Report of the Inspector of Sheep*

43 See *BBNA* for almost every year of the 1890s; the quote is from G.5–'96, p. 28.

44 CPP, G.3–'94, *Report of the Labour Commission 1893–4*, iii, pp. 277–8

45 CPP, G.12–1904, *BBNA* for 1904, report of D. Eadie, magistrate, p. 19

46 *Ibid.*, pp. 23–4, report by H.G. Turner, Inspector of Locations

47 UG 17–'11, Department of Native Affairs, *Bluebook for 1910*, p. 258

48 UG 22–'14, *Report of the 1916 Natives Land Commission*, ii, p. 121, evidence of W.C. Orsmond

49 *1903–5 South African Native Affairs Commission*, v, p. 26, evidence of J. Dovey, Inspector of Native Locations

50 CPP, *BBNA* for 1904, p. 18

51 Macmillan, *Complex South Africa*, p. 147. All the quotations that follow are from the same source, and pagination is indicated in the text, for easier reference.

52 CPP, G.27–'74, *BBNA* for 1874, p. 10, cited on p. 213 above, and CPP, G.6–'92,

Census Report for the Cape Colony, 1891, pp. 448–9
53 See pp. 211–4 above
54 CPP, G.21–'75, *BBNA* for 1875
55 CPP, G.27–'74, *BBNA* for 1874, Report for Basutoland. We also learn that in the same year merchandise worth £150 000 was imported to Basutoland
56 *Bluebook for the Cape Colony 1862*, Civil Commissioner for Aliwal North, p. JJ39
57 CPP, G.12–'77, *BBNA* for 1877, p. 144
58 Macmillan, *Complex South Africa*, pp. 150, 185, and *passim*

CHAPTER NINE

The Cape economy and the expropriation of the Kat River Settlement, 1846–53

Tony Kirk

A central feature of southern Africa's history in the nineteenth century is the displacement of indigenous peoples from their lands by the expansion of white settlement. It should be a commonplace that this process had potent economic causes. S.D. Neumark has convincingly established a direct relationship between economic growth in the Cape Colony and the expansive tendency of its white population in the era up to 1836.[1] But few studies of later periods have cared to approach white expansion from the same angle. For example, between 1836 and 1857 the whites possessed themselves of huge areas across the Cape's north-eastern boundaries. In the process they fought two wars against Nguni chiefdoms occupying the land, crushed a rebellion of coloured people within the colony, and saw the Xhosa people destroy their crops and herds in the disastrous 'cattle killing delusion' of 1857. Studies dealing with these events have largely ignored the state of the contemporary Cape economy and the financial interests of the whites involved in it. Nevertheless, they defend the whites individually and collectively from the charges of economic self-interest which were laid against them whenever territorial expansion occurred.[2] As it stands, their defence is inadequate.

This is not meant to imply that white expansion had purely economic origins. Explanations emphasising political, cultural and other motives have already been persuasively advanced, but they lack the economic dimension essential for a balanced judgment. Instead of concentrating exclusively on politics or economics or social forces the historian needs to try to recreate the Cape's political economy. The attempt reveals the considerable interpenetration of politics and finance which is a feature of the Cape government from the 1840s onward. Again, it demonstrates the extensive commercial and agricultural interests of many advocates for the expropriation of land belonging to indigenous peoples. The influence of such interests on territorial expansion should not be dismissed without rather more careful examination than is usually given to it.

To define the precise interrelationship of political and economic factors between 1836 and 1857 requires a detailed study on a scale which cannot be attempted here.[3] Many angles remain to be investigated before final judgement can be passed. However, by taking a single incident within the period and putting it into an economic context it may be possible to suggest the sort of economic considerations which seem to have influenced the white community's territorial expansion. The example chosen is the rebellion at the Kat River Settlement, in the eastern Cape Colony, in 1851, which led to wholesale confiscations of land occupied by tribesmen and Cape Coloured people. It is a story which brings into sharp focus the nature of external economic pressures on land occupied by indigenous peoples.

The Cape authorities founded the Kat River Settlement in 1829 as a military barrier between white farmers and the Xhosa chiefdoms on the eastern Cape frontier. Lying along the headwaters of the Kat River, it comprised 640 allotments capable of irrigation, with grazing commons attached. The average size of each allotment (known by the Dutch term *erf*) was slightly over six acres. Commonage varied from two to five hundred acres. The Settlement's boundaries also included large tracts of land unsuitable for either grazing or cultivation. Occupancy was reserved exclusively for coloured people. At first they prospered. Later, however, a deterioration set in: the government used the Settlement as a dumping ground for coloureds and tribesmen whom whites had dispossessed elsewhere in the Cape; neighbouring white colonists assailed it as a refuge for 'vagrants'; its military importance declined. Overcrowding created social tensions and economic insecurity among the inhabitants. In 1851 many rebelled, accusing the government of discrimination against the Settlement. The government suppressed the outbreak by force of arms, confiscated all *erven* belonging to rebels, and gave them to the whites.

The internal condition of the Settlement and the grievances of its population in the years before the rebellion have been described in detail elsewhere.[4] Many Settlement people found their grievances harder to support because of the attitude adopted by certain white colonists, who never hesitated to express in public their hostility to coloured civil rights. Such expressions did not originate wholly in white social prejudice and race feeling. In the 1840s they were increasingly inspired by ideas related to the growth of the Cape's woollen industry.

The growth of the Cape's woollen industry occurred in response to the creation of a market for colonial wool in Britain. Broadly speaking, the amount of wool yielded by the domestic clip in Britain declined

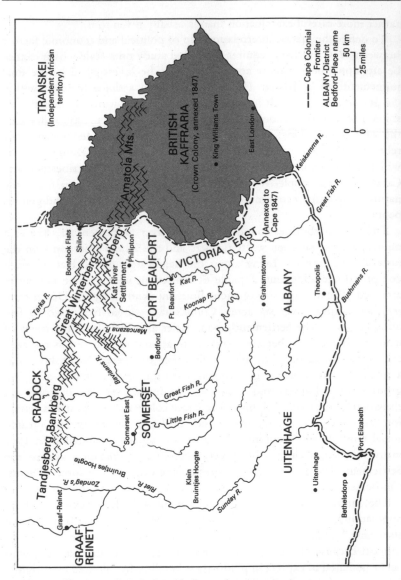

Map 9.1 The eastern Cape in the mid-nineteenth century

from 1840 onwards. Simultaneously the British woollen manufacturing industry entered a forty-year period of expansion during which its raw wool consumption more than doubled. Imports had to make up the shortfall between the British industry's needs and the domestic clip. London rapidly became a central market for imported wool. New machinery introduced into British factories heightened the rate of growth. The amount of mechanisation (and probably of new investment) quickened from 1839 to 1850 and reached its peak in the 1850s and 1860s.[5] Impressed by these advances, men connected with the industry tended to make extravagant forecasts of its capacity to sustain a similar rate of growth indefinitely.

The wool-producing Australian colonies profited most from the growing British demand for imported wool. Continental suppliers—until 1843 the major exporters to Britain—rapidly lost their importance. Cape wool, without approaching the volume exported from Australia, nevertheless gained a significant foothold in the British market. The main expense faced by colonial exporters was ocean freight, and in this respect the Cape, being nearer to London, had an advantage over Australia. Figures for wool exports, computed from accounts kept by Cape customs authorities and port officials, are untrustworthy, but they give an approximate idea of the vigorous progress made by Cape wool farming once it had become established:

Annual Wool Exports—Cape Colony
(rounded to the nearest thousand lb.)

1833	113 000 lb.	
1836	373 000	
1839	586 000	cumulative annual
1842	1 429 000	growth rate: 24%
1845	3 195 000	
1848	3 671 000	
1851	5 447 000	

Of these amounts the quantity exported to countries other than Britain was negligible. Domestic consumption was also low. The welfare of the industry therefore depended heavily on the British market.

Wool was by no means the most important industry in Britain. But at the Cape it rapidly ousted wine as the staple product and export. Cape wools were almost unknown before 1840. In that year the London brokers first began to anticipate 'a large and valuable export from that thriving colony'.[6] The value to the Cape producer varied according to quality and the ruling price on the London market, where sales were held every quarter. Fluctuations in price did not depend so much on supply, which continually increased, as on 'commercial vicissitudes and political circumstances'.[7] Between 1840 and 1870 the lowest point touched was in 1848, when continental revolutions followed the great British commercial crisis of 1847. Generally, however, prices mounted regularly each year until 1860. Thus wool brought more wealth into the colony after every sale. Again the figures are suspect, but it appears that in 1840 total sales realised under £100 000; in 1845 the sum rose to £175 000; and in 1851 it reached £286 000—59 per cent of all Cape exports.[8] Other economic benefits accompanied this growth. After 1840 a new class of wealthy immigrant started to arrive from Britain and elsewhere in the Empire with capital for investment in sheep farms. No comprehensive figures are available for such inflows of capital, but a few examples will show that they made a significant contribution to the development of the industry. In 1841 a number of settlers coming to the eastern districts negotiated bills in favour of the colony to the value of £20 000. Two years later 'several Indian capitalists and others' bought sheep farms in the eastern Cape. An Englishman named Nicholson invested £2 100 in stock in a single year in Uitenhage. A certain Col. O'Reilly sold his commission in the British army for £4 000 to buy on a farm near the eastern frontier.

Towns and villages in the Cape Colony competed vigorously with each other to attract this capital investment. Failure to do so in a period of general economic growth meant stagnation for local business. Pamphlets and newspapers were two favourite tools of businessmen seeking to promote their own area and decry all others. Pamphlets, sometimes the length of large books, purported to give factual information on such matters as the profits to be made from a particular venture. They were often highly misleading.[9] Newspapers could serve the same purpose. The *Graham's Town Journal*, the *Eastern Province Herald,* the *Graaff Reinet Herald* and many others devoted their columns to reporting every promotional scheme, however unlikely to come about, in their particular locality. These editions were then circulated widely in the hope that other editors, in the colony or overseas, would reprint them and so arouse the interest of potential investors. (For this reason the nineteenth-century Cape press should be used as a historical source with great care.) Another promotional technique apparently used by regional business interests was to pad information supplied to government authorities for publication in official reports. This becomes particularly obvious in trying to establish figures for (say) the sheep population of Albany District in the 1840s.

Immigrants, however, did not predominate among the growing numbers of commercial sheep farmers at the Cape. It was established landowners who generally succeeded in converting to wool, although they faced serious obstacles. For example, few had liquid capital to buy the expensive new breeds of sheep. Again, many farmed in remote areas with poor communications and found it uneconomic to transport their produce to distant markets.[10] They overcame these obstacles with the help of the Cape Town merchants, who provided a variety of vital services in the early years of the industry. Among the most important of the merchants were Maximilian Thalwitzer and the two Mosenthal brothers, German Jews who had emigrated to the Cape earlier in the century. Thalwitzer indirectly encouraged wool production in the early thirties by acting as an itinerant wool buyer in the sheep country of the western Cape. After 1840 he became more directly involved, hiring the Cape packet to import Merino sheep and bringing into the colony men from Holstein who could teach farmers how to tend and shear them. As Consul for the Hanseatic cities of Hamburg, Lubeck and Bremen, he encouraged German investment in Cape wool. Through him the Hamburg firm of Lippert & Co. built up a flourishing connection as wool importers.[11] Mosenthal Bros. opened a branch at Port Elizabeth in 1842. To eliminate the collection problems caused by poor communications they established a chain of stores and agencies throughout the eastern districts, where farmers could bring their produce and receive payment without the expense and inconvenience of a long journey. When sufficient quantities were accumulated they could be transported cheaply in bulk to the nearest port or market. The Mosenthals 'created an organized system of commerce by means of which the produce of the individual farmer, in itself perhaps commercially insignificant, could profitably reach the national and world consumer market in the mass'.[12]

The merchants did not confine themselves to acting as middlemen. They also became financiers and bankers to the first generation of eastern Cape wool farmers. When times were hard they provided the credit which kept their clients in business. Their notes began to circulate, drawn on their Cape Town offices. When that practice was discontinued, they became representatives on the boards of banks. 'The role they filled in quickening the economic pulse of the areas they served can hardly be overestimated'.[13] The benefit derived from this relationship between farmer and merchant was mutual. As a western Cape financier and politician observed in 1851,

> a large proportion of the money in Cape Town is derived from mortgages on frontier farms and frontier estates; a large portion of the trade of Table Bay is connected with the frontier; and a great many people in Cape Town have an interest in estates in the eastern province.[14]

Wool farming advanced rapidly in the eastern Cape after 1840. In the season from November 1841 to February 1842 sixty-four additional flocks came into clip. There were several large importations of fresh stock direct from Europe, with married immigrants and servants to carry on sheep farming. Albany District claimed to pasture 200 000 woolled sheep in 1842, so recently introduced that many were unready for clipping. In the following year the numbers rose steadily. As the quality of wool improved, it commanded better prices on the London market. This growth led to a feeling of euphoria among the colonists. The future seemed to lie with what one editor in a characteristic burst of enthusiasm called 'the *golden* fleece—the true and permanent riches of South Africa'.[15] In similar vein a speaker told the annual meeting of the Cape Agricultural Society in 1841 that wool production might be increased 'to an almost unlimited extent'.[16] Many landowners began to look about for the means of making the change to wool farming.

White farmers wishing to raise finance for the expensive conversion to woolled sheep had to provide some form of collateral security. In most cases they seem to have used the title deeds to their farms. Very few Coloureds were in a position to do likewise. Only those at the Kat River Settlement owned land in any numbers, and the terms of the original grant prevented the transfer of erven to whites. Furthermore, although entitled to them, less than one hundred Kat River people ever actually received title deeds for their erven because of 'negligence and dilatoriness' in the Cape Surveyor-General's Office.[17] Their attempts to build up a herd by buying a few beasts at a time were also largely unsuccessful. Because Coloureds could offer no security for purchases on credit the auctioneers at public sales of stock usually demanded cash from them. Also, it must be doubted whether an individual erf and its commonage would have yielded a large enough financial return to justify the level of investment needed for the change to sheep. Herds had to be large to be profitable and the few hundred acres available to the Coloured proprietor could not support them.[18] Inability to obtain credit was therefore an important cause of the Coloureds' general failure to respond to the new economic situation created by the boom in wool.

Lack of response to the opportunities offered by wool did not mean that the Kat River Settlement simply stagnated, maintaining its former level of economic activity but falling behind the white farmers in relative terms. It in fact suffered a steady economic decline. This was partly because, as has been mentioned above, the Cape Government used it as a dumping ground for people dispossessed from other parts of the colony. As the population rose the overall standard of living declined. To many white colonists in the eastern Cape it appeared that the Settlement had become a refuge for 'vagrants' and 'idlers'. They felt this to be intolerable in a colony which was both suffering from a labour shortage and anxious to attract capital investment from overseas. The condition of the Kat River Settlement thus became an issue in the wider debate on the supply of labour, which was a question of 'a very grave and important character' from 1840 onwards.[19]

Cape businessmen and farmers agreed that 'to turn land to advantage a supply of labour must be found'.[20] But at first they differed about the best means of procuring labour. A small but influential group looked to sources outside the colony. Its ablest spokesman, Robert Godlonton, the editor of the *Graham's Town Journal*, published his views in 1842:

> One of the most pressing wants of the colony is that of a better description of labour. All the operations of the field have hitherto been conducted by coloured labourers, but these are found to be quite inadequate to carry out the improvements of the country. Many of them are too independent to engage in service, and others are too indolent to submit to continuous employment. With an influx of European labourers the colony could not fail to make rapid advances in the march of improvement. For want of this, capital is often frittered away in unavailing endeavours; millions of acres of fertile land are lying waste, and useful public works of every kind are neglected, all arising from a scarcity of suitable available labour to carry them forward.[21]

But to rely on immigrants as a source of labour proved impractical. They cost too much to bring to the Cape; and those who did arrive quickly found it possible to earn a living without entering service. For this reason Godlonton and his associates eventually modified their opinion and supported the general cry for measures to force the Coloured people to supply the labour required.

The mass of Cape businessmen and farmers had never agreed with Godlonton's ideas about the inadequacy of Coloured labour. In 1849 a leading Boer politician and landowner told the Cape Legislative Council that Coloureds were the sort of labour most liked by the Boers.[22] What these colonists complained about was the geographical mobility of Coloured labourers, who tended to work only so long as suited their own purposes and then go off to 'squat' on any vacant land they could find.

> The here-today and gone-tomorrow system of Hottentot service [wrote one irate wool-farmer] begets a carelessness of their masters' property on the one part, and a carelessness of the health, morals and comfort of the servant on the other. Can nothing be done to induce a more permanent system of labour?[23]

The colonists proposed to eliminate this mobility by means of a stringent *Vagabond Wet* (Vagrancy Law). Many of them saw any Coloured person who managed to subsist without working for a white as a 'vagrant'. The law they demanded would therefore have a wider application than the title implied:

> What we want is a law to prevent squatting [declared Godlonton]. You may if you please discard the term vagrancy altogether. Only let us have some law which shall protect property against the thefts of these people, which shall encourage industry and repress idleness, and I care not a jot what you call it.[24]

'Squatting' in itself was not the 'evil' which the colonists wished to curb. It was demonstrated in the Legislative Council in 1850 that existing laws were adequate for this purpose.[25] The colonists used 'squatting' as a euphemism for something more: forced labour. As a perceptive British official explained, 'a "Vagrant Law" is, in the general understanding of it in the Colony, contemplated as the means of obliging vagrants to work for private masters'. This understanding of it, the official added, was what made it so generally desired by the whites and so feared by the Coloureds.[26] The British Imperial authorities, who exercised the power of veto over Cape legislation, were opposed to such a measure.

There was one aspect of the Coloureds' reluctance to enter service on which no colonist bothered to comment: the low level of wages. Godlonton argued that labour must be cheap to make investment worthwhile. Wages, he said, should be no more than '*adequate* (i.e. not unreasonable)'.[27] The statistics relating to this topic are rather patchy. It appears that in this period urban 'mechanics' or 'artisans' received equal pay regardless of race. Elsewhere, white workers in the same employment received up to double the rate for Coloureds. Agricultural work paid less than any other kind, and the rate for it remained static, or even declined, between 1830 and 1850. In the district of Albany, the highest wage for unskilled labour on sheep farms was one shilling and sixpence a day or, assuming a six-day week, approximately £2 a month. The rate did not alter between 1842 and 1858. In surrounding districts it was lower. The general practice was for employers to provide food and lodging as well as money, but 'lodging' often consisted of no more than permission to build on an employer's land. There were of course exceptions. A case is quoted of a labourer being offered one shilling and sixpence a month. At the other end of the scale a Coloured shepherd might receive five per cent of the annual profit on the flock he tended, but this practice was not widespread.[28] It is not clear what the average Coloured would have considered a 'living wage' but the universal shortage of labour would suggest that the amounts offered fell below it.

Scarcity of labour, though general, was a less acute problem than some colonists liked to pretend.[29] But its effects were heightened by the reluctance of those Coloureds who did take service to exert themselves to the degree expected by their masters. Many colonists therefore demanded the repeal of laws that protected the interests of labour and the enactment of a strong measure to regulate the relationship between master and servant. When the colonists eventually gained control of the Cape government they carried a 'Masters and Servants Act' which greatly favoured the former.[30] Extending to the minutest circumstances and imposing severe penalties on the defaulting servant, the Act seemed so highly penal to one white observer that (with the characteristic racialism of his age) he hoped no British-born labourer would fall foul of it.[31]

Hand in hand with the colonists' demands for legislation on 'vagrancy' and a Masters and Servants Act went a campaign against the Cape missionary institutions and the Kat River Settlement.[32] The land available for Coloureds at these places, the colonists alleged, allowed Coloureds to live self-sufficient lives free from the need to seek work with the whites. The missionaries were accused of acting in a spirit of 'abominable false Philanthropy' by perpetuating the system. It was asserted that they did not promote the Coloureds' welfare

> by forming them into isolated communities,—by separating them from their more civilized fellow-subjects, and thus giving them distinct, and not unfrequently *opposing* interests to the rest of the community. . . . The separation of labour from capital is equally fatal in its results, and . . . we have at this moment striking examples [of it] both here and in Ireland.[33]

The Coloured leaders at the Kat River were inured to this kind of cant. They saw through the specious benevolence of the argument and grew afraid that their people would be 'enslaved'. Some turned to Britain for protection. In 1849 eight of them petitioned the Aborigines' Protection Society in London for deliverance from the 'insatiable thirst of colonial oppression'.[34] The following year a Coloured priest echoed their sentiments and wrote that 'as the Helots of Sparta were the labourers of the soil and were ruled magisterially with arms, so would the Frontierists like to rule the Natives'.[35] Thus the Kat River people grew unsettled by the whites' constant demand for labour in the aftermath of the large-scale introduction of woolled sheep.

The growth of the Cape woollen industry also posed a threat to the Kat River people in another way. This came about through the Settlement's geographical location. Not all areas of South Africa were suitable for wool farming. Imported sheep needed good grazing and an equable climate to flourish. Conditions were nowhere ideal, and sheep such as Leicesters never managed to established themselves. But Saxons and Merinos quickly adapted to those areas called the 'highveld' in the Orange River Territory and the Cape, where the rainfall varied from sixteen to twenty-five inches a year. The north-eastern regions of the semi-desert Karroo, with a rainfall of under fifteen inches, also proved satisfactory. The uncertainty of rainfall and the prolonged dry season, however, made it essential for every sheep run to have some permanent supply of water in the form of a spring, river frontage or dam. Grazing could be grass or shrubs, depending on the nature of the area. It had to be 'sweet'. In the 'sour' areas (known to the Boers as *zuurveld*) the vegetation proved unsuitable. The best sheep territory did not experience extremes of temperature. The sheep could survive a brief hot spell provided they had water; the snow which often accompanied the last weeks of the cold season rarely lasted long enough to destroy them.

What was considered the best land for sheep farming in the 1840s and 1850s was described at length in contemporary accounts of the eastern Cape. As the zuurveld gave way to the grasslands of upper Albany the traveller entered 'the land of English sheep farming *par excellence.*'[36] Moving further inland he discovered large stretches of productive country. In the Fort Beaufort district sheep farming was the principal occupation, 'much of the country being grassy and suited to the fine woolled sheep which are pastured on it'.[37] The Bruintjes Hoogte area of Somerset, and the lands along the Baviaans and Mankazana rivers as far as the Winterbergen had 'some of the largest and most valuable flocks of wool-bearing sheep that are to be found in the colony'.[38] The district of Cradock was celebrated for the fatness of its stock and the opulence of its proprietors.[39] Victoria East contained large tracts of fine and productive country with pasture particularly healthy for sheep and cattle. This was especially true of the part towards Cradock and the Bontebok Flats, where there was rich grass, permanent water, and clear, open land.[40] Most of the descriptions were written in the exaggerated terms of the financial promoter. But even allowing for this, a glance at the map immediately explains the significance of the above analysis. The Kat River Settlement, with its numerous streams and fertile soil, lay right at the heart of the finest sheep territory in the eastern division.

Originally the settler population in the districts which bordered the Settlement had been overwhelmingly Boer. But between 1834 and 1837 the Great Trek resulted in the wholesale abandonment of the area. The British settlers in Albany took advantage of the exodus to establish themselves in the place of the Boers. Over a twenty-year period there was a marked change in the demography of the eastern districts. In the years immediately following the Trek numerous British settlers made for the areas where sheep farming was most profitable, and thus congregated around the Kat River Settlement. They were afterwards joined by immigrants from Britain who further strengthened the British character of the formerly Boer centres. After the annexation of Victoria East to the Colony in 1847 they were also able to move into the sheep country of the Xhosa. The extent of the movement into Victoria was remarkable. So many farmers from Lower Albany had 'received grants of land between the Fish River and the Keiskamma', the Cape Parliament heard in 1855, that the population of Albany was 'much scarcer' than ten years earlier.[41] Almost all the Victoria farmers were of British origin. The politician Sir Andries Stockenstrom told the Legislative Council in 1850 that there were not fifty Boers in the district. The Kat River Settlement therefore found itself surrounded by its most vehement critics, the commercial farmers—the men most anxious for cheap labour and most conscious of the contrast between their own achievements and the deteriorating state of the Coloureds' land from 1846 onwards.

The eastern Cape commercial farmers were far from united in their political, religious and social outlook. But they had certain attitudes in common. For example, few regarded Coloured aspirations with any sympathy. Again, most believed in the value of material progress. They rated industriousness, business efficiency and private enterprise among the major virtues. Not all had British backgrounds: many Boers had readily adapted themselves to the doctrines and techniques of commercial farming.[42] As a class they looked to the marketing of their surplus produce as a source of income and livelihood, and not to the production of subsistence crops. Nobody questions the importance of their combined contribution to the Cape's economic development. It should not be supposed, however, that their success was achieved without exploitation— as wage-levels indicate. Furthermore, their activities bred a class of businessmen which believed that its financial interests were best served by the pursuit of economic development at all costs. The spokesmen for this business class were the editors and pamphleteers who have been described above. Its membership included numerous 'land speculators' whose operations were a source of continual controversy in the 1840s and 1850s. Using the commercial farmers' criticisms as a pretext, these people tried to bring about the expropriation of the Kat River Settlement.

Land speculation apparently took place on a large scale relative to other financial activity at the Cape. In the areas of densest British settlement many farms were left unoccupied or held on lease by tenants. The exact position is confused because to many colonists 'land speculators' were synonymous with 'absentee landlords' and the analogy was not entirely correct. The real process of speculation was described by a visitor in 1843:

> A spirit of speculation (for it would appear that wherever they go, the English will speculate) gives rise to frequent changes of property . . . and sales of land are often made more upon speculative principles than with a view to farming.[43]

'Speculation' consisted, then, in the buying and selling of land for no other purpose than monetary gain. One of its effects was that as British purchasers penetrated Boer districts the Boers began to value their land more highly.[44] Thus in the eastern Cape a scarcity of land was artificially created. At each successive advancement of the frontier a circle of wealthy men bought farms for speculative reasons and held them until prices rose. Poorer applicants were often excluded. The career of a man named Stanton provides a good example of an individual's operations on this basis: by 1854 he owned three farms, each on a former boundary of the colony.[45] The annexation of Victoria East in 1847 offers a demonstration of the same process on a greater scale. According to one authority the whole affair was 'a regular speculation'.[46] If an examination of land transactions in Victoria is made it is difficult to contradict the statement.

Profitable land speculation depended chiefly on three factors: shortage of available land; an influx of people with capital wishing to buy; and a government competent to issue deeds or register transfers, so that the new owner had watertight title to his purchase. By the mid-1840s practically all the productive farming land in the Cape had been granted by the government to private individuals.[47] In 1846 the total area of the colony was estimated to be 110 000 square miles, or about seventy million acres. Of this approximately forty-three million acres (or three-fifths) was in private hands. Most of the remaining two-fifths comprised 'mountain ranges and arid plains, almost entirely unfit for agricultural or pastoral purposes'. The balance was loan-tenure farms, missionary institutions, town commons, outspan places, lands formerly surveyed but to which title deeds still had not been issued and, finally, the Kat River Settlement.[48] Nobody sought the land unfit for either agriculture or ranching. Although in 1842 there was much vacant land in Graaff-Reinet, Uitenhage and Somerset, it was destitute of water. And many of the areas designated 'unoccupied' formed pockets in the midst of occupied farms and could be of commercial use only if attached to them.

The Cape government placed no restrictions on the sale or purchase of land. The transfer of landed property was 'simple and secure'.[49] The seller had to produce an accurate chart of the property at the Surveyor-General's office in Cape Town. The Transfer Office then made out a deed of transfer in favour of the purchaser, which was registered as soon as the government received payment of transfer dues amounting to four per cent of the purchase money. The land thereupon became the property of the purchaser and his heirs 'forever'—provided the annual quitrent (varying from thirty shillings to £7 10s. according to farm size) was paid to government. Farms could be converted to freehold tenure for the equivalent of twenty years' quitrent paid in a lump sum.

Although Crown Land was virtually exhausted some pamphleteers tried to conceal the fact in the hope of luring immigrants to the Cape. In

1843 J.C. Chase described the colony as 'under-peopled' and alleged that the government had five million 'unappropriated acres' to distribute. With equally little regard for truth he also reported an 'inexhaustible supply' of land across the colonial border in the 'productive, but inadequately-peopled' country of the Xhosa. The tribesmen, he said, occupied over twenty million acres and would 'gladly admit European settlers' to the most fertile parts.[50] In fact when Chase wrote the land for a long way across the Cape's northern and eastern borders had been almost entirely expropriated by emigrant Boers from the colony. The rest was densely populated by Africans. When Governor Smith annexed thirty million acres to the Cape in 1847 he found Boers settled almost everywhere. He wished to sell land in order to raise revenue for the colonial treasury and could only do so by expelling Xhosa tribesmen from their pastures in Victoria East.[51]

Some reasons for Chase's deception are easy to divine. Immigration would heighten the economic activity he wished to promote, and indeed formed part of the body of measures canvassed by those interested in developing the colony. Again, immigrants wishing to buy land helped to create the right climate for profitable speculation. They would be less likely to come to the Cape if they knew the true situation with regard to land—especially while cheap Crown Land could still be had in other British colonies. But there were deeper motives for Chase's activities. A section of the British settlers, with which he sympathised, feared the day when the imperial government would grant control of the colony's internal affairs to the colonists—a step which became a distinct possibility after the publication of Lord Durham's report on self-government for Canada in the late 1830s. The Boers outnumbered the British settlers in the Cape and would therefore gain the upper hand, to the detriment (it was felt) of all interests but their own. Many British settlers engaged in commerce had a low opinion of Boer business capacity. A characteristic expression of such prejudice may be seen in a description of Graaff-Reinet in 1848:

> A vexatious quiet ... pervades everything and everyone; and none of that bustling energy of our countrymen, which is looked upon by these slow-thinking gentlemen as something quite ridiculous, is discernible in the trading operations of the imperturbable Dutchman.[52]

The danger, as certain British businessmen perceived it, was that a colonial government dominated by Boers would give a low priority to economic development. The financial interests of the British community would then suffer.

In the years after 1840 the threat was clear, but did not seem imminent. To anticipate it, Chase, Godlonton and their associates put their trust in the prior economic development of the country, which would attract British immigrants and concentrate all the wealth in their hands. Political dominance, they believed, would then follow. In 1850 an influential British settler named Richard Southey strongly urged the colonial government to help in advancing the policy:

> Were it not for the superior energy of the English, we should long since have been swamped. We should therefore encourage by every possible means the increase of the English population—vote as much as possible to bring out English labour, and in every way encourage capitalists to come.

Albany, like the rest of the Cape, had little established industry—only a few tanneries and a soap factory. Agriculture therefore offered the best hope for fulfilling Southey's plan:

> Open up the resources of the country. Let the attention of all Agricultural Societies and private individuals be directed to improvement in Agriculture and Stock—to the production of exportable articles, wool, cotton, etc., etc. [53]

'Opening up the resources' of the country as Southey wished would involve (among other measures)[54] the conversion of all suitable land to commercial farming. British settlers generally saw themselves and their countrymen in Britain as the only agents capable of achieving such a goal. They confidently anticipated the time when Boer, tribesman and Coloured would each lose his land through inability to compete with the economic enterprise of the Briton. 'Albany must be considered as occupied (speaking generally)', said a visitor in 1844, 'and the Dutch districts are in a state of gradual revolution which will consummate in the occupation of all the most fertile parts by English settlers'.[55] In the event, however, the Boer was not so easily shifted. He had legal title to his land together with the resources to defend his position, and could only be dispossessed by hard economic inducements. But the tribesmen across the colonial boundary had no such defences. British settlers therefore urged the imperial government to seize tribal land by force. It 'must be taken, sold and settled', declared a wealthy wool farmer, 'and [the tribesmen] must be taught to earn their living in an honest, industrious way, which might eventually lead to their Christianisation'.[56] Similarly in 1850 Godlonton presented Governor Smith with a scheme for turning the Xhosa country into cotton farms, although all the land involved still lay outside the Cape colonial boundaries.[57] Similar plans were put forward on other occasions by both Boers and British settlers in the eastern Cape and aired in the frontier press.

Given this background, it is not surprising to find Godlonton calling in his editorials for the opening of the Kat River lands to white settlement.[58] He received public support from Chase and from members of the Southey and Bowker families among others. In 1848 he corresponded with Southey about taking over land in the Kat River Settlement.[59] All these individuals had personal interests in the land question. The Southey family were speculators on a large scale in several districts. Godlonton had bought five farms for speculative purposes in the newly-annexed Orange River Sovereignty. It cannot be said that they craved the Kat River region solely on this account, but the weight of evidence is that their attacks on its Coloured population owed more to their views on the subjects of labour and land than to the actual condition of the Settlement. These views in turn were coloured by their personal financial ambitions.

Their hostility and prejudice would have signified little, perhaps, had Godlonton and his associates been unable to prevail on the government to act in their interests. Events, however, played into their hands between 1846 and 1852. Due to a combination of circumstances they exercised an influence over the government quite disproportionate to their wealth or numbers. First, the imperial authorities sent Sir Harry Smith to govern the Cape. He appointed Southey, T.H. Bowker, Chase, Godlonton and several others of their persuasion to key posts in the colonial administration. Next, the Boer leaders and the citizens of Cape Town mounted a determined campaign for 'representative government' at the Cape. They demanded constitutional changes which would give the colonists a decisive voice in running the country. Smith committed the cardinal political error of trying to build a policy on a minority view. He resisted those colonists calling for representative government for some time, supported only by the business community of the eastern districts and a few Cape Town merchants. In this period government by consent broke down and the colony was ruled by a virtual oligarchy, of which Godlonton and Southey were influential members.[60] Through them government pressures on the Kat River Settlement intensified, and Smith actually went so far as to suggest to his Legislative Council in 1848 that they introduce 'vagrancy' legislation. The Coloureds reacted to the latter with such hostility that a panic occurred among whites in certain areas of the colony and the suggestion was hastily dropped. But Coloured suspicions had been aroused. 'It appears to me', wrote a missionary in October 1850, 'that a spirit of antagonism and bitterness is daily becoming stronger between the colonists and *all* people of colour.'[61] The Coloureds found themselves caught between the devil of the Smith oligarchy and the deep blue sea of a representative legislature dominated by white colonists. In either event their land rights and individual freedoms seemed in jeopardy. Rebellion in

1851 possibly seemed the only method left for them to express their fears in this respect.

The Coloured rebellion led, in a short time, to the confiscation of all rebel-owned erven and the steady displacement of Coloureds by whites in the remaining arable areas of the Settlement. The presence of whites produced a considerable rise in land values. In 1850 a good erf might have fetched £20.[62] In 1858 an erf sold 'for as much as £1 400, the buildings and other improvements forming not a very considerable part of the value'.[63] The Kat River district became integrated with the white economic structure on the terms desired by Godlonton. With few exceptions its former inhabitants were dispersed or forced into service. The ambitions of the businessmen and speculators were thus realised. Their success was no accident. The Settlement's inability to respond to the changing economic situation in the 1840s had left it vulnerable to the criticisms of the white commercial classes. And the propaganda assiduously put out by self-interested parties moved the government to act against the Coloureds in an arbitrary and unsympathetic manner.[64] The Coloured rebellion was thus not in itself the cause of the expropriation of Kat River land by whites. It merely speeded a process which was already threatening to engulf the Settlement.

To sum up: this study suggests that the commercial classes in the eastern Cape believed that productive wool farming required the proper combination of capital, land and labour, and capital would not immigrate unless assured of adequate labour. The leaders and spokesmen of the classes mentioned, who already owned much of the productive land, and therefore stood to profit by an influx of capital, set out to create the conditions for such an inflow, at the expense of the Coloureds. This involved preventing the Coloureds from establishing a foothold in the white economy, by differential legislation (the 'vagrancy' laws). Unable to master the economic forces released by the growth of the woollen industry, the Coloureds therefore became their victims. The link between the operation of white private enterprise and the expropriation of indigenous peoples' land seems substantiated in the case of the Kat River Settlement. It may therefore be assumed that the economic environment is a motivating factor which must be taken into account in any attempt to explain the Coloured rebellion.

The Kat River story illuminates many of the underlying forces at work in eastern Cape society during the middle years of the nineteenth century. It shows the direct connection between the expanding British wool market, the response of the white South African producer and the fate of the Coloured settlers. It demonstrates the effect on Cape society of certain economic theories conceived at the height of Britain's industrial revolution.

It identifies a coherent body of colonial businessmen committed to the same self-confident materialism as their British counterparts. It is important to see the values of these colonists in their historical perspective, and to recognise that much of what they believed was received wisdom in the pre-Marxian world of 1840–50. On the other hand, it must also be observed that the crude, bullying self-interest of Godlonton, Southey and their associates, particularly in relation to the Kat River Coloureds, exceeded the norms of even the brutality of early Victorian Britain. The strength of this colonial group lay in its influence on the Cape government—an influence secured by patronage and nepotism as much as by merit or popularity. The Coloureds and their champions had no counter-vailing voice in official circles, any more than the African tribesmen on the colonial boundary. Power lay with the white settlers, and was being used to fashion a world in which the culture of the Coloured peoples had no part. The expansion and transformation of the pre-industrial Cape economy was about to become a major policy goal. Implicit in the process was the expropriation of 'under-utilised' land, regardless of the social cost to its occupiers, but in the belief that they would ultimately benefit from the change. This being known, the task of explaining such events as the Xhosa Wars of 1846 and 1851, the Kat River rebellion, and the Xhosa 'cattle killing delusion' of 1857 becomes easier.

Notes

1 S.D. Neumark, *Economic Influences on the South African Frontier, 1652–1836*, Stanford, 1957
2 W.M. Macmillan, *Bantu, Boer and Briton*, Oxford, 1963, pp. 278–305; J.S. Galbraith, *Reluctant Empire*, California, 1963, p. 276; M. Wilson and L. Thompson (eds.), *The Oxford History of South Africa*, 2 vols., Oxford, 1969, i, pp. 233–71
3 An attempt has been made to analyse the political economy of the Cape Colony and its relationship with British imperial power in T. Kirk, 'Self-Government and Self-Defence in South Africa: the Interaction of British and Cape Politics, 1846–53', D.Phil., Oxford, 1973
4 T. Kirk, 'Progress and Decline in the Kat River Settlement, 1829–54', *JAH*, xiv, 3, 1973
5 P. Deane and W.A. Cole, *British Economic Growth, 1688–1959*, Cambridge, 1969, pp. 192–201
6 T. Southey, *A Treatise on Sheep* ..., London, 1840, pp. xi–xii
7 A. Hamilton, 'On Wool Supply', *Journal of the Statistical Society*, xxxiii, Part IV, December 1870, p. 498
8 H.B. Thom, *Die Geskiedenis van Skaapboerdery in Suid Afrika*, Amsterdam, 1936, p. 198; Neumark, *Economic Influences*, p. 165

9 See, for example, J.C. Chase, *The Cape of Good Hope and Eastern Province of Algoa Bay* ..., London, 1843, and the criticisms of it in G. Nicholson, *The Cape and its Colonists*, London, 1848, p. 113

10 A demonstration of the difficulties faced by wool farmers appears in M.H. Lister (ed.), *Journals of Andrew Geddes Bain*, Cape Town, 1949, p. xxxiv: 'A farmer lately bringing his wool to market unloaded it at the top of the mountain and rolled it down the precipitous face, following slowly along the so-called road with his empty waggons till he reached the bottom, where he quietly loaded it up again.'

11 Lippert & Co. diversified into Cape diamonds in 1869 and sent Alfred Beit to Kimberley as their agent: Sir A. Beit and J.G. Lockhart, *The Will and the Way*, London, 1957, pp. 4–5

12 G. Saron and L. Hotz (eds.), *The Jews in South Africa—a history*, Cape Town, 1955, p. 350

13 *Ibid.*, pp. 350–1

14 *British Parliamentary Papers (BPP): Reports from Committees, 1851, XIV, (635)*: Report from the Select Committee on the Kafir Tribes—evidence of J. Fairbairn, 12 June 1851; Q.454

15 *Cape of Good Hope Almanac and Annual Register*, Cape Town, 1853, p. 258

16 Quoted in R. Godlonton, *Sketches of the Eastern Districts of the Cape of Good Hope*, Grahamstown, 1842, p. 122

17 CO 48/339, Cathcart to Newcastle, 14 August 1853 (No. 35)—Colonial Office Archives, Public Record Office, London

18 Figures of £1 000 and more are quoted in mid-nineteenth century sources for the expense of setting up a profitable herd. They are probably understated. See Chase, p. 183; Nicholson, p. 60; W. Irons, *The Settlers' Guide to the Cape* ..., London, 1858, pp. 143–4

19 W. Porter, *The Porter Speeches*, Cape Town, 1886, p. 30

20 ?. Gilchrist, *The Cape of Good Hope*, Glasgow, 1844, p. 13. Cf. Chase, *The Cape of Good Hope and Eastern Province*, p. 231

21 Godlonton, *Sketches*, pp. 110–1

22 He added that one of the advantages of employing Coloureds was their willingness to accept inferior provisions to those demanded by white labourers; *Graham's Town Journal*, 26 May 1849

23 J.M. Bowker, *Speeches, Letters and Selections from Important Papers*, Grahamstown, 1864, p. 130

24 Godlonton to Southey, 8 May 1849: B.A. Le Cordeur, 'Robert Godlonton as Architect of Frontier Opinion', *Archives Year Book for South African History (1959)*, Cape Town, 1960, ii, p. 21

25 BPP, *A & P, 1851, XXXVII, [1362]*, Further Papers Relative to the Establishment of a Representative Assembly at the Cape, p. 71

26 [J. Montagu], *Case of the Cape of Good Hope and its Constitution*, London, 1853, p. 15

27 *Graham's Town Journal*, 24 June 1848

28 See Godlonton, *Sketches*, p. 26; Gilchrist, *The Cape of Good Hope*, p. 21; Nicholson, *The Cape and its Colonists*, p. 61; Irons, *The Settlers' Guide to the Cape*, p. 79; Chase, *The Cape of Good Hope and Eastern Province*, p. 182; H. Ward, *The Cape and the Kaffirs*, London, 1851, p. 15; W. M. Macmillan, *The Cape Colour Question*, London, 1927, p. 253; E.A. Walker (ed.), *Cambridge History of the British Empire*,

8 vols., Cambridge, 1963, viii, p. 832

29 Porter, *The Porter Speeches*, pp. 423–4

30 No. 15 of 1856

31 Irons, *The Settlers' Guide to the Cape*, p. 229

32 'Campaign' does not seem too strong a description for, say, the repeated attacks on the Moravian Mission at Genadendal between 1846 and 1854 (which may be followed in B. Krüger, *The Pear Tree Blossoms*, Genadendal, 1966, p. 223, and volumes WO 1/448, 449 and 450, War Office Archives, PRO, London) and the simultaneous onslaught in press, Legislative Council and public meeting hall on the Settlement

33 *Graham's Town Journal*, 20 March 1847

34 *Annual Report of the Aborigines' Protection Society*, London, May 1849

35 J. Read, jun., to Aborigines' Protection Society, 20 October 1850: Anti-Slavery Papers, Rhodes House Library, Oxford—MSS Brit. Emp. s 18, C.21/21

36 Gilchrist, *The Cape of Good Hope*, p. 44

37 Irons, *The Settlers' Guide to the Cape*, p. 88

38 Godlonton, *Sketches*, p. 44.

39 J.C. Byrne, *Emigrant's Guide to the Cape of Good Hope*, London, 1848, p. 47

40 *Cape of Good Hope Almanac and Annual Register*, Cape Town, 1853, p. 254

41 Cape of Good Hope, *Report from the Select Committee of the House of Assembly on Frontier Defence*, 1855, evidence of T.J. Biddulph, Q.14

42 'Account of the Colony of the Cape of Good Hope', *The Colonial Magazine*, London, August/September 1842, p. 430

43 Gilchrist, *The Cape of Good Hope*, pp. 3–4

44 Godlonton, *Sketches*, pp. 43–4

45 Cape of Good Hope, *Report from the Select Committee of the House of Assembly on the Defence of the Eastern Frontier*, 1854, Q.150

46 BPP, *Reports from Committees, 1851, XIV, (635)*: Report from the Select Committee on the Kaffir Tribes, evidence of Sir A. Stockenstrom, Q.1457

47 Godlonton, *Sketches*, p. 123; Gilchrist, *The Cape of Good Hope*, p. 1; Nicholson, *The Cape and its Colonists*, p. 153

48 BPP, *Reports from Commissioners, 1850, XXIII, (1204)*, Tenth Report of the Colonial Land and Emigration Commission, p. 28

49 Gilchrist, *The Cape of Good Hope*, p. 9

50 Chase, *The Cape of Good Hope and Eastern Province*, pp. 221–3, cf. Nicholson, *The Cape and its Colonists*, p. 113

51 BPP, *Reports from Commissioners, 1847–8, XXVI, 961*, Eighth General Report of the Colonial Land and Emigration Commissioners, p. 91

52 Nicholson, *The Cape and its Colonists*, p. 91

53 Southey to Godlonton, 29 July 1850. Cape Colony Letters, Rhodes House Library, Oxford—MSS Afr s 1, f 129. At the time Godlonton had a seat in the Cape Legislative Council

54 The economic theories of Godlonton, Southey and their ilk (a fuller discussion of which is given in T. Kirk, 'Self-Government and Self-Defence . . . ') reflected contemporary British thought about the economic role of the Empire. Broadly speaking, the South Africans believed they could 'open up the resources of the country' by a comprehensive programme involving capital investment from Britain, free-trade within the confines of the Empire, the construction by central and local government of railways and other 'useful public works',

a steady flow of skilled and semi-skilled immigrants from Europe and *laissez-faire* in all spheres of industrial activity save the regulation of labour. It was a formula which later proved brilliantly successful in the 'colonies of settlement' (Canada, Australia and New Zealand). In the Cape Colony it would also achieve much in purely economic terms, though—as this article indicates—certain of its features held an explicit threat for coloured land-tenure in the Kat River Settlement, and for the security and civil rights of the non-whites generally

55 Gilchrist, *The Cape of Good Hope*, p. 6
56 Bowker, *Speeches, Letters and Selections*, p. 237; cf. Porter, *The Porter Speeches*, p. 435
57 Entry for 12 September 1850, *Godlonton's Diary*, Library of Parliament, Cape Town.
58 *Grabam's Town Journal*, 18 December 1847
59 Le Cordeur, 'Robert Godlonton', p. 36
60 *Ibid.*, pp. 80–93; A.H. Duminy, 'The Role of Sir Andries Stockenstrom in Cape Politics, 1848–56', *Archives Year Book for South African History (1960)*, Cape Town, 1961, ii, pp. 111–28; Kirk, 'Self-Government and Self-Defence', chs, 6–8
61 J. Gill to J. Freeman, Fort Beaufort, 24 October 1850, London Missionary Society Archives, London—25/5/B
62 J. Green to J. Freeman, 26 June 1850, LMS Archives, 25/4/C
63 W. Govan, *Memorials of . . . James Laing*, Glasgow, 1875, p. 133
64 Kirk, 'Progress and Decline'

CHAPTER TEN

'The friends of the natives':

merchants, peasants and the political and ideological structure of liberalism in the Cape, 1854–1910

Stanley Trapido

Liberalism in the Cape and the forces which shaped its political manifestations are the central considerations of this essay. It is usual but misleading to write of Cape liberalism: misleading because Cape liberalism has acquired the properties associated with myth. It is often given the accolade of the great but lost tradition, so that it has come to be separated from contemporary liberalism in South Africa. This can readily be explained because, in the judgement of polemicists and historians, the shortcomings of historical liberalism are accounted for in terms of individual hypocrisy, political naivete and betrayal. In this way the conditions which made liberalism in the Cape possible, the purpose which different liberals gave to the institutions which were created, and the changing circumstances which constantly reshaped liberalism in the Cape have come to be disregarded.

To write of liberalism in the Cape would help to free us from the ahistorical treatment of apologists and critics. Apologists of Cape liberalism describe it as a continuous process with all its inconsistencies ironed out, while the critics, in laying bare these contradictions and inconsistencies, neglect the social relationships which produced them.[1] To point to the liberal sentiments expressed by a variety of politicians, administrators and journalists between 1850 and 1910 enables the critic to assert that Cape liberalism is no more than a catalogue of rhetoric.[2] He or she can then produce an alternative catalogue of anti-liberal sentiments expressed during the same period, and, as often as not, by the same individuals. But rhetoric is rarely insignificant, and its presence helps to uncover the social relationships which call it forth. Since these relationships were changing, it is important that the apparent sameness of the rhetoric does not disguise for us the changing alliances and purposes of liberals in the Cape during these sixty years. Moreover, an inventory of inconsistencies brings us no nearer to an understanding of the social relationship which at different times and for different reasons modified liberal institutions.

Liberalism in the Cape is best known for the suffrage it created, more particularly the suffrage which allowed people of African origins, initially Khoisan* and then Nguni, to participate in colonial politics. But it also permitted the much wider enfranchisement of Afrikaners which (though it is taken more for granted by historians than the enfranchisement of Africans), when compared with the franchise then applying in Britain, requires as much explanation as African enfranchisement. This enfranchisement of Afrikaner and African peoples was intended to restore to the colonial state the stability and authority which had been disturbed by the events of the 1840s.[3] In noting the intention we are simultaneously drawn to the guiding principle which determined that parliamentary representation would be extended. William Porter, the Cape Attorney-General, was typical of a significant and ultimately decisive group within the Cape government who, having reviewed the events which had come to threaten the colonial state, concluded that representative government would have to come sooner or later, and therefore it was better that it came sooner since 'all reason and all experience prove that those rulers give twice who give quickly, and that no privileges are so sure to be abused as privileges wrung from reluctant hands'.[4]

Rule from above by a constant adaptation and concession to those below was the hallmark of liberalism in metropolitan Britain. This liberalism had been central to the creation of the conditions which made industrialisation possible, and although this process was in turn dependent on the expansion of empire, it becomes apparent that it was an ideology whose

---

*The descendants of the Khoisan have become known as the 'Coloured' people and it is usual for outsiders to describe their origin as the result of unions between Khoisan, slaves and white settlers. Although there were important Afrikaner-Khoisan unions of which the Baster communities of the north-west Cape and South-West Africa are the most prominent to have survived, the most significant structural factor which relates the 'Coloured' people to white Afrikaners is not race but class. Because Khoisan-cum-slave descended groups became proletarians (i.e. a group separated from their land and with only their labour to sell) in an area dominated by Afrikaner landowners, these African people (for the overwhelming majority of slaves were of Malagasy, Mozambique and West African origin) adopted a working-class variation of the dominant Afrikaner culture. Although Afrikaners do have Khoisan ancestry, those who refer to the 'Coloured' people as 'brown Afrikaners', or even as 'onse bruin mense', make a genetic rather than a structural analysis which confuses rather than clarifies the role and place of the 'Coloured' people in South African society. For a discussion of the problems of terminology, see also S. Newton-King, 'The Labour Market of the Cape Colony, 1807–28', above, p. 201, n. 4.

success carried all before it, even in a colonial situation where settlers were only a part of the population.

The need to incorporate politically both Afrikaners and Africans—first Khoisan and then Nguni—was made necessary and possible by the significant changes which took place in the Cape economy under British rule. These changes—both in the kind of economic activity and its scale—brought new relationships into being not only among British immigrants but also among the non-British and local populations. The restrictive political and administrative institutions which had served a small-scale economy designed to provide meat and grains for ships of the East India trade became, as a result, totally unsuited to an economy geared to large-scale wine and wool production and whose need for growth led to the demand for more facilities necessary for the opening up of the interior, either for further pastoral enterprises or for the more hazardous mineral exploration which marked the 1850s.[5]

Coinciding with these changes in the economy and with the changing relationships which were emerging came an increase in the number of Christian missionary societies which saw new opportunities for their evangelical work. It is, however, difficult to separate the expansion of the missionary frontier from that of the European merchant and trader, and the Christianity of free trade hastened the process of creating the market-oriented peasants which had begun with earlier settler conquests and economic expansion. As Dr John Philip wrote in his *Researches in South Africa* in 1828,

> While our missionaries beyond the borders of the colony of the Cape of Good Hope are everywhere scattering the seeds of civilization, social order and happiness, they are by the most unexceptional means, extending British influence and the British empire. Wherever the missionary places his standard among a savage tribe, their prejudices against colonial government give way; their dependence upon the colony is increased by the creation of artificial wants; so confidence is restored, intercourse with the colony is established, industry, trade and agriculture spring up; and every genuine convert among them made to Christian religion becomes the ally and friend of the colonial Government.[6]

Nor was he alone. Similar sentiments can be found in almost all the missionary journals of the nineteenth century. Thus, the Reverend Joseph John Freeman in 1851 enthused,

> It is something to have changed the old kraal into a decent village—the old kaross into substantial European clothing—idleness into industry, ignorance into intelligence, selfishness into benevolence and heathenism into Christianity.[7]

John Noble writing in 1877 pointed explicitly to the close connections of 'the magistrate, the missionary, the school master and the teacher' in furthering

> the aim of the policy of the Colonial Government since 1855 . . . to establish and maintain peace, to diffuse civilisation and Christianity, and to establish society on the basis of individual property and personal industry.[8]

In addition, for the new entrepreneurs, both within the colony and beyond its borders, small-scale African producers provided substantial opportunities for commercial gain.[9] To quote J.J. Freeman on Zuurbrak yet again, the Khoi inhabitants of the station were 'clad in fabrics of English manufacture',[10] while Philip regarded the increasing sales of the two stores at Zuurbrak as 'evidence of progress not known in the previous one hundred and sixty years'.[11] More strikingly, T. Helm, the missionary at Zuurbrak, was reported in 1850 as stating:

> another proof of the general industry of [his] communicants is the sum realised by persons, who at the request of the people, and in order to obviate the necessity for their resorting to villages where there are canteens, have been encouraged to open shops at the Institution. One has retired having realised in five or six years £800 by his profit on manufactures . . . and I have been shown the books of another by which it appears that he receives about £100 per month in cash, and more than twice as much during harvest and sheep shearing months.[12]

Nor was Zuurbrak alone in this. The Kat River settlement produced 6 900 bushels of grain in 1833 and over 22 000 in 1845. In the same period it doubled its sheep and horses and increased the number of its cattle fourfold.[13] As Andries Stoffel of Kat River told the 1836 *Select Committee on Aborigines*, 'We have ploughing, waggon workers, and shoemakers, and their tradesmen among us'.[14] The earliest mission station, Genadendal, was a substantial producer of agricultural products before it went into decline in the mid-century. The productive activities were not limited to agriculture—'one half of the population subsist by working at mechanical arts, cutlers, smiths, joiners, turners, masons, carpenters, shoemakers, tailors, and so on'.[15] Earlier, in the autonomous tribal economies, the cultivator's surplus had been appropriated by the chief, and while some of the surplus was redistributed, a part was retained to maintain the power and to undertake the religious and administrative functions of the chief.* But the unequal exchange of European trade and the 'new wants' which this trade created

---

*See P. Bonner, 'Classes, the mode of production and the state in pre-colonial Swaziland', and esp. W. Beinart, 'Production and the material base of Chieftainship in Pondoland, *c*.1830–80', pp. 120–47 above.

were incompatible with the chief's role. Trading not only by-passed the chief (or, if the chief were involved in the trading, reduced redistribution) but created inequalities between members of the same clan. Chiefs, or their diviners, attempted to maintain their own power, and sought to restore inequality through accusations of witchcraft and by 'smelling out'. This in turn brought charges of 'barbarism' and 'injustice' from the vanguard of settler society, the missionary, for whom Christian compassion and economic individualism were essential components of the civilisation which he sought to spread. 'Smelling out' also hastened the arrival, even before colonial annexation, of new administrators, with concepts of justice and civilisation based on private property.[16] The expanding Cape economy was in the process of creating free peasant communities. The process was often quite self-conscious and, where possible, missionaries and administrators sought segments of societies where chiefs were weakest.

The free peasant/merchant relationship brought the need for the small workshops—in the Cape ports in particular—with their Khoisan-descended artisans migrating from the missions to the western Cape.[17] At times liberals within the dominant white group whose relationship was with free artisans or labourers rather than with free peasants gained greater prominence, a factor which adds to the difficulty of analysing liberalism in the Cape.

By the 1840s neither commercial nor missionary expansion required territorial expansion. On the contrary, both required a period of consolidation. But to the new settlers from Britain, territorial expansion seemed essential. It provided the opportunities for acquiring not only land and new labour to work the land, but also widespread opportunities for speculation.[18] This expansion disrupted commercial and evangelical activities, and in the second half of the nineteenth century expansionism was generally associated with a move towards illiberal legislation within the colony. It was territorial expansion and commercial conservatism which had led to the breakdown of British authority in the Cape, leaving the security of this strategic colony solely to a military presence. Thus in the early 1850s, the British troops at the Cape numbered more than a third of those in the whole of India—the most prized imperial possession. It was in part to rectify this political disaster that the 1853 constitution,[19] with its liberal franchise, came into being.

Liberalism in the Cape created a great and a small tradition. Centred mainly in Cape Town, liberals of the great tradition were drawn from a variety of sources. The leading financial and commercial enterprises produced a virtual roll-call of liberal names: James Fairbairn, J.H. Wicht,

J.C. Jarvis, J.H. Ebden, P.A. Brand and Saul Solomon were all early directors of one company, the South African Mutual Life Assurance Company.[20] Christian missionaries added their voice. The great administrators from William Porter onwards made decisive contributions to the liberal tradition. The London Missionary Society, with its renowned superintendent Dr John Philip, had its colonial headquarters in Cape Town, but after 1860 the major missionary contribution to the great tradition came from Scottish missionaries, with their educational and mission institute at Lovedale and their influential journal *The Kafir Express*. From the legal profession[21] and the major newspapers of the colony came further support,[22] while almost invariably the government's opponents of the day—whether James Rose-Innes, John X. Merriman, Jacobus Wilhelmus Sauer, Thomas Scanlen, John Gordon Sprigg, Saul Solomon or John Henry de Villiers—could be counted among its ideologues. It is above all through Merriman and Sprigg that the 'contradictions' in liberalism, the changing imperatives of the 'great tradition', can be seen.[23] But all these groups came to portray their decisions, their hopes and their fears in terms which would have been clearly understood by Victorian Britain.

In Britain merchants, administrators, lawyers, newspaper editors and politicians, together with the landed aristocracy, emerged to play autonomous roles in controlling the process of industrialisation. Elsewhere in the industrial countries of Europe their work was very largely accomplished by a strong state. But these industrialising societies were reacting to the expansion of British capitalism. Britain, perhaps because it was first to undergo the transformation, because its empire produced both markets and profit, and because the empire was naval-based, did not have a strong state. British capitalism could, therefore, as we have already suggested, make accommodation from above, using its strategy of containing the new classes which it had created. The Cape's governing elite was both drawn from, and modelled on, the British elite. For the most part, this elite did not question British institutions and their adaptations enabled them to play a substantial and independent part in the maintenance of a colonial state: this, in spite of its use of the military in conquest, was nevertheless without much coercive power on a day-to-day basis. We are not, of course, suggesting that autonomous institutions survived—or even prospered—without there being both a combination of favourable local circumstances and an urgent need for them to survive in the Cape. British settlers did not after all produce an indigenous liberalism in Natal.

It has already been noted that a particular conjunction of group interests made it possible for liberal policies to be propagated. When those in power placed a restraint on territorial expansion and favoured commercial expansion, particularly if it encompassed peasant production, it usually followed that the view that grievances were best contained through elected Parliamentary spokesmen was given high value. But to describe the conditions which made liberalism possible is not to assert that liberal influences prevailed on all occasions. Nor is it to attribute liberal motivation to all members of the coalition which made for the necessary conditions. Those who represented territorially satisfied groups were not invariably liberals, but liberals drew strength from alliances with them and assumed for themselves a mediating role between the colonial and imperial governments. No one exemplified this better than Saul Solomon, the respected 'elder statesman' of the Cape Legislative Assembly. Of Solomon, Anthony Trollope remarked: 'It is not too much to say that he is regarded on both sides as a safe adviser; and I believe that it would be hardly possible to pass any measure of importance to which he offered strenuous opposition.'[24]

Solomon's career, like that of Sauer and Merriman later on, also illustrated the kind of alliances which liberals could construct. More than any other politician, Solomon was seen to be the archetypal liberal, yet when he opposed the British Colonial Secretary's plans for a South African confederation he was ultimately joined in his cause by Jan Hofmeyr and his *Boerenbeschermings Vereeniging* which supported his candidature in the 1879 Cape general election. This it did in spite of Solomon's insistence that he would not vote for the repeal of the excise duty on wine, which was the occasion for the formation of the Vereeniging. Solomon's opposition to the expansionist policies of the British Government, which had led to the annexation of the South African Republic and the war against the Zulu nation, had been the overriding consideration which determined the Boerenbeschermings Vereeniging's willingness to work for his return to Parliament.[25]

The conventional wisdom which assumes that liberalism was imposed in some prefabricated way by a British government fails to comprehend the relationship which evolved in the South African colonial context. Direct British intervention in South African affairs between 1875 and 1880—posited on assumptions which rejected the idea of control by incorporating blacks into settler society—helped to create a local reaction which restated the incorporationist thesis. The Governor of the Cape, Sir Henry Barkly, told the Colonial Secretary, Lord Carnarvon, that his confederation proposals were seen by the local ministry as involving 'the unmerited disfranchisement of the whole of the Coloured races, Kafirs, Hottentots, emancipated Negroes'. Barkly continued:

In the Cape Colony proper, no distinction has been made and the franchise is bestowed irrespective of race or colour, on anyone who possesses the necessary qualifications. Nor do Ministers see how it would be possible to draw any line which should in this Colony exclude persons from the franchise simply on the grounds of colour or race. The exercise of the privilege thus bestowed has been unattended with any inconvenience, and it would probably be unwise to disturb an arrangement which has on the whole worked well by the introduction of a change which could scarcely fail to convey to the minds of those most interested erroneous impressions in which it might very possibly stir up those feelings of race which it has been the object of this government to allay.[26]

This, however, is only part of the story. In February 1876 John Merriman, already serving in a Cape government, presented another aspect of liberalism:

Today the *Volksblad* congratulates Lord Carnarvon on being ready to settle native difficulties 'in a manner agreeable to Africander colonists', which in plain English means to take their land and divide it among White farmers. Froude over and over again hinted at Basutoland, with its 150 000 progressive natives, being handed over to the Free States as a balance for the Diamond Fields.

The Cape Ministry are not, as you know, Solomons: but they do heartily oppose and detest Mr Froude's and Lord Carnarvon's native policy. We are gradually educating the natives. We are introducing individual tenure of land—and European implements. We have four thousand natives at work on our Railways. Gradually the power of the Chiefs is being broken up, and our laws introduced, and I hope this session to get a measure for the modified municipal government of locations. Lovedale has three hundred native boys and seventy girls, very many of whom pay for their own education. They learn trades, and to give you an idea of whether they can do so or not, one of our best carpenters in the locomotive shops at East London is a native. [Natives] may earn forty shillings a week as printers.[27]

Solomon himself, perhaps in the light of his increasingly close association with the Boerenbeschermings Vereeniging, believed that 'the feeling of the country, especially perhaps among the Dutch, is rapidly tending in the direction of humanity and fair play to the Natives all round'.[28]

It was, however, a transient phenomenon. Thereafter, Britain's second withdrawal from the subcontinent coincided with a shortage of labour in the colony in the western agricultural districts and beyond the colony on the goldfields of the Witwatersrand.[29] A new alliance of expansionists came into being once more. In the early 1880s, the Scanlen ministry, which had abandoned Basutoland, also sought to have the Transkei administered by Britain. Scanlen's defeat in the 1884 election by an alliance between the now expansionist Afrikaner Bond and the Upington-Sprigg faction made this impossible. James Irvine, the Ciskeian merchant and one of the members for King William's Town, was a supporter of the Scanlen government. Of this new expansionist alliance he wrote: 'Dutch ascendancy means stagnation in trade and what is worse ceaseless strife between black and white'.[30] At the same time one should not exaggerate the contrast: the Scanlen government was not opposed to annexation in principle, and when the Cape's commercial interests in South-West Africa seemed to be threatened by the possibility of German annexation, Scanlen and Merriman pressed for Cape control.[31]

The new expansionism, however, was not so much to secure markets or acquire land as to push out labour, by gaining control over the economy of the Transkei and thus to inhibit the growth of free peasantries. In the same period, in the older districts of the colony labour tenancy was restricted in order to force Africans into wage labour, through, for example, the passage of Act No. 33 of 1892. The passage of this act marks the beginning of successful statutory attacks on the market-oriented peasantry, but it had taken more than forty years to get a general anti-squatters act onto the statute books. When it was proposed in 1851, popular Coloured opposition prevented it from being passed.[32] In 1860 Saul Solomon wrote to Thomas Hodgkin, a leading member of the Aborigines' Protection Society:

> A bill to prevent Native squatting, based upon a measure submitted by Government but made much more stringent by this [Select] Committee, to whom it was referred, was brought into the House, but met with such determined opposition from a few members that I am happy to say it could not be put through the House.[33]

All these conditions favoured an attack on the franchise, and this came in 1887 and 1892 when the qualifications were changed, with the intention of reducing the number of Africans on the voters' roll. The additional factor which hastened the undermining of the franchise was the growth of Afrikaner nationalism. In the first phase of this nationalism it was fostered by British banks with their control over credit,[34] English merchants with their support for peasant economies,[35] and the constitutional prohibitions upon the use of Dutch in government, limiting Afrikaner recruitment to the civil service.[36] Since the very existence of an African peasantry was under attack by Afrikaner nationalists, the peasantry became involved in the electoral process to a greater degree than ever before.[37] The defence of the franchise was closely related to the defence of the peasantry, and although only a minority of English members of Parliament was involved in this dual defence, the conflict was portrayed as being conterminous with a rigid English-Afrikaner divide.[38] The election statement made in 1887 by Richard Solomon (the future Attorney-General in a government headed by William Schreiner) is typical:

> We English in this country depend to a very large extent upon the Native vote, so I hope the constituencies will wake up in the strongest manner and point out to their representatives that they must resist the Bill to the utmost. If the Bill is carried, the English-speaking section of King William's Town, Victoria East and Fort Beaufort constituency would be represented by Bond nominees and that would be a serious thing for these districts.[39]

The correlation was, however, imprecise. English farmers and the Cape English involved in mining were equally opposed to a free peasantry and to labour tenancy, and sought to limit the franchise. In passing it should be noted that the financially insecure Merriman, with his brief but unsuccessful spell as a Johannesburg mine manager, was more representative of the many Cape English who looked to the Witwatersrand to alleviate their depressed economic condition than the great magnate, Cecil Rhodes. It was at this time (1891) that Merriman told a meeting in Port Elizabeth:

> The question of this country was whether it was going to be a black man's or a white man's country [cheers]. When he saw farmers becoming disheartened or hiring their land out to Kafirs, the Colony becoming blacker and blacker, Natal, a large native location, helped along by coolies, and Cape Town becoming browner and browner every day, then he felt misgivings in his own mind as to the future.[40]

The economic decline of the eastern Cape was, moreover, the result of the Witwatersrand siphoning off both capital and white labour.[41] The alliance between the Afrikaner Bond and the English majority was brought to a rude halt by the Jameson raid, and the polarisation of Afrikaner and English into opposing parliamentary parties and ultimately into protagonists in the South African War (which was, for the Cape, a civil war) halted the attack on the franchise. This was because electoral arithmetic as much as anything else sent both parties to compete for African votes.[42] As Charles Crewe, who had been brought to South Africa because of his professional experience in British elections, wrote:

> I find even in the League there are men, especially those who represent Native constituencies, who say that Rhodes becoming president would cause a good deal of difficulty in the League itself by alienating the native voter.[43]

The slogan 'equal rights for all civilised men' which grew out of this concern for black and Coloured voters in the elections of 1898 and 1904 gave the great tradition its particular shape at this time.[44]

But if electoral arithmetic was crucial in 1898 and 1904, it was unimportant in 1908, and the rhetoric continued unabated. It is difficult to account for the heightened support the franchise was given. It is possible that it was aimed at British policy-makers who wanted assurances that the outward form of the Cape franchise would be secure in a united South Africa. Such an argument is not negated by the British High Commissioner's open invitation to undermine the franchise.[45] There is evidence which suggests that some major politicians had reconciled themselves to a free peasantry, and at the same time were looking with some morbidity at the growing power of white workers in the Transvaal. This power promised to raise the cost of labour, and to the small-scale manufacturers of the Cape employing Coloured artisans it represented an ominous threat.[46] At the same time unrest in Cape Town in 1906 had brought rioting to Parliament's door. Confirmation of the political and civil liberties of Coloured artisans and tradesmen, might, therefore, have been necessary to reduce the tensions which rioting brought. In the sensitive climate which the proposals for a South African federation created, anything less than a restatement of liberal principles would have been provocative. In any event, the period was also marked by a significant rejection of the incorporationist thesis by Coloured political leaders. Whereas before the South African war they had been anxious not to distinguish themselves from the white electorate, after the war there was a growth of 'race pride' which took political form and which went so far as to call for concerted action with African voters.[47]

In addition, Cape politicians and administrators pointed to the upheavals in Natal in 1906 and German South West Africa in 1904 as object lessons of what happened to political systems without direct representation.[48] At the same time, there appears to be little doubt that the liberal ideology had achieved a degree of legitimacy. By the first decade of the twentieth century, Cape politicians and administrators found it difficult to see how franchise rights could be withdrawn.[49] Again the possibility of misunderstanding arises because, if they could not justify disfranchisement, neither could they envisage mass enrolment. Equally, they could barely conceive of Africans sitting in parliament. But in holding these views, they did not step out of the bounds of orthodox liberalism. To liberals in the Cape, a political franchise was directly connected with property and wage qualifications. Since liberals envisaged only the propertied peasantry and the skilled artisans as voters, they were perfectly consistent in supporting a franchise and anticipating a limited enrolment.

Social differentiation among the peasantry was visible from an early date. There were, according to the King William's Town merchant, J.W. Weir, five different strata of rural blacks west of the Kei:

1. Landholders—who are a good native peasantry, and are improving in the mode of farming and habits of industry.
2. A similar class who have not yet titles to their land owing to the opposition of their heathen chiefs.
3. The . . . heathen who subsists mainly on his cattle.
4. The labouring class—who have no land, have lost their stock and depend upon their earnings.
5. The very poor who live with their friends.[50]

From this differentiation, it was possible to assume that the number of peasants who would be sufficiently prosperous to be enfranchised would, for the forseeable future, be small. But it was not simply a matter of numbers. The expansion of the franchise in Britain, which was both accomplished by the liberal hegemony and interpreted by it, left Cape liberals to anticipate a passive and deferential role for the under classes. Political democracy did not create social democracy. J.W. Sauer, one of the best-known liberals and a cabinet minister on four occasions between 1878 and 1913, made this point in the most direct way possible:

> In England the workman and the governing classes both have votes, but there is very little general equality between them—in fact, none at all; I suppose they are just as far apart in some respects as the white man and the native is in this country. Political equality by no means social equality.[51]

Small-scale manufacturing which existed in the ports of the Cape did not bring a mass working class into existence, and the experience of previous colonial industry had not undermined their assumptions. On the other hand, the opponents of liberalism, who talked of 'swamping' were set on creating a mass wage labour force whose freedom they wished to restrict for economic as well as for political reasons. This mass labour force might appear to be a threat to property and to the political order if it were enfranchised, but the liberals had no such labour force in mind. The inability of the liberals to envisage African members of Parliament revealed the limitations of liberalism, but it did not distinguish liberalism in the Cape from Victorian liberalism. It was, after all, not before 1890 that a working class candidate was elected to the British parliament. Equally, the reluctance of liberal missionaries and educationists to divest themselves of the power over African clergy and school teachers is not dissimilar to the attitude of Victorian clergy and educationists in England.[52]

Nor do we need to ponder over the transformation of the major component of liberal ideology—the belief in private land ownership as a civilising agency—into the belief in the dignity of wage labour. Yet again, the mood is caught in the missionary press, the *Christian Express*, with James Stewart of Lovedale exhorting:

The gospel of work does not save souls, but it saves peoples. It is not a Christian maxim only, that they who do not work should not eat; it is also in the end a law of nature and of nations. Lazy races die or decay. Races that work prosper on earth. The British race in all its greatest branches is noted for its restless activity. Its life's motto is Work! Work! Work! And its deepest contempt is reserved for those who will not thus exert themselves. [53]

In the end, there is nothing strange about the death of the liberal Cape. In entering the South African union it tied its fortunes to the creation of a mass wage labour force. Liberalism in its great tradition was mortally wounded.

The small tradition was obviously a microcosm of the great tradition, and, without the social relationships which existed in the constituencies, the great tradition would not have been possible. Equally, the small tradition was dependent on the metropolis as a reference for its values and beliefs. [54] The important difference between the two forms of liberalism in the Cape was the volatile nature of the great tradition when compared with the stability of the small tradition. [55] The great tradition could be submerged, if only temporarily, by the fall of the government or a declaration of the changing intentions of constantly shifting alliances. Alliances were more stable within constituencies. The fall of governments had little local impact and the implementation of policies often took a long time to be effective. Social relationships which made liberal economic and political alliances possible remained constant over a long period of time.

The small tradition evolved most markedly in the constituencies where a combination of peasant and 'town' voters—mostly those associated with the merchant interest—could hold one of the two seats in the two member constituencies. [56] Thus in 1873 the *Kaffrarian Watchman* complained that the merchants with interests in King William's Town, 'Messrs Irvine & Co., Messrs Peacock, Weir & Co., Messrs Whitcher & Dyer, etc., etc.' would determine the outcome of the next election for the Legislative Assembly.

It is quite natural and, let us add, quite legitimate that these great houses, by their innumerable agents and perfect communications throughout Kafirdom, should exercise an influence which may simply be called paramount, and if it so happens that our Kafir merchants and Kafir missionaries agree in choosing two representatives for us in the coming Assembly elections, they need not trouble themselves much about the opinions of a powerless minority, although this minority may consist of the majority of voters with a white skin. [57]

The constitutional arrangement which allowed voters to use only one of their votes was an important factor in the development of the small tradition. Before the evolution of the party system there was usually a large number of candidates, and while African voters could be relied upon to support a single candidate, the same could not be said of the white electorate, the majority of whom were opposed to liberal candidates. However, the existence of African voters needs explaining, and the Constitutional Ordinance provides only a formal and legal answer. Where a qualified franchise exists, the adjudicating of qualifications and the method of registering voters are as important as the legal right to the franchise. The constitution divided the responsibility for drafting the voters' roll between locally appointed field-cornets and civil commissioners, appointed by the central government. The civil commissioner made the final decision, although appeals to be placed on the roll and objections could be raised by any voter. No one pattern emerges for these eastern Cape districts. In some cases field-cornets were sympathetic to African enfranchisement, in others they were hostile, but the existence of registration committees (whose members were African and white), assisted in the final stage in the civil commissioner's court by local solicitors or law agents, went a long way to ensure that Africans would be enrolled.[58]

As for civil commissioners, their need to foster stability gave them a disposition towards maintaining African property owners on the voters' roll.[59] On one occasion a Civil Commissioner, Frank Whitham of Wodehouse, went so far as to propose disqualifying white but not black illiterates. A somewhat bemused Select Committee sought to clarify his position. 'You would' they asked, 'apply the educational test to the European only and not to the Native?' Whitham's reply led to a revealing exchange:

> 'Yes, the European ought to read and write' the Committee was told, 'He cannot afford not to, and he should be made to.'
> 'But unfortunately we are aware that many Europeans cannot read or write.'
> 'Well, I would disqualify them.'
> 'And not the native?'
> 'No, it would be too hard on them. Make their property qualification higher if you like. There are many hundreds and thousands of natives who only know their own language by ear.'[60]

Equally the field-cornet and the members of the registration committee—usually white traders—and the local lawyers had an economic as well as a political motive for aiding the enrolment of African voters. The prosperity of their districts and their own prosperity depended on the marketable surplus of African cultivators.

Thus, W.J. Orsmond (MLA for Aliwal North, 1904–8), who was both a substantial trader and landowner, with a great many African tenants, told a meeting of African voters at Bensonville, Herschel district, in the

Aliwal North Division, in the 1893 election campaign, that they were

> valuable colonists who must be of immense assistance in paying the interest
> on our £25 million debt. Few residents in the Colony realise the importance
> as regards the proceeds of your produce in grain, wool, skins and hides and
> your earning in wages. Your purchasing power is enormous ... the Natives
> are owners of one-sixth of the sheep, a quarter of the goats, half of the cattle and
> half of the horses. The Natives are very great producers and consumers.[61]

A few years earlier, at a public meeting which discussed the proposal to
'break up' the Tambookie Location, the Queenstown general dealer,
A. Morum of Morum Bros., said: 'The natives cultivated ten times more
than the farmers'. T.W. Edkins, a Queenstown merchant, was reported
to have said: 'Gentlemen not in business had no idea of the enormous
trade that was done with these natives, nor of the grain produced by them
in a good season. If the removals took place Queenstown would lose this
trade.'[62]

On the other side attempts to prevent enfranchisement were generally
associated with the wider aim of restricting the growth of peasant economies.[63] To white commercial farmers peasants were anathema. Their
call on family labour meant that there were only irregular supplies of
African wage labourers, and the peasant producer was highly competitive.
In these districts two different forms of production competed, not simply
for resources but for survival.

Under these conditions antagonisms were deeply felt and expressed
themselves in a heightened morality. It was not only in defence of the
franchise that the small tradition manifested itself. For the white liberals,
any local attack on the free peasantry had to be judged by the standards of
a wider liberalism. An attempt to expropriate land denied the rights of
property and was to be challenged. 'Individual tenure' wrote J.M. Orpen,
'has always existed and law and equity requires that it should simply be
recognised as it now exists.'[64] Equally the failure of a jury to convict in
the case of the murder of an African denied the security of the person and
was to be condemned. Hence the renowned case of the Reverend Davidson
Don.* Similarly there must be an end to summary justice against employees which denied them the rule of law. Dr Bisset Berry, a candidate
for the Queenstown Progressive Association in the 1894 election told his
white supporters that he would

> never advocate that a farmer or anyone else should be allowed to wallop his
> servants,[cheers] to carry out the policy generally known as that of walloping

*See N. Hogan, 'The posthumous vindication of Zachariah Gqishela: reflections
on the politics of dependence at the Cape in the nineteenth century', below, ch. 11.

your own nigger. If they were not going to be Bond ridden, they must realise that it was the 'fundamental principle' in English law that the servant works for his master by contract. The Magistrate is the only person to decide between master and servant, and it would be an evil day for this country if it were otherwise.[65]

The rural districts of the western Cape did not produce an ideologically sustained coalition between Coloured and white voters. At first sight this may be surprising since the original accommodation of the 1853 constitution had been made to incorporate Coloured classes. Moreover, for a brief moment in the 1850s it looked as if an alliance between Coloured and Dutch voters—against expansionist English frontier districts— might come into existence in the west.[66] The need to incorporate Coloured groups had resulted from their long and bloody resistance. Before 1800 it seemed possible that the Khoisan would be successful in their attempts to prevent white settlement in the north-east of the colony.[67] Though they failed, the constant fear of Khoisan uprisings meant that the sense of unease among European settlers was sustained in the first half of the nineteenth century. This settler disquiet was not diminished by the creation of legal equality—which was the result both of humanitarian convictions and the belief in the greater efficiency of the 'fair market' which was sustained by the consideration that the new British settlers were likely to acquire wage labour at the expense of the other Dutch-speaking colonists —and the ending of slavery by the British Parliament.* The settlers would have to control their labour by means other than unrestrained coercion or clientage. Attempts to introduce contracts which would carry penal sanctions if servants withdrew their labour brought Khoisan agitation and the possibility of 'armed opposition' to many western districts in the twenty years between 1828 and 1848.[68] The rebellion at Kat River in 1851, and the sympathy among Coloured groups in the west to this rebellion, created a disposition among sections of the colony's political and administrative hierarchies to enfranchise propertied Khoisan. As the Cape Attorney-General said in a celebrated remark: 'I would rather meet the Hottentot at the hustings voting for his representative than meet the Hottentot in the wilds with his gun upon his shoulder'.[69]

Nevertheless, the Kat River rebellion was the last manifestation of Khoisan armed opposition and not, as it was possible to think at the time, one more incident in a long history of resistance. In the two centuries previous to 1853 the Khoisan people and those with whom they had become absorbed had been left with very limited amounts of land. So

*See S. Newton-King, 'The labour market of the Cape Colony, 1807–28', above, ch. 7.

much so that the majority of the Coloured population within the Cape
Colony were probably landless by the mid-nineteenth century. Both
Dutch and then British administrators had made a conscious attempt to
resettle groups of Coloured people on arable land and missionary societies
threw their energies into hastening the transformation from pastoralism
to arable cultivation and production. Writing of the best known of these
institutions, Genadendal, the traveller Lichtenstein had observed at the
beginning of the nineteenth century, said.

> Every Hottentot family has, besides the garden behind the house, in which they
> are instructed to plant vegetables and fruit trees, a certain portion of the fertile
> arable land in this valley, the size of which is determined by the number of
> people under the instruction of the [Moravian] Fathers and receives assistance
> with implements and seed corn. The diligent are rewarded with an increase of
> their land, while the indolent lose part of it. [70]

We have already noted the relative prosperity which marked the lives of
the peasants of the mission-dominated west, but it was prosperity of
limited duration. Lichtenstein was wrong: the 'diligent' could not be
rewarded indefinitely, if only because the mission stations were permitted
to survive while the majority of their inhabitants produced less than their
subsistence. This made it necessary for them to work for surrounding
white farmers at different times during the agricultural cycle. There were,
of course, white farmers who would have preferred to see the mission
stations broken up in the belief that this would reduce either competition
for land, or markets, or the supply of labour. [71] In pointing out the folly
of their agitation the civil commissioner for Namaqualand made clear the
proper and limited purpose of mission stations. The break-up of the
mission stations, he wrote,

> would be attended with serious loss and inconvenience to the bulk of the
> employers of labour, especially the [white] farmers. As a rule the farmers, who
> are by no means a wealthy class in this division, keep but a very small number
> of hands in permanent employ on their farms; but in plough time and harvest
> there is a very general demand for this class of labour. Now the first place they
> send for labour is from these very institutions. [72]

The capacity of the stations to provide for subsistence was greatly
diminished as the years passed and population grew. The tendency was,
therefore, for sections of the mission station population who were better
able to cope with changing fortunes to move to Cape Town and other
parts of the Colony, where, if they were artisans, their prospects of resisting
the downward spiral into abject poverty was increased. The steady loss
of population from the mission stations was, however, a source of constant

anxiety to the majority of white farmers and they attempted by a variety of means, to trap as much labour as possible. One device they used was debt-peonage. This was reinforced by alcohol addiction and according to J.J. Freeman

> A large number of the members of a Missionary Institution had, so lately as in 1829, been inveigled by a neighbouring colonist to serve him, in consideration of debts incurred for brandy. As a first term was working out, he let the men have more brandy at exhorbitant prices, and took from them engagements for forty-nine years—in many others for shorter periods. The wages stipulated were exceedingly low, as the debts were to be paid by the services of the men. The result was great destitution in their families, and general misery. [73]

More than six decades later, the evidence of Johannes April, church warden of Mamre, to the Cape Labour Commission showed that this peonage was still commonplace:

> The man cannot leave the farm because he is in debt to the farmer. The longer he stays the deeper he sinks and frequently has to put his children in the field too, to aid in clearing his liability. [74]

Even if the indebtedness did not lead to peonage the all too familiar picture of producers having to sell their corn immediately after harvesting it and without being able to set aside provisions for the bad years or for sowing the following season was also to be found among the declining peasants of the western Cape. Equally transport riding was not necessarily always advantageous. Draught animals were often lost and income from freight could be insufficient for replacing these animals. [75]

From the mid-nineteenth century impoverishment was far more commonplace among the Coloured population of the rural west than it was among black peasants in the eastern districts of the colony. The resulting antagonisms between white employers of farm labour and their labourers was sufficiently intense to make a strategy of incorporation difficult to set in motion. The advanced stage of proletarianisation, with the very meagre surpluses produced, meant, in addition, that not only was there no group of merchants who had an interest in the survival of Coloured peasants, but that local traders were contributing to their impoverishment.

In addition to economic conditions being unfavourable to the creation of a liberal alliance, there was also the crucial absence of any group committed to a liberal ideology. Rather, the dominant, mainly Afrikaner, groups in the western part of the colony were committed to a defensive reaction to liberalism in all its forms. There was no advantage for these groups in notions of a free market, or in concepts of English law, or in theories of incorporation, or in the selection of a civil service by criteria which, though based on an internal system of merit,[76] necessarily interpreted merit as the ability to uphold English language skills and attitudes. Liberalism played no part in supporting the daily life of either the dominant groups or those who though subordinate to them had related ties of language, religion, kinship and clientage. There was, moreover, a real danger that those with political and religious authority would see their power wane as those who provided for the young in their group chose English education, skills and in many cases even religious communion to attain their own advancement.[77] In this context, therefore, Afrikaner notables led a movement for the revival and creation of these ties which ultimately led to the establishment of Afrikaner nationalist organisations.[78]

But if liberalism could claim neither a base in the material conditions of life in the western regions of the Cape, nor an autonomous ideology, nevertheless constitutional law gave representation to some Coloured men. These were mostly encapsulated in the world of the mission station and this permitted an instrumental form of electoral politics without the trappings of a programme other than the rejection of the white land-owners' candidate.[79] Thus, for example, in the 1854 election in the Clan-william constituency the defeated candidate, F.S. Watermeyr, received no less than 230 of his 262 votes from the Coloured inhabitants of the mission stations of the constituency.[80]

Table: Votes cast in the 1854 election for F.S. Watermeyr in the Clanwilliam Division

Liliefontein Mission Station	100
Wupperthal Mission Station	43
Komgas Mission Station	38
Ebenezer Mission Station	14
Clanwilliam village	62 *
	257

*Clanwilliam village votes comprised 25 white and 37 Coloured electors

Source: *Zuid Afrikaan*, 25 May 1854

For the rest of the century, politics remained the same in constituencies such as Caledon, Clanwilliam, Fort Beaufort, Namaqualand, Paarl, Stellenbosch and Swellendam. The missionary's key role was probably to be found in ensuring the registration of voters. He might be able to deliver the mission station vote to one rather than another anti-landlord candidate, but he could not move without the 'Council of his Community'. This left the field open to a candidate from the local village or town, or more likely a carpet-bagger from Cape Town who possibly had trading con-nections in the constituency. Within these perimeters, the missionary could use elections to increase his influence within the mission station. Thus the missionary at Steinkopf, who, in 1898, offered to deliver not only his own station but those of other missionaries in Namaqualand to the Progressive candidate, did not 'expect any remuneration for any services he might render'. But he let it be known that any 'assistance towards repairing the church and the school, and also adding to the furniture', would be gratefully received.[81] It appears, therefore, that missionaries helped to construct local electoral machines. Thus, if the missionary at Steinkopf favoured the Progressives, his counterpart at the Pniel mission station in Paarl was a Bondsman. The suggestion was made, therefore, that an alternative station be established where Coloured men could worship the Almighty and vote Progressive:

> 'I was talking to Mr Weber of Stellenbosch this morning,' the secretary of the Progressive Party, C.A. Owen Lewis, wrote to Cecil Rhodes, 'and I gathered from him that they are very anxious to start a Coloured Church near Pniel, so as to take the matter out of the hands of the present Missionary, who, the Reverend Weber tells me, is a strong Bondsman'.[82]

By the end of the nineteenth century the growth of population on the static landholdings of the missionary societies led to an ever-increasing antagonism between artisans and cultivators, who were free of overwhelming obligations to local farmers and traders, and the missionary within whose orbit they fell. As we have already noted it was from this group that there was a steady seepage to the towns. For the majority of the Coloured population, however, proletarianisation, whether in an urban or rural environment, was a brutal and brutalising process. Alcoholism remained a social disease among sections of the Coloured population. Not surprisingly, therefore, temperance societies, which arose out of the autonomous urban life of small traders and working-class people, were drawn into a position of hostility to the wine- and spirits-producing Afrikaner farmers of the south-western Cape. This reinforced the anti-Afrikaner Bond position taken by the African Political Organisation, the body formed in 1903 to give programmatic expression to the aspirations of Coloured artisans and small traders.[83]

White liberals, nevertheless, had an ambivalent attitude to the Coloured population in towns, and for a greater part of the nineteenth century most liberals of the great tradition were uneasy about Coloured townsmen, of whom only a minority were artisans. Again Merriman provides a typical statement: 'It was not black [peasant] voters that were to be feared', he told Parliament, but 'the Cape Town coolie—Abdol was the man to play up to at an election, and Abdol was an undesirable element in an election'.[84]

Coloured men were recruited to the electoral machines by a combination of patronage, corruption and intimidation. As early as 1866 Saul Solomon had acknowledged that there were Coloured men in Cape Town who impersonated 'deadmen and living men too', but equally there were widespread reports in the 1850s that 'farmers have resorted to arbitrary acts where Coloured people refuse to vote for their representatives'.[85] In this respect little had changed by the end of the century. The report of voters travelling six hours to an out of the way polling booth so that they could avoid their landlords, as well as the Coloured voters who were evicted by their landlord for refusing to vote for his candidate, seems to have been typical of the Cape political scene.[86]

The cry of corruption led to a call for electoral reform rather than disfranchisement, although the intention may have hardly differed. It was only in the decade before Union that white liberals and urban Coloured voters entered into formal alliances. A new awareness of the importance of the value of Coloured artisans to Cape mercantile and manufacturing interests had by then emerged, as it became likely that white craft unions, with their higher wages, might seek to protect themselves by preventing employment of lower paid Coloured workers. In Cape Town, Port Elizabeth and Kimberley, though usually divided among themselves, Coloured artisans and small traders were sought out by merchant interests and provided the basis of liberal alliances.[87]

Liberalism failed to make a bridgehead in the Cape outside of the eastern districts of the colony and the port towns and Kimberley. Where a bridgehead was established, merchants, missionaries, editors and administrators inhibited the progress of coercive methods of state control and the diminution of civil liberties. This earned them the ambiguous title of 'friends of the natives'. This 'friendship' undoubtedly arose out of their beliefs derived from other societies, and it would be mechanistic to assert that 'ideas once called into being have no life of their own'.[88] But equally, the autonomous life of these ideas would have been significantly shorter if these 'friends' had not had a material and political interest in the survival of the peasantry.

Accordingly liberalism in the Cape was not, as its opponents sought to portray it, merely the opportunistic canvassing of black votes at five-yearly intervals. It was above all a strategy, developed both by colonial administrators and settler politicians, for the political incorporation of a part of the African and Coloured population. It had little popular support, and depended for its legitimacy on its association with the programme of incorporation which the governing classes evolved in nineteenth-century Britain. We get some indication of the strength of this liberal hegemony from the incredulous question asked by the Legislative Council member, J.H. Neethling, after a proposal was made to exclude blacks from sitting in Parliament. 'What would be said throughout the world' he asked, 'if it were made known that on the 15th March 1890 the Afrikaner Bond had passed such a resolution as this?'[89]

Liberalism was, however, more than the sum of its parts. It was firstly the world view of the British ruling class. Thereafter it accomplished political tasks in the Cape, both strategic and tactical. It also sustained notions of property, legal equality and other concepts in keeping with a market economy conceived as being regulated by the 'unseen hand'. When liberals called upon black and Coloured voters to fend off a re-emerging Afrikaner middle-class nationalism, they therefore combined their short-term electoral needs with their long-term social, economic and political strategies. Equally the nationalist ideology of this Afrikaner middle class sought, in the last two decades of the nineteenth century, to redress the imbalance created by British-dominated banks, English merchants, administrators and politicians. If among their opponents there were some who would use black voters to frustrate their objectives, then, not surprisingly, Afrikaner nationalists would set about disfranchising those voters. But disfranchising black voters not only served to win elections, it also weakened the potential of a rising African peasantry. Thus, like the liberals, the strategic purpose of the Cape's Afrikaner middle class also coincided with their short-term needs. When, in the last decade of the nineteenth century, a part of the English settler population tied its fortunes to the gold-mining industry of the Transvaal, liberal possibilities were spent. Unlike liberalism in Britain, Cape liberalism was not posited on the incorporation of wage-labourers. On the contrary, Cape liberalism assumed a small prosperous peasantry which could act as a buffer against poor peasants and the already declining power of chiefs. Black wage-labourers, on the other hand, presented no immediate threat and required no incorporating. Instead the franchise, legal equality and the market place could give them a strength that their early twentieth-century social situation did not justify. Little wonder, then, that liberalism in its incor-porationist form would lose its prominence as an ideology of control in twentieth-century South Africa.

Notes

1 Eric Walker's various works and his *Cape Native Franchise*, Cape Town, 1929;

L.M. Thompson, *The Cape Coloured Franchise*, Johannesburg, 1949; J.S. Marais, *The Cape Coloured People*, Johannesburg, 1939; J.L.McCracken, *The Cape Parliament*, Oxford, 1967; Janet Robertson, *Liberalism in South Africa, 1948–63*, Oxford, 1971. Robertson has a chapter on 'Cape Liberalism' tacked on as an introduction. This is not only full of errors in its detail but is also a good example of the contradiction-free myth

2 E.H. Brookes, *The History of Native Policy in South Africa*, Pretoria, 1927, and R.F.A. Hoernle, *South African Native Policy and the Liberal Spirit*, Johannesburg, 1939

3 S. Trapido, 'Origins of the Cape franchise qualifications of 1853', *JAH*, v. 1964, p. 42

4 British Parliamentary Papers (BPP), 1850 XXXVIII (1137), *Correspondence relative to the establishment of Representative Assembly at the Cape*, p. 11

5 T.E. Kirk, 'Self-Government and Self-Defence in South Africa: the interaction of British and Cape Politics, 1846–54', D.Phil., Oxford, 1973

6 John Philip, *Researches in South Africa*, London, 1828, pp. ix–x

7 Joseph John Freeman, *A Tour in South Africa*, London, 1851

8 John Noble, *The History of South Africa*, London, 1877, pp. 334–5

9 A.E. du Toit (ed.), *The Earliest South African Documents on the Education and Civilization of the Bantu*, Communications of the University of South Africa, Pretoria, 1963, p. 54. J.C. Warner to Sir Harry Smith, 5 May 1848: 'The evil of the former system of Trade in Kaffirland was that it became almost a monopoly in the hands of a few monied men. Men from the lowest rank of Society were mostly employed to take charge of their numerous trading stations'

10 Freeman, *A Tour*, p. 159

11 Cited in W.M. Macmillan, *The Cape Colour Question: a historical survey*, London, 1927, p. 177

12 Cited in Freeman, *A Tour*, p. 25

13 Marais, *The Cape Coloured People*, p. 233; C.W. Hutton (ed.), *The Autobiography of the late Sir Andries Stockenstrom, Bart.*, 2 vols., Cape Town, 1887, ii, p. 421

14 *Select Committee on Aborigines*, London, 1836, p. 360

15 *Ibid.*, p. 355, evidence of Rev. H.P. Hallbeck

16 J. Rutherford, *Sir George Grey*, London, 1961, pp. 331–9

17 Cape of Good Hope G.6–1802, pp. 124–5; G.19–1905, p. 161. Census returns 1891, 1904. The urban Coloured population rose from 106 000 to 183 000 in thirteen years

18 Andrew Duminy, 'The Role of Sir Andries Stockenstrom in Cape Politics, 1848–56', *Archives Year Book for South African History* (AYB), ii, Pretoria, 1960, pp. 153–6

19 Kirk, 'Self-government', p. 503

20 See R. van Selm, *History of the South African Mutual Life Assurance Society, 1845–1945*, Cape Town, 1945

21 See for example, *The Cape Law Journal, 1887*, pp. 137–47, on the 1887 Registration Act. For the role of law agents, see CPP G.4–'88, *Cape Native Laws and Customs Commission*, 1883, p. 9, *Imvo*, 25 August 1886 and 4 January 1888.

22 *Cape Argus, Cape Standard, Cape Times, Cape Town Mail, Diamond Fields Advertiser, East London Despatch, Eastern Province News, Fort Beaufort Advocate, Graaf Reinet Herald, Port Elizabeth Telegraph, Queenstown Free Press, Somerset Budget, South African Commerical Advertiser, South African News*

23 For Merriman's changing rhetoric in response to changing circumstance, see above, pp. 254, 266

24 Anthony Trollope, *South Africa*, London, 1878, i, pp. 96–7. See also, APS C.122/65, Saul Solomon to Thomas Hodgkin, 19 January 1860. Solomon Papers (microfilm), J.A. Froude to Saul Solomon, 10 February 1875: 'Immediately on my return to England, I reported to the Colonial Secretary my conversations with Mr Molteno and yourself respecting the disposition of Langalibale [sic]'

25 Ethel Drus, 'The Political Career of Saul Solomon, Member of the Cape Legislative Assembly 1854 to 1883', unpublished M.A. thesis, University of Cape Town, 1939, pp. 66–7. See also Solomon Papers (microfilm), J.A. de Wet to Saul Solomon, 4 June 1879

26 BPP C1980. 1877, *Further correspondence respecting the proposed confederation of the Colonies and States of South Africa*, Barkly to Carnarvon, 17 April 1877

27 Phyllis Lewsen, *Selections from the Correspondence of J.X. Merriman*, Cape Town, 1960, i, pp. 19, 23–4. JXM to J.B. Currey. Merriman intended Currey to make use of the letter—'If this comes too late for your lecture, recast it and print it as a letter from a colonist'. Cf. Sprigg's attack on Carnarvon's proposals to disfranchise Africans in his confederation, *Cape Argus*, 8 March 1877

28 This was according to Percy Nightingale, the liberal civil commissioner whose conflict with the Cape government led to his being relieved of his post, in a letter to F.W. Chesson, secretary of the APS, APS C.143/275. Cf also C.138/193, J.J. Irvine to Chesson, 3 July 1884

29 CPP. G.3–1894. *Cape Labour Commission*, Cape Town, 1894

30 APS C.138/189; To F.W. Chesson, 3 July 1884

31 Z. Ngavirue, 'Political Parties and Interest Groups in South West Africa, A study of a plural society', 2 vols., D.Phil., Oxford, 1974, i, p. 84

32 P.B. Borcherds, *An Autobiographical Memoir*, Cape Town, 1861, p. 354

33 APS C.122/65, Saul Solomon to Thomas Hodgkin, 19 January 1860; for squatting measures which were brought before Parliament but failed to get a second reading, or were withdrawn, see Bills No. 16–1859, No. 15–1871, No. 9–1875 and No. 38–1875. See also Solomon's and Merriman's successful opposition to a vagrancy bill proposed in 1874: House of Assembly, 8 June 1874. Drus, 'The Political Career', p. 56

34 E.H.D. Arndt, *Banking and Currency Development in South Africa*, Cape Town, 1928, pp. 281–95

35 APS C.138/214, T.W. Irvine to F.W. Chesson, 23 July 1880. 'We are very largely interested in the maintenance of peace in South Africa, in consequence of our extensive business with those trading with various tribes'

36 T.R.H. Davenport, *The Afrikaner Bond*, Cape Town, 1966

37 Stanley Trapido, 'White Conflict and Non-White Participation in the Politics of the Cape of Good Hope', Ph.D., University of London, 1970, ch. 5: The Politics of Registration

38 *Port Elizabeth Telegraph*, June 1886, 21 Dec. 1881; *The Journal* (Grahamstown), June 1886; *Queenstown Free Press*, May, June 1887; *Eastern Province Herald*, May, June 1887; *East London Advertiser*, March, April, May, 1887; House of Assembly Debates 1887, pp. 71–97. 1891, pp. 333–46, 1892, pp. 176–206

39 *Cape Argus*, 27 April 1887

40 *Imvo*, 16 April 1891

41 See, for example, Rose-Innes Papers, 1898, No. 184, n.d., Richard Rose Innes

to James Rose-Innes: 'Kingwilliamstown has been on the decline for some time past and the gold fields have done us nothing but harm—men and money have left for the Transvaal'

42 Rhodes Papers, Vol. 2B, No. 245, C.A. Owen Lewis to P.J. Jordan, 17 October 1900. Various enclosures. CO 48/575, Confidential: Sir Walter Hely Hutchinson to Colonial Secretary, 21 January 1904. Hofmeyr Papers 1617, Queenstown folder, 1898

43 Rhodes Papers, Vol. 2B, No. 140, Charles Crewe to Arthur Fuller, 20 September 1898

44 In 1897, with the franchise qualifications of the South African Republic in mind, Rhodes had proclaimed his belief in 'equal rights for all white men south of the Zambesi'. During the 1898 election campaign, he was dogged by Coloured men and he ultimately revised the slogan by changing 'white' to 'civilised'. There is no doubt, however, that he did so cynically and in response to the needs of the campaign. See J. Flint, *Cecil Rhodes*, London, 1976, p. 214. L.M. Thompson, *Unification of South Africa*, Oxford, 1960, and UG 54/37 *Report of the Commission of Enquiry Regarding the Cape Coloured Population of the Union*, give extensive quotations from the great tradition

45 A.P. Newton (ed.), *Select Documents Relating to the Unification of South Africa*, London, 1924, ii, Informal Suggestions by the High Commissioner on the Question of the Native Franchise, p. 25

46 *South African Native Affairs Commission*, 1903–5, ii, paras. 5155–5346. Evid. J.X. Merriman. This reflects Merriman in his liberal phase

47 African Political Organisation, Minutes of the Annual Conference, Graaf-Reinet, 1904; Cape Town, 1906; Oudtshoorn, 1907

48 Merriman Papers, 1907, No. 111: JXM to Godwin Smith, 26 October 1907; *SANAC*, v, *passim*

49 C. of GH A.4–98, Minutes of evidence taken before the Select Committee on Parliamentary Registration, paras. 940–3; *SANAC*, v. paras. 11070–75.

50 Weir Papers (Rhodes University, Grahamstown), Cory MS 9080, J. Weir to J.G. Sprigg, 15 October 1885. I should like to thank Andrew Purkiss for letting me see his notes and drawing my attention to this letter

51 *SANAC* Evidence, v, paras. 11070–5

52 Richard Johnson, 'Educational Policy and Social Control in Early Victorian England', *Past and Present*, 49, November 1970, pp. 96–119. 'The teacher of the peasant's child', wrote the eminent educationist Dr James Kay Shuttleworth, 'occupied as it were the father's place, in the performance of duties from which the father is separated by his daily toil, and unhappily by his want of the knowledge and skill'. The school inspectorate of the 1840s noted that whereas education for "our own children" occurred mainly through the "associations of home", in respect to the children of labouring men, it must be done, if at all, at school'. 'The school must be an essentially foreign implantation within a commonly barbarized population'. The school teacher was the primary agent of 'civilisation'. Teachers themselves must be emancipated from the local community, made independent of the whims of the parents, more closely linked to local elites (and particularly the clergy), and provided with the financial means of a cultural superiority. They should be raised, but not too far, out of their own class. (*Ibid.* pp. 112–3) Cf. Kay Shuttleworth's prescriptions in A.E. du Toit (ed.), *The Earliest British Documents on Education for the Coloured*

Races: education for 'Coloured races' was to 'civilise races emerging from barbarism', to enable them to become a 'settled and industrious peasantry' with habits of 'self-control and moral discipline'. Education should provide 'the mutual interests of the mother country and her dependencies, the rational basis of their connection, and the domestic and social duties of the coloured race', together with 'the relation of wages, capital, labour and the influence of local and general government on personal security, independence and other'

53 Cited in James Wells, *Stewart of Lovedale*, London, 1913, pp. 216–7, who quotes Stewart from the *Christian Express*

54 Saul Solomon papers (microfilm), various letters to Solomon, from small-town correspondents

55 Morris Alexander and Bisset Berry are good examples of 'small tradition' members of parliament who retained their liberalism throughout their parliamentary careers, which lasted well into the 1930s

56 Constituencies which returned liberal-cum-merchant supported members: Aliwal North: J.W. Sauer, J.M. Orpen, E.G. Orsmond, W.J. Orsmond. Fort Beaufort: C.W. Hutton, J.J. Yates. King William's Town: James Irvine, Richard Solomon, William Hay. Queenstown: Bisset Berry, J.M. Orpen, Wodehouse: J.M. Orpen, J.X. Merriman. Victoria East: James Rose-Innes, H.T. Tamplin. Cape Town, with its four seats and its plumping system, enabled Coloured voters to help return at least one member in most elections: Namaqualand 1898, Stellenbosch 1904, Caledon 1854–68. *Cape Mercury*, 13 November 1888. *Queenstown Free Press*, 2 February 1894, 8 August 1888. James Rose-Innes, *Autobiography*, ed. B.A. Tindale, Cape Town, 1949, p. 52. *Cape Times*, 5 August 1893, reported a meeting in Aliwal North district at which W.J. Orsmond failed to persuade a meeting of African voters to nominate him for the forthcoming election because they felt he would split the African vote and that neither he nor Sauer would be returned

57 *Kaffrarian Watchman*, 10 November 1873

58 Richard Rose-Innes: Victoria East and King William's Town, *Imvo*, 24 December 1884. F.W. Lance (of East London): Fort Beaufort, *Imvo*, 4 January 1888. H.T. Tamplin (Grahamstown): Queenstown. For election committees, see S. Trapido, 'African Divisional Politics', *JAH*, ix, 1, 1968
Cape CO 2557, Percy Nightingale to Cape Colonial Secretary, 16 October 1872. CPP G.4–1884 *Report and Proceedings of the Commission on Native Laws and Customs,* 1883, Appendix F, Circular No. 1 Section D, pp. 49–68, 111, 166, 181, 195, 203 CPP A.9 of 1888, *Proceedings in the Case of Theunis Jacobus Botha, Applicant and Egbert Garcia, William Hughes and William Wakeford.* CPP A.19 of 1888, *Select Committee on Queenstown Registration Minutes of Evidence,* Telegraphic Submission, Chief Magistrate Transkei to Under Colonial Secretary, Cape Town, 13 December 1887; Rhodes Papers Vol. C.2A, The Cape; i, No. 40, 22 December 1881. CPP A.4 of 1898 *Minutes of Evidence Taken Before the Select Committee of Parliamentary Registration,* p. 101, paras. 940–3. Evidence of F.C. Whitham, *South African Native Affairs Commission,* 1903–5. v. Only five of the fifteen civil commissioners giving *written* evidence to this commission were hostile to the existing African representation. Eight of these were positively in favour of it when giving written evidence. It is of some significance that those giving verbal testimony were less ready to acknowledge its supposed virtues. The commission, it should be said, generally found the evidence that it set out

to find. See also CPP A.3 of 1907, *Report of the Select Committee on the Biennial Registration of Parliamentary Voters*, para. 11

60 CPP A.4 of 1898, p. 101, paras. 940–3

61 *Cape Times*, 5 August 1893

62 *Queenstown Free Press*, 2 October 1889. See Colin Bundy, 'The Emergence and Decline of a South African Peasantry', *African Affairs*, lxxi, October, 1972, pp. 369–88. See also APS C.147/49, G. Silberbauer to F.W. Chesson, 9 December 1885. Cf. the correspondence of T.W. and J.J. Irvine of King William's Town, and Richard Rose-Innes's statement: 'The native goes in and out amongst us, our commercial welfare is largely bound up with his prosperity. He is an extensive property holder in the district, he is a peasant proprietor and a producer on our markets', *Cape Times*, 18 February 1909

63 Commenting on the implications of the 1887 Registration Act, whose prior purpose was the disfranchisement of Africans occupying 'communal' land, Jabavu wrote to F.W. Chesson, 'The people were alarmed that in first declaring that the lands they hold do not belong to them—as the new Act declares implicitly—it is sought to deprive them of the lands when the supremacy of the Dutch in Parliament, sought to be assured by this measure, is assured. This opens up such a stupendous question relating to the settlement of land by natives which ought to go together with the relation of wages, capital, labour and the influence of local and general government on personal security, independence and order'. (APS C.139/19, Jabavu to Chesson, 28 November 1877)

64 Joseph Millerd Orpen, *Some principles of Natives Government, the petitions of the Basuto tribe regarding Cape law, representation and disarmament to the Cape parliament considered*, Cape Town, 1880, p. 43

65 *Cape Times*, 8 December 1893

66 'Your petitioners' wrote the Coloured signatories of Kat River in 1857, 'cannot keep back the expression of the fact that the great majority of the Frontier inhabitants are opposed to the interests of the coloured inhabitants; whereas the inhabitants of the West, and especially those of Dutch origin, have shown a liberal feeling in and out of Parliament'. Cape Parliamentary Papers, *Votes and Proceedings of the House of Assembly*, 1854. Appendix 1. For 'English' expansionism. See A.H. Duminy, 'The Role of Sir Andries Stockenstrom', *AYB* 1960, i, p. 156

67 Shula Marks, 'Khoisan resistance to the Dutch in the seventeenth and eighteenth centuries', *JAH*, xiii, 1, 1972

68 In 1800 the Khoi joined with the Xhosa. In 1836 Fairbairn wrote: 'There is no doubt that the alarm and agitation caused by Wade's Vagrant Law induced the Kafirs to believe that the Hottentots would not be very hearty in the colony's defence', and, as Macmillan noted, D'Urban's action in vetoing the Vagrants Law saved the country from a Hottentot rebellion. W.M. Macmillan, *Bantu, Boer and Briton*, London, 1929, p. 145. In 1848 Sir Harry Smith decided against a new vagrancy act, after widespread Coloured agitation. T.E. Kirk, 'Kat River', MS., n.d. p. 61, citing *The Colonial Intelligencer*, February 1851, p. 147. In 1852 further agitation prevented legislation against Coloured squatters. Borcherds, *Memoir*, p. 354. See also S. Newton-King, 'The labour market of the Cape Colony', above, ch. 7, and Tony Kirk, 'The Cape economy and the expropriation of the Kat River Settlement', above, ch. 9

69 BPP LXV 1853 Cd. 1581, *Further Correspondence Relative to the Establishment of*

a Representative Assembly at the Cape of Good Hope, p. 219

70 H. Lichtenstein, *Travels in Southern Africa*, Cape Town, 1928, p. 193
71 Cape of Good Hope, *Report from the Select Committee on Granting Lands in Freehold to Hottentots*, Cape Town, 1854, p. 25; C. of GH A.26–1879, *Report of the Select Committee on the Supply of the Labour Market*, p. 68
72 G.41–89, *Correspondence on Lands for Natives in Namaqualand*, p. 10
73 Freeman, *A Tour in South Africa*, pp. 136–7
74 G.39–93, *Cape Labour Commission*, para. 4068
75 G.41–89, p. 7. J.S. Marais, *The Cape Coloured People*, p. 81
76 *Zuid Afrikaan*, 10 April, 15 May, 7 September 1854; 7 April 1856
77 *Zuid Afrikaan*, 31 Aug. 1857, for a statement on the relationship between 'language, nationality and religion'. Saul Solomon, who constantly proffered his good feeling for his 'Dutch fellow-citizens', nevertheless led the campaign to end state grants to the colony's churches. This 'disestablishment' campaign was deeply resented by Afrikaner clerics. *Grahamstown Journal*, 13 February 1869; *The Cape Argus*, 17 March 1870
78 Davenport, *The Afrikaner Bond*, pp. 3–53
79 See, for example, *Zuid Afrikaan*, 25 May 1854 on Clanwilliam; also 20 March 1856 CPP A.9–1864, *Minutes of Evidence of Select Committee on Standing Rules and Orders on the Subject of Clanwilliam and Caledon Elections*; Rhodes Papers, B.2 No. 167, Frances Bennet to Francis Oats, 11 November 1897; and *Cape Times*, 6 August 1898 for Namaqualand
80 *Zuid Afrikaan*, 25 May 1854
81 Rhodes Papers B.2 No. 167
82 Rhodes Papers B.2, No. 222, C.A. Owen Lewis to Cecil Rhodes, 29 September 1899
83 *Minutes of the African Peoples Organisation Conference*, Oudtshoorn, 1907, p. 10; *Izwi*, 8 October 1907
84 *Cape Times*, 28 June 1887. Cf CO 48/521, No. 160. November 1892, minute by James Rose-Innes, who expresses similar sentiments
85 *Cape Argus*, 8 November 1866
86 *Cape Monitor*, 18 February, 1 April 1894; *Zuid Afrikaan*, 20 March 1850; CPP A9a–1863. *Report of the Scrutineers Appointed to Examine Votes for Members of the Legislative Council; Cape Times Law Report*, iv, 1894, p. 190; x, 1899, p. 46; CPP A.1–1907
87 *Minutes of the APO Conference*, Oudtshoorn, 1907, p. 4; *South African News*, 29 January 1908
88 E. Genovese, *In Red and Black: Marxian explorations in Southern and Afro-American History*, New York, 1972, p. 34
89 *Afrikaner Bond Notulen*, 1890, pp. 21–2; *Cape Times*, 20 March 1890; *Imvo*, 27 March 1890

CHAPTER ELEVEN

The posthumous vindication of Zachariah Gqishela:

reflections on the politics of dependence at the Cape in the nineteenth century

Neville Hogan

This essay is constructed around a story and a moral. The story tells of the death of Zachariah Gqishela and its sequel. The moral is implied in a Nietzschean rejection of an alien legitimacy of domination. In the essay as a whole I try to do three things: to say why I am interested in the politics of dependence; to reconstruct a tragedy of South African life; and to document an instance of the workings of that alliance between independent African producers and white merchant-traders which Stanley Trapido has called the 'small tradition' of Cape liberalism.[1]

The historical importance of the groups around such individuals as Tengo Jabavu and Walter Rubusana has been recognised in the general literature of South African political history, but almost solely from the point of view of their being proto-nationalists or the forerunners of the South African Native National Congress.[2] In the most comprehensive account of African politics in South Africa to date, Peter Walshe's *The Rise of African Nationalism in South Africa* (1970), the nineteenth-century origins of modern African political consciousness are summarily dealt with in the space of a single chapter; and the ideologies developed by the leading figures are most often referred to in the process of building up a critique of their vitiating effect on post-SANNC political action.[3] The explanation of this relative neglect of the nineteenth century lies in the belief, current since Ranger's pioneering efforts of the 1960s, that the study of African history is properly and almost exclusively a study of nationalism.[4] Because the ideology of nineteenth and early twentieth-century politicians like Tengo Jabavu 'falls outside the context of African nationalism', it is deserving only of 'retrospective comment'.[5] The historiography of nationalism has been subject to a widespread *ex post facto* prejudice against what it has labelled 'collaboration', and if there is a commonly held idea of nineteenth-century African politicians at the Cape, it is that they were collaborators in helpless thrall to their white associates.[6]

My own approach to this group is partly influenced by what has been called post-independence gloom. It was to be expected, at a time when African societies appeared to be throwing off the shackles of their colonial overlords and asserting their right to an independent national existence, that historians should have rediscovered the African past in terms of resistance and nascent nationalism. It became clear, contrary to the wisdom of conventional colonial historiography, that there was an African past; that it had been made by Africans; and that during the colonial episode Africans had remained the subjects of their own history. Soon, however, contrary to the hopes engendered at independence, it became clear that dependence was deeply embedded institutionally and intellectually in the most important areas of economic and social life; that colonisation was not merely an interlude in the unfolding of African history, but introduced structural changes which altered its course in a profound way. What was thought to be development came to be seen as underdevelopment; what the nationalist-evolutionists had hailed as a new era of state-building turned out to be an era of national stasis and breakdown.[7] The very apotheosis of nation-building came to be regarded by such radical pessimists as Fanon and Sartre as nothing but despotic parasitism. So it is that historians are having to re-investigate the colonial period in order to provide more balanced interpretations of African history. More specifically, resistance and nationalism as themes of study must give way to a deeper understanding of the importance of co-operation and assimilation.

This is not to recommend a return to an historiography which assumes the absence of African initiative. What is required is an approach which, while moving away from these categories altogether, includes the notion that without collaboration there could not have been colonisation, and also that collaboration is itself a matter of choice and initiative. Even the Cape schoolmen, who appear at times to take over in unquestioned form the ideology of their colonisers, undoubtedly regarded their success at becoming assimilated as instrumental to their own purposes; and they sometimes pursued those purposes to the point of open rebellion against their earnestly proclaimed allegiances. While they came to share the British assumption that 'there were universal standards, that those standards resided in British culture, and that the merit of other cultures rested on their approximation to those standards',[8] they were caught up in the contradictions which their identity as black Victorians entailed in the colonial context.

Thus the columns of *Isigidimi SamaXhosa*, under the editorship of Elijah Makiwane and then Tengo Jabavu, could make the struggles of 1877–81 appear to the Xhosa reader as a clash between Christendom, represented by 'our troops, the troops of Victoria Child of the Beautiful', and heathendom, in which those Africans who were defending their lands and their right to carry weapons were cast as villains engaging in 'hostility to the Word'; and at the same time carry a poem by *Hadi* in which the image of Victoria is made to undergo a radical metamorphosis:

> Awake, rock rabbits of the Mountains of the Night
> She darts out her tongue to the very skies
> That rabbit-snake with female breasts
> Who suckled and fostered the trusty Fingoes
> Thereafter to eat them alive.[9]

What is revealed here and throughout the last quarter of the nineteenth century is a complex interplay between the poles of rejection and co-operation. At times both are in play at the same moment. It is this complexity, called by Shula Marks 'the ambiguities of dependence', which a history of the spectacular fails to take into account.[10]

There are many levels at which this ambiguity can, and should be, explained because there are so many levels at which it operates. What is entirely absent from the existing published literature is any attempt to link dependence in its ideological manifestations to what underlies it in the political economy. Ideological ambiguities arise out of structural ambiguities, and cannot be explained at the level of ideology alone. Ideology is not self-explanatory. When it is treated as though it were, the result is a moralising psychologism. Under such an historiographical regime ideological inconsistencies become betrayals and ideological shifts hypocrisy.[11] As Brian Willan has shown in an important article on Sol T. Plaatje, that is precisely what comes about when the early growth of modern African political consciousness is treated exclusively as the result of 'missionary education, the impact of Christian values, the beginnings of urbanisation, and the influence of British, Negro American and liberal ideas'.[12] Missionary education and the existing ideological milieu are important in shaping African attitudes at the level of individual socialisation, but they remain influences only. They do not constitute the ideology of an undifferentiated elite, much less explain it; and they have been concentrated on to the neglect of a wider analytical investigation which must be firmly rooted in the historical processes which shaped society in (mainly) the eastern Cape in the last quarter of the nineteenth century. Constitutional developments apart, this indicates a methodology which will attempt to explain the ideology and the political behaviour of the elite in terms of its structural situation within the colonial political economy—an approach used so far only by Stanley Trapido, Colin Bundy and, for a later period, Brian Willan.[13]

Stanley Trapido has pointed to the need for a deeper understanding of the social relationships which produced that ideological complex known as Cape liberalism. In differentiating between what he calls the 'great' and 'small' traditions of liberalism at the Cape, he identifies the latter as arising out of a relatively stable alliance between African peasant producers and white merchants and traders—most clearly identifiable in those districts of the eastern Cape annexed between 1847 and 1865. In such areas, where prosperity depended to a great extent on the marketable surplus of African cultivators, attacks on the rights of Africans were (rightly) associated with an attack on the peasant sector. Defending the peasant sector therefore involved defending the rights of Africans in general as members of the constitutional polity.[14] Colin Bundy, too, has demonstrated that there were individuals with important mercantile interests, who were adherents of liberalism, who were in favour of the growth of a producer/consumer class of peasant proprietors, and who 'identified their self-interest with the development of an African peasantry'.[15] These insights and analyses have added greatly to our understanding of a very important aspect of Cape political life, and by relating ideology to its material base have begun the work of explaining African political ideology in a more comprehensible way. In the remainder of this essay I want to illustrate an instance of the way in which the alliance which constituted Trapido's 'small' tradition was reinforced and redefined at the level of ideology.

At a time when Africans as independent peasant producers were coming under increasing pressure from Bond-dominated ministries in Cape Town, and when successive governments were proving themselves 'a sort of political Baal to the entreaties of the natives',[16] their fears for the security of their land ownership and their rights as British subjects were from time to time allayed by public displays of continuing support from spokesmen for the other side of what had become an established if informal alliance.

By the middle of the 1870s King William's Town was already the centre of the burgeoning peasant trade,[17] and it was there in 1884 that the alliance between peasants and traders was made concrete with the founding of *Imvo Zabantsundu*.[18] It was also in King William's Town that the Presbyterian minister there, the Rev. John Davidson Don, created an issue around which the alliance coalesced and found one of its high points of solidarity.

On the morning of Friday 16 January 1885, Zachariah Gqishela of Tambookie location was sent out by his master, a stone mason of Burghersdorp, to look for a horse which had gone astray. He followed the railway line out of Burghersdorp and approached the farm 'Rooidebergsvlei'. On the way he met two men called James Fischer and Grahamstown (sic) who were working on the telegraph construction between Queenstown and Aliwal North. After greeting them and having a smoke, he moved on to the farmhouse where horses were tethered in an enclosure.[19] He inspected them and went on to the tramp floor nearby where the farmer, Willem Jacobus Pelser, his cousin and brother-in-law, and several labourers including Martinus David senior and Abo were threshing corn.[20] Abo was the only fluent Xhosa speaker present, and Zachariah asked him if he had seen a black horse. Abo replied that he had not. Zachariah asked Martinus David, who made the same reply. Pelser then asked Abo what it was Zachariah wanted. Zachariah asked Abo to tell Pelser that he was in search of a black horse. Pelser did not answer directly, but asked Zachariah through Abo whether he had a pass. Zachariah replied that he had not, and Pelser ordered him to go back and get one. Zachariah replied that he could not as the horse was not his but his master's. Pelser did not reply.[21] Zachariah then left the tramp floor and passed out of sight over a ridge in the direction of the farmlands.

Pelser left the tramp floor and stood on the land wall to observe the direction Zachariah had taken. Threatening to fine Zachariah fifteen shillings, he jumped off the wall and went to the house. After a while he emerged with a telescope and mounted an eminence behind the house from where he watched Zachariah's progress through his lands. He then returned to the house, and after strapping on his revolver and talking a while to his father, he came out once more, mounted a horse, and rode in the direction Zachariah had taken.[22] As he passed the tramp floor he called out to Martinus David junior to ride after two policemen who had passed in the direction of Burghersdorp earlier.[23] About an hour had passed since Zachariah first appeared at the tramp floor.

When Zachariah left Pelser and the labourers he walked back past the house towards a small dam some distance on the other side of the railway, where there was a group of horses. On his way he met up with more workers on the telegraph construction. He first greeted Alfred Peters, who was digging a post-hole, and moved on to where Veldtschoen Gcwacweka was similarly occupied. He sat down there for a while and was joined by Zwartboy Mdlunya, a friend of his. A third worker, Ntolyiya, left his hole and joined the others in conversation. After about half an hour Zachariah left in the direction of the dam. Not long after he had left them, the telegraph workers saw Pelser gallop after him. Ntolyiya and Alfred Peters gathered at Veldtschoen Gcwacweka's pole to watch what would follow.[24] Alfred Peters:

There were some horses out beyond the dam, and in the direction in which Zachariah was going. I saw Mr Pelser, riding on a black horse, go up to him, and then they both stood still for about five minutes, after which they turned and came in my direction, the native in front and Pelser behind. Suddenly, while watching them, I saw smoke hanging around them, and then I heard the report of a pistol, and saw the native fall down in front of the horse. The native shouted three times after he was shot. 'Hey! hey! come this way!' ... I told my fellow workmen that if I had not been frightened also of being shot, I would have gone to examine the deceased.[25]

Ntolyiya:

He went to turn the Kafir. I saw him turn him then they stood a little while and then both came back; the white man behind the native. While I was looking I saw smoke. I was looking towards them. And then I heard the report. Then the man dropped. The horse stood and the white man, after looking a little, galloped towards the house.[26]

Veldtschoen Gcwacweka:

After getting through the dam the white man overtook him. They spoke a little. I could not hear it. The white man had gone ahead of him, and they faced each other. Then the native turned and came towards us. Then they walked along, the white man behind mounted, and the native walking three yards in front of the horse. When they got near to the dam there was a gun's report. It came from the white man. After I heard the report the horse swerved with the white man on it. Then he turned and galloped home. . . . I was afraid.[27]

Frederick David, who was taking sheep to midday water, saw Zachariah near the dam. He was lying with his legs crossed and was waving his hand. Frederick did not go to him because he was afraid.[28]

Pelser's bullet had entered above Zachariah's left shoulder-blade about two inches from the spine. It had travelled obliquely without deflection and fractured the second vertebrae of the spine, compressing the spinal marrow.[29] That afternoon the District Surgeon, accompanied by Pelser and the Chief Constable, Edward Williams, made a *post mortem* examination. On Saturday morning police constable Jacob Sulemane together with some prisoners buried Zachariah at the spot where he had fallen.[30]

After the shooting Pelser rode back to the house, and then into Burghersdorp, where he made statements to the Magistrate's Clerk, Alfred Harmsworth, and to the Chief Constable. The gist of his statements that afternoon was that he had been out riding, had come across Zachariah, asked him to show a pass, and, when he did not, had tried to turn him off his land. Zachariah, he said, had then resisted and struck out at him with an iron bar which he was carrying. Pelser then drew his revolver and shot him.[31]

After taking all the evidence during hearings on 20 and 27 January the magistrate was in two minds whether to indict Pelser for murder or for culpable homicide. He sent the evidence to the Solicitor-General, A.F.S. Maasdorp, in Grahamstown and asked for instructions. On 31 January Maasdorp instructed the magistrate to indict for culpable homicide. On 9 February, Prime Minister Upington, who was also Attorney-General, addressed a telegram to Maasdorp enquiring what stage the case had reached.[32] Maasdorp wired back that the magistrate had been told to indict for culpable homicide. On 11 February Pelser made another statement saying that the pistol had fired accidentally as his horse shied away from Zachariah's blows. On the same day the magistrate at Burghersdorp wrote to Maasdorp that there was 'very considerable excitement in the District' and that he anticipated 'very serious excitement' if the trial of Pelser were not moved to another district. On 16 February Maasdorp wired Upington: 'On seeing the examination as completed, have declined to prosecute'.[33]

There the matter rested until, on 24 March, George Hay, editor of the anti-ministry, anti-Bond *Cape Mercury* published a leading article entitled 'Justice and Party Politics'. In it he attacked Upington, suggesting that he had quashed the case against Pelser in order to retain the support of the Afrikaner Bond in parliament. The article denounced the government for introducing party politics into the administration of justice. Hay suggested that if Pelser had been an English farmer, or had Zachariah been a white man, the case would not have been dropped.[34]

Hay's initiative was greeted with general public silence until 14 April, when *The Mercury* published what was afterwards to become a famous letter from the Rev. Don. In his letter Don called Zachariah's death a foul crime for which Pelser should have been tried. As the government had not rebutted Hay's charges, Don was 'reluctantly compelled to come to the conclusion that our rulers have been influenced by political instead of . . . legal considerations'. He demanded that justice and decency be satisfied:

> I belong to no party; I am not a politician; I never was in Burghersdorp; I know nothing of its people and never heard of Pelzer before. But I am a member of the community which has to bear the responsibility in the last resort of its Government's unchallenged acts, and a minister of a religion which knows no distinction of race, caste, class or colour; and my conscience refuses to put up silently with this offence.

This is the eloquent voice of compassionate liberalism. Unlike Hay, Don is not making overt political mileage out of Zachariah's death. He is genuinely outraged that Pelser should be allowed to get away with it:

> That poor man's blood cries to heaven, not merely against the wretched mur-

derer, but against the Government which refuses to prosecute, and the country which condones such conduct.[35]

By the end of April the affair had become a major political row, with the whole of the Cape press involved. Papers such as the *Kaffrarian Watchman* which supported the Ministry, took Pelser's side—or made out at least that the decision not to prosecute was the Solicitor-General's, and not the government's. The opposition papers denounced the Upington ministry and called stridently for 'justice and fair play' and an enquiry. The *Burghers-dorp Gazette* published a letter by 'Bondsman' which called the *Cape Mercury* 'one of the greatest detestors of the Boers and a champion of the most rabid Jingoism'.[36] Hay published letters from missionaries and opposition politicians supporting Don.[37] On 2 May Richard Rose-Innes had the whole of the evidence given at the preliminary hearings printed in the *Cape Mercury*.[38] A question on what had become known in the opposition press as the Pelser case was raised in parliament on 19 May, and in the ensuing debate Upington was cleared of any interference with Maasdorp. Hay's comment was 'so much the worse for Maasdorp'.[39]

Public comment died away until early in July when, on the affidavit of Pelser, the Attorney-General started proceedings against Don and Hay for criminal libel.[40] The allegedly injurious part of Don's letter was the final paragraph quoted above. The case was set down for a hearing on 23 July, and it raised tremendous public interest.[41] The hearing was stopped on a technicality, and after further appearances on 25 and 27 July, Don was finally remanded until 11 November. Six days before the commencement of the trial the case against Hay was dropped. Don now stood alone.[42]

When Don heard early in July that he was to be charged with *criminal libel* he was outraged that he should be so traduced by Upington. Nevertheless he saw the impending trial as an opportunity to uphold his principles. By August when he had been committed for trial, he was no longer concerned with 'that poor man's blood', but was trying hard to justify himself to the Foreign Missions Committee (FMC) of the Free Church of Scotland.[43] In a long letter home he set out the course of events and explained to his Scottish superiors why he had got into such a parlous position. According to Don, Pelser was not prosecuted

a) because of racial discrimination, and
b) because of 'Dutch' power in government.

He was being prosecuted:

a) to appease the Dutch voters,
b) because Upington was an Irishman,
c) because the government was tyrannous,

d) for political reasons of state,
e) because he had become the plaything of powerful forces, and
f) because he spoke the truth.[44]

So that by now Don, like Hay, saw the 'Pelser case' as a government/ Bond conspiracy, and his own trial as a political one.[45] Don's letters to the FMC became increasingly shrill before they became resigned. On 19 August he implied that the African population was so disturbed over the Pelser affair that they were threatening the destruction of the colony, and reminded the FMC of his plight as a victim:

> It is not Pelser, however, who is striking at me, but the head of our Government, a disreputable, false, disloyal man, who holds his place by pandering to Dutch prejudice, ignorance, and disloyalty.[46]

The whole liberal establishment in the eastern Cape—or rather, all those who thought of themselves as loyal British subjects—gathered around Don in support, interpreting his prosecution in much the same way that he did: as an attack on their position by the Bond. James Stewart, the powerful principal of Lovedale, wrote to the FMC that 'There is nothing very surprising in this case, as a result of the dominance of Afrikanerdom'.[47] The Presbytery of Kaffraria, representing all Scottish missionaries west of the Kei, sent a long minute to the FMC setting out their view of the case and endorsing the stand taken by Don as being 'necessary in the interests of justice and right'.[48] As the trial approached Don took a more resigned tone and moved from political vituperation back to a consideration of his original impulse in writing to the *Mercury*. In mid-October he characterised the trial as the test of a 'great question': 'for it is a great question involving the sacredness of life, the equality of men before the law, and the purity of Justice'.[49] Because he was pleading 'justification', a more dangerous course legally than the more usual 'fair comment', in order 'that the case could be more fully aired', he recognised that he might have to go prison:

> But should the result be a purifying of our atmosphere, and healthier views on the great questions involved, the price paid will not have been too great.[50]

The trial opened in Grahamstown on 11 November. It was a disaster for the prosecution. The African witnesses stood firm. Pelser was made to contradict himself.[51] The medical evidence showed that Zachariah could not have been in the act of striking at Pelser when the shot was fired.[52] The jury returned a verdict of not guilty, and the Judge-President, Sir J.D. Barry, acquitted Don and congratulated him 'on the position he had taken to uphold justice in this country'.[53]

This was the signal for colony-wide rejoicing by all those who considered themselves 'liege subjects of Her Majesty in South Africa'.[54] As the verdict was announced:

> Such a burst of applause breaks out through the Court house as had never been heard before. It is not suppressed. It is the universal assent of true-born Britons to the fact that one man had dared to stand forth and vindicate, at terrible cost, and at the peril of being cast into a felon's cell, the principles of truth and justice and the sacredness of the life of all who claim to be the subjects of our Gracious Sovereign Queen Victoria.[55]

King William's Town had never been so excited. The townspeople decided to do honour to the 'hero of the hour'. Shortly after five o'clock on the afternoon of 20 November, 'a number of well-filled vehicles and many horsemen' went out to meet Don, arriving in the Royal Mail cart, at the borough boundary. They arrived to discover that they had been anticipated. Already with Don was a 'troop of native horsemen, who had ridden out as far as Crowe's (sixteen miles) to greet one who, in this trial, had championed their race!' Don was transferred to a private coach and the cavalcade set off for a triumphal entry into the town. Their approach was heralded by two African horsemen, one of whom carried his many-coloured handkerchief tied to a kerrie as a flag. 'Remember!', exclaimed George Hay at his purplest, 'this was their Runymede!'[56] As the Mail appeared African schoolchildren raised a song of joy. The town pressed forward eagerly, then rushed back to the square when it was discovered that Don was not on it. Finally he arrived, preceded by the Mayor's carriage, and was given three 'lusty British cheers'. When he could make himself heard the Mayor read an address in celebration of Don's 'great victory'. The address (expensively bound to show what could be done by local printers) with eight hundred signatures attached was presented to him with ceremony. Then at the height of what a Bondsman might have been justified in calling a jingoistic orgy, Tengo Jabavu, supported 'by several other influential native men', stepped forward and read 'with a very clear enunciation' a tribute on behalf of 'the natives of King William's Town'.[57]

The tribute paid by Jabavu to Don on this occasion expresses very clearly how deeply impressed the African community was with his willingness to sacrifice himself for a principle of which they believed they would be the chief beneficiaries. But Jabavu also took the opportunity to point out to his audience how important and timely the stand taken by Don had been in averting wholesale African disaffection:

> This, the triumph of your act, has allayed our suspicions as to the soundness of the system of government; it has subdued our excitement and alarm, which had reached their utmost tension, and it has grounded and re-established the

faith of the wavering, who had begun to fear that even religion itself was a political dodge intended to weaken the minds of men into submission.[58]

This is a direct statement of the way in which the notion of justice, as an ideological instrument in the hands of the colonial ruling class, had been used in this affair to manipulate popular consciousness. It was on such occasions that rampant inequalities in the law took on the appearance of Equality before The Law—achieving precisely that cathartic reconciliation with the existing order of things brought about in eighteenth-century England by the hanging of men of property and position. If these cases were 'persuasive evidence that the law treated rich and poor alike', then Don's acquittal was an equally useful demonstration that in the Cape Colony, the law was blind to colour.[59] Don, like Jabavu, saw very clearly that it was only by such occasional tests that white over-rule could be maintained. In his reply to Jabavu's speech he interpreted the core of what had been achieved in his struggle:

> The vindication and maintenance of these principles ['the *sacredness of human life*, the *equality of all before the law*, and the *purity of the administration of justice*'] is of vast moment. ... It is only thus that the white and black races which exist here side by side can preserve a satisfactory relation to each other, working together, and each contributing its share to promote the prosperity of the country. If these are jealously maintained and faithfully preserved there is no reason why there should not be that harmony which is necessary to the comfort and well-being of both.[60]

Reading the correspondence between Don and his Home Committee it becomes clear that public adulation turned his head somewhat. He was led by self-congratulation to see himself as a kind of lone hero led by God to defend the interests of the weak.[61] But most of all, it was Don and a system of legal inequality which were vindicated in this affair. In all the public celebration and the correspondence, the name Zachariah Gqishela is not mentioned. From the time Hay took the case up, the debate centred upon establishing a principle. Once that had been achieved those involved were satisfied. Pelser was not prosecuted. Like so many others at the time he did in fact 'get away with it'. The legal system having once been celebrated in its ideological guise as The Law, could with safety reassume its ordinary predatory course. Those who administered it could henceforth be allowed to protect agents of social terror like Pelser with greater assurance of acceptability. The public argument was only obliquely relevant to the defence of African rights, and its legal resolution resulted merely in those who considered themselves to be British and virtuous gaining a temporary victory over the 'Dutch element', who they fervently believed would abolish The Law altogether—thus inviting retribution from the masses.

By January 1886 a Don defence fund had been started. Africans at Osborne station, Mount Frere, sent a donation of £2. Thirty-nine 'Natives of Theopolis' sent a contribution of £1 14s. with an address eulogising Don: 'WE, as natives, feel that you are our friend, and pray that the number who would be like-minded with you may increase.'[62] It was the small tradition's finest hour. That wider liberalism to which it appealed had been publicly upheld.

But what had been established legally could not be sustained politically. White commercial farmers were to win out against a peasantry rendered increasingly uncompetitive by legislation; and with the growth of the Rand new and different opportunities prised merchants from their failing peasant base. They found other allies, new partners. The Ciskei peasantry had had sufficient voting power in the middle 1880s to be a significant force electorally in a handful of constituencies, but unlike their white partners they did not have access to political power. As their electoral and economic base was eroded, they became more dependent on the goodwill rather than the self-interest of their erstwhile allies. Even in 1885 there was no doubting who the senior partners in the alliance were. In expressing to Don 'the deep gratitude we all owe to you as a race', and informing him that 'we are the burden that is on thee laid',[63] Jabavu expressed a pattern of dependence which had already entered into his interpretation of the alliance.

The ambiguity of Jabavu's response to Don's act is an echo of the double-edged reality of the latter's liberalism. On the one hand it consolidated the relationship between peasants and traders; and on the other it revealed the unequal nature of that relationship. There is for this reason a very real sense in which liberal rhetoric and action disarmed African suspicions and led them to a greater contentment with their allotted place in the colonial order of things than might otherwise have been the case. Again, Jabavu expressed this directly in the address to Don quoted above: 'This, the triumph of your act, has allayed our suspicions'.

Let us look for a moment more closely at Don. Throughout the century the Foreign Missions Committee urged the Scots missionaries to form independent African pastorates so that they themselves could be freed to establish new mission stations away from the more settled areas. The Presbytery of Kaffraria consistently avoided the issue, and this gave rise to rather sharp exchanges between the two bodies.[64] The missionaries in the field did not trust even ordained African ministers to carry out the work of a pastorate properly without direct supervision. As clerk to the Presbytery, Don was in the forefront of exchanges on this subject with his home committee; and he was one of those who stood out against an African ministry on the ground that Africans were not competent to do the job:

> I do not think that the native churches possess men capable of guiding, govern-
> ing, and successfully developing a church's work if thrown entirely upon
> themselves.[65]

And again:

> We cannot afford to act upon the assumption that the native is really equal to
> the European. There is something wanting in the best of them. . . . I have been
> . . . a partisan of the native ministry, but have sorrowfully modified some of
> my earlier ideas . . . they are at their best . . . working under the surveillance of
> Europeans.[66]

In 1901 the retiring convenor of the FMC, Dr Lindsay, complained that
of all Free Church missionaries those in South Africa 'do not seem to have
grasped the idea of a Native Presbyterian Church'.[67] They did not grasp
it because, together with other settlers, their liberalism 'did not depart
from the major consensus of white South African politics, that power shall
be retained by the white groups'.[68] That, ultimately, is what Don meant
when he spoke of white and black 'preserving a satisfactory relation to
each other'. Trapido's judgement, that Cape liberalism was a brand of
conservative paternalism, is correct, even where it was a direct expression
of class interest.

I do not want to suggest either that liberal churchmen like Don were
not on occasions courageous in their defence of African rights, or that
African leaders were altogether their hapless victims. Yet their activities
did reinforce a pattern of dependence and trust which is discernible in any
group who have undergone a process of dispossession and colonisation.
When faced with the problem of the economic and political pauperisation
of their own people, African intellectuals held fast, like the children of
freed slaves in the Southern States, to the belief that 'the troops would not
permit it'.[69] In their case the troops were that legion of Cape and later
Union liberals who marched through their lives, after whom they named
their sons, and in whom they placed their hopes for the future.[70]

As this essay has shown, those hopes were not always misplaced. Nor
were Africans slow to realise the treacherous nature of their dependence.
For the Cape, I would not fully endorse Genovese's remark on post-
reconstruction negroes in the United States—that they sealed their fate
by relying on the protection of others.[71] The formation of the Congress
Youth League in 1943 and the emergence of the South African Students'
Organisation in the mid-sixties were a summation of ideas and feelings
which had been present in the articulated political consciousness of Africans

for well over half a century. It is S.M. Molema, a man who felt very keenly the ambiguities of dependence, who, in quoting from Nietzsche in 1920, expresses what was and is necessary for a counter-thrust against a morality of political and social strangulation:

> I say: as long as your morality hung over me I breathed like one asphyxiated. That is why I throttled this snake. I wished to live. Consequently it had to die. [72]

Notes

1 See above, Stanley Trapido, '"The friends of the natives": merchants, peasants and the political and ideological structure of liberalism in the Cape, 1854–1910'

2 This is the approach of Walshe, Roux, Benson, Carter, Thompson, Denoon, Kuper, and H.J. and R.E. Simons. The category 'general literature' excludes those theses and papers devoted entirely to African politics and societies in the nineteenth century. Instances are Stanley Trapido's 'White conflict and non-white participation in the politics of the Cape of Good Hope 1853–1910', Ph.D. thesis, London, 1970; Colin Bundy's 'African Peasants and Economic Change in South Africa, 1817–1913, with special reference to the Cape', D.Phil., Oxford, 1976; R. Hunt Davis's continuing work on education and the educated in the eastern Cape; and Christopher Saunders's work on the Cape eastern (or western) frontier

3 Leo Kuper, 'African Nationalism in South Africa 1910–64' in M. Wilson and L. Thompson (eds.), *The Oxford History of South Africa*, ii, Oxford, 1969, p. 443

4 Although Ranger has with some justice denied that this was the thrust of his own work or that of his colleagues at Dar es Salaam. See his reply in *African Affairs*, lxx, 1971, to the critique by D. Denoon and A. Kuper, 'Nationalist Historians in search of a Nation: the "new historiography" in Dar es Salaam', *African Affairs*, lxix, 1970

5 Kuper, 'African Nationalism', p. 425

6 See for instance the chapter 'Tengo Jabavu and the Bantu Liberals' in E. Roux, *Time Longer Than Rope. A History of the Black Man's Struggle for Freedom in South Africa*, Wisconsin, 1964

7 Ranger expresses it this way: 'When the discussion of these issues began, most people were concerned with African *nationalism* . . . Five or six years ago, even, the mass nationalist party seemed the dominant and triumphant, in some sense the final, form of African political organisation and activity. Today the more interesting question seems to be that of African *politics*. African states have turned out to be less united than the mass nationalist emotion seemed to promise'. T.O. Ranger, 'The Development of African Politics in East Africa, with special reference to Tanzania', *Workshop on the Teaching of Central and East African History*, Lusaka, August 1970

8 H.A.C. Cairns, *Prelude to Imperialism*, London, 1965, p. 98

9 Quoted by Sheila Brock in 'James Stewart and Lovedale: a reappraisal of missionary attitudes and African response in the Eastern Cape, South Africa,

1870–1905', Ph.D., Edinburgh, 1974, pp. 222–3. From the time of Jabavu's editorship in 1881 *Isigidimi* carried a great deal of condemnatory material which its missionary proprietors found extremely alarming

10 Shula Marks, 'The ambiguities of dependence: John L. Dube of Natal', *Journal of Southern Africa Studies*, i, 2, 1975, pp. 162–80

11 One instance among many is Edward Roux's treatment of Tengo Jabavu's political career from the time he allied himself with the Afrikaner Bond until the 1914 Cape Provincial Council elections: *Time Longer Than Rope*, ch. 6

12 Brian Willan, 'Sol Plaatje, De Beers and an Old Tram Shed: Class Relations and Social Control in a South African Town, 1918–19', *JSAS*, iv, 2, 1978, pp. 195–215, citing Peter Walshe, *The Rise of African Nationalism in South Africa*, p. xi

13 Trapido, '"The friends of the natives"'; Colin Bundy, 'The emergence and decline of a South African Peasantry', *African Affairs*, lxxi, 1972; Willan, 'Sol Plaatje, De Beers and an Old Tram Shed'

14 Trapido, '"The friends of the natives"'

15 Bundy, 'African Peasants and Economic Change in South Africa', p. 114

16 Tengo Jabavu to Chesson, 6 May 1880, Aborigines Protection Society (APS) papers, Rhodes House, Oxford, Mss. Brit. Emp. S.18, C.139/1

17 Bundy, 'African Peasants and Economic Change', p. 103; see also Trapido and Bundy in this volume

18 Richard Rose-Innes and the prominent local traders J.J. Weir and T.J. Irvine provided security for and assisted Tengo Jabavu, himself a small farmer in the Peddie district by 1885, in setting up *Imvo Zabantsundu*. *Imvo* was printed weekly on William Hay's *Cape Mercury* press, and was never short of advertising copy inserted by local shopkeepers and traders. See D.D.T. Jabavu, *The Life of John Tengo Jabavu, Editor of Imvo Zabantsundu, 1884–1921*, Lovedale, 1922, pp. 13–15

19 Evidence of James Fischer and Grahamstown, *Regina v. Don*, Eastern Districts Court, Grahamstown, 13 November 1885; published in *The Cape Mercury*, King William's Town, 19 November 1885

20 Cape of Good Hope, *Annexures to Votes and Proceedings, A.1–'85, Evidence taken at a preliminary hearing before the magistrate of Burghersdorp on Tuesday 20 January 1885*, printed by order of the Cape Parliament, 1885 (henceforth A.1–85 Cape), and published in *The Cape Mercury*, 2 May 1885

21 Evidence of Abo and Martinus David, 20 January 1885, A.1–85 Cape, and *The Cape Mercury*, 2 May 1885. It is not clear whether Zachariah was in this case legally required to carry a pass

22 *Ibid.*, Evidence of Willem Jacobus Pelser and Abo, *Regina v. Don*, printed in *The Cape Mercury*, 17 November 1885

23 Evidence of, among others, Martinus David junior, 20 January 1885, A.1–85 Cape and *The Cape Mercury*, 2 May 1885

24 Evidence of Alfred Peters, Veldtschoen Gcwacweka, Zwaartboy Mdlunya, Ntolyiya, Breakfast, Canteen, A.1–85 Cape and *The Cape Mercury*, 2 May 1885

25 Evidence of Alfred Peters, *Regina v. Don*, 13 November 1885; *The Cape Mercury*, 19 November 1885

26 *Ibid.*, Evidence of Ntolyiya, *Regina v. Don*, 13 November 1885

27 *Ibid.*, Evidence of Veldtschoen Gcwacweka, *Regina v. Don*, 13 November 1885

28 Evidence of Frederick David, 20 January 1885, A.1–85 Cape and *The Cape*

Mercury, 2 May 1885. It is notable that of the three eyewitnesses and the four others who heard the shot, not one went to the spot where Zachariah lay because they were frightened. That is hardly surprising. Pelser had been charged several times with assaulting Africans, and his reputation would have been enough to discourage even mild curiosity. See his evidence, *Regina* v. *Don*, 12 November 1885, *The Cape Mercury*, 17 November 1885

29 Evidence of Ferdinand Paul, 20 January 1885, A.1–85 Cape and *The Cape Mercury*, 2 May 1885

30 *The Cape Mercury*, 2 May 1885

31 Evidence of Edward Williams and Alfred Harmsworth, 20 January 1885, A.1–85 Cape and *The Cape Mercury*, 2 May 1885. An iron bar was found next to Zachariah's body. It is a notable feature of the evidence that both Pelser's cousin and brother-in-law, who saw Zachariah at the tramp floor, swore that he had been carrying such a bar. Pelser's employees swore the same, with the exception of Abo, who insisted that he had been carrying a switch. Each of the independent witnesses swore that his hands were empty as he left them and walked to the dam. Pelser's statement to Harmsworth was: 'I was riding on my farm when I saw a Kafir going through the veldt. I rode up to him and asked him what he wanted there, he answered "I have come to look for a horse". I then demanded to see his pass, but he said he had none. I told him to leave my veldt, as I did not allow natives to roam about there without passes. I then went away . . . and on looking back saw the Kafir still in my veldt. I thereupon rode up to him and told him that . . . I would give him into custody . . . he then said "You'll not stop me". He had a bar of iron in his hand, and with this he struck my horse a blow on the nose. My horse . . . became unmanageable . . . I turned the horse around and as I did so I saw his arm raised again to strike me, and I thereupon shot him.'

32 'Urgent. The Attorney-General is anxious to know at what stage the proceedings in the case against Pelser at Burghersdorp for shooting a native have arrived. Please wire at once.' A.1–85 Cape

33 A.1–85 Cape. The completion of the examination refers to Pelser's second statement, which contradicted his first: 'When the deceased came to me I asked him for a pass. . . . Deceased was determined to go into our veldt. Upon this I went to fetch him back. When I got to him he would not come back. At last he did go a few yards in the direction of the house, but he suddenly turned back and struck at me three times, in such a way as to show me my life was in danger. I had already my revolver out for the purpose of frightening him. The horse got restless, and when the horse gave way for the deceased, the revolver went off and hit the deceased', *The Cape Mercury*, 2 May, 1885

34 Hay quotes the case of a Mr Filmer who had at the last circuit been charged with wounding an African in the hip 'for which he was charged £30, but then he had the misfortune to be an English European farmer, and therefore had to stand his trial', *The Cape Mercury*, 24 March 1885. In this article Hay was less concerned with the 'demands of Justice' than with using the case as a stick with which to beat Upington's ministry and Afrikaners in general. On 16 April in the *Mercury* he commented 'A man named Beer has been sentenced to seven years hard labour at Somerset East for the murder of a native. If he had only put de before his name or called himself Pelzer, he would probably not have been prosecuted.'

35 Letter dated 14 April 1885

36 *Cape Mercury*, 21 and 23 April 1885, and *Kaffrarian Watchman*, 20 April 1885

37 Letters from Bryce Ross and Richard Rose-Innes, *Cape Mercury*, 21 April 1885

38 His brother James Rose-Innes had been returned to parliament in 1884 largely on the strength of African votes

39 Leader headed 'Law and the Solicitor General', *Cape Mercury*, 26 May 1885.

40 *The Cape Mercury*, 7 July 1885

41 The courthouse in King William's Town overflowed with the interested: 'The ladies were accommodated in the seats provided for the jury, and occupied the whole space at the left of the bench. The right-hand side was occupied by townsmen, and the whole space allotted to the Side Bar was taken up, and the body of the hall being also well filled.' *The Cape Mercury*, 23 July 1885

42 *The Cape Mercury*, 5 and 12 November 1885

43 Don was not a missionary proper, but as clerk to the Presbytery of Kaffraria he reported to the FMC

44 Don to George Smith, 10 August 1885, Foreign Mission Records of Church of Scotland, National Library of Scotland, Edinburgh, MS 7797 folio 33 (hereafter NLS). Upington is plainly not to be trusted in Don's book because his nationality distorts his loyalties: 'Our present Premier ... Upington, an Irishman of very questionable loyalty to the British Crown, will snatch at every means of fostering a feud between the Dutch and the English'

45 Don to Smith, 19 August 1885, *ibid*. 'This prosecution, though nominally by Pelser, is instigated by the Government, and there is every reason to believe that this is really a political trial.'

46 Don to Smith, 19 August 1885, NLS, MS 7797 folio 39

47 Stewart to Smith, 11 September 1885, NLS, MS 7797 folio 54

48 Presbytery of Kaffraria to Smith, 2 September 1885, NLS, MS 7797 folio 56

49 Don to Smith, 14 October 1885, NLS, MS 7797 folio 68

50 *Ibid*.

51 At one stage he claimed that it was 'usual for Kafirs to walk about with pieces of iron in their hand': evidence of Willem Pelser, *Regina* v. *Don*, 12 November 1885, printed in *The Cape Mercury*, 17 November 1885.

52 Evidence of Drs Greathead, Ross, and Paul: *Regina* v *Don*, 13 November 1885, *The Cape Mercury*, 19 November 1885

53 *The Cape Mercury*, 17 and 19 November 1885

54 *The Cape Mercury*, 17 November 1885

55 'Waiting for the Verdict', *Cape Mercury*, 24 November 1885

56 'Vindicated', *Cape Mercury*, 21 November 1885

57 *Ibid*.

58 *Ibid*., and *The Christian Express*, December 1885

59 Douglas Hay, 'Property, Authority and the Criminal Law' in D. Hay, P. Linebaugh and E.P. Thompson (eds.), *Albion's Fatal Tree*, London, 1975, p. 33

60 *The Cape Mercury*, 21 November 1885

61 See Don to Smith, 27 Nov. 1885, NLS, Ms 7797 folio 76: 'The great trial is over and has ended with a complete victory for truth and right. God has maintained His own cause. I recognise His Hand very clearly in all that has happened. Though our cause was good, yet to the very end, the jury was a source of anxiety ... one man stood out for three hours against the rest, and was only shamed into acquiescence. He had been seen drinking with Pelser. ... But he

who holds all hearts in his hand was on our side. The Judge behaved nobly. . . . The plea of justification is deemed a dangerous one: but I was anxious to have that course taken as the only mode of probing the whole matter to the bottom. . . . Now, with few exceptions, the press of the country is on my side . . . the interest of the whole country has been aroused, and public opinion was swung around to my side'. William Hay, recently returned from a stay in England where he had tried to get publicity for Don, wrote to George Smith claiming that Don was 'the most popular man in South Africa': Hay to Smith, 28 December 1885, NLS, MS 7797 folio 80

62 *The Cape Mercury*, 21 November 1885. The donations were sent to the offices of *Imvo Zabantsundu*

63 *Ibid.*

64 The problems posed for the Free Church of Scotland in establishing African pastorates at the Cape were very much the same ones faced by the London Missionary Society in West Africa. In neither field were European missionaries initially prepared to leave the congregations they had gathered to African pastors; and what African pastors there were they tended to regard as their rivals. See J.E.A. Ajayi, *Christian Missions in Nigeria, 1841–91: the making of a new elite*, London, 1965

65 Don to Smith, 4 September 1886, NLS, MS 7797 folio 134. At this time Elijah Makiwane and Pambani Mzimba had been ordained for ten years

66 Don to Dr Lindsay, 24 September 1898, NLS, MS 7798

67 Sheila Brock, 'James Stewart and Lovedale', p. 50. Instead, they were confronted with one in the shape of Pambani Mzimba's independent African Presbyterian Church in 1898

68 Trapido, 'White conflict and non-white participation', p. 206

69 'When Whitelaw Reid asked black schoolchildren what they would do if someone tried to enslave them, most responded that the troops would not permit it', Eugene Genovese, *In Red and Black*, London, 1971, p. 140

70 Ultimately, of course, they placed their hopes in the British parliament, whence they directed many useless appeals. That was very much the liberal style also, and the correspondence between Don and the FMC, for instance, is packed with calls by Don for the arousal of 'healthy public opinion at home'. Don and others believed as fervently as any loyal Africans in the certain efficacy of such appeals. See NLS, MS 7797, *passim*

71 Genovese, *In Red and Black*, p. 140

72 Quoted by S.M. Molema in *The Bantu Past and Present*, Edinburgh, 1920, p. 325

CHAPTER TWELVE

Migrant labour and the Pedi, 1840–80

Peter Delius

In recent years, the subject of migrant labour has excited an increasing amount of attention from students of southern African history and society. An understanding of the process whereby African societies became exporters of labour and increasingly dependent on goods and cash secured in this fashion is critical to the understanding of the wider process of the underdevelopment of rural areas, which accompanied the emergence of the dominant capitalist mode of production in South Africa. While there has been a depressingly uniform 'slow decline into rural stagnation' of the areas from which migrant labour has been drawn,[1] the early stages of the participation of African societies in labour migration presents a diverse picture, both in terms of the effect on the society and the chronology of participation. In the latter respect, it has recently been suggested that 'the willingness of some African societies to accept their role as exporters of labour from an early date, while others resisted until the 1890s and after, still presents a considerable problem in South African history'.[2]

Pedi involvement in migrant labour dates back to the 1840s. During the 1850s and 1860s there was a significant increase in the numbers migrating, and in the 1870s large numbers of Pedi responded to the demand for labour created by the opening of the diamond fields. The Pedi example is thus one of very early labour migration. Their participation predates the conquest of the Pedi polity, and major economic reverses, such as rinderpest and east coast fever, factors which played a central role in promoting large-scale migration from other societies.[3] This essay seeks to explore the complex and changing interaction of factors which prompted this early Pedi involvement. A note of warning must be sounded, however. The period covered is one for which documentation on the society is scanty, and for which oral tradition is equally lacking in detail. There is an almost total lack of statistical information and what there is has to be treated with considerable caution.

The term Pedi, already liberally employed above, presents a number of problems. It has, in existing usage, been utilised variously to indicate virtually all the peoples of the northern Transvaal; restricted to the Rota paramountcy, and its offshoots;[4] and used to refer to these groups within the area of hegemony of the paramountcy. It is in the latter sense that it is employed here. Even this usage is, of necessity, a loose one. The Pedi polity was not a geographically static entity, and the period under consideration witnessed marked changes in the area and people under its control. Equally, the influence and control of the paramountcy was not uniform, and tended, in particular, to diminish toward the perimeters of the polity. Within the area of the Pedi domain a multiplicity of groups of diverse origins lived, who have been categorised as Tau, Kwena, Roka or Koni, largely on the basis of their totemic affiliation and traditions of origin. This already existing diversity was compounded in the nineteenth century by the movement of groups of refugees into the area of the polity, from all over the northern and eastern Transvaal and beyond. The term is retained, however, because at the political level, the paramountcy itself played an important role in labour migration as will be shown below. Further, although differences of self-identification and culture remained even among the more long-standing groups within the polity and political and cultural boundaries were not conterminus, a common 'Pedi' culture was emerging out of the interaction of these groups.[5]

The Rota, an offshoot of the Kgatla in the south-western Transvaal, were not the first arrivals in the north-eastern Transvaal, nor were they initially the dominant group.[6] It is possible in fact, that the name 'Pedi' was appropriated by the Rota from the name given to the area by the preceding groups. The period after the arrival of the Rota in the area witnessed the twin processes of, on the one hand, an elaboration of the powers of the chief within Rota society, and, on the other, an increase in the power of the Rota relative to the other groups in the area. During the regency of Mampuru, the Rota successfully challenged the ritual and 'judicial' supremacy of the Mongatane chieftaincy and began in turn to extend their dominance over the neighbouring chieftaincies, while at the same time elaborating the powers of the paramountcy. The most celebrated and perhaps most fundamental innovation was the practice of ensuring that subordinate groups took the principal wife of their chiefs from the Rota lineage, thus ensuring both political leverage and inflated bridewealth.

The apogee of early Pedi power and prestige was achieved during the reign of Thulare (1780?–1820). During this period combined armies, under the leadership of the Rota, raided over a wide area of the Transvaal capturing cattle and temporarily pressing men into service in their regiments. It is likely that the extension of the area of hegemony and raiding that occurred at this time was, in part, related to the position of the Pedi polity in patterns of local and long-distance trade.[7] The reign of Thulare is remembered as one during which direct contact was established with the Mozambique coast, and the Pedi area also straddled trade-routes running from that coast to the west. It is equally probable that the paramountcy played a role both in the control of the production of iron goods, and their trade, locally and to the south.[8]

The authority of the paramountcy, already weakened by the internal dissension which followed the death of Thulare, did not survive the *difaqane* in the Transvaal. The Pedi polity, with which this essay is most directly concerned, emerged out of the conditions in the Transvaal consequent on that period of disruption. The authority of the Rota group was partially re-established under Sekwati in the 1830s and 1840s. Sekhukhune succeeded Sekwati in 1861 and his reign witnessed a further extension of the power of the polity, so that by the 1870s, it had become a major alternative focus of power to both the Zuid Afrikaanse Republiek (ZAR) and the Swazi for Africans in the north-eastern Transvaal. The nineteenth century, however, probably witnessed a continued reduction of the role of the Pedi in trade networks. While the polity remained linked, largely through Tsonga middlemen, to the east coast, and a virile iron trade continued between the north-eastern Transvaal and the southern Sotho area until at least the 1860s, increasing penetration of the interior by traders from the Cape and Natal considerably reduced the importance of the older established routes running from east to west and north to south.[9] Nor was the polity, even at the height of its power in the 1870s, in a position to dominate trade-routes in the way it had during the reign of Thulare.

During the chieftainship of Thulare, the Rota capital was situated in the rich agricultural and pastoral lands of the Steelpoort River valley, and much of the population under its sway resided in the south. The heartland of the polity that was established under Sekwati in the 1830s and 1840s, on the other hand, was the rugged and consequently more easily defensible area between the Olifants and Steelpoort Rivers. While the numerous valleys and mountains of this predominantly bushveld terrain provided the combination of resources required by Pedi agriculture and cattle-keeping, it did not equal the lush environment that had provided the context for the earlier development of the polity. Although in the early 1860s the German missionary, Merensky, commented on the luxuriant fields and abundant grain in the area around the Leolu mountains, much of the region was not arable and agricultural success was dependent on the vagaries of rainfall. The effect of the Drakensberg rainshadow on this area meant low, erratic and highly localised rainfall. The missionary record bristles with complaints relating to rains, in particular their absence or insufficiency during critical phases of the agricultural cycle.[10]

The first detailed accounts of Pedi labour migration become available after the arrival of the Berlin missionaries in the area in 1861. By 1862, Merensky was writing about the hundreds of men who travelled from the north-eastern Transvaal to the Cape Colony each year, and who with the money they earned, bought guns and ammunition before returning home.[11] Indeed, this movement of men southwards was so regular that Nachtigal attempted to use it as a way of getting post back to Germany.[12] The Pedi contributed significant numbers to the flow of men, and Merensky maintained that it was regarded as established practice among members of the Pedi polity that each youth, on reaching maturity, went to the Cape Colony for one or more years.[13] This comment may well have involved an element of exaggeration, but it does give an indication of the extent of Pedi participation in migrant labour, and it seems probable that of the major groups in the northern Transvaal, the Pedi were the most committed to the system at this stage.

They were, however, by no means the only society to participate; they constituted an important part of a much wider system which included significant numbers of Sotho and Tsonga from north of the Olifants River.[14] While the Venda do not appear to have been involved, some Lobedu certainly were,[15] and by 1870 the Zoutpansberg was peppered with individuals who had had some grounding in *Nederlands Gereforemeerde Kerk* teachings in the Cape and Natal.[16] To the north-west, the Transvaal Ndebele under Mapela participated, and there are also references to migrants from just north of Pretoria.[17] On the southern periphery of the Pedi domain, both the Kopa under Boleu and the Transvaal Ndebele under Mabhogo were involved, as were the Pai and Pulana.[18] Men from the north and north-east passed through the Pedi area *en route*, and Merensky believed, in 1862, that it was no exaggeration that in many of the preceding years up to a thousand guns with accessories had been brought back to the area and through it to the groups living to the north.[19] By 1869 Merensky's colleague, Nachtigal, calculated that a thousand of Sekhukhune's subjects passed his mission station outside Lydenburg on their way south annually.[20]

Men travelled from the Pedi area in groups as large as two hundred.[21] They had to travel for fifteen arduous days before they reached the first homesteads under Mshweshwe in the Basotho kingdom, by which time there was little, if anything, left of the bag of cooked maize that each man carried as provision for the journey. [22] From the southern Sotho area, after securing the necessary exit permit or pass from Mshweshwe or the French missionaries in return for service or tribute, they moved on into the Cape Colony. [23] While there are references to Pedi labourers in Colesburg, Victoria, Graaff-Reinet and even in Cape Town, the main concentration appears to have been in the environs of Port Elizabeth. [24] Natal was also a destination in the late 1860s and probably also the 1850s for men from the northern Transvaal. [25] They appear to have worked as long as they needed to save sufficient money to buy a gun, although they also brought back a range of other commodities, prominent among which were cattle, blankets and ammunition. [26] Thus, for example, Jonas Podumo, on the first of his two trips to the Cape Colony, worked for eight months, in which time he is reputed to have earned three heifers and six sheep. With the proceeds of the sale of one of these heifers he bought an 'old English soldier's gun'. [27] Other individuals spent as much as two years away before returning. It is difficult to establish precisely how guns were procured. Some migrants may have received them directly in exchange for service, but in the main the pattern seems to have been that individuals used either cash or stock earned to buy guns elsewhere. Podumo, on his second trip, was defrauded by a Koranna of approximately three pounds with which he was attempting to purchase a gun. This particular piece of dastardliness took place in the environs of Philippolis. [28] There are also accounts of Pedi returning from Port Elizabeth, who travelled to the Griqua before returning home, and it may be that the Griqua were an important source for the supply of guns. [29] Firearms were also probably purchased from gun-traders in the eastern Cape, and from the southern Sotho.

Returning migrants usually waited in Mshweshwe's area until sufficiently large numbers assembled to make the hazardous journey north. Merensky suggests that these returning groups consisted of between two hundred and five hundred men. Nevertheless smaller groups were clearly also making their way back, no doubt at considerable risk. [30] One of the most detailed descriptions of a returning group is of Transvaal Ndebele, subjects of Mapela: 'There were 130 men. They all carried guns over their shoulders and besides these they also had a variety of kinds of baggage . . . the group also had fifteen horses with it.' [31]

The large size of these parties was dictated, in part, by the dangers of attack. Apart from the prohibitions in the ZAR on Africans possessing guns and horses, in 1852 A.H. Potgieter had concluded that the bulk of guns secured by Africans were procured by working in the English colonies. A *Krygsraad* (Military Council) decision of the same year forbade

Africans to cross the Vaal River. Draconian punishments were proposed for those who breached the prohibition or were found in possession of firearms. Veldcornets in border areas were ordered to organise regular patrols and, if necessary, mount commandos to track down groups of returning migrants.[32] The extent to which these measures were implemented is unclear, but the probability is that, as with much of early ZAR 'native policy', there was a marked disjunction between the real and the ideal. Certainly, initially, some of the smaller parties were attacked and disarmed. As a result migrants travelled through areas of white settlement by night, and the larger parties put up effective resistance to attempts to disarm them.[33]

By the 1860s, one's major impression is of the inability of the authorities at Lydenburg and elsewhere to do much more than harass them. Indeed the recurring complaint was not of attacks by whites, but of attacks by Mabhogo and, to a much lesser extent, Boleu on returning migrants.[34] Mabhogo's stronghold lay on the route followed by migrants to and from Mshweshwe, and he staged regular attacks on labour parties. The object of these attacks was clearly to secure guns and other goods and not to practise cannibalism, as outraged Pedi informants told Nachtigal. It is also possible that Mabhogo was attempting to contest Sekhukhune's hegemony over the migrant labour system. By the second half of the 1860s there is strong evidence, that, while members of Trekker society may have effectively abandoned attempts to stop the flow of men and arms, they were not averse to seeking to profit from it. Subjects of Mabhogo and Lydenburgers collaborated in joint ambushes on smaller parties, sharing the spoils.[35] Sekhukhune was plagued by complaints from his subordinate chiefs and members of groups from further north about these attacks, and they appear to have been an important factor in persuading the Pedi to join forces with a commando sent to attack Mabhogo's stronghold in 1863.[36] The desire to keep a route to the south open, and to reduce or eradicate attacks on groups of migrants, was, in fact, a fundamental component of the policy pursued by the paramountcy throughout the 1860s and 1870s.

The 1870s produced a welter of legislation in the ZAR aimed at controlling and taxing African labour.[37] In the second half of the 1860s complaints of labour shortage took on a new stridency in the Republic. This 'shortage' related to the increasing ability of African societies to resist labour demands, a movement away from the use of apprentice labour by the Trekkers, the growth in the numbers of settlers in the ZAR, and the increasing stratification of ZAR society.[38] The large-scale flow of labour to the diamond fields posed severe problems for the ZAR, both accelerating the already advanced process of the arming of African societies and, as importantly, reducing still further the numbers of Africans prepared to work on white farms. This happened at a time when the market for produce created by the diamond fields and the alluvial gold fields in the north-eastern Transvaal provided a much needed stimulus to agricultural and pastoral production.[39] To a state desperately short of revenue, the earnings of migrants also provided a tempting potential source of hard currency. Prominent among the measures introduced were those insisting on the purchase and carrying of passes by Africans, with the proviso that those who had been in employment with white farmers for six months or more should receive their passes free. Once again, however, while these measures had some impact, the ZAR had neither the administrative nor the coercive machinery to implement them effectively. In the case of the more powerful African societies, such as the Pedi, there was no possibility that they could be applied, and the Republic's attempt to apply this legislation to weaker societies simply caused the smaller chiefdoms to identify more clearly with the effectively independent African polities.[40]

An intriguing example of the changing relations of power in the northern Transvaal is provided by the deceit and ultimate demise of one D. van der Merwe. After agreeing to transport a number of guns back from Natal for a group of Pedi migrants, van der Merwe subsequently refused to hand them over. Sekhukhune, using Nachtigal as an intermediary, threatened dire consequences for the Lydenburgers unless the guns were returned. The landdrost returned the guns and the *Uitvoerende Raad* (Executive Council) approved his action, and further stipulated that van der Merwe stood in breach of the law and should be tried.[41] There were clear advantages in being a subject of the Pedi polity in the turbulent Transvaal of the 1870s.

The opening of the diamond fields provided a new market for labour to a society already deeply involved in migration. The Pedi responded to the demand with rapidity and on a large scale. In 1872 a system of registration of 'native' labour was established on the fields. While the categories employed to indicate origin are vague and the figures provided are dubious in the extreme, the returns do suggest that Pedi and Tsonga were major sources of the supply of labour to the fields.[42] In the context of an already existing labour system, the diamond fields offered a number of advantages to the Pedi. The wages paid to African labourers on the fields were reputedly the highest in South Africa.[43] The result was that the amount of time spent away from home was reduced. The time that the Pedi spent on the fields varied between four and eight months. Again the work period appears to have corresponded, broadly, with the length of time required to purchase a gun.[44] While the journey to the diamond fields was an arduous and dangerous one, and Pedi arrived there in a weakened state, it is unlikely that it was any more taxing than the long haul to Port Elizabeth had been. The flourishing arms trade that existed at the fields presumably reduced the level of effort and risk involved in the purchase of guns. Lacking precise information on the previous conditions under which the Pedi had laboured, it is difficult to make comparisons of working conditions, but, this aside, it would seem probable that the diamond fields represented a marked improvement on the previous options open to the Pedi. However, while the Pedi response to this new demand for labour can be partly accounted for in these terms, clearly wider questions about the reasons for Pedi participation remain unanswered.

Probably the first people from the Transvaal to go to the Cape for work were those impoverished and/or displaced by the ravages of the difaqane and its aftermath. Some of these individuals subsequently returned and were integrated into the societies emerging in the post-difaqane environment. Prominent among these emerging foci of power was the Pedi polity. The movement of refugees into its area of hegemony was an important aspect of the consolidation of the Pedi polity throughout the period under consideration. The early period of Trekker settlement in the Transvaal was characterised, in particular, by a highly coercive relationship between Trekkers and African societies and this generated a flow of refugees into the Pedi domain. There are indications that refugees, especially in the early stages, were more prone to migrate and were also more likely to engage in more than one spell of migration, although lacking any statistical material it is impossible to demonstrate this conclusively.[45] Again this may have stemmed from the need to secure the resources necessary to integrate into the societies they had joined, and to do so, without entering into too constricting a relationship of dependence on and clientage to men of wealth and power within Pedi society. Equally, the opportunities for social mobility offered by the hunting economy may have been particularly important to new entrants into Pedi society, as may have been the kinds of affinal relationships they were able to establish. Hence the acquisition of both firearms and cattle may conceivably have been more important to members of Pedi society of low status than to the longer established members of that society.

While, however, migration stemming from these causes may have played a critical role in the earliest phase of migration, and no doubt continued as a sub-theme throughout the period under consideration, the scale of migration from the Pedi area in the 1850s, 1860s and 1870s suggests that a substantially wider involvement was entailed than simply that of new and low status members of the society. The desire to accumulate guns appears to have been a factor of critical importance. The beginning of substantial Pedi participation in labour migration in the early 1850s coincided with a period in which the Pedi were under severe threat from the Zulu, the Swazi and the Trekkers. The attacks which the Pedi experienced and survived, though narrowly, at this stage, amply demonstrate the effectiveness of the limited number of firearms which they then had in their possession[46] particularly in the essentially defensive military strategy which they employed, which involved the ability to withstand long sieges in fortified strongholds. Equally, the opening of the diamond fields coincided with a period of mounting tension between the Pedi and the ZAR which was to culminate in the attack launched on the Pedi by President Burgers in 1876.

Apart from their military significance, guns were obviously equally important in hunting. Modern ethnographers tend to project the current absence of hunting in the area into the past.[47] The documentary record suggests a very different picture. The cattle losses which the Pedi experienced in the 1820s presumably increased the importance of hunting, and by 1839 they lived 'chiefly by the chase, on millet and on beans'.[48] The gradual re-accumulation of cattle reduced this dependence on the hunt but in accounts of the region in the 1860s, hunting is given equal prominence with agriculture and cattle-keeping as constituting the economic bases of local societies.[49] Apart from playing an important part in day-to-day subsistence and being critical at times of crop failure, skins, horns, feathers and ivory were important trade-goods, and it was probably in hunting for trading purposes, if such a distinction can be drawn, that guns were most important, given the problems and cost of the supply of ammunition. It is clear that individuals within the society gained prominence specifically in the role of hunters.

The fascinating life story of Jakob Makoetle is a case in point. He does not appear to have been born of high rank. Having secured a gun, he operated as a hunter in the area round the Steelpoort River, where, because of the prevalence of tsetse fly, big game still abounded. He appears to have hunted with a group of followers; but just what the composition of this group was, unfortunately is not clear. His greatest feat was to shoot five elephants in one day, and he became 'der liebling des Konigs Sekhukhune'.[50] In the long run, however, the twin processes of cattle accumulation and the eradication of game in and around the Pedi domain probably reduced the importance of hunting throughout the period covered by this essay.

While the Pedi's acquisition of firearms increased their military and hunting potential, it probably hastened the eradication of game. It also meant that the society became dependent on a changing technology that it could not reproduce. In order to retain the advantages which the possession of firearms afforded, especially in military terms, the Pedi were forced to attempt to keep pace with changes in gun technology. Although they were extensively armed by the 1860s, Pedi firearms were largely old muskets or elephant guns.[51] The arms trade in Griqualand West, while dealing in the usual selection of obsolete and decrepit firearms, also made available more modern rifles, and Merensky suggests that the Pedi made use of this to rearm extensively, trading off their older firearms to groups to the north of them.[52]

Although the 'conventional' explanation, that it was demand for firearms which promoted the early involvement of groups like the Pedi in migrant labour, appears to be substantially correct, the problem remains of why the Pedi adopted this strategy to secure them. The demand for firearms, which existed among all African societies in southern Africa, did not lead automatically to labour migration. The Mpondo, Zulu and southern Sotho, for example, acquired substantial numbers of guns largely through trade in cattle and grain.[53] The key variable would appear to be the absence of accessible markets for these commodities in the north-eastern Transvaal until the 1870s, unlike the situation further south. Some trade in grain existed between Boer and Pedi society, but the basic similarity of their produce meant that trade consisted in the main of evening out inequalities of production. The distance of the Lydenburg district from markets, and the difficulties and high cost of transport, ruled out the large-scale export of grain for Trekker and Pedi alike. While cattle could walk to market, even the cattle trade from the Lydenburg area appears to have been limited.[54]

It is difficult to construct any coherent picture of Pedi cattle holdings in the period prior to 1880 from the documentary record. The subject of cattle excited much less comment from missionaries than did agriculture. What does emerge is that throughout the period in question the Pedi were intent on accumulating cattle. Their area had been denuded of cattle in the 1820s by Ndebele and other raiders and one of the consequences of this depopulation was the reappearance of tsetse fly in parts of it.[55] By 1839 cattle holdings do not seem to have recovered markedly, although the suggestion of a Pedi visitor to the southern Sotho that there were no cattle in his homeland at all more probably reflected a caution born of the experience of the consequences of loose talk about cattle to strangers than reality.[56] In the early 1850s the Pedi were once again stripped of substantial amounts of cattle, this time through Zulu and Trekker raids.[57]

The later 1850s and 1860s were largely years of freedom from attack and presumably witnessed an increase in stock holdings, although other enemies of Pedi cattle, prominent among which was 'lungsickness' (bovine pleuro-pneumonia), continued to take their toll. It appears unlikely, however, that the Pedi ever accumulated sufficient cattle to participate in the cattle trade to the extent that the Mpondo did.[58] R. James, for example, armed with his experience of trading cattle from the Mpondo, set out to reproduce this trade in the Lydenburg area in 1872, but discovered 'The natives in those days all wanted young cattle. I had men trading in Swaziland for cattle which we then sold to the Basuto tribes' (i.e. northern Sotho).[59] According to Merensky, the opening of the diamond fields led to the widespread purchase of cattle from white farmers of the Lydenburg area by Pedi and others returning from the fields. Information as to the distribution of cattle within the society is unfortunately even more scanty. The probability is, however, that wealth in cattle was restricted to relatively few individuals.

The Trekkers' attempt to establish and maintain a monopoly of arms in the Transvaal involved prohibitions on Africans owning guns or horses, and trading in these items to Africans was illegal. These restrictions were consistently flouted by Trekker and African alike, but attempts were made to enforce them, particularly in the case of traders from the Cape and Natal. The hazards of gun-smuggling inflated their cost and it was initially only ivory and later cash which provided sufficient incentive and return to make the trade an attractive proposition.[60] Trade did, nonetheless, play a role in the supply of guns to the Pedi, and ivory was a critical item in this trade.[61] The amount of ivory which the Pedi could secure, however, declined with the eradication of elephants in the area and in and around the Pedi domain. As the centre of the ivory trade moved to the Zoutpansberg, the Pedi were bypassed, and the opportunities which their earlier collaboration with hunters from Ohrigstad had presented for acquiring guns either temporarily or permanently were reduced.[62] The complaints of Lydenburgers in the latter half of the 1850s about the difficulty of attracting traders to the area,[63] probably reflected the dwindling supply of ivory, although some ivory was to be traded from there until the late 1860s.[64]

Given the distances, hazards and commodities involved, trade was unlikely to have led to the widespread acquisition of arms which the Pedi achieved through labour migration. Recent informants maintain that chiefs had rights to all ivory acquired by their subjects, and that they also had control over the organisational requirements of elephant hunting.[65] Thus, the extent to which firearms were diffused through the society as a consequence of trade in ivory depended on how far chiefs chose to redistribute them among their subjects. It was also presumably only chiefs, and the relatively few others with considerable herds of cattle, who would have been willing or able to trade cattle against guns. It would seem that the cash that traders demanded in return for guns by the late 1860s came, at least in part, from tribute payments made to chiefs by returning migrants. Where external enemies were less threatening, chiefs may have attempted to retain control over the firearms introduced into their society, but in the turbulent Transvaal it was in the interests of both chiefs and subjects that guns should be as widely distributed as possible, and, short of a massive investment of chiefly resources, migrant labour was the only way of achieving this end. To some extent, control over the use of firearms was retained by chiefs, through their accumulation of stores of ammunition which were distributed among subjects only in the event of military action and perhaps large-scale hunts.[66] Chiefly resources were invested in the purchase of superior arms, which were loaned or given to favoured subjects.[67]

With the opening of the alluvial gold fields in the north-eastern Transvaal, the early 1870s witnessed a minor economic revolution which gave rise to a new demand for labour and grain. However, while some Pedi responded to this local demand for labour, on the whole the white miners were compelled to secure most of their labour from other sources.[68] Although there was a more or less open arms trade on the gold fields, which had the sanction of President Burgers, the probable reason why the Pedi were reluctant to work on them revolved around the lower rates of pay than at the diamond fields, and the higher prices for firearms and the inferior quality of the guns available in the north-eastern Transvaal.[69] Grain prices on the gold fields were extremely high and the Pedi did trade some grain to traders at the fields, particularly in exchange for ammunition.[70] The opening of both the gold and diamond fields, however, coincided with a period of mounting pressure on land within Pedi society and this, at the least, militated against the large-scale production and sale of grain.

The absence of anything resembling accurate population figures for the area makes speculation about population increase hazardous at best, but it does appear likely that there was a steady build-up of population in the Pedi domain. The polity provided a partial haven from the plundering and coercive activities of the Zuid Afrikaanse Republiek that occurred to a greater extent beyond Pedi borders than they did within. Hence, apart from any 'natural' increase, the population of the domain was swelled by a constant stream of refugees.[71] By the early 1870s there is evidence that a perception of land shortage existed within the society. This is revealed by the reports of Nachtigal, the increased vigour with which land claims were pursued by the paramountcy, and by the movement of groups out of the area after the power of the Pedi polity was broken in 1879.[72] The security in the heartland of the Pedi polity had probably encouraged settlement in marginal agricultural areas by the 1870s. It is likely that there was not an absolute shortage of arable land but rather a shortage of better quality land and an increasing difficulty in securing the combination of grazing and agricultural resources favoured by the Pedi. While the favoured soils were black peat or turf and red clay, when these were fully subscribed or when they were exhausted, less fertile soil had to be used.[73] Thus the 1870s may well have seen the Pedi being increasingly forced to utilise lands of poorer quality with resultingly reduced yields.

The vulnerability of the Pedi to drought may also have been increased by the introduction of maize, a crop less resistant to drought than the sorghums and millets that had been the dominant cereals cultivated earlier. Arbousset's informants at Morija in 1839 told him that maize was not grown in the Pedi area. Although it had been experimented with, it was abandoned in the face of chiefly disapproval.[74] By the beginning of the 1860s some maize was being grown, but it does not seem to have challenged the dominant position of the older crops.[75] During the mid-1860s maize cultivation spread still further, but its extent is not clear.[76] The increased planting of maize may have represented a response to population increase. From 1869 to 1877 the Pedi experienced a number of years in which inadequate rainfall and locusts, presumably in combination with the factors outlined above, resulted in shortfalls of grain. In 1869 Nachtigal reported that, in order to preserve grain stores, beer-brewing had ceased. In 1870 he reported widespread hunger, and in 1872 Sekhukhune made the same complaint.[77] The picture for the years 1873 to 1875 is not clear, but in 1876 and 1877 the Pedi were forced to import large quantities of grain, partly in exchange for cattle, the result of poor rains and the ravages of war.[78]

Quite apart from ecological pressures, Pedi rulers appear to have played a critical role in the initiation and control of the kind of movement of men to the south which existed by the 1860s and 1870s. With the settlement of Trekkers in the north-eastern Transvaal from 1845 onwards, the Pedi rapidly discovered that the Trekker monopoly of fire power, so attractive in alliance, was costly in the event of dispute. Merensky suggests that Chief Sekwati saw the importation of guns and horses as the main way to resist whites (and no doubt other African societies as well).[79] This implies that Sekwati initiated the large scale flow of labour to the south;

and it is also borne out by my informants, who stated that Sekwati, while still at Phiring (his capital till the mid-1850s) sent out three regiments, two to the Cape and one to Delagoa Bay, and that they returned with firearms.[80] While it is unlikely that entire regiments were dispatched with any regularity, by the time the missionaries arrived in the 1860s, groups as large as two hundred men were leaving the area on occasion.[81] Pedi almost always left and returned in organised groups, and men of high rank appear to have travelled with them.[82] The bulk of men going south did so shortly after initiation, and it seems likely that elements of regimental organisation were being utilised. Although information is not available to elaborate this point, regiments were a fundamental component of chiefly power within Pedi society. Sekhukhune also appears to have exercised control over the departure of men for the south, and in the 1870s referred, in conversation, to men he had 'sent out' to work.[83]

In this process of labour migration to white enterprise, the southern Sotho ruler Mshweshwe played a key intermediary role. Moreover both Sekhukhune and Mshweshwe were able to play a critical role in the movement of men to the Cape Colony because of their position as rulers of major independent African areas bordering on areas of white control. This was a situation which both could exploit to their material and political advantage. Pedi passing through Mshweshwe's area had to work in his 'gardens' before he would grant them an exit permit, although this could possibly have been circumvented by the payment of tribute. On the return journey from the Cape, Mshweshwe had 'the right to take the chief's portion out of their earnings, and this invariably consisted of munitions of war', although to what extent this right was exercised in not clear.[84] Sekhukhune, equally, probably derived benefits from tribute payments made by individuals passing through his domain and by returning Pedi.[85]

Throughout the period under consideration, it appears to have been the practice that returning migrants made gifts to their chief, although the precise form that this tribute took is not clear. By 1862 Sekhukhune had in his possession considerable quantities of cloth and blankets—as well as his own arsenal.[86] It also seems that Mshweshwe and Sekwati (and later Sekhukhune) had come to some kind of mutual arrangement. There is the suggestion that Sekwati had formed a matrimonial alliance with Mshweshwe, and such a marriage would have provided for institutional expression of the relationship between them.[87] Mshweshwe's significance in Sekhukhune's view of power in southern African relations is reflected in the two letters he dispatched on his accession. One went to Lydenburg, the other to Mshweshwe.[88] Maletsul, who carried the letter south, subsequently returned with two individuals, 'sons of Mshweshwe', who were fêted and entertained to military displays by Sekhukhune.[89] On their departure 'Mshweshwe's sons' were accompanied by two hundred Pedi going to the Cape Colony to work.[90] Presumably part of the purpose of the letter and the visit was to renew the arrangement regarding the flow of men and arms.

The control of the paramountcy appears to have extended to the areas in which groups of Pedi found employment. Nachtigal, visiting Port Elizabeth in 1865, encountered a community of Pedi living around a London Mission Society station on Hospital Hill. Prominent in the community was one Morutane, 'brother' to Sekhukhune, who sent gifts back to Sekhukhune and who dispatched letters to him through the missionaries.[91] At the diamond fields J.B. Curry commented that some chiefs had unofficially accredited ministers who kept them informed by returning parties of what was going on among their men working on the diggings.[92] Sekhukhune had at least two men, Mamaree and Timian, on the fields in this role.[93] Mamaree was probably the man known to the missionaries as Mamaricha and to the Boers as Windvogel. He was Sekhukhune's brother and prominent in Pedi politics throughout the 1860s and 1870s.

The demand for labour which existed at the diamond fields and for Cape railway construction gave rise to a number of attempts at labour recruitment, and the Pedi were a favoured target. The method of recruitment revolved, to a considerable extent, around enlisting the aid of chiefs. Prominent among the recruiters was one J. Edwards, who had previously traded in the Pedi area, and who, in 1873, concluded an agreement with Sekhukhune by which the latter agreed to supply 'constant labour to the fields at current wages'.[94] After the negotiations were completed, Edwards set off for the fields accompanied by forty-seven of Sekhukhune's subjects.[95] Although chiefly power was an important factor in Pedi labour migration, it is unlikely that the levels of coercion involved were high. Apart from the incentives of new commodities and perhaps, by the 1870s, the relief of pressure on grain supplies, if labour migration was an accepted norm by the 1860s, as Merensky suggests, this was presumably even truer by the 1870s and it was in this context that chiefly powers of persuasion were applied.

It is not only in terms of recruitment that the 1873 agreement between Sekhukhune and Edwards is of interest. It also marks an intriguing attempt on the part of the paramountcy to tighten its control over Pedi migrants. In the agreement it was laid down that 'Each man was to be contracted for six months at the current wages payable . . . £1 to be paid by the employer as royalty to Mamaree and Timian . . . the amount as royalty . . . to be deducted from wages'. Further, no man was to 'receive a permit for a gun without the sanction of Mamaree and Timian and not until after the royalty has been paid'.[96] The number of Sekhukhune's subjects on the fields, and hence subject to the agreement, was calculated at 'about three thousand'.[97] In practice the agreement broke down because it failed to secure the support of Robert Southey, Lieutenant-Governor of Griqualand West, who quite rightly saw it as being designed to 'squeeze £1 each out of every labourer of the tribe'.[98] This agreement marks a clear attempt on the part of the paramount to tighten his control over the earnings of migrants and possibly also to increase the proportion of their earnings which accrued to him. But, perhaps more importantly still, it raises a number of questions concerning the nature of the relationship between paramountcy and subordinate chiefdoms.

One of the dominant themes in Pedi politics in the period 1830 to 1880 was the conflict between the paramountcy and subordinate chiefdoms, with the paramountcy attempting to maintain and extend its authority and the more powerful chieftaincies seeking to expand their independence and to establish their hegemony over the chiefdoms in their own areas of the polity. It seems probable that while Sekwati and Sekhukhune controlled the flow of men from the immediate area of the capital and secured tribute from them, subordinate chieftaincies exercised similar control over men from their own areas, while remaining responsive to overall direction from the paramount. Moreover, while in the early part of his reign Sekhukhune did much to consolidate the position of the paramountcy, by the early 1870s a number of the more powerful chieftaincies were acting increasingly independently of the paramountcy, and it is doubtful whether Sekhukhune exercised any significant control over labour migration from them. Men from the chieftaincies on the periphery of the area of Rota hegemony would in the normal course of events experience little in the way of direct control or exaction from the paramountcy even if they fell under the general appellation of 'Sekukuni Basuto's' which was employed on the diamond fields. The agreement of 1873 rested in part on an inaccurate conception by Edwards of the nature and extent of the power of the paramountcy within Pedi society and on an attempt on the part of Sekhukhune, through manipulating this misconception, to secure a degree of control over Pedi migrants that his internal resources of power could not provide. If the agreement had been fully implemented it may well have marked an important turning point in the relationship between paramountcy and subordinate chiefdoms. It was not, however, and in 1879 British and African (mainly Swazi) troops, under the command of Sir Garnet Wolseley, stormed the Rota capital and put an end to Pedi independence.

The unpublished sources on which this article is based are, in the main, located in the Berlin Missionary Archives (BMA), East Berlin; the Transvaal Archives (TA), Pretoria; and the Cape Archives (CA). Information gained through interviews conducted in Sekhukhuneland in October and November of 1976 has also been employed.

Notes

1 W.G. Clarence-Smith and R. Moorsom, 'Underdevelopment and Class Formation in Ovamboland, 1845–1915', *JAH*, xvi, 3, 1975, p. 365

2 P. Kallaway, 'Black Responses to an Industrialising Economy: labour shortage and native policy in Griqualand West, 1870–90', unpublished paper presented to the Conference on South African Labour History, University of the Witwatersrand, April 1976, p. 1

3 See, for example, W. Beinart, 'Rural Production and Stratification in South Africa: Pondoland, *c*.1894–1930', unpublished African History seminar paper, London, ICS, October 1975

4 H.O. Monnig, *The Pedi*, Pretoria, 1967, pp. v. and vi

5 *Ibid.*, p. v. While Monnig is intent on demonstrating that cultural differences remain, his work does not contradict the suggestions that a common culture was emerging

6 The following paragraphs are based in the main on A. Merensky, 'Beitrage zur Geschichte der Bapeli', *Berliner Missions Berichte*, 1862, 21; J.A. Winter, 'The Tradition of Ra'lolo', *South African Journal of Science*, ix, a, 1972; D.R. Hunt, 'An Account of the Bapedi', *Bantu Studies*, v, 4, 1931

7 This is not a novel approach; see M. Legassick, 'The Sotho-Tswana Peoples before 1800' in L. Thompson, *African Societies in Southern Africa*, London, 1969, p. 108. While there are far more complex problems in relating trade to political expansion than either Legassick or the remainder of this paragraph confront, this is, perhaps, not the place to tackle them

8 Hunt, 'An Account', pp. 283–4, and P. Delius, 'Migrant Labour and the Pedi before 1869', *CSP*, vii, 1977, p. 44

9 T. Arbousset, *Narrative of an Exploratory Tour*, Cape Town, 1868, p. 175 and Delius, 'Migrant Labour', p. 44

10 A. Nachtigal, 'Das Tagebuch des Missionars', UNISA library typed transcript, Pretoria, 1975, pp. 38, 42, 67 and 73 for example

11 *Berliner Missions Berichte* (hereafter *BMB*), 1862, 21, p. 356

12 Berliner Missions Archiv. (hereafter BMA), Abt.11, Fach 3, 1, letter from Nachtigal to his father, 10 September 1861

13 *BMB*, 1862, p. 357

14 T. Wangemann, *Die Berliner Mission im Bassuto-Lande*, Berlin, 1877, p. 48; and BMA, Nachtigal's Tagebuch, 3 September 1861, Abt.11, Fach 3

15 A. Merensky, *Erinnerungen aus dem Missionleben in Transvaal*, Berlin, 1899, p. 143

16 R. Wagner, 'Zoutpansberg: the dynamics of a hunting frontier', see below, ch. 13

17 *BMB*, 1865, p. 99 and Merensky, *Erinnerungen*, p. 211

18 *BMB*, 1862, p. 377, and 1864, pp. 260 and 263

19 *BMB*, 1862, p. 356

20 *BMB*, 1870, p. 388

21 *BMB*, 1862, p. 258
22 *BMB*, 1862, p. 357
23 A. Atmore and P. Sanders, 'Sotho Arms and Ammunition in the nineteenth century', *JAH*, xiii, 4, 1972, p. 538
24 T. Wangemann, *Lebensbilder aus Sudafrika*, Berlin, 1876, pp. 15, 28–9 and Wangemann, *Die Berliner Mission*, p. 48. See also *BMB*, 1868, p. 233, and 1862, p. 357.
25 *BMB*, 1862, p. 377
26 *BMB*, 1862, pp. 356–7 and Transvaal Archives, LL179, Nachtigal to Landrost of Lydenburg, 26 September 1865; also LL179, 13 June 1866. Migrants also brought money back with them
27 *BMB*, 1868, p. 233
28 *Ibid.* p. 237
29 Wangemann, *Lebensbilder*, p. 29
30 *BMB*, 1862, p. 357
31 *BMB*, 1865, p. 99
32 *South African Archival Records*, Transvaal No. 1, Bylaag 32, Krygsraad Decision, signed by A.H. Potgieter and seventeen others, 18 December 1852
33 *BMB*, 1862, p. 357
34 BMA, Abt.11, Fach 3, 1, Nachtigal's Tagebuch, 20 October 1861, and *BMB*, 1862 p. 382
35 Nachtigal, Tagebuch, p. 413
36 BMA, Abt.11, Fach 4, 2, Merensky, Tagebuch der Station Khalatlolu, 31 December 1862
37 See T.S. van Rooyen, 'Die Verhoudinge tussen die Boere, Engelse en Naturelle in die Geskiedenis van die Oos-Transvaal tot 1882', *Archives Year Book for South African History* (AYB) xiv, pp. 194–7, and TA, SN1, No. 239 Memorandum and Translation of Laws regarding Natives, H. Shepstone, October 1879
38 This is a rather truncated version of an argument that will be elaborated in my forthcoming Ph.D. thesis (London)
39 P. Naude, 'Boerdery in die Suid-Afrikaanse Republiek', unpublished D.Litt. thesis, UNISA (Pretoria), 1954
40 TA, SS152, Supl.82/71, Memorandum in Zaken der Kaffer Kwestie in de Zuid Afrik. Republiek, A. Merensky, Botsabelo, 17 October 1871
41 TA, LL3, 155, Merensky to Jansen, 29 December 1871; LL4, no no., Nachtigal to R. Botha, 12 March 1872; LL4, 114, Gov. Sec. to Landdrost, Lydenburg, 26 June 1872
42 R.F. Sieborger, 'The recruitment and organisation of African labour for the diamond mines', unpublished M.A. thesis, Rhodes University (Grahamstown), 1976. In an appendix to this thesis Sieborger presents a compilation of returns of registered labour on the fields. His thesis was further of great value in directing me to material in the Cape Archives on Pedi at the diamond fields
43 Sieborger, 'Recruitment', p. 18
44 *BMB*, 1872, p. 197 and Sieborger, 'Recruitment', p. 10
45 See for example the life history of Jonas Polumo, *BMB*, 1868, pp. 235–52
46 van Rooyen, 'Die Verhoudinge', p. 98; *BMB*, 1882, p. 354
47 Monnig, *The Pedi*, pp. 174–5
48 Arbousset, *Narrative of an Exploratory Tour*, p. 172
49 T. Wangemann, *Maleo en Sekukuni*, Cape Town, 1957, p. 35 for example
50 Merensky, *Erinnerungen*, pp. 120–2, Wangemann, *Lebensbilder*, pp. 184–202 and

especially p. 195. See also R. Wagner, 'Zoutpansberg: the dynamics of a hunting frontier', below, pp. 329–30
51 Merensky, *Erinnerungen*, p. 30
52 *Ibid.*, p. 293
53 W. Beinart, 'Economic Change in Pondoland in the nineteenth century', *CSP*, vii, 1977; Atmore and Sanders, 'Sotho Arms'
54 Merensky, *Erinnerungen*, p. 291
55 *BMB*, 1862
56 Arbousset, *Narrative*, p. 172
57 *BMB*, 1862, p. 355
58 Beinart, 'Economic Change'
59 University of the Witwatersrand, Church of the Province Library A.55, R.T.A. James, 'The Diary of Trader James,' 1926, p. 4
60 TA, SS 938/67, C. Potgieter to U.V.R., 7 September 1867
61 van Rooyen, 'Die Verhoudinge . . .' p. 96
62 Wagner, 'Zoutpansberg'
63 TA, L.I. Volksraad Notule, July 1857, Art.31
64 James, 'The Diary of Trader James', p. 2
65 Interview with Jonathan Sekwati and William Sekhukhune, Sekhukhuneland, 3 November 1976
66 A. Nachtigal, Tagebuch, p. 569
67 C.2482, N.158, Statement of Tamakana, 26 October 1879
68 H.T. Glynn, *Game and Gold: memories of over 50 years in the Lydenburg district, Transvaal,* London, 1938, p. 100
69 TA, Eerste Volksraad, 220, Petition J.A. Erasmus and thirty eight others, 26 April 1873
70 TA, LL4, State Secretary to Jansen, 3 October 1873; SS 207 R.893, Scoble to State Secretary, 24 April 1876
71 *BMB*, 1862, p. 365
72 TA, SS 187, R.807 Nachtigal to Landdrost of Lydenburg, 13 April 1875; SS 189, R.1351, G.S. Schoeman to State Secretary, 22 June 1875 and SN3, N.40, G. Schultze to Secretary for Native [Affairs], 2 February 1880
73 Merensky, *Erinnerungen*, p. 27
74 Arbousset, *Narrative*, p. 172
75 *BMB*, 1862, p. 366
76 *BMB*, 1865, p. 215
77 Nachtigal, Tagebuch, pp. 807, 905, 928
78 TA, SS 258; R.4654, A. Aylward, 31 December 1877
79 *BMB*, 1862, p. 356
80 Interview with Rev. F.M.E. Mothubatse, Sekhukhuneland, 8 November 1976
81 *BMB*, 1862, p. 255
82 *BMB*, 1862, p. 347 and BMA, Abt.11 Fach 3, 1, Nachtigal's Tagebuch, 20 October 1861
83 C.1883, No. 22 M. Clarke to T. Shepstone, 13 June 1877
84 Atmore and Sanders, 'Sotho Arms', p. 538
85 A. Merensky, *Beitrage zur Kenntniss Sud-Afrika*, Berlin, 1875, p. 106
86 Merensky, *Erinnerungen*, pp. 130–2
87 Atmore and Sanders, 'Sotho Arms', p. 538
88 Merensky, '*Erinnerungen*, p. 84

89 *BMB*, 1862, pp. 253–4
90 *BMB*, 1862, p. 255
91 Nachtigal, Tagebuch, pp. 218 and 278
92 Sieborger, 'Recruitment', p. 31
93 Cape Archives, Griqualand West (GLW) 184, R. Southey to Barkly, 6 March 1975
94 CA, GLW 17, 'Memo of an agreement made by Mr John Edwards with Sekhukhune paramount chief of Sequati's people', 3 August 1873, and Receipt from M. Skinner, Landdrost Pretoria, 11 September 1873
95 *Ibid.*
96 *Ibid.*
97 CA, GLW 184, R. Southey to Barkly, 6 March 1875
98 *Ibid.*

CHAPTER THIRTEEN

Zoutpansberg: the dynamics of a hunting frontier, 1848–67

Roger Wagner

'Zoutpansberg' is the name given by the Boers in the nineteenth century to a range of mountains in the far north of the province of Transvaal.[1] Literally 'Saltpan Mountain', it takes its name from a large saltpan at the western extremity of the range. With its close relation Blouberg—'Blue Mountain'—fifteen miles further west, it forms a ragged curtain roughly one hundred and fifty miles east-west dividing the Transvaal highveld from the lowveld of the Limpopo basin. 'Zoutpansberg' was also once the name of a village about three miles south of the mountains, and of a Boer colony whose market place and administrative centre it constituted. Better known now by its other name, 'Schoemansdal', the village long ago was reclaimed by the bush, and is commemorated only by a sleepy railway stop nine miles west of the modern town of Louis Trichardt, and by a graveyard, rank upon rank of anonymous stone tumuli in mute testimony that once here was a place.[2]

In its time, Schoemansdal was such a place that reverend gentlemen grew dark and shook their heads. The Berlin Society missionary, Bernhard Beyer, passed this way in March 1872 when the graveyard might still be approached through the ruins of the deserted dorp. His reflections aptly summarise the mixture of emotions which the place inspired:

> Despite the devastation we took pleasure in the old gardens, still with many kinds of fruits, particularly quinces and apples. The dorp lies in a magnificent valley on the south side of the mountains, visible afar on almost all sides. The dorp itself now makes a gloomy impression on the visitor. No wonder too, for wickedness formerly had its residence here in the highest degree. Here, drunkenness and gluttony were the order of the day with the buyers and sellers of many valuable African products among which slaves too were numbered. The market and site of the town hall were manured by the thousands of tears and the blood of poor blacks who were lashed unmercifully, and of these doubtless a good many gave up the ghost under the beating. The Lord scented this offence; to that the ruins of the formerly prosperous spot now testify. At

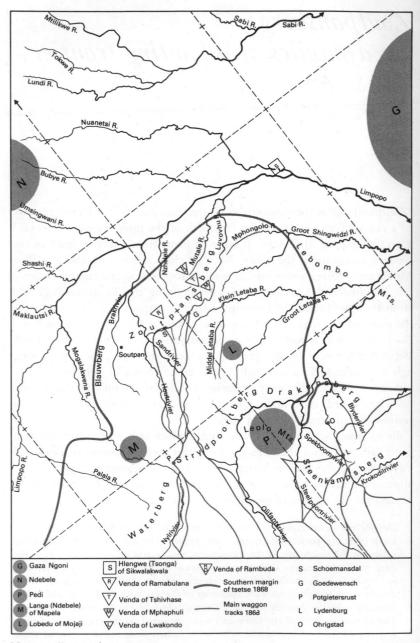

Map 13.1 Zoutpansberg 1848–75

the east end is found the churchyard, richly provided mostly in consequence of fever.[3]

Before he viewed its ruins, Beyer knew Schoemansdal only by repute, and we may excuse his picture of a transported Carolina slave mart, excited by the association between Schoemansdal and allegations of a Transvaal slave-trade, as merely fanciful. The most celebrated cases of slave-trading in the Boer republics did feature Zoutpansbergers, but no-one has suggested the prosperity of their village was founded upon it.[4] That honour is reserved for another valuable African product—ivory.

In its time the colony of Zoutpansberg was two hundred miles deeper in Africa than its closest neighbour, further cut off from the south by a mountain curtain, Waterberg-Strydpoortberg, rising like the Zoutpansberg itself one thousand metres above the plain and easily crossed by ox-wagon only at two points, Makapanspoort and Strydpoort. Beyond the Zoutpansberg it was useless to take either ox-wagon or horse, because to the north in the Limpopo basin lay fly-country, home of the tsetse, transmitter of *nagana*, a form of *trypanosomiasis* or sleeping sickness, fatal to domestic animals. The whole area beyond the southern passes was fever country, inhabited by mosquito carriers of malaria, to whose annual human devastations Schoemansdal's churchyard stood witness. And yet to Frans Lottering, an old hunter, 'it was once a splendid region, a true land full of Milk and Honey'.[5]

For almost twenty years Schoemansdal dominated trade in the one great export item of Transvaal prior to the discovery of gold. A resident of Potchefstroom estimated the total export of ivory from that region for the year 1864 at 1 200 cwt. Of that, fully 930 cwt came from Zoutpansberg. If one counts the figure he gives for Pretoria as also originating in the north, the total is 1 030 cwt, 85 per cent of the annual export.[6] Such figures are fallible, but the proportion goes some way toward explaining why the rest of Transvaal, and subsequent historians, called the colony of Zoutpansberg, *'n jagtersgemeenskap*, 'a hunters' community'. Every winter, merchants came from the Cape and Natal, from Potchefstroom, Pretoria, and Lourenço Marques, to set their mark on the season's plunder. Every winter, hunters went out to cull the elephant herds as far away as Lake Ngami to the north-west, in present Botswana, and the river Sabi to the north-east, in present Zimbabwe and Mozambique. When Carl Mauch 'discovered' the Zimbabwe ruins, one hundred and fifty miles beyond the Limpopo, in 1871, it was a Zoutpansberg hunter, Adam Render, whom he found living there.[7]

Sometimes old Zoutpansberg seems as seldom visited by academic research as its graveyard is by modern tourists.[8] This appears a strange omission in view of the assumptions about the role of 'the frontier' in the formation of modern South Africa which underlie both the 'Afrikaner' and 'liberal' interpretations of its history. 'The frontier', we are told, was the dynamic element in the history of European South Africa, largely determining its spread and its peculiar characteristics, such as its innate conservatism and its attitude to race. A strange omission, that is, until we recall—or have recalled for us, as Martin Legassick's seminal essay, 'The frontier tradition in South African historiography' in this volume does— how little tested generally are these assumptions about the influences and tendencies of 'the frontier'.[9]

Other factors, too, contribute to the reluctance to treat the northerners seriously. If Zoutpansberg was for two decades a frontier, in 1867 it became an abandoned one, a casualty of the pioneering days when a white population of less than 30 000 spread itself so thinly north and east from the Vaal River as to overreach itself. With only limited resources and extended supply lines, the Transvaal Boer republic could not sustain its foothold in the far north against determined African resistance in the mid-1860s, and the centre of gravity of northern settlement moved permanently southward to the passes through Waterberg—Strydpoortberg. There began a more orthodox agricultural development, based initially on the villages of Potgietersrus and Marabastad, the latter being a new establishment from which the district headquarters was again transferred more securely to Pietersburg on that village's foundation in 1885. Moreover, the hunting from old Zoutpansberg attracted elements which have tempted commentators to regard the early white settlements in the north as unrepresentative of Boer colonisation generally. The original settlement had been of Boers led by Hendrik Potgieter who had been unable to adjust to the pattern of affairs evolving in the white settlements further south. They were joined from the first by a swelling complement of hunters, traders, and adventurers, among whom figured English, Scots, and Irish, Dutch, Belgians and Germans, Portuguese of European and Asian extraction, and Cape Coloureds.[10] Even Frans Lottering felt the need to apologise: 'Zoutpansberg formed the outermost inhabited frontier of the Boer country and the elements which colonized it did not belong without exception to the best'.[11]

It seems to me disingenuous, to say the least, to suggest a frontier momentum behind the history of European South Africa and then scorn a frontier on the grounds of its 'disreputable' inhabitants. If Frederick Jackson Turner had gone looking for reputable frontiersmen, there never would have emerged a frontier interpretation of American history. Neither does it seem entirely honest to include those elements in one's consideration only when they have ceased their independent striving and become reconciled with a wider convention: in the case of the impoverished Zoutpansbergers, when their former lands were sold to foreign land speculators and their community converted from the independent Transvaal to the Cape Synod of the Dutch Reformed Church, from the *Nederduitse Herformde Kerk* to the *Nederduitse Gereformeerde Kerk*.[12] Indeed, such an approach implies that the really momentous forces acting on the history of the European in South Africa came from quite another direction than the frontier. It seems only incidentally unfair that the Zoutpansbergers should be tainted with domination by 'foreigners', when they invariably sent men with stern Afrikaner surnames as their representatives to the volksraad, to sit with members such as Evans of Potchefstroom, Robinson of Rustenburg, Struben and Bührmann of Lydenburg, and Johnstone of Wakkerstroom.[13]

It would be premature to advance any alternative general theory of the nature and effects of the European frontier in southern Africa, but in any serious reassessment, the northern frontier of the South African Republic in the period 1848–67 is potentially significant in at least two respects. First, in origin it was an authentic Boer colonisation of the Trek period, derived from the same pool of frontier white communities in the eastern Cape which after 1836 colonised Natal, the northern Free State, south-western and eastern Transvaal, and carrying the same cultural portmanteau of Dutch-Afrikaans language, Calvinist religion, and Roman-Dutch law, and characteristic patterns of social relations and economic preoccupation. Thus any vagaries in its development must be subsumed within a general assessment of the Great Trek and its consequences. Secondly, in its demise it set in motion what was arguably an African resurgence in the Transvaal, culminating in the 'Sekhukhune Wars' of the late 1870s, from which the Boer settlements were rescued by the British annexation of 1877. The Pedi kingdom of chief Sekhukhune was one of the most important with which the Boer settlers shared Transvaal. At the beginning of the troubles with Sekhukhune, in 1874, the father of the Berlin Society's Transvaal mission, Alexander Merensky, traced a line stretching back through a series of African defiances and retreats of Boer settlement in the north and north-east to the abandonment of Schoemansdal in 1867:

> Sekukuni had seen with inner joy that the Dutch Boers lost ground to north and north-east .... Now, he thought, the moment had come when he, who was already equipped with over 5–6000 guns and a considerable store of ammunition, could also settle accounts with the Boers and could drive them out of the land of his fathers once and for all.[14]

Thus the pattern of frontier relations evolved on the hunting frontier of old Zoutpansberg was momentous for the African as it was for the European.

In the third quarter of the nineteenth century the South African Republic was not the only state between the Vaal and the Limpopo Rivers, and the dominion of its white citizens over the black communities whose environment they shared was by no means assured. Although the Boer state was recognised by Britain in 1852, it did not command the allegiance even of all the white communities in Transvaal until 1860. Agreement on constitutional forms then was followed by four years of armed dispute—the *Burgerkryg* or Civil War—to decide the personnel occupying the citadels of constitutional power and the question of wider association with the Boer communities dwelling south of the Vaal. The republic north of the Vaal was more properly an association of three district Boer colonies, Potchefstroom, Lydenburg and Zoutpansberg, separated by nature and on occasion as profoundly by man.

From one viewpoint Zoutpansberg was the youngest of these. Potchefstroom, within twenty miles of the Vaal, was founded in 1838, and Ohrigstad—from which the focus of Boer settlement in eastern Transvaal was transferred to Lydenburg about 1850—in 1845. The village of Zoutpansberg, later Schoemansdal, was laid out in the winter of 1848. From another viewpoint, however, Zoutpansberg was the oldest Boer colony on the highveld. Some former citizens of Cape Colony, the Buys brothers, half-caste sons of an eastern Cape frontiersman of some notoriety in the generation before the Great Trek, had been living there from the early 1820s.[15] In 1836 they were joined by the celebrated first trek of Louis Trichardt, which was camped in the Schoemansdal area at the foot of the mountains for fourteen months. There Trichardt was visited by a reconnaissance from the body of the trekkers south of the Vaal led by Hendrik Potgieter, and it is clear that the first prospectus for settlement in Transvaal, the so-called Bronkhorst Memorandum which arose from this reconnoitre, has the resources of the northern bushveld at its centre.[16] Many of those who came to form the nucleus of the northern colony in 1848 had been with Potgieter when he founded the settlement in the grassveld of the south-west a decade before on his return from Natal, and had moved with him into the eastern bushveld to Ohrigstad in the mid-1840s.

While in the south and east of Transvaal the original trekker population became overlaid with latecomers from the Cape and backtrekkers from Natal after British annexation, in the north the Zoutpansbergers preserved some of the characteristics of an original trekker maatskappy—literally 'company'. In their secession from the Ohrigstad colony, the followers of Hendrik Potgieter are usually presented as those who preferred a 'patriarchal' to a 'democratic' form of government, as represented by the followers of the Nataler, 'Kootjie' Burger, or 'Volksraad party'. The Portuguese Vice-Consul to the South African Republic, himself a trader in the north and a notable in the councils of the colony, continued to discern a 'Potgieter party' among the Zoutpansbergers long after Potgieter was dead, which he opposed to a 'Pretorius party' drawing its support from the settled south.[17]

When the first census of the white population of Transvaal was taken in 1873, something like seventy per cent lived in the south-western area circumscribed by Potchefstroom and its daughter settlements—Klerksdorp, Zeerust, Rustenburg, Pretoria, and Heidelberg. The two northern districts, Zoutpansberg and Waterberg, between them mustered precisely 1376 people, barely five per cent.[18] In the period of the hunting frontier before 1867 we can safely suggest that the absolute numbers and proportionate weight of white population in the north were greater. The Vicar of Inhambane, who visited Zoutpansberg on a diplomatic mission in 1855–6, was told that of 12000 whites beyond the English frontier—presumably the Vaal River, which constituted the boundary until the British withdrew from the Transorange highveld in 1854—1800 dwelt in the northern colony.[19] Although this figure probably surpassed 2000 by 1860, it is doubtful if the north ever challenged the demographic preponderance of the south-west.

Politically, however, the Zoutpansbergers were able to exercise quite a degree of autonomy. While affairs in the south became dominated by the personalities of two returnees from Natal, Andries Pretorius the father and Marthinus Pretorius the son, the latter from the end of 1855 as first President of the South African Republic, Zoutpansberg between 1848 and 1860 was successively the personal fief of three Commandants-General. Until an emotional reconciliation between Hendrik Potgieter and Andries Pretorius at Rustenburg in March 1852, it was technically independent. And again, between November 1855 and February 1858, by virtue of its opposition to the new *Grondwet* (Constitution) sponsored by Marthinus Pretorius, the north was technically in a state of rebellion. Whatever their legal status within the South African Republic, the writ of Hendrik Potgieter (1848–52), his son Piet (1852–4), and Stephanus Schoeman (1854–60) was virtually unchallenged by whites up to the passes.[20]

From his acceptance of the republican Grondwet in 1858, Schoeman was the first supreme commander of the civilian militia, as Commandant-General of the South African Republic although at the time this did not include Lydenburg. However, he was the last full Commandant-General to dwell in the northern district, and though he ruled it in patriarchal style he never truly made it his own. A late settler in the Potchefstroom area, he rose to prominence there as an ambitious commando leader. On Piet Potgieter's untimely death in the 'Makapan War', he clinched his elevation to the Potgieter seat by sealing the dynastic match of the age, lending his name to both Piet's widow and Hendrik's village. However, his rule increased the influx and influence of outsiders, who were not always welcomed by the older established settlers. Nor did his pretensions to a grander role in the politics of the whole highveld sit well with the desideratum of a Zoutpansberg patriarch. There is evidence of growing, but only occasionally coherent, defiance of his rule before his departure in 1860—in one memorable incident the village artillery, a cannon named 'Ou Grietje', was turned on the Commandant-General's residence.[21] During the Burgerkryg after 1860, when Schoeman made his play for the Presidency as the candidate of the 'Revolutionary' or pro-confederation party, he could not count on his former dominion, and after January 1862 anti-Schoeman elements were in complete control.[22]

It would thus be a mistake to see the alternative centres of power which emerged in the 1860s, simply either as a descent into anarchy, or as a distorted northern image of the civil war. Opposition to Schoeman grew, as we shall see, for reasons more satisfactorily explained in connection with changing circumstances in the *jagveld*, the hunting grounds, and it predated the Burgerkryg. Marthinus Pretorius, the architect of the greater Boer republic experiment and original sponsor of Stephanus Schoeman as Presidential twin north of the Vaal to himself south of it, abandoned the attempt in the 1864 and climbed back to power in Transvaal over the broken reputation of his former ally. The Commandant-General of reconciliation, Paul Kruger, was a Rustenburger, and in the absence of a resident patriarch in the far north a power vacuum was created. Quite naturally, the occupants of the existing secondary levels of lawful authority were in the best position to take advantage of it. These effectively reduce to three: the district Commandant, in charge of the civil militia organised through the local veldcornets; the district Landdrost or magistrate, in charge of civil and judicial administration; and the Superintendent, properly the *Superintendent van Kafferstammen* or Superintendent of Kaffer Tribes, in charge—for the moment to beg a lot of questions—of 'native affairs'. It is this institution, original to the colony of Zoutpansberg and in its last year of life represented in three offices, which provides one of the keys to understanding the development of the colony as a whole. It was lack of co-operation between the Commandant, Landdrost, and Superintendent that was made to bear a substantial proportion of the weight of the Volksraad's condemnation in the aftermath of the retreat of 1867.[23]

The office of *Superintendent van Naturellen*, or Superintendent of Native Affairs, of the South African Republic, was a British invention dating from the annexation of 1877–81, when a central Department of Native Affairs for Transvaal was first created. The office of Superintendent van Kafferstammen in Zoutpansberg had an independent pedigree. It arose in the informal and special relationship between the Buys brothers and Hendrik Potgieter, although as a title it was never borne by them. That honour went to João Albasini, by all standards a most remarkable white trader from Delagoa Bay, who lived in the north virtually continuously from 1853 until his death in 1888, and who occupied the office of Superintendent from 1859 until 1868. However, the heart of the office was the responsibility shouldered by the Buyse under the Potgieters and Schoeman, responsibility for the *opgaaf*. In the Cape this term was used to describe the annual assessment paid by holders of loan-places to the government, but in Zoutpansberg it was used exclusively in connection with the tribute paid by African chiefs and headmen. The Buyse, and the Superintendent, were collectors of tribute.[24] Not entirely coincidentally, they were also the controllers of considerable armies of African collaborators.[25]

With the Superintendent we are wrenched back from the frontier as margin, the outer edge of colonisation, to the frontier as zone of interaction. The highveld at the time of the Great Trek is often pictured as a world providentially cleared of African inhabitants by the series of devastating migrations in the 1820s, emanating from the area of Nguni population in the south-eastern coastlands, known in the Sotho language as the *difaqane*. If this was at any time true of the open grassveld of the south, which seems increasingly doubtful,[26] it was manifestly not true of the bushveld of the east and north which the Boers penetrated in the 1840s. Hill country, with which these areas are eminently provided, was the natural refuge of the pre-difaqane population, and in entering it the Trekkers entered a disturbed but crowded African world. Exactly how crowded can only be guessed, but by an admittedly late estimate from the annexation period, a single Venda chiefdom in the mountains above Schoemansdal, that of Makhado, would command as many as two thousand warriors.[27]

Even granted the Boer monopoly of the horse and the gun, the presence of a Boer colony in this world for over twenty years depended upon the acquiescence, and even collaboration, of African neighbours. Undoubtedly the circumstances of the difaqane in north Transvaal contributed to its initial success. Southerners experienced the Ndebele kingdom of Mzilikazi in their midst, were incorporated in it between 1823 and 1837, and were relinquished completely by it to the Boers thereafter. Northerners in contrast experienced the Ndebele kingdom—and other wandering Ngoni[28]—in occasional devastating visitations, and in this sense the threat remained the same whether the raids came from south of Makapanspoort before 1837 or north of the Limpopo after 1840. The fact that Mzilikazi did not descend upon Zoutpansberg after 1840 in no way diminishes the importance of this observation, as is evidenced by the panic which could be caused by the appearance of even a small party of Ndebele south of the Limpopo as late as 1871.[29] The guns of Hendrik Potgieter, who had twice successfully raided Mzilikazi south of the Limpopo and raided him again north of the Limpopo in 1847, might at least provide a powerful intimidation, or a useful factor, in relations with the Ndebele raiding state in Rhodesia and the Gaza raiding state taking shape in the same period in southern Mozambique.

Indeed, the Zoutpansberg colony itself was experienced by Africans as a raiding state, exercising hegemony over them through annual tribute levies and meeting obduracy with destructive forays, funded out of the attendant plunder. Admittedly it had several crucial special features which distinguished its development from that of its difaqane counterparts, and engaged itself equally in the plunder of nature herself as of man. But it is interesting to note the careful association between Potgieter and two other freebooters of the difaqane era in his migration to the north. He conducted at least one raid into the region from Ohrigstad in alliance with Sekwati, father of Sekhukhune,[30] who made his name as a raider there before returning to the Leolu mountains to found the post-difaqane Pedi kingdom. And his more permanent allies in the north were the Buys brothers.

The African context of the white colony of Zoutpansberg may be further outlined thus. The mightiest of its African neighbours were fairly remote: the Ndebele kingdom beyond the Limpopo fly-zone to the north, the Gaza kingdom beyond the same natural boundary to the east, and the Pedi kingdom beyond the Strydpoortberg and the Olifantsrivier to the south-east. The Zoutpansbergers appear to have had few relations to speak of with the closest of these, the Pedi, after a testing of each other's strength in 1852 which seems to have been mutually chastening. With the Ndebele they concluded a peace treaty in 1853,[31] and maintained fairly cordial relations thereafter. With the Gaza Ngoni close relations were maintained until 1859 and deteriorated seriously thereafter, a development of the utmost consequence for the colony.

Within the region bounded on the north by the Limpopo River and on the south by the Waterberg-Strydpoortberg range, the African population consisted of a large but diffuse Sotho element dominated by three hubs of political interest of non-Sotho origin occupying the mountain recesses so coveted during the difaqane. In the case of the Lobedu who lived in the east where the Strydpoortberg merges into the edge of the highveld, the hegemony was cultural rather than strictly political, based on the cult of Mojaji, the rain-queen.[32] During the difaqane and after, in contrast, Mapela, chief of the Langa section of Transvaal Ndebele in the Waterberg, had established an ascendancy over the Ndebele and Sotho peoples around him which placed him in control of the crucial Makapanspoort gateway to the north. After 1867 Mapela's successor, Mmankopane, was even able to dislodge the whites for a time from their settlement in Makapanspoort, Potgietersrus, and in the Langa chiefdom's regular defiance of Boer authority there is more than a hint of support from further south, from the Pedi and from the even more remote southern Sotho kingdom of Mshweshwe.[33] Even so, the strategic position of the Langa was only a function of the European's desire to reach the north, and communications, though sometimes difficult,[34] were never severed.

The position of the Venda in the Zoutpansberg itself was the key.[35] Not a united kingdom but a series of populous chiefdoms, each based upon a mountain fastness, the Venda controlled the veld around the Zoutpansberg range, by virtue of their occupation of its length. In particular, they controlled access to what were to become the most important elephant grounds in the tsetse region of the Limpopo basin. With all three African groups, Lobedu, Langa and Venda, relations deteriorated fatally in the 1860s. But in 1867 it was the Venda alone who set the seal on the Boer collapse.

This pattern of deteriorating relations in the 1860s reveals a basic characteristic of the hunting frontier: its tendency to enlarge. 'Potgieter's people' came to Zoutpansberg initially to exploit elephant from horseback. They went out into the veld in large parties with wagons, oxen, drivers, and often appreciable numbers of African followers.[36] And they committed great slaughter,[37] with the result that although certain areas continued to harbour pockets of elephant outside the tsetse areas, such as Blouberg and Mojaji's veld, the quarry retreated rapidly from much of the territory into the relative sanctuary of the fly-zone behind the Zoutpansberg.[38] Perhaps the mounted expedition to Lake Ngami by Zoutpansberg Boers in 1852 marks the point at which local resources of elephant which could be shot from the saddle were becoming scarce.[39] Certainly the hunt law of 1858 describes a jagveld for elephant which was clearly in the fly-zone, where no horse or ox-wagon might tarry.[40] What is equally certain is that the Zoutpansberg Boers were not slow to take to their feet in pursuit of ivory and ranged far beyond the Limpopo fly-zone into the lowveld of Rhodesia and Mozambique. Indeed Hendrik Potgieter's son, Andries, recalled hunting on foot on the Rhodesian Sabi even before his father's death in 1852.[41]

The tendency of the frontier zone to enlarge multiplied the points of interaction between white colonists and African politics such as the Lobedu, the Venda, and the Gaza Ngoni. Though the Translimpopo veld to the north-west of the colony provided substantial reserves of elephant they were more easily exploited by the well-known fly-free 'Hunters' Road' through present-day Botswana into Matabeleland; the greatest enlargement of the Zoutpansberg frontier took place in a north-easterly direction into the Gaza dominion and the area of semi-independent Shona chiefdoms between the Gaza Ngoni and the Ndebele.

More exactly, the Boers of Zoutpansberg should not be described as the first to exploit these hunting grounds, either in northern Transvaal or in southern Translimpopo, rather the first to extensively apply a piece of European technology—the gun—to it. Ivory from an area the Portuguese called 'Beja' arrived at their Delagoa Bay factory at least from the early eighteenth century, and the Tsonga peoples of southern Mozambique had developed both as the carriers of this trade with the interior and as commercial hunters in their own right.[42] 'Beja' is the equivalent of Bvesha, the Tsonga name for the Venda, and at the time of the Great Trek four main routes led to it from the east coast, two from Lourenço Marques and two from Inhambane, converging at a point nearby the present Elim hospital.[43] Venda traditions suggest that skill in elephant-hunting brought social standing even before the influx of firearms gave free rein to such expressions of individuality.[44] The Inhambane routes to 'Beja' led through a region on the east bank of the Limpopo which also acquired a Portuguese designation, 'Chinguine'.[45] Again it was a straightforward descriptive nomenclature derived from the inhabitants of the area, the Hlengwe, a widespread northern division of the Tsonga, who like the Venda have strong elephant-hunting traditions.[46] Thus the jagveld of the Zoutpansbergers by the 1860s coincided with the east-coast oriented hunting grounds of 'Beja' and 'Chinguine'.

The establishment of Ngoni dominion over the Tsonga coastlands and the penetration of the South African highveld by Boer hunters were broadly contemporary with another development of crucial significance for the evolution of the hunting frontier in northern Transvaal: the appearance among the Tsonga of parties of commercial hunters armed with guns by Lourenço Marques traders.[47] There is no indication this was on any massive scale, and indeed the implication is that merchants were enlarging their control of the system of ivory production into the hunting operation by supplementing the existing piecemeal cottage industry with their own selected African 'contractors'. The outstanding figure in this development was the same João Albasini who, in 1859 became Superintendent in Zoutpansberg, although the whole Portuguese enclave at Schoemansdal was its issue, as was, more permanently, the sizable Tsonga colony in the eastern portion of the district.[48]

Tsonga had tended to migrate westwards along the trade-routes for decades, and this migration received impetus from the difaqane incursion of Ngoni into the coastlands, so that much of the Transvaal lowveld became colonised, though sparsely. It was among these fragmented refugee bands that Albasini, a trader at Lourenço Marques from 1831, built up the nucleus of a personal following in the late 1830s and established an advanced base in the interior. In 1846 this base was on the Sabie River, about sixty miles south-east of Ohrigstad at the kraal of the Kutswe chief Magasule.[49] From there Albasini moved north to Zoutpansberg in 1853, eventually settling down at the fortified homestead of Goedewensch, which became the terminus for the Tsonga carrying-trade.[50] Western Venda tradition recalls that the first Tsonga to settle in the Venda highveld, as opposed to visiting it as traders, were the Maswanganyi of Munene.[51] The Maswanganyi were incorporated in the Ngoni army as Tsonga auxiliaries, but Munene's refugee section found a protector in Albasini and was associated with him at Magasule's before moving further into 'Beja'. The Maswanganyi were one of the principal constituents of Albasini's Tsonga following at Goedewensch.[52]

There were several potential conflicts in this situation. What is remarkable is that so few of them came to light, for the Zoutpansberg frontier achieved a rough but workable harmony of interest between a Boer hunting and trading complex linked with British havens in the Cape and Natal, and a Tsonga one linked with Portuguese havens in southern Mozambique. Before considering the ramifications of this system, however, it is necessary to mention the single external conflict which could not be avoided.

Incorporation of the Tsonga who were involved in the Delagoa Bay trading complex probably involved the relative eclipse of the Inhambane route. This was disrupted anyway by the establishment of the Gaza kingdom on the lower Limpopo, but it is useful to recall that the second trader to establish himself at Zoutpansberg village after its foundation was Antonio Augusto de Carvalho, a merchant of Inhambane.[53] If the Inhambane connection still had some vigour in 1848, it had lost it by the time the Inhambane delegation led by Fr Joachim de Santa Rita Montanha visited Zoutpansberg in 1855–6. De Carvalho had died of fever and the delegation was entertained by Albasini, of whose honourable intent Fr Joachim was patently suspicious by the end of his stay. The Inhambane mission came to try to re-invigorate the trade route to Inhambane and actually proposed a military alliance to clear the Gaza kingdom out of the way, but to no avail.[54] Gaza and Zoutpansberg were later said to be linked by an agreement or undertaking.[55]

At this stage, we may surmise, Manukuza, the initiator of the Gaza state, was prepared to tolerate the mounting exploitation of 'Chinguine' from west of the Limpopo if it prevented a Boer alliance with the Portuguese of Inhambane. Under his successors, Mawewe (1858–62) and Mzila (1862–83), however, this policy clearly changed, a change in itself partly provoked by the opportunist involvement of Zoutpansberg elements in the politics of the Gaza succession. After he fled the Gaza kingdom in 1859, Mzila was sheltered by Albasini,[56] who meanwhile canvassed an ambitious scheme of alliance for the spoliation of Gaza in Schoemansdal and Lourenco Marques, now from the vantage of the accredited Portuguese Vice-Consul to the South African Republic, a post he held quite happily with that of Superintendent.[57] In January 1860 Albasini took his Tsonga followers into 'Chinguine' and collected tribute from Sikwalakwala, the most important of Mawewe's Hlengwe liegemen, clearly signalling his intention of laying claim on behalf of the jagtersgemeenskap to its trans-Limpopo jagveld.[58] Equally clearly, Mawewe was concerned not just to uphold Nguni hegemony, but to make effective its right to a share of the plunder of its dominion by a more rigorous enjoyment of a long-established custom of his Tsonga subjects, the suzerain's right to the 'ground tusk', or the tusk nearest the ground of a dead elephant. In the face of clear provocation—the protection of his rival and the attack upon the integrity of his domain—at the end of 1860 his raiding parties closed the disputed veld to the Zoutpansbergers and by March 1861 were threatening to cross the Limpopo.[59]

Albasini's projected alliance, despite its approval by the Governor of Lourenço Marques, ultimately foundered, not merely in sudden squalls of the Transvaal Burgerkryg which distracted the whole Boer community, but more ominously in the shoals of the internal politics of the Zoutpansberg colony.[60] Albasini's failure to effect a consensus in support of an 'offensive policy' in 1861 was repeated in 1864 when his line had become 'defensive'. Mzila, the refugee, who can have had few illusions either about the plunder being effected in 'Chinguine' or the role for which Albasini had intended him in an emasculated Gaza kingdom, slipped quietly back across the Limpopo and transformed himself in the course of 1862 into Mzila the conqueror.[61] Early in 1864 he felt secure enough to resume the pressure upon the hunting community, and neatly turned the tables on Albasini.

Mzila again closed the trans-Limpopo jagveld, and demanded in return for its reopening, the surrender or execution of Munene and the repatriation of the Maswanganyi.[62] By thus pursuing what was technically a Tsonga rebellion against Gaza dominion, albeit after an interval of nigh on twenty years, Mzila struck at the heart of Albasini's power and Zoutpansberg's capacity to exact tribute in 'Chinguine'. It is a measure of Mzila's percipience that Albasini did prepare to betray one of his main Tsonga headmen: hunting even on Mzila's terms was preferable to season after season of lost profits.[63] Albasini's pawns, however, had a nasty habit of turning into queens, and Munene, warned in advance, switched his allegiance—from the Superintendent to the Commandant and the Landdrost.

When Schoemansdal was a charred ruin and the Volksraad tried to apportion blame for the tragedy of 1867, the commission appointed to examine the documents began its account with the Munene affair—'from which great jealousy and, one may say, rancour arose between Superintendent Albasini and a part of the officials and officers of the district Zoutpansberg'.[64] Faced with a mountain of circumstantial detail, the Volksraad was unable to comprehend the circumstances of the central government—its inability to marshal and equip a force of citizens prepared to aid their northern cousins or to adequately order and define an administrative and judicial system suited to them. Sitting over two hundred miles away in Pretoria without any representative of the jagtersgemeenskap among them, they can hardly be blamed for not even attempting to comprehend the mechanisms behind the conspiracy of 'overlapping' official jurisdictions, 'irresponsible' whites, and 'treacherous' blacks which enlisted and ultimately defeated the government's involvement in the Zoutpansberg after 1864.

The crucial sequence of events in 1864 and 1865, which led to a Venda war and the dissolution of the jagtersgemeenskap, reveals tensions which transcend the conventional demarcations of Boer and African society. In April 1864, Commandant Frederik Geyser and Landdrost Jan Vercueil were not only prepared to defend Munene against the Superintendent, but to exploit the split in Albasini's Tsonga following on behalf of an alternative puppet candidate as tribute-gatherer. Since their quarrel, Munene broadcast in the homesteads around Goedewensch that it was not Munene and Albasini but Munene and Jacob de Couto, a former secretary of Albasini, who were appointed 'to order and govern the land here'. The Superintendent was ordered to attend a judicial inquiry into his dealings with the colony's African subjects: Munene was, after all, not just the servant of the trader Albasini but an important leader of the African auxiliaries to the Zoutpansberg militia. Albasini refused and appealed to the central government.[65]

The *Uitvoerenderaad* (executive council) responded in the form of a commission headed by President Pretorius and Commandant-General Kruger which deliberated at Schoemansdal in August. Munene was removed from the vicinity of Goedewensch—he had been on de Couto's farm, Morgenzon—and placed in the care of Landdrost Vercueil, while negotiations were opened with Mzila over his fate.[66] Since Geyser had retired through ill-health, there was also a new Commandant, Stephanus Venter, but the Landdrost and Superintendent remained.[67] On 28 March 1865, having learned Mzila's inevitable reply to the Superintendent's emissaries, the Uitvoerenderaad issued an order for the surrender of Munene and the repatriation of his following.[68] On the same day Munene, who had been whisked into the custody of the militia as soon as Mzila's attitude was known, burst out of gaol with the connivance of Landdrost Vercueil and took to the hills.[69] Venter and Albasini roared after him in vain pursuit and in the process raised a hornet's nest among the various Venda chiefdoms whose homesteads they raided.[70] As a result not just 'Chinguine' but the remaining hunting grounds of 'Beja' were to all intents and purposes lost, and from April 1865 until July 1867 when the Commandant-General returned to lead them south, the Zoutpansbergers were almost continuously in laager.

What needs to be remarked immediately is the central government's inability to dispense with the personalities who figure most prominently in this drama. Albasini remained Superintendent throughout. Vercueil, though replaced as landdrost by a Hollander, Reginald Alphonse van Nispen, in December 1865, joined Albasini, his rival, and a neighbour of Geyser's and former veldcornet, Abraham Duvenhage, in a triumvirate of Superintendents.[71] Venter remained Commandant, as did the veldcornet, Jan du Plessis, another prominent member of the militia who came under criticism for his dealings with Africans. Even Frederik Geyser reappeared in June 1865 as Kruger's assistant Commandant-General in the northern districts, a temporary appointment.[72] Whatever its preferences might have been, the Uitvoerenderaad found it could only deal with the jagtersgemeenskap through these individuals, whose power was thus vested only partially in their office.

Further we find an equally powerful Venda theme running through the Munene affair, and not just entering at its climax. 1864 is also the year of a succession dispute in the royal Venda chiefdom, which occupied the western end of the mountains above Schoemansdal. Ramabulana, a weak candidate in Venda law who had come to power in 1836 with the aid of the guns of Doris Buys and Louis Trichardt and had slain the then chief, his brother Ramavhoya, died, probably in 1863.[73] The Venda attach a special sacredness to the person of the chief and his death is usually concealed until his will with regard to a successor may be spoken through his womb-sister, the *makhadzi*.[74] In 1864 Ramabulana's makhadzi, Nyakhuhu, nominated another weak candidate in Venda law, Makhado. The eldest son of the first or great house of Ramabulana was Davhana: Makhado was merely the youngest son of the second house. Subsequently he was to base his claim to the succession upon the technicality that by cattle (i.e. by Venda marriage law) he was the son of the great wife of Ramavhoya, taken by Ramabulana after his brother's murder. Indeed, Makhado's chief Venda supporter was his uncle Madzhie, called by the Boers 'Katlagter' or 'Katse-Katse', who in 1836 had supported Ramavhoya. At any rate, Davhana seems to have been unpopular even beyond the chiefdom of Ramabulana, and was driven out of the mountains.[75]

In this dispute Vercueil particularly was aligned with Makhado and Madzhie, while Davhana found a protector in Albasini. In June 1864 the former were permitted to attack the latter at Goedewensch with the aid of Africans led by Tromp, an employee of the landdrost, and Michael Buys, whose position in the district militia implicates the Commandant also.[76] In March 1865 Commandant Venter was as anxious to assure Makhado and Madzhie of his indifference to the fate of Davhana should they consider attack on Goedewensch as he was to ensure the efficient disposal of Munene, and revealed only that part of his plan to the Landdrost and the Superintendent which convinced each of the impending discomfiture of the other.[77] Munene for his part, was not just an opponent of Albasini but of Davhana as well, and as such was welcomed by the Venda.[78] And Albasini in co-operating with Venter in his pursuit, was careful to include Davhana in his force and to direct the Commando's attentions to the homestead of Nya-khuhu.[79] The death of the makhadzi no doubt granted Davhana the compensation of revenge, but it made any solution short of violence unlikely. Thus a crucial division in the white community coincided with another among its black associates.

We have already noted the tendency of the hunting frontier to enlarge, multiplying the points of interaction between white colonists and African polities. The Munene affair and its obverse, the Venda succession dispute, reveal enlargement of a different kind. The jagtersgemeenskap began as a close trekker maatskappy and in many ways maintained itself against other Boer communities, ultimately to its cost. When called upon to fight in the north, a Rustenburg veldcornet spoke for many when he wrote:

> and so I see no occasion for me to put my men to the expense of opening up the elephant hunters' way, from which I and all my men have nothing. And there are the kaffers and the flies and the unhealthiness too. And then the men must twist the dagger there and who pays the cost?[80]

And in the east a missionary commented after visiting the lowveld beyond the Lepalule (Olifantsriver): 'They see the land as their property; no Boer from the Leidenburg kind dares hunt there'.[81]

Yet through its main economic pursuit it enlarged not only its external relations but itself. It incorporated other hunter-traders who ensured the channels of commerce with the outside world—Cape traders like Jan Vercueil and Delagoa Bay merchants like João Albasini. It incorporated African allies having the same commercial orientation, such as the personal followings of the Buyse and Albasini, who helped ensure its military dominion. Finally, it began to incorporate elements of the African societies around it who ensured its continuing commercial effectiveness, particularly Tsonga and Venda. To all it vouchsafed the symbol of that incorporation: the gun.

The gun was the basis of Boer power on the highveld: to the Boer hunter it was also the tool of his trade, a 'mystery' of which only he was master, to be enjoyed by him alone. And yet by the 1860s so many Africans had acquired guns in the north that a distinct stratum of the jagtersgemeenskap arose, composed of *swart skuts*—literally 'black shots' or 'black marksmen'. The Venda in particular so benefited from this proliferation that they were able to turn it to effective political use. In 1865, 1866, and 1867 the whites asked for their guns back and the Venda said 'no'. And in refusing they were led by a man who was himself a swart skut, Makhado.[82]

The occasion of the rise of the swart skut was the transition to foot-hunting. We have seen above that the profits from ivory had already led to the controlled proliferation of guns in the area hunted on foot from Delagoa Bay, that 'Potgieter's people' were in contact with the system at Ohrigstad, and permitted its independent expansion into the fly areas of 'Beja' in the early 1850s. When elephant was plentiful and could still be shot from the saddle there was no competition in the veld. When the retreat of elephant into the fly and into ever more remote regions beyond it forced even the Boers on to their feet, they became assimilated to the Delagoa Bay mode of hunting with African 'contractors'.

The transition can be illustrated in the accounts of two English traders who were well acquainted with Schoemansdal. Fleetwood Churchill visited from Potchefstroom in 1856, at a time when white hunters were still the predominant element in hunting expeditions:

> The Hunters all go out on *foot* with six, eight, or ten Kaffers along with them carrying a kettle, small bag of coffee and biscuits, and a couple of elephant guns from four to eight the lb. Their hunts last from ten to thirty days at a time. It is certainly hard work for them, especially if they are unfortunate and bring back nothing.[83]

Harry Struben of Pretoria, on the other hand, knew the jagtersgemeenskap better in the 1860s:

> In the early days of Schoemansdal (a trading village under Zoutpansberg) there was a recognized system under Government permits of supplying native hunters with guns, ammunition, blue salempore, brass wire, and Venetian glass beads. Each hunter according to his recognized value was given a certain number of carriers to take his truck in and the ivory out, and the hunters got a percentage on the ivory delivered. Some of these men were good elephant shots and made lots of money. Many Boer hunters went themselves taking bearers with them. It was a hard life, fraught with danger.[84]

Some white hunters continued to go out year after year hunting elephant in country increasingly more remote from their home base. Perhaps most kept on making forays into the sub-Limpopo lowveld. But Struben's account makes clear the importance of the swart skut.

The development has certain similarities to that noted in the English woollen cloth industry of the early modern period between the 'guild' and the 'domestic' system. The membership of the original trekker maatskappy, analogous to the cloth guild, developed from monopolists of a particular craft, hunting with firearms, into 'mercantile capitalists', owning and loaning the equipment of the hunt to Africans, and collecting and disposing of the result in the manner of a sixteenth-century English clothier. The difference is that a gun, unlike a handloom, is both portable and lethal. A clothier's ownership of the means of production was enough for him to control the supply of cloth: white ownership of a gun in the hands of a black marksman twenty-five miles the other side of the Limpopo ultimately signified very little.

In fact this mode of hunting was strictly illegal. Although from 1851, in recognition of his special situation in the lowveld at that time, Albasini was allowed to equip his 'apprentices' with guns for the protection of his travelling parties, no more than five per party, the law applied to other citizens of the republic always strictly referred to white supervision where Africans were in possession of guns. The hunt law of 1858 insisted that no black might be sent on the elephant hunt without the presence of a white; that all such black hunters should be properly registered with the land-drost; that black hunters straying from their white supervisor in the course of the chase must be back with him the same evening; and that no white might take more than two swart skuts into the veld with him.[85] In practice, the supposed controls upon swart skuts were more honoured in the breach. Already in 1857 when Schoeman promulgated the regulations which were elaborated in the republican hunt law there was an immediate outcry that the new law was 'disadvantageous' from petitioners in the south of the district.[86] By the end of 1865 the law had become so ineffective in Zoutpansberg that petitioners for relief from fines incurred through its re-implementation there could claim that it had never been applied, indeed they thought it had lapsed; moreover its reapplication now would ruin them. The number of these petitions would seem to indicate that non-compliance was fairly general and involved some of the most prominent men in the district. One old hunter later went so far as to say, *especially* the most prominent.[87]

The decisive role of the landdrost in the elaboration of such a system is obvious: the landdrost who presided from 1862 to 1865 was said, two years before his election, to be one of the most prominent of those who consistently traded with Africans without bothering to purchase a licence.[88] Nevertheless, even Jan Vercueil would not have embarked upon such a development if he believed it was destined to spin out of his grasp. Swart skuts were accommodated within the existing labour system of white Transvaal, which consisted in essence of two components, tribute labour and apprentices.[89] No comprehensive analysis of the workings of this system in the north is possible here, and the occurrence of an illegal form, the swart skut, within a system that already had its shady aspects is particularly difficult to chart accurately. On the face of it, it would seem more logical to employ hunt labour under the tribute system, since it was essentially seasonal employment. On the other hand, a servile element such as the apprentice, who was bound to a particular master technically until majority but practically—since there was no mechanism providing for emancipation comparable with the book which recorded the original bond—for substantially longer, might be more amenable to the kind of control required for a swart skut.

African apprentices, or *inboekselings*, were formally those African children 'orphaned' and subsequently 'rescued' by a Boer commando: slavery as such was strictly forbidden. Undoubtedly some swart skuts were apprentices. Albasini is supposed to have registered five hundred black 'slaves' when he came to Transvaal in the 1840s.[90] One of the most famous of them, 'Albasini zyn apprenties Manungu', remained with him till death, and certainly belied that lowly designation's usual attributes, leading the Tsonga auxiliaries into battle in the 'Makapan War' of 1854, acting as Albasini's amanuensis in the veld, and treating on behalf of the republic with the Gaza kingdom.[91] Harry Struben's brother, Alex, met him in Albasini's laager in 1865 and referred to him as 'the head chief'.[92] As captives, apprentices developed social ties within the fellowship of the Boer farm, which provided some guarantee of their return to it, even with the master's gun.

On the other hand, references to captives in the north are often refreshingly without pretence. Hardly ever do we read of *weeskinderen*—'orphan children'. Where they are not plain *kinderen* they are either *kleingoed* —'little ones' and with irony literally 'little goods'—or *zwarte ivoor*—'black ivory' in contrast to the 'white ivory' obtained from the hunt.[93] The terms are more suggestive of commerce, and at least one visitor to the north in the aftermath of the retreat—the German explorer Carl Mauch in 1871— interpreted the collapse in terms of the growth of illegitimate at the expense of legitimate commerce.[94] Further, captives involved two categories rather than one—*kinderen* or children and *meiden* or girls.[95] Women had no place among the swart skuts or their attendants, and the pairing of children and young girls is more suggestive of an ultimately more orthodox function within the agricultural systems of Zoutpansberg or the other white communities of Transvaal.

Harry Struben's description finds echoes elsewhere, in presenting a hunting system based squarely on tribute labour.[96] In that the foothunting system of swart skuts developed out of a saddle-hunting system whose requirement was for additional hands, this has an internal logic: some of the bearers of the previous mode were translated into fully-fledged 'team leaders'. The law viewed tribute labour as a two-tier system. Labour could be required from a tributary homestead for up to fourteen days without payment. Otherwise the term of employment was for a year. Such *huurkaffers* were entitled to demand reward after their year's service, whose conditions of hire were controlled by the veldcornet who allocated them.[97] Fourteen days would have needlessly restricted the hunt and prevented the development of a proper working relationship between a hunter and his team. Consequently tribute labour for the hunt was overwhelmingly in the form of huurkaffers. The northern veldcornets divided the Africans under them into those who simply paid opgaaf and those described as *dienstdoende*—'doing service'. The great majority of homesteads came into the latter category and were thereby relieved of the obligation to pay the hut-tax part of the opgaaf.[98]

The problem with tribute labour entrusted with guns was to ensure its loyalty. It was only liable to solution if rewards were adequate and the threatened annual turnover of hunting 'teams' headed by the swart skuts was permitted to evolve into more permanent clientship. Clearly this was the preference of many of the older white residents, but connections with particular African homesteads, however long established, were periodically renewed only at the behest of the veldcornet, who might decide for a variety of motives, economic or political, to interfere. As the boom-times attracted more whites to the district, the annual division of homesteads caused mounting unrest. A typical instance is the complaint of N.M. Jansen van Rensberg in 1863. Landdrost Jan Vercueil had taken a homestead under 'Captain Sasra' away from him to do government work cutting stones. Van Rensburg complained that Vercueil was a newcomer who already had 'hundreds' of Africans in his service without his permission. As an old resident he was outraged that 'uitlanders' were now receiving homesteads after only three or four days' residence while 'de oude dienst-doeners'—the old servicemen—who regularly turned out at their own expense in defence of the community were passed over.[99] Harry Struben's brother, Alex, was one such 'uitlander'. He was resident only during the hunting season and had no farm. Arriving for the 1864 season he received almost as a matter of course the allocation of a Venda homestead, consisting of a homestead and thirty men, from the veldcornet of Schoemansdal.[100]

By 1865 the need to stabilise the workforce in the interests of the old established white residents by providing for proper clientship of tribute labour caused Abraham Duvenhage, then veldcornet of Rhenosterpoort, to propose a new system of regulating African tribute labour which pivoted on the requirement of the employer to provide ground for settlement and cultivation.[101] The next year as Superintendent he and twenty-four of his neighbours set their faces resolutely against further division of the homesteads in their area, which would only benefit those who had been unable to keep their previous labour force from deserting.[102] But by this time the jagtersgemeenskap was coming apart at the seams.

What we have, therefore, is a formal labour system which was unable to adapt to the system of relations evolving through the economic pursuit of the hunt. In this situation it is quite understandable that prominent figures in the white community should at least wish to ensure the elevation of parties sympathetic to them to power over one of the principal pools of tribute labour, for both Madzhie and Makhado in 1864 were described as 'dienstdoende kaffers'.[103] Certainly there was an element of stability if the developing gun culture among the Venda could be successfully kept under chiefly control. The missionary Bernhard Beyer visited chief Tshivhase in 1872 and remarked:

> The veranda of his house, his dwelling place, is also his work place, furnished with vice, hammers, files, etc. The master is himself, that is to say he mends all

gunlocks, so far as his skill permits, himself. Thus he is no idler as are most other Basutho kings.[104]

Makhado's position as a swart skut before 1864 may have developed in him a similar ability. Guns were distributed to and reclaimed from African hunting teams through the highest African authority over them, as we might expect,[105] suggesting many chiefs and headmen joined the stratum of swart skuts like Makhado.

However, this fragment of security evaporated if any coincidence of interest could actually create cohesion within the swart skut stratum. There is at least a strong suggestion that such an alliance of forces, articulated through the swart skut system, was beginning to form around Makhado in the disturbed conditions of the 1860s. Makhado became a swart skut, according to Venda tradition, by befriending two such black marksmen, Tromp and Stuurman, who took him on as their assistant and taught him how to shoot. When he was skilful enough they found him a white man to work for and bearers of his own. Tromp was the 'schut van Landdrost Vercueil', but Makhado's employer is unknown.[106] Makhado's involvement with the swart skuts of Schoemansdal extended to his entry into one of their circumcision lodges. This was an extraordinary step for a high-born Venda of the 'royal' clan at the time, the practice being very newly arrived among them and carrying with it what might have been fatal for a weak candidate for the succession, the taint of illegitimacy and madness.[107]

The step is only explicable in terms of the alliance it brought with elements, by no means all Venda, who would aid him in his bid to oust Davhana. Tromp was noted as present in the raid on Davhana in June 1864, when many of the swart skuts present were Tsonga. A year later he stood by Makhado in his defiance of the white authorities.[108] Another of Makhado's commanders in 1865 was called Fleur, indicating another former African employee of the whites. Fleur told the government commission sent up in that year that Makhado would not give up his firearms, for his people had earned them by three years' service among the whites.[109] Desertions by black marksmen, taking their masters' guns with them to the Venda, suggest there were others like Fleur who felt the rewards and conditions of service under the Boer system were inadequate.[110] Whites by inclination and by law limited themselves to hunting in the fever-free winter: no such restriction applied to the Venda, and Makhado is credited in Venda tradition with introducing off-season hunting even before the death of Ramabulana.[111] The opportunity would be denied to Tsonga and Sotho hunters who dwelt among the whites. By 1866 Makhado's control of the hunting resource was being driven home in no uncertain terms. The occasional daring soul who ventured into the veld found the Venda charged a protection levy even to let him cut timber, let alone shoot game.[112] Thus the advantages of a remodelling of frontier relations, dispensing with white settlements and the irksome obligations they entailed and reducing white participation to the essentials of servicing and external commerce, indeed reasserting African control of the hunting resource through the positive application of its emergent gun culture,[113] might present attractions to the quite disparate elements of the swart skut stratum.

At least two independent Venda traditions state something as positive: that the impulse to Makhado's circumcision and *coup d'etat* came from his companions of the hunt. Makhado's son, Tshamaano, in particular, recalled that Makhado was admitted to the circumcision lodge at Mashan's among Venda commoners with the prophetic words, 'that today they had made a new chief.'[114]

Hunting was a preferred occupation among the whole male section of the white immigrant population of the highveld, and was as intrinsic to Boer culture as *boerdery* (farming) itself. One preferred to hunt for one's meat than cull carefully husbanded domestic stock. A natural by-product of subsistence hunting was a certain quantity of hides, straps, whips, and so on for domestic use or export.

Ivory, however, was different. On an elephant it was the meat which was the by-product, and that was often left to the other occupants of the veld, human and animal. Ivory had no other use than as an article of commerce, and its acquisition and disposal required the eye of a marksman to be combined with the nose of a businessman. Like gold, ivory was always saleable and of sufficient worth to warrant expensive transportation from remote areas. It was sufficient prize to tempt the Potgieter maatskappy and its adherents into a remote and pestilent corner of Africa, and there to dismount.

Ivory ensured, as no other product could, the annual attendance of the *smous* (hawker), granting each hunting household access to those culturally required goods which its lack of cash might otherwise deny— cloth, sugar and groceries, especially coffee and tea, and most of all, *skietgoed* (guns and ammunition). Skietgoed provided the Boer community with both the means of political coercion necessary to ensure a labour supply for its rural economy, and the wherewithal—ivory—to perpetuate that facility. Around this central articulation of ivory and firearms moved the jagtersgemeenskap of Zoutpansberg: without it, it was meaningless.

To the African too, however, ivory was a means of acquiring European trade goods—cloth, metals, beads, even firearms—and in following the retreating elephant resource into the fly-zone the Zoutpansberg jagters-gemeenskap ran up against the conflicting aspirations of the Gaza Ngoni state, which was able to exclude it from the most valuable hunting grounds in 'Chinguine' completely from 1864. Moreover, the logistics of foot-hunting encouraged Boer entrepreneurs to adopt the methods of the pre-existing east-coast system, equipping their African clients as swart skuts. Failure to utilise the supplies of cheap labour available would have led to a steady reduction in the quantity of ivory extracted as the elephant resource: the proliferation of guns as a form of mercantile capital in the hands of huurkaffers and inboekselings, nevertheless, meant a dispersal of the means of political coercion. Power in this elaborated jagtersgemeen-skap accrued to those who controlled entrance to it and directed its supplies of hunt labour—the landdrost, the Superintendent, and the officers of the civil militia. But power to direct hunt labour rested now, not on a monopoly of the means of coercion, but on the acquiescence of the swart skuts them-selves. The disturbing effect of the closure of the 'Chinguine' jagveld and the competition between white notables for African clients, caused a signi-ficant withdrawal of that acquiescence, a development whose chief bene-ficiaries were the Venda. With the ruin of Schoemansdal, the Venda and the Tsonga swart skuts who joined them, having in effect now acquired the technology previously denied them, resumed control of the resources of 'Beja', and excluded the Boer entrepreneurs who for twenty years had intervened. Venda autonomy was not finally stifled until 1898, by a resur-gent Boer republic whose own day had but a few hours to run.

Notes

1 Throughout the period under discussion, this name is correctly spelled in Dutch, Zoutpansberg. However, the local pronunciation was already ac-quiescing in the 1860s in the transformation which produced modern Afrikaans, almost bereft of all 'z's. When agents of the Berlin Missionary Society pushed into the area, they innocently called the new field 'Distrikte Soutpansberg', and where they complied with official orthography, were often moved to explain 'Zoutpansberg (spr. Sautpansberg . . .)': see, e.g. *Berliner Missions Berichte (BMB)* 1866, p. 69; 1869, p. 263
2 Only two graves bear memorials, those of the wife of the (Nederduitse Her-vormde Kerk) predikant, Ds. N.J. van Warmelo (died 1864) and of the trek leader Andries Hendrik Potgieter (died 1852)
3 *BMB* 1874, pp. 125–6. Translations from German, Dutch, or Afrikaans, unless otherwise stated, are by the author
4 See, e.g. J.A.I. Agar-Hamilton, *The Native Policy of the Voortrekkers,* Cape

Town, 1928, pp. 211–2; and related sequence in the Transvaal Archives (TA): R.1280/65, copy G.J. Steyn (Potchefstroom) to Sir P.E. Wodehouse, 4 December 1865; R.1289/65, Notulen Uitvoerenderaad (Doom Draaij) 5 December 1865, Art.1; R.1291/65, Verklarings (Doorn Draaij) (i) P.J. van Staden, (ii) M.L. Prinsloo, 5 December 1865; R.1292/65, Verklarings (Doorn Draaij) (i) P.C. de Clerk, (ii) M.L. Prinsloo, H. zoon, 5 December 1865; R.1295/65, F. Jocks (Doorn Draaij) 5 December 1865

5 C.J. Moerschell, *Der Wilde Lotrie: Fahrten, Abenteuer, and Beobachtungen des Buren Bernard François Lotrie*, Würzburg, 1912, p. 129. G.S. Preller, 'Baanbrekers' in *Oorlogsoormag*, Cape Town, 1923, p. 165, identifies 'Lotrie' as Bêrend Lottering. Internal evidence suggests that he was better known as Frans, the brother of Gert and Cornelis, who all three crop up pretty regularly in official and missionary (BMS and NGK) correspondence from Zoutpansberg

6 P.J. Potgieter, 'Die Vestiging van die Blanke in Transvaal, 1832–86' in *Archives Year Book for South African History (AYB)*, Pretoria, ii, 1958, pp. 87, 145

7 Carl Mauch, *The Journals of Carl Mauch, 1869–72*, translated by F.O. Berhard and edited by E.E. Burke, Salisbury, 1969, pp. 134–40

8 The most notable work on the jagtersgemeenskap, a D.Litt. thesis for the University of South Africa by J.B. de Vaal, was published as 'Die Rol van João Albasini in die Geskiedenis van die Transvaal' in *AYB*, i, 1953, pp. 1–154. There is also a conventional and unpublished M.A. dissertation for the University of South Africa by P. Naudé, 'Die Geskiedenis van Zoutpansberg, 1836–67', 1938

9 See above, ch. 2

10 In TA: A.81 (Afrikaans translation), 'Account of Father Joachim de Santa Rita Montanha', p. 60, there is mention of a Russian, 'Jannes Werbes', who might provide the list with a rhetorical flourish, were it not that this is more probably a rendering of Johannes Herbst, whose descent is nowhere else described so exotically. Cf. Leonard Thompson, 'Cooperation and conflict: the High Veld' in L. Thompson and M. Wilson (eds.), *The Oxford History of South Africa*, Oxford, 1969, i, p. 441

11 Moerschell, *Der Wilde Lotrie*, p. 55

12 For an account of the spiritual revolution in 1876–7, among the remnant of the jagtersgemeenskap, known as the *Groot Opwekking*, see the missionary's published correspondence, S. Hofmeyr, *Twintig Jaren in Zoutpansberg*, Cape Town, 1890, pp. 144–80, and an unpublished but complementary sequence in the archives of the Cape Synod of the NGK, Cape Town, archive of the Sending Kommissie (henceforth NGKS), 15/8/3, Hofmeyr Versameling. An interesting personal account of the Opwekking, by Alida Susanna Margrieta Vorster, is in PA, W.126, 'Herinneringsboek van Barend Jacobus Vorster'

13 These examples are taken from a single Volksraad, that of September–December 1867, reconvened February–April 1868, see *South African Archival Records, Transvaal* (henceforth *SAAR, Transvaal*), 7, pp. 3–154

14 *BMB*, 1875, p. 151

15 The Buys clan still lives in Zoutpansberg on the four farms, Mara, Buisdorp, Buishoek, and Buisplaats, given them in 1888. They are the descendants of Gabriel (1808–55), Theodorus Cornelis, or Doris (1810–?51), and Michael

(1812–88), three sons of the famous Cape hunter and freebooter, Coenraad de Buys (1761–?1822), who crossed the Orange in 1814 and disappeared over the Limpopo in the early 1820s. The author is at present preparing a study of the role of Coenraad and his three sons in the history of four South African frontiers between 1784 and 1867

16 J.C. Chase, *The Natal Papers*, Grahamstown, 1843, pp. 73–4

17 TA: 'Correspondencia Official do Consulado Portuguez' (henceforth COCP), 27–34, to Govr. Lourenço Marques, 4 March 1860, 34–42, to Sec. Gen. Moçambique, 8 March 1860

18 Potgieter, 'Die Vestiging van die Blanke', *AYB*, 21, ii, 1958, pp. 106–7

19 TA: A.81 'Account of Fr. J. de S. Rita Montanha', information in answer to questions dd. 18 September 1856. 12 000 for Transvaal seems an underassessment, especially since 4 500 of this number were said to be males between the ages of sixteen and sixty (capable of carrying weapons). The 1 800 in Zoutpansberg were composed of not much more than 260 households, and could muster at the most 300 armed men. Another Portuguese visitor in 1861 counted about 70 houses in the village of Schoemansdal; see D.F. das Neves, *A Hunting Expedition to the Transvaal*, London, 1879, pp. 140–1

20 The central position of the patriarchal Commandant-General in the commercial system of the original Zoutpansberg *maatskappy* is graphically described by G.G. Munnik, *Kronieke van Noordelike Transvaal*, Pretoria, 1921, pp. 12–13, and by G.S. Preller, ''n Vergane Voortrekkerdorp', in *Oorlogsoormag*, pp. 201, 203. He fixed the price of all commodities in the market, and particularly with regard to ivory acted as general broker, while controlling the distribution of guns and ammunition to hunting households

21 Moerschell, *Der Wilde Lotrie*, pp. 66–7. This incident was precipitated by Schoeman's hunting regulations of 1857—TA: R.1380/57, Publieke Byeenkomst (Zoutpansberg), 11 March 1857. See also the rebellion of Veldcornet Piet Elof in 1859, for which there was considerable popular support, when Schoeman attempted to mobilise the district militia and remove the village artillery for use in the south-west against the Tlhaping chief, Mahura: TA: R.2883/59, Veldct. P.J. Elof (Schoemansdal) to Pres. M.W. Pretorius 10 January 1859; R.1897/58 (misplaced), Elof to acting Landdrost A. Landsberg, 1 February 1859; R.2576/59, Byeenkomst, 4 February 1859; R.2633/59, Burgers van Zoutpansberg to Pres. M.W. Pretorius, 2 March 1859

22 TA: R.4848/61. Hof van Landd. en Heemr. (Schoemansdal), 6–7 November 1861 (opened to the general public by Comdt. F.H. Geyser); R.48/62, Order Comdt. F.H. Geyser, Veldct. A.P. Duvenhage,—provisional Veldct. T.P. le Grange (Zoutpansberg), 22 January 1862; R.127/62, Landd. A.F. Fick (Schoemansdal), n.d. (from internal evidence to acting Pres. Schoeman, February 1862); R.131/62, ditto to acting Pres. Schoeman, 28 February 1862

23 *SAAR, Transvaal*, 7, pp. 47–54. Volksraad, 15 November 1867, Art.166. 'Rapport omtrent de zaak van Zoutpansberg'

24 I here prefer the Afrikaans plural, which the Buyse used themselves to the more clumsy English 'Buyses'. Albasini was appointed 'Superintendent van Kafferstammen' in June 1859, see de Vaal, 'Albasini', p. 64. Doris Buys was closely associated with Hendrik Potgieter at Ohrigstad, and collected tribute for him: *SAAR, Transvaal*, 1, pp. 58–9. Ekstra Volksraad, 10 December 1864, Art.6; *Voortrekker Argiefstukke* (henceforth *VA*), pp. 251–3, R.119/47 'Onderzoek

der Commissie van enege Kaffers Opperhoofden'. After he quarrelled with Potgieter, the 'Volksraad party' too found him a useful ally and appointed him 'Opperhoofd of groote Capitein over alle de Kafferstammen in zo verre onze, lemieten zich uitstrekt, eksept na de kant van Zoutpansberg onbepaald' (chief or great captain over all the kaffer tribes as far as our boundaries extend, except in the direction of Zoutpansberg undefined): *SAAR, Transvaal*, 1, p. 93, Volksraad, 7 March 1849, Art.5; *VA*, p. 369, ad. R.169a/49, Pùblieke Bekendmaking, 8 March 1849, Art.3. Gabriel Buys too collected tribute in the north for Potgieter at Ohrigstad: *VA*, p. 272, R.1216/47, A.J. de Lange (Olyvandsrevier [sic]) to L. Erasmus (tot Steelpoord), 2 June 1847. Gabriel remained loyal and continued in this capacity until his death in 1855, e.g. *SAAR, Transvaal*, 2, p. 473, VR.337/53. Verslag van Comdt. Gen. P.J. Potgieter, 19 September 1853. There is one extant formulation of their role as tribute-gatherers from the time of Michael Buys—*PA*: R.307/63, 'Regulation en Conditien agter volgens welke Michael Buis Capitein by deze . . . aangesteld en geauthoriseerd wordt, opgaven van kaffers hoofden voor Rekening van het Gouvernement der Zuid A. Republiek in te vorderen' (regulations and conditions under which Michael Buis by this is appointed captain and authorised to collect tribute from Kaffer chiefs on behalf of the government of the ZAR). For the tribute formula see PA: R.774/55, Besluiten, 27 February 1857

25 Albasini could field a force of 700 in 1864—see TA: R.900/64, Superintendent J. Albasini to Uitvoerenderaad, 14 October 1864. We are less certain of the Buys force, although its nucleus was probably assembled during the aftermath of the difaqane, as a band of brigands: see J.A. Winter, 'A History of Sekwati', in Report of the 10th Annual Meeting of the *South African Association for the Advancement of Science*, Cape Town, 1913, pp. 329–30. The first service at Michael Buys's kraal at Schoemansdal held by the NGK missionary Alexander MacKidd was attended by 300 people and 15–20000 people were said to own his 'Opperhoofdschap'—paramountcy—in 1865: NGKS, 15/8/4. Briewe Alexander MacKidd, to Rev. Alexander Murray, 3 September 1863, and 27 February 1865

26 See, e.g. W.F. Lye, 'The Sotho Wars in the Interior of South Africa, 1822–37', Ph.D. thesis, University of California, Los Angeles, 1969, pp. 232–8, 256–9; by the same author, 'The Distribution of the Sotho Peoples after the Difaqane' in L. Thompson (ed.), *African Societies in Southern Africa*, London, 1969, pp. 191–206

27 TA: SN1/233/79, 'Statements about the population in the North of Zoutpansberg', BMS missionary C. Knothe (Mphome), 16 September 1879. This is a conservative estimate—compare e.g. SN1a/187/79, 'Approximate Estimate of Able-bodied armed Kaffirs in Zoutpansberg District', Oscar Dahl, Native Commissioner (Eerstelling), 20 July 1879, whose estimate of 5000 warriors was favoured by the Secretary of Native Affairs in SN2/297/79, 'Memorandum on the Native Population of the Transvaal'

28 Both the Maseko Nguni of southern Malawi and the Zwangendaba Nguni of Tanzania made incursions into Venda territory on their way north. See, G. Liesegang, 'Nguni Migrations between Delagoa Bay and the Zambezi, 1821–39', in *African Historical Studies*, iii, 2, Boston, 1970, pp. 317–37

29 *BMB* 1872, pp. 250–1

30 *SAAR, Transvaal*, 1, pp. 21–2. Ekstra Volksraad (Ohrigstad), 26 September

1845; Winter, 'Sekwati', pp. 331–3; A. Merensky, 'Beitrage zur Geschichte der Bapeli' in *BMB* 1862, pp. 339–40

31 *Transvaalse Argiefstukke (T. Arg.)*, pp. 294–5. R.483/53, Vredesonderhandeling (Zoutpansberg), 8 January 1853

32 The Native Commissioner, Oscar Dahl, in 1879 estimated that with 10 000 warriors at her disposal, Mojaji's was the largest single chiefdom in the district. This opinion seems to have been shared by the BMS missionary Knothe and the Landdrost, though their numerical estimates vary considerably. Dahl comments that her supposed powers as a rain-maker drew a large revenue from the tribes of the northern districts and that three Boer raids had made little impression on her, but her land was mountainous and inhospitable, so was only visited by hunters and traders. TA: SN1a/187/79, 'Approximate Estimate' and 'Supplement to Estimate', Oscar Dahl, N. Comm. (Eerstelling), 20 July 1879; SN1a/129/79 C. Knothe, 3 June 1879; SN2/(no number, placed after 233/79), Landd. Zoutpansberg, 27 November 1879. Further see E.J. and J.D. Krige, *The Realm of the Rain Queen*, London, 1943, esp. pp. 303–14

33 The Special Commissioner for Waterberg and Zoutpansberg, Sir Morrison Barlow, estimated the chiefdom of Mapela could field 5 000 fighting men in 1879. Again the Landdrost of Waterberg and missionary Knothe differed on either side of this figure, but not in their estimate of its importance. In 1864 when Berlin missionaries first visited Mmankopane, they rode for five hours on only one side of the mountains he inhabited, almost continuously through cultivated land, which they estimated alone supported over 10 000 souls. TA: SN1a/187/79, 'Approximate Estimate of able-bodied and armed Kaffirs in the Waterberg District' and 'Supplement to the Estimate', Sir Morrison Barlow, S. Comm. (Eerstelling), 5 August 1879; SN1a/129/79, C. Knothe, 3 June 1879; SN2/276/79, Landd. Waterberg, 4 November 1879. Also *BMB*, 7, 1865, pp. 104–5. For relations with the Pedi kingdom, see T. Wangemann, *Maleo en Sekoekoenie*, 1868, Van Riebeeck Society, xxxviii, Cape Town, 1957, pp. 169–70, and the essay by Peter Delius in this collection. Mmankopane, chief of the Langa Ndebele of Mapela, must be distinguished from Mugombhane, chief of the Muledlana Ndebele of Mugombhane, his contemporary and ally, who is commemorated in the placenames Makapanspoort and Makapansgat. Both Mmankopane and Mugombhane were at war with the Republic, not for the first time, in 1867–9. When peace was concluded at the BMS station of Ga Lekalekale, missionary Wilhelm Moschütz wrote: 'As the Boers required neither service nor tribute from the Kaffers, the latter were very soon satisfied'. *BMB*, 1870, pp. 106–7. After a particularly virulent outbreak of malaria in the following year, Potgietersrus was abandoned for the next decade. See Potgieter, 'Die Vestiging van die Blanke', p. 70

34 See e.g. PA: A.17, J. Fleetwood Churchill (Rhenosterpoort), 13 September 1856, pp. 4–7

35 The Venda form a culture complex, distinct from but clearly related to the Sotho of Transvaal and the Shona of trans-Limpopo, of unusual homogeneity. The western section owing allegiance to the royal house of Nzhelele, in the mountains on either side of Schoemansdal, was ruled in the period under discussion by Ramabulana (1836–?63) and Makhado (1864–95), although at least as important a figure was Ramabulana's brother, Madzhie, called 'Katlagter' or 'Katse Katse' by the Boers. Indeed, there is some ground for

regarding him as semi-autonomous in the mountains west of the Sandrivier/
Waterpoort, and in 1877 he and his 'thousand warriors' were placed in the
jurisdiction of the Waterberg rather than the Zoutpansberg Native Commission. See SN1, Sir Morrison Barlow, S. Comm. Waterberg and Zoutpansberg
(Gert Ruth's Farm near Katlakta's Stadt), 2 October 1877; SN1a/187/79,
'Approximate Estimate' and 'Supplement to the Estimate', S. Comm. (Eerstelling), 5 August 1879. There is also a southern section, fragmented and mixed
with Sotho and (from the 1850s) Tsonga elements in the rolling landscape of
the Spelonken south of the Zoutpansberg, and an eastern section in the
mountains above Albasini's Goedewensch which contains several powerful
chiefdoms, particularly those of Tshivhase and Mphaphuli. See further, N.J.
van Warmelo, *A Preliminary Survey of the Bantu Tribes of South Africa*, Department of Native Affairs Ethnological Publications (henceforth DNA-EP),
5, Pretoria, 1935, p. 117; *Contributions towards Venda History, Religion, and
Tribal Ritual*, DNA-EP, 3, 1932; *The Copper Miners of Musina and the Early
History of the Zoutpansberg*, DNA-EP, 8, 1940. Also H.A. Stayt, *The Ba Venda*,
London, 1931

36 See, e.g. TA: W.126, 'Herinneringsboek van B.J. Vorster', pp. 15–16, 36–7
37 J. Chapman. *Travels in the Interior of South Africa, 1849–63*, ed. E.C. Tabler,
i, 1867, Cape Town, 1971, 'Notes on the Elephant', 1856, pp. 185–6; H.W.
Struben, *Recollections of Adventures, 1850–1911*, Cape Town, 1920, p. 86;
Moerschell, *Der Wilde Lotrie*, pp. 68–9, 71–4. Also PA: A.17, J. Fleetwood
Churchill (Rhenosterpoort), 13 September 1856, pp. 12–13; J.A. Breedt (1914)
in G.S. Preller, *Voortrekkermense*, iv, Cape Town, 1925, pp. 146–7
38 See e.g. TA: A.17, J. Fleetwood Churchill (Rhenosterpoort), 13 September
1856. pp. 3, 11
39 *T. Arg*, 252–3, R.442/52, Veldt. H.P. Potgieter to Hoofd. Comdt. A.H. Potgieter, 25 October 1852; 260–2, R.450/52, Verklaring, P.D. du Preez, 9
November 1852, also TA: W.126, 'Herinneringsboek van B.J. Vorster',
pp. 15–16, 36, 'B.J. Vorster se Eerste jag deur dorsland in April 1852'
40 *SAAR, Transvaal*, 3, pp. 599–602, 'Wet tot beter regelen der jagt . . .', 22
October 1858, Art.1
41 Preller, *Voortrekkermense*, iii, Cape Town, 1922, p. 12
42 G. Liesegang, 'Eighteenth Century Documents on the Kingdom of the Venda',
a draft of which was kindly loaned to me in 1975 by the author; H.A. Junod,
The Life of a South African Tribe, 1912, 2nd edition, 1927, reprinted New York,
1962, ii, pp. 59–60, 140–5; A. Smith, 'Delagoa Bay and the Trade of South-
eastern Africa' in R. Gray and D. Birmingham (eds.), *Pre-Colonial African
Trade*, London, 1970, pp. 165–89
43 de Vaal, 'Albasini', p. 2
44 Stayt, *The Ba Venda*, pp. 76–7
45 das Neves, *A Hunting Expedition*, pp. 122–3
46 See also F.W.T. Posselt, *Fact and Fiction*, Bulawayo, 1935, pp. 32–3; A. Wright,
Valley of the Ironwoods, Cape Town, 1972, pp. 53, 143, 200, 372, 394. On the
extent of Hlengwe dispersion, see A. Smith, 'The Peoples of Southern Mozambique' in *JAH*, xiv, 4, 1973, pp. 576–9
47 Junod, *South African Tribe*, ii, pp. 60, 143–4; de Vaal, 'Albasini', pp. 5–7
48 The Tsonga in Transvaal went under a variety of names. They called themselves
ma Gwamba, which the Sotho and Venda rendered *maKwapa*. The Boers in the

nineteenth century referred to them as *Knopneusen*, which the English translated as 'Knobnoses', from the habit of the northern clans of tattooing their faces with large blisters. The whites of Transvaal today generally call them 'Shangaans', from the well-known surname of the Gaza Nguni king Manukuza, i.e. Soshangane, which may itself have a Tsonga origin. Native Commissioner Oscar Dahl estimated that, apart from those under several Venda and Sotho chiefdoms, there were about thirty independent Tsonga headmen in his district in 1879, mustering between them perhaps 10 000 warriors. See TA: SN1a/187/79, 'Approximate Estimate' and 'Supplement to Estimate', Oscar Dahl, N. Comm. (Eersteling), 20 July 1879. Further on the composition of the highveld Tsonga population, see van Warmelo, *Preliminary Survey*, pp. 91–5; Junod, *South African Tribe*, i, p. 19 and map

49 de Vaal, 'Albasini', pp. 5–7. For Kutswe genealogy see van Warmelo, *Preliminary Survey*, iii, G. Liesegang, *Beiträge zur Geschichte des Reiches der Gaza Nguni im Südlichen Mozambique*, Ph.D. thesis, University of Cologne, published by the author, Bromberg, 1967, p. 66, constructs a table based on 'Mappa Nominal das Nações vizinhas do districto de Lourenço Marques ...' in the Arquivo Historico Ultramarino, Lisbon, Papeis de Sá da Bandeira, Maço 2. Here 'Macachule' is described as tributary to Portugal, ruling in the region of 'Beja'. Moreover, Dr Mabel Jackson-Haight has brought to my attention a contract in Arquivo Historico Moçambique, Maputo, fol. 80v–82v., dd. 7 July 1846, establishing 'João Bernardo Jubert' (Johannes Barend Joubert, an inhabitant of Ohrigstad) as the agent at a business house in the territories called 'Macazula' of the entrepreneurs 'João Albazini' and 'Carlos João Trigardt'. This is an intriguing reference to a business association between Albasini and the son of the trekker Louis Trichardt, Carel, for the development of trade from Lourenço Marques with the new Boer colony of Ohrigstad and beyond into 'Beja'

50 de Vaal, 'Albasini', pp. 19–39

51 M.M. Motenda in van Warmelo, *Copper Miners*, pp. 68–9

52 TA: R.210/64, Comdt. F.H. Geyser, with Veldcts. J.H. du Plessis and J.C.J. Herbst, to Uitvoerenderaad, 14 April 1864, enclosing Vergadering (Zoutpansberg), 11–14 April 1864

53 G.G. Munnik, *Kronieke van Noordelike Transvaal*, p. 11; Preller, ''n Vergane Voortrekkerdorp', *Oorlogsoormag*, p. 208; A.H. & W.J. Potgieter in Preller, *Voortrekkermense*, iii, p. 10

54 TA: A.81, 'Account of Fr. J. de S. Rita Montanha', pp. 33–60

55 TA: R.3171/59, Verklaring, Manhunde and Guanhane (Spelonken). 8 October 1859

56 Liesegang, *Gaza Nguni*, pp. 74, 77–8: de Vaal, 'Albasini', p. 57; PA: UR.1, Uitvoerenderaad (Schoemansdal), 26 May 1859, art.5. Ninety-eight white inhabitants objected to Mzila's settlement, fearing the effect the settlement of *Kaalkaffers* (Ngoni) would have on the *Macatees* (Sotho and Venda) who attended their hunt. The latter, on whom they depended for the successful completion of the hunt, would not continue to venture from home leaving their families open to the depredations of the newcomers. See TA: R.2993/59, Inwoners (Renosterpoort) to President and Uitvoerenderaad, 8 August 1859

57 TA: COCP, pp. 17–20, 22–4, 24–7, 27–34, four letters to Governor of Lourenço Marques, 4 March 1860; pp. 34–42, to Sec. Gen. of Mozambique,

8 March 1860. There is no certainty that Albasini advanced the scheme of alliance at Schoemansdal until March 1861, but the opinions he expressed about Mawewe in TA: R.3406a/59, to Comdt. Gen. S. Schoeman, 10 October 1859, suggest in the light of the action he subsequently took in January 1860 (discussed below) that he had Schoeman's tacit approval of a 'forward' policy in trans-Limpopo. See also R.4325/61, J. Albasini to Acting Pres. S. Schoeman 30 March 1861; COCP, 84–7, to Governor of Lourenço Marques, 31 March 1861

58 TA: R.3515/60, J. Albasini, 'in nationale dienst' (Singwi lagerplaats) to Comdt. Gen. S. Schoeman, 30 January 1860; das Neves, *A Hunting Expedition*, p. 122

59 TA: R.4243/61, Landd. N.J. Grobler (Schoemansdal) to Acting Pres. J. Schoeman (Pretoria Klein Schoemansdal), 4 February 1861, and enclosure, J. Albasini Goedewensch to Landd., 1 February 1861; R.4298/61, J. Albasini to Acting Pres. S. Schoeman, 2 March 1861; R.4322/61, ditto, 29 March 1861; COCP, 84–7, to Governor of Lourenço Marques, 31 March 1861; also Junod, *South African Tribe*, i, p. 406; TA: microfilm D/S.13, 'Account of the wanderings . . . of one Alexander Betts Struben' (typescript in possession of Pretoria Municipality), p. 30

60 From May 1861, Albasini advocated a joint operation to supplant Mawewe with Mzila, see TA: R.4404/61, J. Albasini to Acting Pres. S. Schoeman, 13 May 1861; COCP, pp. 100–102, to Gov. Lourenço Marques, 23 May 1861; pp. 102–3, to same, 11 July 1861; pp. 106–8, to same, 6 November 1861. However, his colours had clearly flown beside those of the aspirant President Schoeman, and the anti-Schoeman elements which were eventually to triumph in early 1862, though by no means hostile to the Portuguese Government, viewed Albasini with suspicion. In their view the 'forward' policy in the hunting grounds was a mistake. Mawewe had been provoked and was best assuaged now by the surrender of Mzila, whose presence in Zoutpansberg was anyway a disturbing influence on the Sotho and Venda who had suffered the incursions of the difaqane. They hardly warmed to Albasini when they discovered he had accepted thirty-eight tusks from Mawewe, as a pledge for the reopening of the hunting grounds once Mzila was killed, but made no attempt to execute his part of the bargain. See TA: Supp.5.27/61, Onderzoek, Comdt. E.H. Geyser (Vlagvonteyn), 1 October 1861; COCP, pp. 106–8, to Gov. L. Marques, 6 November 1861

61 Liesegang, *Gaza Nguni*, pp. 79–82. Also, TA: R.4753/61, J. Albasini to Acting Pres. S. Schoeman, 31 October 1861; Supp.S.9/62, J. Albasini; Portuguese Vice-Consul to Acting Pres. S. Schoeman, 8 January 1862; R.170/62, ditto, 15 March 1862; R.171/62, Extract, Journal, Portuguese Vice-Consul, 15 March 1862

62 TA: R.183/64, Memorandum, Superintendent J. Albasini, 2 April–25 May 1864; R.210/64, Comdt. F.H. Geyser and Veldcts. J.H. du Plessis and J.C.J. Herbst to Uitvoerenderaad, 14 April 1864, with enclosure, Vergadering (Zoutpansberg), 11–14 April 1864. In the meantime Albasini had been posing as Mzila's ally, raising an African force to re-enter 'Chinguine' in April 1862. In that other white inhabitants contributed Africans to this force, Albasini had even effected momentarily the long sought 'consensus' among the white notables. Mzila later demanded the repayment of a bribe he had paid Albasini to forge this alliance—some cattle, twenty-seven elephants' tusks, and 'vyf

groot meiden en klein kaffers'—because it had simply chastised Sikwalakwala and reasserted Zoutpansberg control in the hunting grounds, without materially affecting his own position. Ironically, this force had been led into 'Chinguine' by Munene. See TA: COCP, p. 147 to Veldct. J.H. du Plessis and Comdt. F.H. Geyser, 14 March 1862; pp. 148–9, two letters to Acting Pres. S. Schoeman, 15 March 1862; p. 150, to Landd. A.F. Fick and Veldct. J.H. du Plessis, 16 March 1862; pp. 151–2, three letters to Comdt. F.H. Geyser, 15, 21 and 21 March 1862; pp. 154–5, to A. de Paiva Rapozo, J.C. Couto and other Portuguese citizens in ZAR, 21 March 1862; pp. 155–9, Address to Public Meeting (Goedewensch), 21 March 1862 (enclosure to 7 April to Gov. L. Marques); p. 152, to J.C. Couto, L.M. Nunes, B.P. Pereira, 22 March 1862; p. 153, to Acting Pres. S. Schoeman, 2 April 1862; pp. 159–66, to Gov. L. Marques, 7 April 1862

63 PA: R.183/64, Memorandum, Superintendent J. Albasini, 2 April–25 May 1864; R.210/64, Comdt. F.H. Geyser and Veldcts. J.H. du Plessis and J.C.J. Herbst to Uitvoerenderaad, 14 April 1864, with enclosure, Vergadering (Zoutpansberg) 11–14 April 1864

64 *SAAR, Transvaal*, 7, 47, Volksraad, 15 November 1867, Art.166, 'Rapport omtrent de zaak van Zoutpansberg'

65 As n.63. Also R.551/64, Superintendent J. Albasini to Uitvoerenderaad, 5 August 1864. Jacob Christovao Xavier de Couto, like the majority of the Portuguese in Zoutpansberg apart from Albasini, was an Asian, probably of Goanese descent. He was the public notary at Lourenço Marques who drew up the contract for Albasini in 1846, mentioned in n.49. He joined Albasini at Goedewensch in 1859 as his Consular secretary, but was sacked in December 1861, in circumstances which suggest a fierce quarrel, after which he continued to act in a hostile manner towards his old associate. He was married to a Boer and owned Morgenzon, the farm immediately east of Goedewensch. See de Vaal, 'Albasini', p. 42; also TA: COCP, pp. 422–4, to Gov. L. Marques, 15 April 1869; pp. 425–7, to Gov. Gen. Mozambique, 18 May 1869

66 No official account of the visit of this Uitvoerenderaad commission to Zoutpansberg exists, but de Vaal reconstructs a fair narrative from the extant correspondence generated by the trip, see 'Albasini', pp. 79–81. Vercueil appears to have brazened out an attempt to examine his conduct, see TA: R.558/64, Landd. J. Vercueil to Pres. M.W. Pretorius, 8 August 1864; R.559/64, J.J. Strydom to Pretorius, 8 August 1864; R.758/64, Vercueil to Pretorius, 11 September 1864. For bristling exchanges between Albasini and Vercueil over their respective jurisdictions over Munene, see R.594/64, Correspondence, Vercueil to Albasini, 18–20 August 1864, and R.593, 604, 603/64 (split and wrongly ordered by the compiler of the Staatssekretaris Argief), Correspondence, Albasini to Vercueil, 18–20 August 1864

67 TA: R.348/64. Landd. J. Vercueil to Pres. M.N.. Pretorius, 15 June 1864

68 TA: UR.1, no.2, Uitvoerenderaad, 28 March 1865, Art.77, R.290/64, Verslag. Dodanbana and Majolome (Goedewensch) 13 March 1865

69 TA: R.363/65, Veldct. S.J. Jansen van Rensburg to J. Albasini, 28 March 1865; R.369/65, Landd. J. Vercueil to van Rensburg, 28 March 1865; R.300/65, Verslag, Veldct. van Rensburg, 14–29 March 1865. Vercueil had been particularly annoyed by the manner in which Munene had been removed from his custody; see R.307/65 and R.308/65.to van Rensburg, 15 March 1865; R.317/65,

ditto, 16 March 1865; R.336/65, to Pres. and Uitvoerenderaad, 21 March 1865. Munene took guns with him which belonged to Vercueil and a business associate

70 M.M. Motenda in van Warmelo, *Copper Miners*, pp. 57–8. TA: All to Uitvoerenderaad; R.519/65, C.J. Rake, 1 May 1865; R.528/65, Superintendent J. Albasini, 2 May 1865; R.536/65, Landd. J. Vercueil, 5 May 1865; R.538/65, Comdt. S.M. Venter, 5 May 1865

71 de Vaal, 'Albasini', p. 88

72 Commandant-General Kruger was operating along the Zulu border of Utrecht; see J.J. van Heerden 'Die Kommandant-General in die Geskiedenis van die Suid-Afrikaanse Republiek', Ph.D. thesis, University of Pretoria, 1949, in *AYB*, ii, 1964, pp. 73–5; de Vaal, 'Albasini', p. 85

73 S.M. Dzivhani in van Warmelo, *Copper Miners*, p. 39; M.M. Motenda in van Warmelo, *Copper Miners*, p. 55; Tshamaano in van Warmelo, *Contributions*, pp. 15–22; G.S. Preller (ed.) *Die Dagboek van Louis Trichardt*, Bloemfontein, 1917; 2nd edition, 1938, entries for December 1836, pp. 19–23

74 A short discussion of the role of the makhadzi in Venda inheritance law is contained in Stayt, *The Ba Venda*, pp. 167–8

75 Tshamaano, son of Makhado, in van Warmelo, *Contributions*, pp. 18–23, 29–32; S.M. Dzivhani in van Warmelo, *Copper Miners*, pp. 39–40; M.M. Motenda in van Warmelo *Copper Miners*, pp. 56–7. Also TA: R.287/64, Driemaandelyksch Verslag, acting Veldct. S.J. Jansen van Rensburg, 14 May–19 August 1864. Tshamaano told van Warmelo that Ramavhoya's Great Wife had died childless, so her father by custom was obliged to supply another wife from his family, who happened to be Limani, his grand-daughter. Limani was thus Ramavhoya's replacement Great Wife under the same lobola agreement. Before she could be married to Ramavhoya, however, Ramabulana murdered him and took Limani for himself, and she subsequently bore him Makhado

76 TA: R.316/64, Copies of correspondence between Albasini and Vercueil, 3–4 June 1864; R.328/64, Superintendent Albasini to Uitvoerenderaad, 9 June 1864; R.292/64, Superintendent's Memorandum, 26 May–9 June 1864; R.287/64, Driemaandelyksch Verslag, acting Veldct. S.J. Jansen van Rensburg, 19 May–19 August 1864; R.348/64, Landd. Vercueil to Pres. Pretorius, 15 June 1864. Also S.M. Dzivhani in van Warmelo, *Copper Miners*, p. 40

77 The Krygsraad records have not been preserved, but its decisions are revealed in various correspondence. See TA: R.293/65, Comdt. S.M. Venter (Spelonken) to Veldct. S.J. Jansen van Rensburg, 13 March 1865; R.295/65, J. Albasini, S.M. Venter, W.J.H. Potgieter, and others (Goedewensch), to Uitvoerenderaad, 13 March 1865; R.528/65, Superintendent Albasini to Uitvoerenderaad, 2 May 1865; R.536/65, Landd. Vercueil to Uitvoerenderaad, 5 May 1865

78 Munene had shown himself hostile to Davhana at the time of his association with de Couto in 1864, see TA: R.183/64, Superintendent's Memorandum, 2 April–25 May 1864. He was ultimately sheltered by Tshivhase, whom M.M. Motenda in van Warmelo, *Copper Miners*, p. 70, says made him headman over his Tsonga

79 TA: R.495/65, Verslag. Veldct. A.P. Duvenhage, 28 April 1865; R.1349/65, assistant Comdt. Gen. F.H. Geyser to Staatssekretaris S.J. Meintjes (Schoe-

mansdal), 22 December 1865
80 TA: R.4514/61, Veldct. G. van Rooyen (Roodekrans) to Comdt. S.J.P. Krüger, 22 July 1861
81 Alexander Merensky in *BMB*, 1863, 'Reise im Norden des Lepaluleflusses', p. 10
82 Makhado's induction into the swart skut college is discussed above, pp. 335–6
83 TA:A.17, J. Fleetwood Churchill (Rhenosterpoort), 13 September 1856, p. 12
84 Struben, *Recollections*, p. 86
85 *SAAR, Transvaal*, 2, p. 25; Volksraad (Lydenburg), 5 May 1851, Art.6; *SAAR, Transvaal*, 3, pp. 599–602, 'Wet tot beter regelen der jagt ...', 22 October 1858. Potgieter's hunt law is not extant, but it is supposed to have provided for limited arming of African attendants in the veld as a protection against lions; see Munnik, *Kronieke*, p. 10. Schoeman's hunt law anticipated the provisions of the 1858 regulations, and referred to Potgieter's law under the date 20 October 1850. See TA: R.1380/57, Publieke Byeenkomst (Zoutpansberg), 11 March 1857
86 TA: R.1814/57, Hof van Landd. en Heemraden (Zoutpansberg), 7–8 December 1857, Art.1
87 Moerschell, *Der Wilde Lotrie*, p. 28. The petitions against Landd. R.A. van Nispen's reapplication of the law are in TA: R.1374/65, H.R. Schnell and others, 28 December 1865; R.1355/65, 22, L.M. Nunes, 4 January 1866; R.732/66, J.A. Weeber and others, 25 July 1866. Also *SAAR, Transvaal*, 6, pp. 101–2, A.H. Potgieter and others, 9 January 1866; p. 102, G.J. Snyman and others, 15 January 1866
88 TA: R.4179/60, acting Landd. N.J. Grobler to Comdt. Gen. S. Schoeman, 10 December 1860
89 See particularly S. Trapido, 'Aspects in the transition from slavery to serfdom: the South African Republic, 1842–1902', in *CSP*, vi, 1976, pp. 24–31
90 Munnik, *Kronieke*, p. 34
91 E.g. (military), de Vaal, 'Albasini', p. 21: (commercial) TA: R.183/64, Superintendent's Memorandum, 2 April–25 May 1864; (diplomatic) R.997/56, Landd. A.C. Duvenhage (Zoutpansberg) to Comdt. Gen. S. Schoeman, 6 March 1856, and R.171/62, Extract 'Journaal van den Portuguesche Vice Consul', 15 March 1862
92 TA: microfilm D/S.13 'Account of ... A.B. Struben', p. 38
93 Typical instances: in February 1856 Commandant Jan Jacobs returned from an attack on the stronghold of the Venda chief Rasikhuthuma in which twenty-five Africans were shot, with 76 head of cattle, 108 sheep and goats, and 13 'jonge kaffers' captured. In January 1861 Michael Buys was sent against 'Makakabula' and brought back 14 'klyn goet'. When 'Makakabula' sued for peace, Landdrost Nicolaas Grobler felt his way clear to offer to return the 'klyn goet' if the chief delivered ten tusks to defray the costs of the patrol. See TA: R.995/56, Verslag, Comdt. J.H. Jacobs (Zoutpansberg) to Comdt. Gen. S. Schoeman, 29 Feburary 1856; R.4224/61, Landdrost N.J. Grobler to acting Pres. S. Schoeman, 24 January 1861. Harry Struben once accepted some oxen, some ivory, and a boy aged twelve in settlement of a debt, and wrote of dealings in 'black ivory':
    During the annual petty wars in Zoutpansberg district in the fifties and sixties, native children were brought out and disposed of, the average value being about two hundred Rixdollars (£15)

See Struben, *Recollections*, p. 87

94 Mauch, *Journals*, 113–4

95 Typical instances: in November 1854 at the seige of Makapansgat, Comdt.. Gen. Marthinus Pretorius amassed 400 'myde en kinders' in his laager, who had surrendered from the Muledlana Ndebele of Mugombhane. An attack on the Langa Ndebele of Mapela by Comdt. Gen. Stephanus Schoeman in April 1858 yielded, in a long list of loot, 239 'kleine kinderen' and 75 'meiden'. See TA: R.719/54, Comdt. Gen. M.W. Pretorius (Makapanspoort) to Comdt. S. Schoeman (Mooirivier), 12 November 1854; R.2041/58, Lyst van buit (Zoutpansberg) 29 April 1858

96 E.g. Preller, ''n Vergane Voortrekkerdorp', in *Oorlogsoormag*, pp. 210–1; Munnik, *Kronieke*, p. 36

97 *SAAR, Transvaal*, 1, p. 117. Volksraad (Potchefstroom), 23 January 1850, Art.34

98 TA: R.521/64, Veldcts. J.H. du Plessis and J.H. Duvenhage, 2 August 1864. Of 919 'under-captains' of named chiefs in three northern 'wyke' (Veldcornetcies) counted in this document, 828 were in the diensdoende category, including Madzhie and Makhado. The practice of exempting them opgaaf is mentioned in Supp.S.63/65, Veldct. A.P. Duvenhage, 'Voorstel van Wetten voor de Kaffers Stammen', n.d. (marked received by the office of Staatssekretaris, 16 May 1865)

99 TA: R.300/63, N.M. Jansen van Rensburg to Pres. Uitvoerenderaad, 10 April 1863. See also letters to Comdt. Gen. S. Schoeman, R.3305/59, W.A. Marais, 1 December 1859; R.3306/59, James Moulder, 1 December 1859; R.3309/59, A.J. Marais, 2 December 1859; R.3311/59, B.J. Vorster, 3 December 1859. Also R.466/63, J.H. Jacobs to Pres. W.C. Jansen van Rensburg, 16 June 1863

100 TA: microfilm D/S.13. 'Account of ... A.B. Struben', p. 30

101 TA: Supp.S.63/65, Veldct. A.P. Duvenhage, 'Voorstel van Wetten voor de Kaffers Stammen', n.d.

102 TA: R.370/66, Superintendent A.P. Duvenhage to Uitvoerenderaad, March 1866; R.371/66, Inwoners van wyk▸Rhenosterpoort to Uitvoerenderaad, March 1866

103 TA: R.521/64, Veldcts. J.H. du Plessis and J.H. Duvenhage, 2 August 1864

104 *BMB*, 1874, p. 131. Beyer, like other Berlin missionaries in the 1860s and early 1870s, made no distinction between the western Venda and the northern Sotho

105 E.g. TA: R.528/65, Superintendent J. Albasini to Uitvoerenderaad, 2 May 1865; R.918/67, enclosure no. 1, 'Memorandum van eene overeenkomst met de Kaffers Magato en Tromp by de kraal van Katlagte', 5 June 1865. Also Munnik, *Kronieke*, p. 36

106 Tshamaano in van Warmelo, *Contributions*, pp. 24–7. Also TA: R.328/64, Superintendent J. Albasini to Uitvoerenderaad, 9 June 1864; R.292/64, Superintendent's Memorandum 26 May–9 June 1864, identifying Funyufunyu as Tromp

107 Tshamaano in van Warmelo, *Contributions*, pp. 25–7, 30

108 TA: as n.106. Also R.918/67, enclosure no. 1, 'Memorandum', 5 June 1865. Makhado's other mentor, Stuurman, remained close to Michael Buys and later became a prominent African evangelist of the NGK mission to Zoutpansberg; see Hofmeyr, *Twintig jaren*, pp. 77–8

109 TA: R.831/65, assistant Comdt. Gen. M.J. Schoeman (Rustenburg) to Pres. M.W. Pretorius, 26 July 1865

110 TA: R.370/66, Superintendent A.P. Duvenhage to Uitvoerenderaad, March 1866; R.371/66, Inwoners van wyk Rhenosterpoort to Uitvoerenderaad, March 1866. Also Preller, "'n Vergane Voortrekkerdorp' in *Oorlogsoormag*, p. 211

111 Tshamaano in van Warmelo, *Contributions*, pp. 27–8

112 TA: R.1116/66, Landd. R.A. van Nispen to Uitvoerenderaad, 9 November 1866

113 Compare description of the inception and effects of a gun culture among the Shona after 1865, at the instigation of the Venda, in D.N. Beach, 'The Rising in South-West Mashonaland, 1896–7', Ph.D. thesis, University of London, 1971, pp. 143–7, 150–1

114 Tshamaano in van Warmelo, *Contributions*, p. 26; S.M. Dzivhani in van Warmelo, *Copper Miners*, p. 39

CHAPTER FOURTEEN

Reflections on land, office and wealth in the South African Republic, 1850–1900

Stanley Trapido

The emphasis on nationalism in the study of Afrikaner people in South Africa has meant that important, probably crucial, social relations in the South African Republic (between 1850 and 1900) have been very largely ignored. In particular there has been little or no examination of property relationships and the forms of production which these created. By focusing our attention on these relationships we may gain new insights not only into the development of classes within Afrikaner society but also into the state which supported and maintained those structures. This essay must serve as a tentative and preliminary attempt to outline some important aspects of these social relationships.

A partial market in land existed from the beginning of white Afrikaner occupation of the territory north of the Vaal River, which led to rapid accumulation among Afrikaner notables but also to landlessness among their clients. The major source of profit from agriculture (and the source of support for both notables and clients) lay in the various forms of rent paid by African producers who had often been the cultivators of the land prior to its seizure by Afrikaner settlers. The state which emerged from these property relations was created by the dominant, quasi-feudal notables who, with their functionaries, used their dominant position to acquire more land. In addition to the accumulation of land by Afrikaner notables, speculative land companies owned by South African-based entrepreneurs with European financial connections, contributed to the proletarianisation of sections of the Afrikaner population.

Partly in an attempt to alleviate intra-Afrikaner conflict, Afrikaner notables who controlled the state used their position to make irregular exactions upon the internationally financed deep-level gold-mining industry which was established in the last decade of the nineteenth century. Because profits from deep-level gold-mining investments were delayed, these exactions caused intense anxiety about costs. In addition, the system of land-holding (determined by custom or speculative ownership) led to under-utilisation and made it impossible to meet the need of the gold mines for cheap food. The systems of agricultural production and gold-mining production were incompatible, and after the South African War of 1899–1902, property relationships in agriculture swiftly changed. But while the notables were transformed into capitalist farmers, the proletarianisation of their former clients continued to its ultimate conclusion.

In 1850, ten years before the final unification of the four major Voortrekker communities north of the Vaal, the white settlers were a relatively homogeneous population committed to providing large tracts of land to members of their *maatskappy*. The leaders of the several parties of pastoralists were already wealthy and they and their kin were as a result in an advantaged position when the original distribution of land took place. The result was the reproduction of relationships of power and property which had existed in the Cape Colony from which they had migrated.

In the Dutch settlement at the Cape, popular elections played no part in the institutions of government and the major offices were held by metropolitan officials of the Dutch East India Company. These transient officials sought the assistance of the wealthy settlers in administering the colony. Both in the advisory *Burgerraad* in Cape Town and in the courts of *heemraaden*—the institutions created for the settlement of local disputes—in the districts of the interior, it was the wealthiest property owners who received the company's nomination. Similarly, the landdrosts, the chief administrators in the district, were also drawn from the Cape Town economic hierarchy to which they ultimately retired. Their reasons for being willing to undertake this service were twofold. First, it was the outlying districts which contained grazing lands for cattle which were either owned by, or would have to be sold to, the monopoly butchers of Cape Town. Since the meat trade provided the colonial elite with a major part of its wealth, it had a crucial interest in the maintenance of frontier stability, for when this stability broke down, so did the cattle trade. Secondly, service to the company was rewarded by grants of land in the districts in which they served and helped the already economically dominant group by providing it with additional grazing facilities.[1]

Serving the courts of heemraaden and the landdrost was the veldcornet. In law, veldcornets were appointed by the landdrosts but it was the heemraaden who selected them. Though more representative of the whole population, the veldcornets were men of greater substance than their fellow burghers. The major function of the veldcornet was the organising of the commandos, the mounted militia in which every male burgher had by law and custom to serve. The main role played by the commando was the acquiring of forced labour and the seizing of stock from Khoisan and then Nguni people. It is interesting, however, that these activities were not sufficiently legitimate to go without the justification that they were acts of retaliation. When the events known as the Great Trek of 1834–8 took place its leaders emerged from the wealthiest of the migrants. This leadership ultimately derived its power from its ability to maintain the commando in the field, to provide it not only with food but also with largely imported arms and ammunition which had to be paid for in negotiable currency.[2]

The administrative machinery of the embryonic Transvaal state was incapable of collecting sufficient revenue to finance both military expenditure and the barest essentials of civil administration, including the collecting of taxes. Between 1850 and 1876 the cost of acquiring and defending land was far more than the republican exchequer could pay, and payment was therefore made by securing land against debts. This in its turn inevitably involved the state in the search for new land with further expenditure which was again secured by the provision of land against Republican currency. Land used to secure debts was no longer available for burgher occupation, and provided a further reason for the conquest of more land.

In an attempt to solve the financial problems caused by military expenditure and the initial inability to raise revenue, two related sets of financial manipulations were attempted. Within the first set of proposals the simplest aspects involved providing land in lieu of salaries for administrators and directing creditors to taxpayers who were in arrears. More complex was the issuing of exchequer bills or *Mandaaten* for services rendered to the state. Mandaaten were not legal tender, but were secured by government farms.[3] The next measure, taken in 1865, five years after all the Transvaal burgher communities had combined to form the South African Republic, was the issuing of paper currency. The notes also were secured by government farms and were intended to recall the Mandaaten. The number of Mandaaten issued exceeded the notes issued by the Republic, and a further issue again secured against governments farms—three hundred on this occasion—was made in 1867. These notes were insufficient to meet new government expenditure and in 1868 a finance commission was established which proposed, among other things, the issue of more notes against no less than one thousand farms or 3 million morgen.

It is extremely difficult to summarise the variations of these schemes which were introduced not only by the Volksraad, but also by landdrosts who issued an unrecorded number of Mandaaten and failed to recall either their own or the state's issue when required to do so. In addition clergymen, traders, and private individuals issued credit notes which became known as *good-fors* because of the monetary chaos. It is hardly surprising that the Republic's currency was unacceptable in most commercial transactions and there were occasions when even government departments refused to accept currency which was supposedly legal tender.[4]

The second set of financial proposals concerned attempts to establish a bank among the burgher communities. These had less impact than the monetary programme but they help to illustrate the use to which land was put. The earliest proposal was made by a Hollander, Jacobus Stuart, who had very close connections with Amsterdam merchants involved in the South African trade.[5] Stuart's proposals, accepted by the Potchefstroom Volksraad in 1853, involved his being given the right to sell a hundred 3 000 morgen farms in Holland for £450 each. The capital raised by the sale of these farms was to be invested in the *Landsbank* and the Dutch settlers Stuart hoped to attract were to be invited to subscribe additional share capital to the bank. Stuart had no success in Holland. Whatever chances of success he may have had were in any case reduced by the scepticism of rival Dutch merchants.[6]

Similar proposals were made a decade later in 1865 by a Scottish adventurer, Alexander McCorkindale, who advocated the establishment of a *Bank der Zuid-Afrikaansche Republiek*. McCorkindale had previously undertaken to establish the London and South African Commercial, Agricultural and Mining Company which was to purchase two hundred farms from the government at £40 each and settle these with European immigrants. Eventually eighty farms were purchased—in all about 110 000 morgen—in an area of the eastern Transvaal named New Scotland. McCorkindale made a variety of industrial and commercial proposals to Pretorius and the Volksraad. He proposed building a harbour on Delagoa Bay and making the Maputa and Pongola Rivers navigable. In addition he proposed constructing roads, improving the postal service, and attracting engineers, mechanics, doctors and teachers from Europe to the Republic. To undertake these schemes he required that the government provide him with a hundred farms as security for the raising of a loan of £250 000 and for his services he proposed that the government give him two hundred farms. Nothing came of these later proposals but they indicate the profligate way in which commercial adventurers were ready to dispose of land.[7]

The Republic failed to establish a bank of its own but its new President, Thomas François Burgers, was able to negotiate a favourable loan with the Cape Commercial Bank and the state was therefore able to redeem its outstanding debts. The bank was heavily involved in supporting the Burgers regime for what de Kiewiet describes as 'political and not financial' reasons.[8] Burgers's attempt to raise a further European loan was apparently intended to free himself from the Cape Bank's tutelage. It was also intended that capital be raised for building a railway from Delagoa Bay to the Republic which would have freed the Republic from dependence on the ports of British colonies. No sooner had Burgers made these attempts, however, than the Republic was involved in another and very costly war against the Pedi. The Commercial Bank despaired of recovering its loans and the Republic's creditors played an important part in persuading the British Government to annex the territory, which was also at that time part of a wider imperial political programme in South Africa. Annexation did not save the Cape Commercial Bank which went into liquidation in 1881, claiming land worth £400 000 which it had been given as security for its loans.[9]

The administration of the Transvaal (as the annexed Republic was called) was placed under Theophilus Shepstone, the powerful Natal Secretary for Native Affairs. Shepstone made J.C.A. Henderson his honorary financial Commissioner, which promised little for a change in the Transvaal's property relations. The latter had been a banker, was one of the prime movers in attempting to raise capital for a railway from Durban to the Transvaal which left him hostile toward Burgers's Delagoa Bay proposals, and, while in Shepstone's service, established what de Kiewiet has called 'one of those land-jobbing companies'. Henderson's Transvaal Board of Executors and Trust Company included the Government secretary, two managing officials of the Cape Commercial Bank and George Moodie, 'the entirely dishonest promoter of the Lebombo Railway Company'.[10] Before the Cape Commercial Bank went into liquidation Henderson had appropriated British funds to give its claims preferential treatment. His activities undermined British policy and went a long way toward creating the conditions which rallied republicans to overthrow the regime, but his association with the Transvaal was not to end there. In 1900 Henderson's Consolidated Corporation Limited owned eighty farms in the Transvaal, and it is very probable that he was himself a director of other land companies.[11]

In 1900 when the Lands Settlement Commission took evidence it was told that 1 400 farms were owned by land companies. Intelligence reports, however, indicate that at least another seven hundred farms were owned by companies.[12] J.S. Marais reports that in 1899 the Colonial Office received a letter from a committee claiming to represent companies who owned over eight million acres in the Republic. The view that these land companies were merely ancillary to mining activities is not well founded. The prospectus of the Oceana Land Company, published in London in 1891, offered 105 farms suitable for agricultural purposes and by 1900 the

Company owned 224 farms.[13] Many of the Transvaal Consolidated Land Exploration Company's 656 farms were acquired before 1883, and it offered a large number of farms suitable for agricultural purposes for sale in 1894. For its part the Republic continued to use land to secure its debts; Paul Kruger was reported, for example, to have given 'a large amount of land' to, among others, the Netherlands Railway Company.[14]

It should be apparent that the usual explanation for 'landlessness' in the Transvaal is unsatisfactory. It is not enough to posit a group of unprogressive farmers lacking initiative, but set on providing a landed inheritance for all their sons by subdividing land until it was no longer economically viable. Rural impoverishment should be set against land accumulation and the relationship between the two should be noted.[15] The process by which land became the Republic's major resource in its dealings with outsiders was initiated in its dealings with its own officials. Land accumulation began among officials who were given land in lieu of salaries and who were thereby gradually encouraged to perceive land as a marketable asset. To begin with this may have created hardship.[16] But it was ultimately perceived as gain when land values increased. When we ask what kind of people within the various communities became officials we see that the situation was one which provided opportunities for certain members of the community to consolidate already existing advantages. Most officials were elected and the landdrost—the only appointed official— was dependent upon local approval for the confirmation and retention of his appointment.[17] The veldcornet who had most local authority was almost inevitably elected from a family of local notables. Status was acquired from wealth in cattle, and wealth in cattle enabled the owner to settle down and hire others to do the arduous task of herding. Thus, with large herds, activities were centralised, and kin and others were employed to take cattle to widely-dispersed pastures. In a community where there was constant movement among burgher farmers, some of them abandoning old and seeking new pastures, few other people were settled long enough to acquire local prestige.

The veldcornet—the pivotal official of the burgher state—played interchangeable military and civil roles. He was responsible to the *Krygsraad* (Military Council) and to the administrative and judicial authority of the landdrost. In his military role, he was entrusted with maintaining a list of combatants in his ward and for summoning these for military service. But, above all, the veldcornet was responsible for inspecting claims to farms to enable them to be transferred from the state to citizens of the republic, and for placing in service every coloured person not subordinate to any of the African chiefs.[18] It is apparent, therefore, that whatever the rules of the constitution (and for all that he was usually a benign paternal figure),[19] the veldcornet, with so much power in the apportionment of land and African labour in a community of constant flux, was well placed for accumulating landed property. The landdrost, who was responsible for putting up for sale land for which taxes had not been paid, had access to valuable information about land on the market. His responsibility for the issuing of licences to 'shopkeepers, itinerant foreign traders, auctioneers' and his role as chief judicial officer enhanced his authority. Moreover the office of veldcornet was most often a stepping stone to higher office and a very high proportion of those who became members of the legislature, the Volksraad, began their careers as veldcornets.[20]

In the two decades between 1850 and 1870 the burgers of the Transvaal were relatively prosperous and one should not equate the condition of the state's finances with those of its citizens. Ostrich feathers, ivory, cattle, hides and wool provided substantial exports, particularly from the Potchefstroom district.[21] The traders who came originally as *smouses* to *nagmaal* remained to establish permanent stores. They exchanged their goods for agricultural products or products of the hunt which they sold or passed on to their principals in the coastal ports. Despite their hinterland, Transvaal dorps had a solid core of English businessmen who were joined or replaced at the end of the nineteenth century by East European Jews.[22]

The combination of President Burgers's loan, the discovery of gold in the Lydenburg district and the experience of administration made for greater efficiency, and by 1870, for example, officials were receiving their salaries in cash. In the main, however, an improvement in administration primarily meant an improvement in tax-collecting. It coincided with a general decline in prosperity among the republic's citizens which was possibly intensified by relatively efficient tax-collection. Game was now a wasting asset, and those who had primarily been hunters abandoned or sold farms and followed the diminishing elephant herds. Between 1850 and 1868 various Volksraads attempted to raise taxes by exhortation, fines, proclamations and hectoring instructions to landdrosts, with little or no effect.[23] By 1873 the situation had changed dramatically. It is significant that the Volksraad found it necessary to pass a resolution instructing landdrosts not to sell free-hold farms of debtors for less than the owners owed the state.[24] For those who owed the state money and were faced with having to leave their farms, to sell was more to their advantage than merely to abandon, and who was better placed to know that an owner wished to sell (or barter) his farm than local officials involved in tax assessment and collection?

Although the imminent auction of abandoned farms had to be advertised in the *Staats Courant*, and later also in the local papers, local officials were in the best position to know whether land was coming on to the market.[25] As a young veldcornet Paul Kruger is said to have acquired several farms 'by barter' before 1846 and before he came president he acquired much land at a time when it 'went begging'. His major biographer, D.W. Krüger, reports that he received a large number of farms for services rendered to the state. In addition, between 1855 and 1866, he bought and sold at least fourteen farms.[26] By the late 1850s Kruger no longer had the time for hunting, and like other burghers 'hat by hom reeds geruime tyd op grond-spekulasie toegelê'. The future Commandant-General of the Republic, Piet Joubert, had, as a veldcornet, acquired over a dozen farms by 1871. A veldcornet and a native commissioner in Vryheid, Louis Botha, acquired or purchased six farms, in all 16 000 acres, before he was elected to the Second Volksraad in 1895, to begin a political career which culminated in his being the first Prime Minister of the Union of South Africa.[27]

In the last two decades of the century the dominant group of Afrikaner landowners had established an informal network which provided them with information and enabled them to accumulate profitable land-holdings.

Piet Joubert was in a fortunate position since 'persone wat hulle vaste eiendom wou verkoop het hom dikwels, en selde te vergeefs om 'n aanbod genader'.[28] Paul Kruger 'immediately saw the possibility of good specu-lation' when gold was discovered on the Witwatersrand. In August 1886, together with his son-in-law, Frikkie Elof, he bought the farm, Geduld Springs, for £700. In July 1891 he bought Elof's share for £4000, before ultimately selling the 4000 morgen farm to the Springs Real Estate Company for £107 700. By the last decade of the century, Piet Joubert owned no less than twenty-nine farms, most of them in the established districts of Piet Retief, Wakkerstroom, Lydenburg, Potchefstroom and Middleburg.[30] The Republic's last Registrar of Deeds said of one of Kruger's close associates, Alois Nellmapius, who bought a large number of farms at public auctions after 1883, that he 'knew the country well him-self and obtained good information'.[31] But who could have had better information than the very same Registrar of Deeds, Christoffel Minhaar, who was a director of the Transvaal Land Exploration Company, or the Surveyor-General of the Republic, Johannes Rissik, who was the com-pany's chairman?[32] Similarly, Louis Botha 'had his connections every-where'. He not only managed a 'land syndicate' with his patron, the first Volksraad member for Vryheid, Lucas Meyer, but his syndicate, we are baldly told, 'yielded its thousand pounds from time to time'. Immediately after the South African war he was able to profit from selling land and 'indulging his speculative bent'.[33]

Because the rich are always with us, so are the poor. The device to which the republic's governments always resorted in an attempt to cope with poverty was expansion into African areas, whether within or beyond the state's customary boundaries. This was never more than a palliative measure, and ultimately it made the situation worse. If land acquired from Africans provided a tolerable surplus from agriculture or mining, then it was almost certain to fall into the hands of rich burghers or land companies. Expeditions undertaken to seize new land—supposedly for the landless—were as often as not financed by speculators who received a half share from each of the freebooters whom they had provisioned.[34] If new land did not attract the attention of notables or speculators, then the poor who were settled on it—'de arme klas waar uit onze bevolking grootlyks bestaat'[35]—were unlikely to succeed in getting the necessary attention of the central government.

New settlements at the very least need administration to establish access to water and to secure the issuing land-titles. Yet it is evident from the experience of the burghers granted land in that territory known to them as the 'Mapoch's gronden' that without the ability to influence the president, his executive or the Volksraad, even minimum administration was not forthcoming. The Mapoch settlers, although they owned little property were not without political energies, and it was the unresponsiveness of the administration which wore them down.[36] Their attempts to acquire title deeds were frustrated for more than twenty years and were only finally granted after the fall of the Republic and the establishment of Crown Colony rule. It took the central administration of the Republic ten years to make provision for the issuing of 'occupation-farm' title deeds. This was partly the result of the Executive Council's failure to inform the Volksraad of the need to provide for this modified form of tenure. Between 1883 and 1889 the settlers constantly petitioned the Volksraad to look into their affairs. Finally in 1895 they were asked to provide transfer fees which were beyond their means. These were quickly waived, but the Volksraad resolution doing so was not published for another eighteen months. In the meantime, the settlers were asked to pay survey costs, stamp duties and for title deeds.

There were other examples of government inertia and inefficiency which had a debilitating effect on the settlers. Regulations were required for the distribution of water in order to stop disputes which began immediately after the first settlers took possession. The Executive instructed local officials to settle all disputes out of court, but when this was found to be impossible the local veldcornet and the landdrost of Middleburg proposed draft regulations to the Volksraad at regular intervals between 1884 and

1889—the year in which these were finally adopted. Even then the regulations were printed but never distributed. It is inconceivable that burghers with large landed and other interests would have been neglected in the way in which the Mapoch settlers were.[37]

Although the subdivision of land and the diminution of game may have left many to eke out a precarious livelihood, it is probable that many burghers never owned land at any time. Not all of these can be described as 'indigent'.[38] Many who arrived after the initial land grants had been made, became tenant- or squatter-farmers on the land of large owners. The form of tenure by which these tenants held land varied considerably though it was always informal, and although all tenant-squatters are now categorised as 'bywoners' it is probable that a number of relationships are subsumed under this heading. It may well be that the usual description of bywoner is derived from observations made during the crucial period of change when land was being transformed from non-capitalist to capitalist production. Grosskopf reported that 'several of the old Transvaalers objected to the word "bywoner". "We used to say [he was told] "that we obtained *'vergunning'* (concession) on the farm."'[39]

Many who were to become known as bywoners came from the Orange Free State and from the Cape in the last quarter of the nineteenth century and were men with movable property. They provided the landowner with a share of their crops and added to his status; the landlord was able to call upon his bywoners for commando service and they provided his family with affinal society. The bywoner's status declined and his tenure became more precarious, not because there was a shortage of land, but because land became commercially viable. The bywoner who previously had added to the landlord's status in a changed situation became an encumbrance. The South African war provided the opportunity for many landlords to refuse to resume patronage for those bywoners who had left the land to serve with Boer commandos.[40] As the Dutch Reformed Church Minister, the Reverend Kestel, revered among Afrikaner nationalists for his activities during and immediately after the South African war, told the 1938 Peoples Economic Congress called to consider measures to alleviate the lot of the poor whites,

> Our forefathers had time for *bywoners*. The children learned to respect the *bywoner*. He ate at the same table as the landowner and he could feel that blood crawls where it cannot run.
> After the Second War of Independence a new spirit was abroad, a spirit of each for himself, Then we had no more time for *bywoners*.[41]

In addition, land which was worked by the extended family, and which for practical purposes was treated as a single farming unit, became the source of considerable rural misery and poverty when some members of the family sought to establish legal rights to sections of a farm. Then the greater part of those resident on the land were left as the owners of miserable holdings which were ultimately purchased, often under guise of charity, by those with the largest holdings.

By the last decade of the nineteenth century, when capital intensive gold-mining was well under way, the dominant class had maintained non-capitalist property relationships for a quarter of a century. The gold-mining industry at Barberton and then on the Witwatersrand created new entrepreneurial opportunities for this class. In order to raise revenue for the state after independence was regained in 1881, Paul Kruger's concessions policy was brought into being, the intention of which was to encourage those with capital and technical and managerial skill to come to the Republic by granting them monopolies to produce industrial goods. 'As far as internal policy is concerned', Kruger declared in 1883,

> the first essential is the development of the resources of the country, so that our imports are reduced and our exports increased; or to speak more clearly, so that we export goods and import money, and not (as happens too frequently now) import products, to pay for which money flows out of the country. . . . Why should our products, such as wool, etc. be processed in foreign countries and expensively re-purchased by us. Already, under the government's protection, factories are being erected to manufacture our own gunpowder and ammunition, from the products of the country; a concession has been granted for a wool factory; and others have been requested for the preparation of leather. I shall always, insofar as it does not interfere with the freedom of trade, advance the cause of factories . . .

Mining concessions, Kruger continued, would ensure that 'proper machinery' was imported 'and that the mines would run in the best way, with less costs and more profit'. Moreover, the concessions policy would mean that the mining population was brought 'under the better control of responsible persons'.[42]

In many ways these proposals were a revival of the McCorkindale schemes.[43] Kruger envisaged that the concessions would provide the state with substantial revenue, create a market for local raw materials, and allow the concessionaire to make a handsome profit from his monopoly position. In practice the policy did not have this effect. From the very beginning concessions were granted to those who were close to the President's coterie (the so-called 'third Volksraad') or were members of it, to members of the Executive Council or the Volksraad (both to those who supported the policy and to those who were its bitterest critics) and to high officials of the government. Without the requisite skills, most concessionaires treated their concessions as one more resource with which to speculate. And speculation brought them into conflict with mining capital.

Within the agrarian economy, the major productive groups were African cultivators, who either worked their own lands and paid tribute or farmed rented land[44] or worked—largely under duress—as labourers where white farmers were engaged in productive activities. This resulted in Africans, most of whom came to the gold fields from outside the Republic, having to run a gauntlet of veldcornets set on acquiring labourers for themselves and their fellow burghers. Those who controlled the state in the South African Republic came into conflict with mining interests at every point in their economic activities. The concessions policy (particularly the dynamite concession) added significantly to the cost of gold-mining and delayed their becoming profitable. A struggle for power between the governing class and mining capitalists became inevitable, but this is not to argue that the form which it took was inevitable.

The weakening of client-patron relationships and this growing, but regionally uneven, impoverishment might have led to intra-Afrikaner class conflict. Afrikaners had taken to arms against Afrikaners before, and they were to do so again. The Lichtenburg commando which took to the field during the 1914 rebellion was made up of impoverished cultivators, while the Afrikaners of the eastern Transvaal who rallied to Botha's call were from a prosperous region which was benefiting from their Parliamentary leader's agrarian policy. Intra-Afrikaner class conflict was delayed by the mining capitalists, who were new men of economic and political power. They were unversed in the pragmatic politics of older capitalist classes, and the extent to which power was concentrated in their hands had given them the belief that they could do anything. The result was the Jameson raid which, when combined with later agitations, helped to create a climate which prepared both sides for war, and for a time reduced intra-Afrikaner tensions. At the same time the post-war policy of conciliation was intended to blur the antagonistic divisions which had emerged in Afrikaner society.

The results of the South African war were, as we know, many and far-reaching. Although much emphasis has been placed on the explicitly political consequences of the war little attention has been given to the change in property relationships in agriculture and to the attendant increase in food production.[45] The colonial state, established in the Transvaal after the war under the direction of the British High Commissioner, Lord Milner, sought to create a class of commercial yeoman farmers. The political aspect of this policy which is always given the greatest prominence was the attempt to anglicise the countryside and the failure of this aspect of his policy. But far more important was the outcome of the overall policy which resulted in substantial state involvement in agriculture.

This statism was explicitly enunciated by F.B. Smith, Milner's director of the Transvaal Department of Agriculture and permanent secretary of the Union Department of Agriculture from 1910 to 1920. 'If the agriculture of a country is to be developed,' he wrote in 1908, 'it must be by radical measures.' These radical measures were to be initiated and directed by a department of state. Smith claimed that

> with the exception of Great Britain, where centuries of experience and enterprise of private individuals and societies have atoned for the short-comings of the Government ... the condition of the agriculture of a country can be gauged with a fair degree of accuracy by the quality of its Department of Agriculture.[46]

The resurgence of the dominant group of Afrikaner landowners, meant that they, rather than the British yeomen, were the beneficiaries of an ideology and a state apparatus intended to bolster commercial agriculture. This was not, however, a passive acceptance of useful institutions. Because of their accumulation of land the dominant Afrikaner agrarian class was the only group capable of taking advantage of British statism. In one crucial respect, moreover, the Afrikaner leaders had to improve upon their inheritance from the Transvaal colonial government. They had to see to the procuring of labour. It was the apparent failure of the colonial government to bring about the conditions which would create an indigenous labour force which had been one of the causes of Afrikaner resurgence. When the Transvaal government accepted the demand by the mining houses to 'recruit' outside South Africa, particularly in China, the hostile reaction from Afrikaner leaders had as much to do with the implications of this policy for the procuring of labour within southern Africa, as it had to do with the racial implications of a Chinese labour force.

Shorn of their commando system, both by the defeat of their state and by the decline of the social relationship which made it possible, the dominant landowners had to make a bid to share state power if they were to have available non-economic mechanisms for the procuring of labour. In successfully gaining a share of state power the Afrikaner landowners were not only to acquire the mechanisms for obtaining labour but also many of the resources originally intended for British yeomen.

The most important resource of all was the Transvaal Land Bank, with its initial capital provided by the British Government. In addition the Transvaal had a Department of Agriculture, which its director claimed was the 'only department in South Africa that at all answers to the description of what a department should be'.[47] It is of some consequence, therefore, that the first Afrikaner government after the defeat of the republic was led by Louis Botha who filled not only the office of Prime Minister but also that of Minister of Agriculture. In these circumstances it is hardly surprising that the ubiquitous Johan Rissik was Minister of Lands.

Production increased dramatically and from being a large importer of maize before the South African war, the Transvaal soon became a substantial exporter. After the unification of South Africa, the Transvaal retained the greatest share of state assistance to agriculture. In 1917 Transvaal farmers owed the Land Bank £367 000, while their counterparts in the Orange Free State owed the bank £49 000, those in Natal £6 000, and because of Cape law—which was only changed in 1923—farmers in that province were unable to obtain loans from the bank at all.[48] Moreover, all these loans were for the most part never repaid and were to be written off in less than a decade.

In addition, the state used its resources not only to provide capital but also to intervene in the marketing of maize, with the result that existing marketing channels as well as sources of supply for the market were at least partially by-passed. The Transvaal maize co-operatives—which came into being under the Botha government in the years immediately before Union—were not able to dispose of their crops successfully and the largest purchaser of maize, the mining companies, were initially unwilling to accept a joint tender from them. Before they would do so they required a guarantee, acquired from the Land Bank, that the co-operatives would not only provide maize at the price which they had tendered, but also that the Bank would make good any shortfall in the quantity which the mining companies had commissioned. To ensure the purchasing and delivery of co-operative-produced maize, a central agency was established with state aid.[49] These facilities reduced competition from the then most productive white maize farmers, the large Afrikaner producers of the Orange Free State. It was surely not mere coincidence that in the year in which the Orange Free State members were to break away to form the first post-independence Nationalist party, the secretary of the Co-operative Division of the Department of Agriculture, A.E. Marks, should note that there were hardly any Free State farmers involved in the Maize Agency. 'The explanation of this apparent apathy' he wrote,

> probably lies in the fact that facilities similar to those afforded to the Transvaal Societies for receiving expert advice and assistance in the formation and carrying on such undertakings have not been placed at the disposal of Free State farmers by the Government. It is probable that until such time as a government depart-

ment of sufficient capacity and numerical strength effectively to supervise operations in the two provinces is established, the movement will make very little progress in the Free State.[50]

Against this background it is possible to see that much conflict between Afrikaners has been as a result of a struggle, not simply for patronage, but for the control of the State.

Notes

1 The famous van Reenen family would appear to illustrate many of the points made in this paragraph. As the most progressive farmers in the late eighteenth/ early nineteenth century Cape Colony, its members were nevertheless heavily dependent on their income from their meat contract to the government based on their farms in the interior. Their various services to the government were not infrequently rewarded with the grant of further lands. See W. Blommaert and J.A. Wiid (eds.), *Die Joernaal van Dirk Gysbert van Reenen*, Cape Town, 1937, pp. 1–8, Biographical Sketch

2 E.H.D. Arndt, *Banking and Currency Development in South Africa, 1652–1927*, Cape Town, 1928, pp. 94–121. In 1854 the ammunition used at the battle of Boomplats in 1848 had not yet been paid for and the Volksraad called for public subscriptions. C.J. Uys, *In the Era of Shepstone*, Lovedale, 1933, noted 'The Sekukuni War had taken a big slice out of the revenue of the state and in August 1876 the Government was obliged to mortgage the private properties of its members to raise sufficient money for purchasing ammunition ... As [Paul Kruger's] property had already been bonded for the loan of £19 000 raised by the Government, he suggested that the members of the Executive Council should forfeit their salaries to enable the Government to purchase ammunition', (p. 439)

3 Arndt, *Banking and Currency Development*, p. 96

4 In the three years before 1867 commandos had been called out against the Ndzundza Ndebele under Mabhogo in the eastern Transvaal, the Republic had been involved in a war against the Basotho in 1865 which considerably undermined the new currency since it cost the government Rds. 83 000, and, before the full effect of this expenditure was felt, further commandos against the Zulu and the Basotho resulted in Rds. 162 000 being spent on ammunition and clothing for the combatants. There were further military expenses incurred in the Zoutpansberg in 1867 and the calling out of commandos once more in 1869. *Ibid.*, pp. 98–104, Arndt notes 'It further appeared while they had budgeted for an expenditure of £15 883 in 1866 the actual expenditure amounted to roughly £46 000. They had budgeted for £1 500 in contributions from the natives and £3 000 for fines, whereas the corresponding receipts were £3 5s. 9d. and nil' (p. 104)

5 Stuart was one of the many Hollanders influenced by U.G. Lauts. For Stuart's merchant connections and his various schemes to raise capital in Holland see T.A. du Plessis, 'Jacobus Stuart en die Transvaalse verdeelheid van 1855–6', *Historiese Studies*, June 1947

6 Stuart's major Dutch commercial rival was Johannes Smellekamp who had arrived in Natal in 1842 to work for the Amsterdam trading-house, J.A. Klijn and Co.

7 D.W. Krüger, 'Die Weg na die See', *Archives Year Book for South African History, (AYB)*, iv, 1, Pretoria, 1938, pp. 174–85

8 C.W. de Kiewiet, *The Imperial Factor in South Africa*, Cambridge, 1937, p. 104

9 G.T. Amphlet, *History of the Standard Bank of South Africa Ltd., 1862–1913*, Glasgow, 1914, p. 85

10 de Kiewiet, *Imperial Factor*, p. 143

11 *List of Farms in Districts of Transvaal (Intelligence Department)*, Pretoria, 1900; British Parliamentary Papers (BPP), 1901 XXIV, Cd 626, *Report of the Land Settlement Committee*, p. 58

12 BPP, 1901 XXIV, Cd 626, p. 58

13 Oceana Land Company Prospectus 1891; BPP, 1901 XXIV, Cd 626, p. 58, evidence of Johannes Christoffel Minnaar, Registrar of Deeds, South African Republic; J. S. Marais, *The Fall of Kruger's Republic*, Oxford, 1961, p. 5

14 BPP, 1901 XXIV, Cd 626, p. 58, evidence of H. Struben. In 1903 the Transvaal government claimed 29 million acres of land, 19 million being unsurveyed. Of the 11 000 farms in the new colony 2 861 were registered in the name of the state, BPP, 1903 XLV, Cd 1551, *Progress of Administration in the Transvaal*, p. 96

15 The original land grants were for two 3 000 morgen farms, one pastoral, the other for cultivation. *Law of the Transvaal up to 1899*, Volksraad Resolution (VRR) No. 149 of 28 September 1860 ('Wordt besloten dat alle Emigranten in dezen staat ingekomen tot en met het einde van jaar 1852 geregtigd zullen zijn voor twee plaatsen van het Gouvernment te ontvangen, en wel eene zaai—en eene veeplaats'). The extent of accumulation can be gathered from successive resolutions concerning taxation to be paid on land being surveyed. In 1875 the Volksraad resolved that for all farms 'surveyed by land surveyors of a greater extent than one hour this way or that, or 3 750 morgen, a tax of 2/6d shall be paid for every 100 morgen over 3 750'. VRR No. 118 of 24 May 1875. By 1891 surveyors were provided with a table indicating the state fees for holdings ranging from ten to ten thousand morgen and including a method for easily arriving at the cost of surveying land exceeding ten thousand morgen. Act 9 of 1891, Annex. No. 1. It is of some interest that Kruger purchased large tracts of land 'near Zoutspansberg for poor whites' in the decade after 1890. BPP, 1901 XXIV, Cd 626, pp. 55–8

16 F.A. van Jaarsveld, 'Die Veldkornet en sy aandeel in die opbou van die Suid Afrikanse Republiek tot 1870', *AYB*, II, Pretoria, 1950. In 1865 one veldcornet wrote 'als ik den nog myne groote salaris narekenen die nimmer betaald wordt, dan kan ik door moedeloosheid mijn wagen oppakte en dit district verlate', *ibid.*, p. 338

17 *Ibid.*, p. 333. 'Wanneer veld-kornette egter nie een van hulle (landdrost) gehou het nie, het geen burger vir hulle gestem nie, Honderd-agt-en-sewentig burgers het in 1853 versoek dat P.J. van Staden landdros van Rustenburg moes word maar die vier veld-kornette was daarop teë, so dat die aanstellung gekanseller is'

18 G.W. Eybers, *Select Constitutional Documents Illustrating South African History*, London, 1918, pp. 384–97, Grondwet (1858), Articles 96–145

19 Van Jaarsveld, 'Die Veldkornet', p. 331. 'In die oog yan die Volk was die veldkornet hulle beskermer, opsiener, vader en nie in die eerste plek 'n amptenaar op 'n kantoor wat die regerings belange behartig het nie'

20 *Ibid.*, pp. 341–7

21 F.J. Potgieter, 'Die Vestiging van die Blanke in die Transvaal, 1837–86', *AYB*, Pretoria, 1958, ii, p. 195

22 A. Aylward. *The Transvaal of Today*, Edinburgh/London, 1878, p. 155. J.A. Agar Hamilton, *The Road to the North: South Africa, 1852–86*, London, 1937, p. 247, wrote, 'as in the rest of South Africa, the town population was pre-dominantly British. It is only of late years that the descendants of the African farmer has become a dweller in towns, and until the twentieth century was some years old even such places as Potchefstroom, Bloemfontein and Pretoria were markedly British in character'. F.J. Potgieter, 'Die Vestiging', observes that the storekeepers in Rustenburg in the 1860s were said to be of English, Dutch, German and French origin

23 *VRR*, 26 November 1864, Article 318. The instructions to landdrosts on the collection of taxes evolved gradually. In outline they required taxes to be paid by the first of July each year. If they were not paid the landdrost was required to issue a writ to attach movable and immovable goods of taxpayers without judgment, and to sell them for the state treasury. This writ had to be shown to the taxpayer and payment was required before it was executed. If the address of the owner was unknown the writ had to be advertised three times in the *Staats Courant*. The execution of the writ could be suspended by a protest accompanied by reasons for the protest. The landdrost could then give judgment but no appeal could be allowed so long as the tax remained unpaid. Law 10 of 1885; amended by Law 11 of 1896

24 *VRR*, 5 June 1873

25 C.T. Gordon, *The Growth of Boer Opposition to Kruger 1890–5*, Cape Town, 1970, pp. 91–108, has shown that in the case of the Johannesburg stands scandal, the fact that land had to be advertised did not mean that it was. Although local conspiracies for self aggrandisement may have taken place it was equally probable that inefficiency on the part of either the landdrost or the office of the *Staats Courant* would lead to the advertisements failing to appear in print

26 D.W. Krüger, *Paul Kruger*, 2 vols., Johannesburg, 1961, i, pp. 76–8. In the ten years between 1858 and 1868 the Rustenburg *Registrasieregister* showed Kruger taking possession of the farms Kleindoornspruit (1858), Kookfontein, Boschfontein (1859), Beeskraal, Welgevonden, Modderkind, Middelkuil, Losperfontein and Koedoespruit, Beesfontein (1860), Bavianskrans, Saulspoort, (1866) Turfontein. In 1866 Kruger gave the farm Saulspoort for his services to the state, and sold it to Henri Gonin in 1868. Gonin was a missionary acting on behalf of 'kaptein Magamajan en sy volk'. The asking price for the farm was £900. This was paid for partly in cattle valued at £360 (at £3 sterling a head), £240 in Transvaal notes and three payments of £100 in sterling

27 C. Jeppe, *The Kaleidoscopic Transvaal*, 1906; J.A. Mouton, *General Piet Joubert in die Transvaalse Geskiedenes*, *AYB*, Pretoria, 1957, p. 201; F.V. Engelenburg, *General Louis Botha*, London, 1929, p. 34. Mouton reports of Joubert that 'In Januarie 1874 het hy deur middel van 'n advertensie in die pers aan immigrante wat te arm was om grond in die Republiek te koop, elf van sy plase en 'n groot aantal erwe aangebied om te kom bewoon "onder goede en billike voorwaarden

voor 'n lange reeks van jaren, aangesien hy die plasen nimmer wil verkoopen maar als erfins aan zyn kindered, die nog zeer jong zyn, wil laten zoodat deze goede kans is" '. (*Ibid.*)

28 Mouton, *General Piet Joubert*, p. 201
29 Krüger, *Kruger*, p. 79
30 Mouton, *General Piet Joubert*, p. 201
31 BPP, 1901 XXIV, Cd 626, p. 51, evidence of Johannes Christoffel Minnaar. Nellmapius was a Hungarian mining engineer who made his way from Kimberley to the Lydenburg gold-fields. He established a transport service from Lydenburg to Delagoa Bay for which he received 'several grants of land'; S.P. Engelbrecht, *Thomas Francois Burgers*, Pretoria, 1946, p. 144. Later Nellmapius became an associate of Sammy Marks and Frikkie Elof, Kruger's son-in-law
32 BPP, 1901 XXIV, Cd 626, p. 50, evidence of J.P. Fitzpatrick
33 F.V. Engelenburg, *Botha*, pp. 21 and 35
34 Agar-Hamilton, *Road to the North*, pp. 129, 310, 442
35 François Stephanus Cillie, 'The Mapoch's Gronden: an aspect of the Poor White Question', unpublished M.A. thesis, Pretoria University, 1934, p. 66
36 *Ibid.*, p. 95
37 *Ibid.*, pp. 43–50
38 Even within a poor community there was some differentiation. This is brought out by Cillie in his reporting the exchange relationships which the plotholders had with the neighbouring Pedi. 'If a plotholder had cattle he would slaughter an ox and barter the meat to the natives for 25 to 30 bags of grain; or he would purchase a bag of salt in Middleburg and barter that for 8 to 10 bags of grain. If he did not have meat or salt he would plough for the Natives in Seccuniland at the rate of two buckets of grain per 1 200 square yards ploughed' (p. 76)
39 J.F.W. Grosskopf, *Rural Impoverishment and Rural Exodus*, i, (*Carnegie Report on the Poor White Problem*), Stellenbosch, 1932, p. 38. But this suggests confusion with the state loan farm system. In a *Volksraad Besluit* (decision), 5 June 1869, the word 'afstand' is substituted for 'vergunning'. According to *Cassel's Dutch Dictionary* 'afstand' can be used to mean 'cede', while 'vergunning' is defined as concession
40 BPP, 1903, XLV, Cd 1551. *Progress of Administration in the Transvaal and the Orange Free State*, PE5. Enclosure 4 in No. 1 states 'During September and October numerous reports were received showing the ex-Military Burghers of the poorer class who had, at an early stage, taken advantage of Repatriation Aid in order to proceed to farms on which they had previously lived as *bywoners* were finding life upon such farms socially unpleasant. The owners in some cases were returned prisoners-of-war of others, whose political feelings were opposed to the residence upon their farms of men who had served on our side during the war. Of actual violence but few cases were reported, and these were unimportant in themselves. But a spirit of unfriendliness, developing in cases of more isolated farms into actual boycott, was common'

Appendix C of this enclosure (pp. 75–91) provides evidence which undermines the assertion that bywoners were less committed to the republican cause than landowner. Of the 127 heads of families settled under Burgher Land Settlement schemes—most of whom had been bywoners or tenants before the war—twelve had been National Scouts, fifteen had surrendered before the war ended, and had been allowed to return to the Transvaal and can be described as *hensoppers*, fourteen were either invalids or too old to fight and eighty-six had either fought to the war's end or had been taken prisoner. These last had refused to swear an oath of allegiance to the British Crown and had been held in prisons or camps in South Africa, India, Ceylon, St Helena and Bermuda.

41 *Press Digest*, Memorandum 433, Appendix A speech by Reverend J.D. Kestell, quoted by Laurence Salomon, 'Socio-Economic Aspects of South African History, 1870–1962', Ph.D., Boston University, 1962, p. 127

42 J.P. La Grange Lombard, *Paul Kruger die Volksman* (1925), pp. 147–8, quoted in Gordon, *The Growth of Boer Opposition to Kruger*, p. 36

43 They are also reminiscent of latter day development programmes. In some ways the Uitlanders of the Witwatersrand were expatriates who stayed.

44 See S. Trapido, 'Landlords and Tenants in a Colonial Economy: the Transvaal, 1880–1910', *JSAS*, v, 1, 1978, pp. 26–58

45 'The Union of South Africa has become known to the principal markets of the world as one of the foremost fields for the production of maize of good quality'. So wrote the *Official Year Book of the Union of South Africa* (Union Office of Census and Statistics, 1, 1917, p. 398. Whatever the exaggerations in this statement, it is nevertheless true that before the South African war South Africa was a maize-importing region. By 1910 South African maize exports were valued at £693 413

46 F.B. Smith, *Some Observations upon the probable effect of the Closer Union of South Africa upon Agriculture*, paper read at the meeting of the South African Association for the Advancement of Science, Grahamstown, 1908, p. 11

47 *Ibid.*, p. 19

48 *International Review of Agricultural Economics*, 1918, p. 493

49 A.E. Marks, 'Agricultural Cooperation in South Africa', *Monthly Bulletin of Economic & Social Intelligence*, International Institute of Agriculture, Rome, September 1914, p. 28

50 *Ibid.*, p. 35

Index

compiled by Valerie Lewis Chandler